THE ANTHROPOLOGY
OF SPORT

THE ANTHROPOLOGY OF SPORT

An Introduction

Kendall Blanchard
and
Alyce Taylor Cheska

Introduction by Edward Norbeck

BERGIN & GARVEY PUBLISHERS, INC.
Massachusetts

Library of Congress Cataloging in Publication Data

Blanchard, Kendall, 1942-
  The anthropology of sport.

  Bibliography: p. 281
  Includes index.
  1. Games, Primitive.   2. Sports—History.   I. Cheska,
Alyce Taylor.   II. Title.
GN454.B56 1985   306'.483   84-12395
ISBN 0-89789-040-X
ISBN 0-89789-041-8 (pbk.)

Cover photos: (right) by David Riecks, courtesy of Illinois
Sports Information; (left) by Phillips Stevens Jr.; photographed in
Imbura, Gongola State, April 1970.

Text photos: (p. xiv) Phillips Stevens, Jr.; (p. 6) Don Clebb, courtesy of
Illinois Sports Information; (p. 28) Kendall Blanchard; (p. 62) Richard A.
Gould; (p. 90) courtesy of the Smithsonian Institution, National
Collection of Fine Arts; (p. 123 & 166) Francis Clune; (p. 124) G.
Whitney Azoy; (p. 198) Curt Beamer, courtesy of Illinois Sports
Information; (p. 232) courtesy of University of Illinois News Bureau,
Urbana-Champaign.

First published in 1985 by
Bergin & Garvey Publishers, Inc.
670 Amherst Road
South Hadley, Massachusetts 01075

56789   987654321

Printed in the United States of America

Contents

List of Tables:

List of Figures:

Preface

Sociologist George Sage (1974:5) has observed that

> Sport is such a pervasive human activity that to ignore it is to overlook one of the most significant aspects of contemporary American society. It is a social phenomenon which extends into education, politics, economics, art, the mass media, and even international diplomatic relations. Involvement in sport, either directly as a participant, or indirectly as a spectator, is almost considered a public duty by many Americans. It has been observed that if there is a religion in America today, it is sport.

The 1980s have been virtually overwhelmed by a wave of athletic excitement: the "soccer madness" in Brazil (Lever, 1983); the intensity of Wimbleton tennis enthusiasm; the millions of dollars being spent on recreation in the Middle East; the devotion to Olympic training in the Soviet bloc, China, and other countries around the world; the burgeoning magnitude of female involvement in sport activities once reserved for males; and a special genre of sport literature that has captured major portions of the newspaper, the newsstand, and the bookstore.

As though they were afraid they might be left out, the social and behavioral sciences are rushing to be part of the show. Big-time sport has its big-time academic complement; sport psychologists, sport sociologists, sport economists, sport geographers, sport historians, and sport anthropologists. Like a mob of anxious reporters swooping down on the winning pitcher for a post-game interview, social scientists now chase stories of their own, looking for that one document, set of data, or exotic performance that will shed new light on the craziness that is sport.

One measure of the growing interest in sport scholarship can be seen in the Social Science Citation Index. In the period from its inception in 1971 , through 1981, the number of references to "sport" or sport-related terms (e.g., sports, sporting, sportsmen) increased by 510 percent while the total number of index citations increased by only 56 percent.

At the forefront of the growing legitimation of sport studies in the social and behavioral sciences are the sociologists, psychologists, and historians. Anthropology has gotten into the game only recently. However, in the past decade, a significant representation of that discipline's membership has begun to take the subject seriously (see Chapter 1). As a result of this new enthusiasm, the resulting development of a body of literature, and the potential application of anthropological techniques in the several sport program fields (e.g., physical education, recreation), an anthropology of sport is emerging -- and justifiably so.

In the first place, anthropology provides a unique theoretical perspective from which to analyze any facet of human behavior, from subincision rites among the Walibiri in Australia to ostrich rides in central Africa. The theoretical models and insights developed in its focus on primitive or small-scale societies and its scientific approach to prehistory are of particular value in the attempt to understand sport behavior. In this sense, a distinctive anthropology of sport is a logical complement to existing specialities such as the sociology of sport and the psychology of sport. Frederickson (1960:637) has suggested this in her plea for a specifically "cultural study of sports," noting that

> there is no relation of simple function between specific organic needs rooted in the body and mind of man, or in his environment, and his cultural activities. Although organic factors are always present and operative, another set of factors intervenes between the impulse and the act. These are the factors represented in the ideas, beliefs, and practices of the particular culture of which the individual is a part.... Cultural research in sports is pointed toward a clearer understanding of the degree to which cultural living has blocked, modified, encouraged or redirected the energies that are operative primarily at an animal level.

In the second place, sport is such a broad and highly visible phenomenon in today's world that anthropology cannot afford to simply relegate it to occasional comments and papers or to a small chapter in the back of a general ethnography. The fact that sport repeatedly impinges on the daily lives of most people in one fashion or another gives it a seriousness that demands special attention, similar to that accorded other general categories of behavior by the discipline (e.g., economic anthropology, anthropology of law, educational anthropology, anthropology of religion).

Finally, and perhaps of greatest importance, the issues addressed in the anthropological study of sport often have ramifications of direct or indirect applied value. The solutions and potential solutions to general social or particular logistical programs made possible by the anthropological perspective should be of great interest and value to persons involved in the more explicitly sport-related professions; for example, coaches, physical educators, intramural directors, and recreation leaders. The development of a specialized anthropology of sport is making these contributions more visible and accessible to such persons.

The anthropology of sport is simply the anthropological analysis of sport behavior. Its distinctiveness is manifested through its characteristic theoretical persepectives and major concerns. These concerns include such things as the meaning of play and sport, the description of sport in small-scale, preliterate, or tribal society, the prehistory of sport, sport and culture change, and the possible applications of sport data.

The assumption that sport is a significant element of cultural behavior is fundamental to the anthropology of sport. It is a part of culture. As such, sport is subject to the same developmental forces and processes as the other components of the cultural system (e.g., religion, art, law). Likewise, sport is subject to the same basic styles of anthropological investigation and interpretation. Given all this, it is simply assumed that sport, along with games and play in general, deserves the serious attention of social science, in this case, anthropology.

This volume is a general introduction to the developing field of sport anthropology. It exposes the student to a particular perspective on sport, the contributions that anthropologists have made to sport studies, and the possibilities of future research. Much of everything one wants to know about anthropology is addressed, from basic conceptual problems and theoretical models to prehistory, sport ethnography, and applied sport studies.

The term "primitive" is used in this text as a value-free concept to refer to all societies at prestate and preliterate levels. The word "tribal" is often used interchangeably with "primitive," although it usually pertains to systems that are more complex than the simplest forms of hunting-and-foraging societies.

The singular form "sport" is used instead of "sports" as a generic term for all such activities. Also, "sport anthropology" is used occasionally in the text in lieu of the "anthropology of sport." Both refer to the same anthropological subdiscipline.

This work should be of interest to the physical educator, recreation director, leisure consultant, and coach, as well as to the students of anthropology and sociology. Also, it should appeal to the curiosity of the sophisticated layman or sports fan who happens to be intrigued by the intricacies of the athletic event and for whom the game goes beyond the bouncing ball and playing field boundaries to include the total pattern of interactions among spectators as well as between participants. It is hoped that having read the book the sport enthusiast will never again take sport at face value, nor the sport critic ever underestimate its importance.

In Memory of
B. Allan Tindall
1943 – 1976

Acknowledgements

The authors are indebted to many of their students and colleagues. Amy Earls and Martha Sharp played active roles in the data collecting stages of the project. Wannie Anderson, Ralph Balleu, Ralph Bolton, Thomas Cureton, Beulah Drom, Claire Farrer, Frank Glamser, John Loy, Barry McPherson, Andrew Miracle, James Misner, John Roberts, Allen Sack, Michael Salter, Brian Sutton-Smith, Marilyn Wells, and Mari Womack provided various forms of assistance, from article reprints and reference suggestions to critical comments and words of encouragement. Anthropologists G. Whitney Azoy, Francis Clune, Richard Gould, Harriet Kupferer and Phillips Stevens, Jr., were generous in providing relevant photographs from their own collections. Judith Hall, in the Publications and Graphics division of the Learning Resources Center on the Middle Tennessee State University campus, combined her sense of artistic detail and quiet patience to turn our sloppy lists and awkward doodlings into camera-ready tables and figures. Evelyn Jared and Rosemary Wampler typed and retyped parts of the manuscript several times, but were kind enough to protest only in good humor. Editor Ellen Foos was firm yet considerate in helping us hammer the wrinkles out of the manuscript in preparation for publication. Middle Tennessee State University, the University of Illinois, and the University of Southern Mississippi are to be thanked for their provision of several forms of institutional support. Special thanks is reserved for Edward Norbeck. His willingness to take time to read the manuscript and write an introduction in the midst of an already crowded schedule illustrates the old adage that if you want something done right you should find someone to do it who already has too much to do.

Young men in Nigerian kingdom of Bachama compete in wrestling bouts as part of ceremony (see Stevens 1973; 1975).

Introduction

The authors of this book may be described accurately as pioneers in their field of scholarly specialization. To be sure, the large bibliography included in the book lists various writings on the study of sports, all of which may also be called pioneering efforts. Earlier volumes come principally from the field of sociology. To my knowledge, this book is the first on its subject by cultural or social anthropologists that covers a broad range of sub-topics. The authors describe their work as an introduction to the growing field of the anthropology of sport.

The history of this subject of anthropological investigation is short and intimately linked with the history of the study of human play in all of its various forms, a topic generally given little attention by the biological and social sciences until recent years. Anthropology, both physical and social/cultural, has probably been the tardiest discipline to take up the topic of play with any vigor. Once play became established in anthropological consciousness as worthy of study, however, published research on the topic has grown rapidly in quantity and quality and has developed many facets. The Association for the Anthropological Study of Play, founded in 1974 and holding its first annual meeting in 1975, is an indication of the rising prominence of this subject in anthropology. It is also indicative of the growth of scientific interest in play that extends to an ever-widening number of fields and sub-fields of study in the biological and social sciences. The growth of interest seems to tell us that scholars have not only recognized sport and other forms of play as being universal and conspicuous human behavior but also have ceased to regard this behavior as being trivial, a form of indulgence, a sign of weakness and immaturity, or--an increasingly old-fashioned view--as being immoral and sinful. The general conclusion, rarely stated, is surely that if the goal of our study is to gain an understanding of humanity then we must study this outstanding kind of human behavior. Partially restating my thoughts, I shall say that the grip of the Protestant ethic has been weakened by scientific curiosity. In our nation it has now long been acceptable to acknowledge that people have sexuality and sexual relations as well as many other attributes and kinds of behavior on the man-animal level, that is traits resting upon biological proclivities and capabilities like those of other members of the animal world. We are also aware that these attributes are modified by culture in a way that is unique to human beings. Among our forms of man-animal behavior, play has been the slowest to gain recognition as being scientifically meaningful. The position today of the scientific/scholarly world with regard to the study of play seems much like that of the early history of the ideas of Sigmund Freud concerning the unconscious and the relevance of its study to gaining an understanding of human behavior. Although published in 1900, Freud's *The Interpretation of Dreams* reached few readers in the following decade or longer. We all know of the subsequent spread of his ideas and their elaboration by others, and we regard him as a pioneer.

Although forging in new directions, this book on sport follows anthropological tradition in a number of ways. Preeminently, it deals with similarities and differences of peoples of the world in their sport. Anthropology may reasonably be described as the study of similarities and differences in all aspects of humanity and human existence and attempts to account for those likes and unalikes on the basis of biological and cultural circumstances. This book is thus also distinctively anthropological in being pan- or cross-cultural in its coverage, embracing accounts and interpretations of sport among societies geographically and culturally remote from our own and from each other. The range is great, including various Indian societies of the Americas, Australian native peoples, Polynesians of Samoa, Tonga, New Zealand, and Tikopia, Eskimos, Assamese, Andamanese, Vietnamese, the Chukchi of Siberia, a native society of New Guinea, several African societies, Afghanistanians, and the Japanese, as well as the ancient or prehistoric societies of India, Greece, Egypt and Central America.

This book also follows anthropological tradition in presenting interpretations of inter-societal differences in sports that are seen to rest upon differences in other aspects of culture and in seeing the whole of learned behavior or culture as composing a system of related parts that mutually affect each other. The "same" sport is seen to take distinctive forms and have distinctive significance in different societies and these circumstances are explained on a cultural basis. To some readers the preceding statements are perhaps truisms, but I wonder if it is obvious to them that baseball in Japan differs from baseball in the United States in both form and significance. Still another strain of anthropological tradition evident in the book is application; that is, the authors aim to apply their understanding to the amelioration of troublesome social problems and, in general, for the betterment of human conditions of life. Sport -- and play in general -- are seen as adaptive behaviors that have survival value.

In my opinion, the greatest contribution of the book does not concern the adaptive value of sport, which constitutes a major but not its dominant theme. From the far-ranging descriptions and accompanying interpretations of inter-societal differences presented by the book, the reader must certainly gain a strong impression of the extent to which other elements of culture, notably including the ideological, mold the forms of sport and give meaning to them in different societies.

In their efforts to reach this goal of understanding, the authors deal with various subjects that are necessary or useful preliminaries. One such preliminary consists of identifying the field of study -- defining and discussing distinctive traits of sport and various related or seemingly related forms of behavior such as play, work, recreation, leisure, games, and ritual. These passages will doubtless evoke critiques by professional colleagues, a result which seems most desirable at this point of progress in research on sport. In defining sport, emphasis is given to the trait of competition and sport is described as meta-play by analogy with Gregory Bateson's concept of meta-communication. This idea might profitably be further explored.

After discussion of anthropological approaches to the study of sport and an account of prehistoric sport in Greece, Egypt, India and other societies known from either early history or archaeology, the authors present an account of the evolutionary development of sport which must surely be the first of its kind. Linkages are drawn between traits of sport and five categories of societies ranging from small bands to primitive states, following the evolutionary sequence of societies formulated by Elman R. Service (1962). Most of the conclusions presented by the authors as representing general trends of evolutionary change in sport will probably meet with little objection on the part of readers. It seems reasonable to think that as societies and cultures evolved over the millenia, sport would also do so, tending to follow paths common to culture in general of growing secularity and bureaucratization as well as becoming increasingly quantified as mathematical systems, clocks, and other measuring and recording devices were invented. The adaptive significance of sport in a biological sense, however, is far from clear. As fostered by sport, the adaptive value of developed musculature and skilled coordination of movement seems obvious for members of hunting and gathering societies in making their life secure. The value to members of modern civilizations, however, appears to lie elsewhere. For each of the evolutionary categories of societies the functional significance of sport undoubtedly varies, if one accepts the idea that both form and function are influenced by various cultural factors. What is held in common in all circumstances, in all types of culture, is not wholly clear, although the authors in numerous passages throughout their book point to inter-societal differences in both form and function. Although not so labeled, a number of such passages, particularly in the two concluding chapters, have evolutionary significance.

The authors treatment of the subject of applying knowledge of sport to the conditions of human life will also evoke among readers questions, concurrences of opinion, denials of validity, argument, and -- perhaps the most profitable reaction -- speculation and further examination. One topic that has often struck the attention of observant people is the frequent similarity between war and games. But is it possible, as the authors suggest, to establish sport as an alternative to war? The authors' ideas of the functional value of "multi ethnic" sport, as exemplified by the Olympics, might similarly be questioned. Are its negative or disruptive, competitive aspects truly outweighed by its roles in effecting cultural exchange and promoting cross-cultural understanding? Knowing that the growth of science has never led to the development of precise techniques of quantifying the pros and cons of such issues, I shall guess yes. However, my attempts to imagine competitive sport as an alternative to war fail completely even though I am aware that sportlike single-champion athletic competition has been used in some societies to settle issues of contention. But let us note that questions of this sort are not obstacles in the path of the growth of knowledge but a normal part of the process of growth.

The concluding chapter of this book, entitled Contemporary Issues and the Anthropology of Sport, concerns the role of women in sport, and the relationship of sport to aging, violence, and international affairs, and, as noted earlier, relates to earlier discussions of both applications of knowledge about sport and the evolution of sport. The account of women in sport is informative and otherwise interesting, and includes a brief history of the image of femininity from the time of the early classic civilizations of the West. A fairly detailed history of the changed and changing role of women in sport is indeed what it is labeled, a contemporary issue, but it is also an example of cultural evolution, related to such events of modern times as the changed economic positions of females and other changes in female-male relations and relative statuses, developments which, in turn, relate to alterations in many other elements of culture. The changes relating to sport are not limited wholly to attitudes and other totally cultural matters. We are told that females in sport are "adopting the male kinetic model," an observation that bemuses me in considering the future, of sport and of the human condition in various other aspects.

The authors state that their work is intended for students. Professional scholars, perhaps particularly those in disciplines other than anthropology,will also find it useful. For them, part of its value will surely be heuristic, stimulating questions, arguments, and, in short, further thinking and research. This, I believe, is a major if unstated goal of the authors.

The preceding words lead to a question about the future, what the state of the study of sport and other kinds of play might be one, two, and five decades from now. We have noted that the study of play has already gone far beyond sport, the topic to which the writers of this book confine themselves. As in other fields of science, it has become increasingly difficult to be a generalist in the study of play. Investigation has branched into avenues that only specialists may follow, and new relevances, new avenues, continue to be recognized. Only several years ago, for example, it was difficult to imagine that research on hemispheres of the brain is relevant to our understanding sport and other activities of play as well as to other human behavior. Biologists have provided much information on the play of non-human mammals and primatologists have similarly contributed to our knowledge of the play of non-human primates, in which prototypes of various features and kinds of human play seem evident. These and other sources of biological and neurophysiological data as well as the growing accumulation of relevant fact and theory in the social sciences suggest that we may in the fairly near future have a clearer answer to the question of the adaptive significance of play. With reference to the functional value of play for human beings, I think we can now see that human beings have by far the largest repertory of kinds of behavior of any living form, a condition that may readily be seen as adaptive. We call various of those kinds of behavior by such names as sport, games and play. I think we can now also see that the processes of human biological evolution have led to an organism so constituted in anatomy and physiology that varied behavior is biologically necessary for the healthy life of the individual and the continuation of the species -- and we know that the various kinds of play are an important constituent of the range of variation.

What appears to be needed in order to gain a broad understanding of play, its genesis, forms, and significances, is what I believe we are now witnessing in one of its vital states of growth, research along many lines by specialists. The process must then combine specialized knowledge and theory, synthesizing and resynthesizing. We can thank the authors of this book for their contribution to the process.

Edward Norbeck

Women's collegiate track competition

1   Sport and Anthropology

A curious custom exists in Australia -- that of the ball game.

"A game of ball-playing was a favorite pastime of the Victoria tribes, of which the Wotjobaluk, Wurunjerri, and the Kurnai will serve as examples. The ball used by the former was made of strips of opossum pelt rolled tightly round a piece folded up and covered with another bit sewn tightly with sinews. The ball used by the Kurnai was the scrotum of an "old man" kangaroo stuffed tightly with grass. This was called *Turtajiraua*.

"The Wurunjerri called their ball, which was like that of the Wotjobaluk, *Manguri*. In playing this game the two sides were the two classes, two totems, or two localities. For instance, in a case which I remember in the Mukjarawaini tribe, the Garchula (white cockatoos) and the Batyangal (pelicans) played against each other. But this was in fact the class Krokitch against Gamutch. The Kurnai played locality against locality or clan against clan, their totems being merely survivals.

"Each side had a leader, and the object was to keep the ball from the other side as long as possible, by throwing it from one to the other. Such a game might last for hours."

Howitt remarks that the ball game is a useful index as to the class of a particular totem group. He says that "in games played with a ball, the two segments of one class will play together against those of the other; or when the whole tribe is gathered together on some ceremonial occasion, the two pairs of subclasses will camp on opposite sides of a creek. In

7

ceremonial or expiatory encounters, one pair of fellow
subclasses will always side together against the other two."
The ballgame is mentioned here because it will turn up again
in other places as part of the dual organization. This
remarkable custom will help much to understand the cultural
nature of the dual organizaton, and to counteract the
tendency to imagine that it sprang up independently in
various parts of the region. (Perry, 1923:213-313)

This passage is taken from W. J. Perry's well-known ethnography,
The Children of the Sun, a general description of the aboriginal
peoples of Australia that was published in 1923. Perry, a noted
British anthropologist, took most of the material on the ballgame in
this selection from an earlier work by A. W. Howitt, *The Native
Tribes of South East Australia* (1904). In general, Perry's treatment
of this particular athletic event is typical of the way that
anthropologists tended to deal with sport behavior during the early
phases of its one hundred and twenty-five year history. The
description is brief and more or less incidental to other issues. The
data is secondhand; in other words, it is taken from another published
source rather than from the actual obervations of the writer. In
addition, sport is viewed only as a means of understanding another
facet of culture, not as something to be studied in and of itself.

However, the timidity characteristic of earlier anthropological
ventures into the description of sport is being supplanted by a new
boldness. Anthropologists are taking sport behavior seriously,
analyzing it with systematic flair, and recognizing its importance as a
phase of the total life style among the people with whom they work.
This book is a declaration of the importance of sport as a category of
cultural behavior to be appreciated and studied by anthropologists. It
is also a description of changing attitudes within the discipline,
selected analyses, various sport-related theoretical problems, and the
potential application of sport studies.

ANTHROPOLOGY

Anthropology, from the Greek *anthropo logos,* is the "study of
man," in the generic sense of that term. The most comprehensive of
the social sciences, the discipline treats every imaginable facet of
human behavior, past, present, and future. Although other techniques
have been used to categorize the different phases or subsystem of
anthropology, the method most often employed among American
anthropologists is that of subdividing the discipline into four major
parts or areas: physical anthropology, archeology, linguistics, and
cultural anthropology.

Physical Anthropology

Physical anthropology dates from the year 1859, the year Charles Darwin published his monumental *Origin of Species,* and deals primarily with the problem of human evolution. Significant dimensions or phases of this branch of anthropology include the general science of body measurement, population genetics, human biology, paleontology, paleopathology, primatology, and human engineering. This latter is the most "applied" facet of physical anthropology, as its practitioners design airplane cockpits and automobile interiors, and use other insights gained from studying the human anatomy and its adaptability in order to facilitate more comfortable and safer man-machine relationships.

Many of the body measurement techniques that have been developed by physical anthropologists are used by sport physiologists. One such use is the measurement of athletes' bodies and the attempt to correlate body types with particular sport skills. For example, Kukushkin's (1964) article on "Growth, Physique, and Performance" describes the results of a study that was undertaken in 1960 by the Soviet Union State General Institute of Physical Culture in which "adult sportsmen" in the country were subjected to a series of measurements. The results suggested that "each type of sport has its own specific peculiarities and influence upon the physical development and function capability of man" (Kukushkin, 1964:255). Hammer-throwers, weight-lifters, and wrestlers were found to have the largest chest circumference, although basketball players had the largest chest expansion. On the other hand, swimmers tended to have the greatest lung capacity.

Although physical anthropologists themselves have rarely dealt with sport-related questions, the procedures they have developed for measuring and classifying body types have been applied many times in the athletic arena in ways similar to that described above. One of the anthropological resources of significant value in this context is Brozek and Henschel's (1961) *Techniques for Measuring Body Composition.*

Physical anthropologists also study growth and the way that it affects and is affected by athletic activity. Many problems that an aspiring athlete might encounter in the process of growing up can be avoided by the proper utilization of anthropological technique. Robert Malina (1972) describes this process in detail in his instructive article, "Anthropology, Growth, and Physical Education."

Another area of physical anthropology contributing to the general study of sport is comparative primatology, one of the most popular of the discipline's specializations. Comparative primatology, the study of nonhuman primate behavior, has recently turned some of its attention to the study of play among monkeys and apes and has added to the general understanding of this behavior and its development and function among human beings (see Fagen, 1981).

Archeology

Archeology, historically the oldest of the four anthropological subdisciplines, is at its simplest level defined as the "study of the past." However, archeology is done within other academic circles besides anthropology (e.g., historical archeology, classical archeology) and has a more specialized meaning for those archeologists who are trained in anthropology and consider their work to be uniquely anthropological in nature. In this context, archeology becomes "the anthropology of extinct peoples." The so-called "new archeologists" contend that the science can describe prehistoric cultures with the same level of specificity achieved by the cultural anthropologist who studies contemporary cultures.

While individual bits of behavior, specific events, or particular periods of time are retrieved by the archeologist, the greater concern is the reconstruction of the "culture process." The latter is the mechanic of the underlying changes in human history and prehistory, and the archeologist views each event in cultural time as a part of that process. As one better understands the mechanics of that process he or she can in turn more effectively interpret data from the past, understand the present, and predict the future.

Important aspects or specializations within archeology include lithic analysis (lithic referring to stone, e.g., stone tools), paleo-osteology, paleobotany, paleozoology, palynology, and ceramic analysis among the many specialty areas that have significant contributions to make to the comprehensive study of the past.

Another critical phase of archeology is the "science of dating." Many methods for determining either the relative or absolute age of sites, artifacts, or other archeological remains have been developed in recent decades. The proper use and interpretation of the results of these techniques are vital to the continued importance and reliability of archeological analysis. Some of the more commonly used dating methods in archeology include radiocarbon (C-14), potassium-argon, dendrochronology (tree-ring), stratigraphy, and paleomagnetism. (For a complete description of the goals and methods of scienfitic archeology, see Hole and Heizer, *Introduction to Prehistoric Archeology*, 1977).

Archeology's most important contribution to the study of sport has been its occasional treatment of the phenomenon's prehistory and evolution (see Chapter 4 on the prehistory of sport). Archeologists have been relatively verbose in their analyses of some prehistoric athletic contests, such as the Middle American ball game, but have given little attention to sport as a general category or as a prehistoric behavior in other areas of the world.

Linguistics

Linguistics is the scientific study of language and, like archeology, it is broader than its specific role within general anthropology. Of the many variations or types of linguistics, the most common are descriptive, comparative-historical, and ethno-linguistics. Anthropological linguists may actually do any or all of these in one context or another.

Descriptive linguistics is the science of describing languages, often those not having formal writing systems. The descriptive process begins with the linguist's isolating and recording a grammar and collecting a corpus (a body of recorded data in the native language being studied). Learning the language of the people they study is essential to anthropologists, but in many cases information about a particular people's language is limited, forcing the anthropologist to do a language description before he or she can communicate adequately with native speakers. For this reason, the descriptive process is vital to anthropology (For a complete discussion of the descriptive linguistics process, see Samarin, *Field Linguistics*, 1967.)

Comparative and historical linguistics is the analysis of language relationships, changes, and origins. This process usually results in the reconstruction of protolanguages, languages that are no longer spoken by any group of people and have not been recorded historically, but have been reconstructed by comparing historical languages. For example, Proto-Indo-European (PIE) is the parent language of all the Indo-European languages, the largest language family in the world, encompassing all the Germanic tongues, including English, the Romance and Slavic languages, as well as Sanskrit and still other languages. PIE has been reconstructed by comparing these many languages and isolating common sounds and meanings. As a result of these efforts, linguists have put together not only a language, but also a picture of the culture of its speakers. The early Indo-Europeans were hunters and gatherers who roamed an area of northern Europe about 5000 years ago. Comparative and historical linguists have developed a range of techniques and have discovered a variety of "laws" governing language change. Anthropologists find much of this data useful in the attempt to reconstruct regional prehistories and specific intercultural relationships, although the findings of the linguists sometimes conflict with those of the archeologists.

Ethnolinguistics is the study of the interrelationships between language and its cultural and social milieu. For example, the ethnolinguist might do an analysis of the ways that a partricular group of people structure and verbalize its plant world (ethnobotany) and the way that these words are grouped or classified in the speech process. The assumption is that this information, essentially language data, is useful in the attempt to understand the culture of the

speakers themselves. Ethnolinguistics has its roots in the language-
and-culture tradition in anthropology and is still an important phase
of the discipline.

Anthropological linguists have rarely devoted any time to the
study of sport. However, some cultural anthropologists with general
training in linguistics have been fascinated by the nature of sport
language and its relation to other aspects of sport behavior. For
example, one of the authors of this text has analyzed the conflict
language that the Mississippi Choctaws use in association with
basketball (Blanchard, 1975). While Choctaw is a first language for
the majority of basketball participants, players and spectators alike,
among this group few native words or phrases are used to express
antagonism or hostility in a sport context. Most of the epithets or
slang hurled by Choctaw sport enthusiasts at opponents are items
borrowed from English (e.g., "Kill him!" "Throw him out!" "Bust his
ass!"). However, when actual usage patterns were analyzed and
compared with those of typical white, English-speaking sports fans, it
was discovered that the Choctaws, though using the same expression,
do so with different intent. Specifically, when a Mississippi Choctaw
uses the English conflict term or phrase he does not imply the same
level of hostility or actual aggression. This conclusion has been
reinforced by other analyses of Choctaw sport behavior.

In general, the analysis of language can be very useful to sport
studies.

Cultural Anthropology

Cultural anthropology is the study of human social and cultural
behavior. While traditionally the dsicipline has focused on the
small-scale or primitive society, it has also treated more complex
social groupings, from the tribe and chiefdom to the urban state.

Cultural anthropology is distinct from sociology and the other
social sciences in several important ways. It tends to focus on
"culture" rather than on "society" as its basic unit of study. It
stresses the importance of participant observation, a process in which
the field worker actually lives with the people he or she is studying,
participating in daily activities while at the same time maintaining a
degree of objectivity in actual data collection. Cultural anthropology
also tends to focus initially on the exotic or unique elements in the
full gamut of human behavior. It is believed that the "strange" or
"unusual" tell us as much about that noble species *Homo sapiens* as
does the "normative" or the "usual." Finally, cultural anthropology is
different in the sense that it has a unique history and is practiced
within the general theoretical framework created by all of the four
subdisciplines of anthropology.

Cultural anthropology is rooted in an ideology called "cultural
relativism," a doctrine that suggests a cultural system or any aspect
of that system can only be evaluated on its own terms. In other

words, any behavior can only be judged right or wrong from within its own cultural context. For example, whereas polygyny, the marriage pattern that allows one man to have more than one wife at any given time, is "wrong" in some systems, it may be "right" in others. Who would question the wisdom of King Solomon? The doctrine of cultural relativism suggests that members of one system have no right to judge those of another. Cultural values are relative, and in this sense, truth becomes a by-product of culture.

Associated with cultural relativism is anthropology's opposition to ethnocentrism, the notion that one's group and its sense of values are superior to those of all others. Ethnocentrism, though generally a characteristic of all peoples to one degree or another, runs counter to the principles of cultural relativism, and is often at the roots of man's inhumanity to man. In sport studies, an awareness of the dangers of ethnocentric attitudes can lead to a greater appreciation of the games and recreational activities of other people, while at the same time allowing researchers to look more critically at their own.

Cultural anthropology is often referred to as social anthropology. Though there are minor differences between the two, the major distinction is a historical one. The British School of Social Anthropology has traditionally perceived itself as doing "sociology among primitive peoples" and used the title "anthropologist" with some reservation. Thus, anthropologists who want to identify with the British school tend to call themselves social anthropologists. On the other hand, the American school has been less explicit in admitting that it is similar to sociology and generally uses the title "cultural" anthropology.

Cultural anthropology is also referred to as *ethnography* and *ethnology*. Ethnography is the description of a particular culture, while ethnology is the comparison of behaviors across cultural lines. The former is descriptive, while the latter is theoretical and depends on the data collected within the context of the first. Cultural anthropologists often refer to themselves as ethnographers or ethnologists.

Cultural anthropology has many theoretical, geographical, and topical specializations. Among the latter are areas such as economic anthropology, culture change, political anthropology, the anthropology of religion, and so on. Actually, any aspect of culture can be studied to the point that a unique literature and conceptual tradition develop, at which point the field can legitimately be called a subdiscipline. This is the process underlying the recent emergence of the anthropology of sport.

While the anthropological study of sport is a process that combines the specialized methods and data of the four major areas of the science, it is primarily an undertaking of cultural anthropology. Physical anthropology, archeology, and linguistics each make contributions, but ultimately the focus is on sport behavior. The cultural anthropologist studying sport is interested in the ways that his or her science can increase the understanding of sport and ways in which these insights can be applied to improve the utilization and administration of the sport process in fields such as recreation, physical education, and leisure counseling. The importance of the cultural factor in athletic performance is recognized by Malina (1972:301), and his observation underscores the significance of such a focus in sport studies.

> Just as there is need for study at the biochemical level to supplement the evidence of body morphology and composition, there is likewise need for study of relationships within the complexities of the psycho-socio-cultural milieu in which the individual lives and performs. The biological data are fascinating as they stand; nevertheless, there is more to performance than sheer muscle and bone.

SPORT AND GAMES IN THE HISTORY OF ANTHROPOLOGY

The treatment of sport, defined here as a game-like activity having rules, a competitive element, and requiring some form of physical exertion, has generally been included within the broader category "games" in the history of anthropology. During the early years of the discipline, the mid to late 1800s, the evolutionists dominated the cultural anthropology literature. Limited by their dependence on second-hand field data and an adherence to an evolutionary model of culture that viewed the industrialized West as the apex of human accomplishment, the classical fathers were generally preoccupied with issues such as the origin of religion, the mechanics of cultural evolution, and the diffusion of cultural ideas between continents. Some of these nineteenth-century scholars, however, found time to treat the function of games in human society.

Sir Edward Burnett Tylor, often called the father of anthropology, was one of the first social scientists to recognize the importance of games as a subject of scholarly investigation. In particular, Tylor realized that activities such as sporting events might provide the anthropologist with important clues about the nature of prehistoric culture contact. In a classic article entitled "The History of the Games" (1879:63) he argued that while some simple and natural games (e.g., tossing a ball or wrestling) had "sprung up of themselves," there were others that were "distinctly artificial" with some peculiar trick or combination not so likely to have been hit upon twice" that can be traced from a common geographical center. In other words, certain games can be used as evidence of diffusion and contact between cultural centers in different parts of the world. Tylor (1879:66) illustrates this observation by describing the characteristics and historical movements of the ball game:

Following up the clues that join the play-life of the ancient modern worlds, let us now look at the ball-play, which has always held its place among sports. Beyond mere tossing and catching, the simplest kind of ball-play is where a ring of players send the ball from hand to hand. This gentle pastime has its well-marked place in history. Thus the ancient Greeks, whose secret of life was to do even trivial things with artistic perfection, delighted in the game of *Nausikaa,* and on their vases is painted many a scene where ball-play, dance, and song unite in one graceful sport. The ball-dance is now scarcely to be found but as an out-of-the-way relic of old custom; yet it has left curious traces in European languages, where the ball (Low Latin *balla*) has given its name to the dance it went with (Italian *ballare, ballo,* French *bal,* English *ball*), and even to the song that accompanied the dance (Italian *ballata,* French *ballade,* English *ballad*). The passion of ball-play begins not with this friendly graceful delivery of the ball into the next hand, but when two hostile players or parties are striving each to take or send it away from the other. Thus, on the one hand, there comes into existence the group of games represented by the Greek *harpaston,* or seizing-game, where the two sides struggled to carry off the ball. In Brittany this has been played till modern times with the hay-stuffed *soule* or sun ball, as big as a football, fought for by two communes, each striving to carry it home over their own border. Emile Souvestre, in his *Derniers Bretons,* has told the last story of this fierce game in the Ponthivy district -- how the man who had had his father killed and his own eye knocked out by François, surnamed le Souleur, lay in wait for that redoubted champion, and got him down, soule and all, half-way across the boundary stream. The murderous soul-play had to be put down by authority, as it had been years before in Scotland, where it had given rise to the suggestive proverb, "All is fair at the ball of Sconce." The other class of hostile ball-games differs from this in the ball having not to be brought to one's own home, but sent to the goal of the other side. In the Greek *epikoinos,* or common-ball, the ball was put on the middle line, and each party tried to seize it and throw it over the adversary's goal-line. This game also lasted on into modern Europe, and our proper English name for it is hurling while football also is a variety of it, the great Roman blown leather ball (*follis*) being used instead of the small handball, and kicked instead of thrown. Now as hurling was an ordinary classical game, the ancients need only have taken a stick to drive the ball instead of using hands or feet, and would thus have arrived at hockey. But Corydon never seems to have thought of borrowing Phillis's crook for the purpose it would have so exactly suited. No mention of games like hockey appears in the ancient world, and the course of invention which brought them into the modern world is at once unexpected and instructive.

In the same article, Tylor discusses the history of polo and croquet. He also treats the significance of sport language, its impact on other areas of a particular vocabulary, and how "Metaphors taken from sports may...outlast their first sense" (1879:68). For example, he notes that the English word chicanery (trickery) is from the French *chicane*, in turn a corruption of the Persian *chugan*, a game played by hitting a boxwood ball with a long mallet, similar to polo on foot. Also, the word bandy (as in "Don't bandy words with me.") comes from an early form of hockey in which the club was called a *bandy*.

In another article, entitled "On American Lot-Games as Evidence of Asiatic Intercourse Before the Time of Columbus" (1896:93), Tylor discusses the similarities between the ancient Hindustan game of *pachisi*, which we know today as parcheesi, and the Mexican game of *patolli*, arguing that this parallel is solid evidence of pre-Columbian contact between the New and the Old Worlds, specifically, "communications across the Pacific from Eastern Asia."

Typical of the anthropologists of his era, Tylor tended to treat the sport phenomenon as a vehicle for the analysis of broader cultural processes. And, though his periodic study of games represented a valuable contribution to present-day understanding of sport, it did not generate a theoretical framework within which future studies of sport and games could be constructively conducted.

Other nineteenth-century anthropologists occasionally mentioned sport activities in ethnographies or within the context of general introductions to culture (e.g., A. C. Haddon, 1898, *Study of Man*). These events remained items of only secondary interest but there were a few exceptions.

One such exception was an article written by anthropologist James Mooney of the Bureau of American Ethnology, a description of the Cherokee racket game that was published in the *American Anthropologist* in 1890. This lengthy treatment of the "Cherokee Ball Play" begins with a discussion of "the Indian game of the ball play" which Mooney (1890:105) contends is "common to all the tribes from Maine to California, and from the sunlit waters of the Gulf of Mexico to the frozen shores of Hudson Bay."

The racketball game, often referred to as "the parent game of lacrosse," is played by the Cherokees in a way similar to that of the other Southeastern tribes (see Table 3). Each participant uses two "ball sticks," hickory staffs with netted pouches of twisted bear sinew. The ball is less than two inches in diameter and is made of closely packed deer hair covered with deer hide. Two teams of Cherokee ball players compete in the attempt to carry or throw the ball up and down a lengthy field and strike goal posts at opposite ends. The first to accumulate an agreed-upon number of points in this fashion is declared the winner. The only rule that is enforced consistently is one that prohibits a player from touching the ball with anything other than his ball stick.

The formal ball game is a very important community event. It involves extensive preparation, ritual fasting, religious ceremony, and heavy wagering on the event's outcome (For a more detailed description of the "Indian ball game," see Chapter 5 and the section on Choctaw stickball).

Mooney (1890:108-32) focuses on one particular ball game he witnessed among the Cherokee in September, 1889. He recounts the myth underlying the ball play performance, describes the ritual preparation, translates the music, and paints a vivid picture of the game's entire process. Throughout the article, Mooney elaborates on the importance of the ball play as an integral aspect of Cherokee culture.

Despite the detail of his own description, Mooney (1890:108) admits that "it may be said without exaggeration that a full exposition of the Indian ball play would furnish material for a fairsized volume." It is significant that since Mooney's work, several major pieces of research have been conducted that have focused on the ball game. In 1962, anthropologist Raymond Fogelson, now at the University of Chicago, wrote a Ph.D. dissertation entitled "The Cherokee Ball Game: A Study in Southeastern Ethnology" that is an extensive and well-documented analysis of the phenomenon. In many ways, the latter research can be viewed as an indirect product of Mooney's (1890) early work and interest in sport.

Another important figure in the history of anthropology's interest in sports and games is Stewart Culin. Culin, who has been called the "major game scholar of the past 100 years...in the field of anthropology" (Avedon and Sutton-Smith, 1971:55), was born in Philadelphia in 1859 and educated at Nazareth Hall in Pennsylvania. As a business man in his late twenties he became interested in archeology. His own extensive study in the discipline resulted eventually in his appointment as director of the Museum of Archeology at the University of Pennsylvania in 1892. In 1903, Culin became curator of ethnology at the Brooklyn Museum, where he remained until his death in 1929.

Culin's interest in games was first manifested in published form in his *Chinese Games with Dice* which appeared in 1889. In 1895 he published an important monograph entitled *Korean Games with Corresponding Games of China and Japan.* Eight years later, one of the most significant of the many articles he wrote on games and sports appeared in the *American Anthropologist,* "American Indian Games." In this short piece he classified these activities into two general classes: games of chance and games of dexterity. In turn, he divided the latter into five categories: games that involve (1) archery, (2) shooting at moving targets, (3) sliding javelins on the ground or ice, (4) a ball, and (5) racing. All of these can be legitimately defined as "sports" (Culin, 1903).

Culin's most important contribution to anthropology in general and the study of games in partricular was his *Games of the North American Indians* that was published by the Bureau of American Ethnology in 1907, in its twenty-fourth *Annual Report.* This 846-page volume systematically classified and described the games and sport activities of 225 different Native North American tribes. According to one Culin biographer:

> *Games of the North American Indians* has stood as a classic and the vast undertaking has to be admired by the man's strongest critics. The identification and description of the gaming implements accompanied by sketches, measurements, Indian names, playing rules, scoring systems, and even mythical origins when known, plus credits to the collectors, dates of acquisitions, museums where objects were housed with their catalogue numbers, along with many photographic reprints of artifacts, participants playing games, and paintings represented a monumental effort. This volume has stood on such an esteemed pinnacle that few challengers have done battle with Culin's theories, methodology or facts. (Cheska, 1975:4)

Culin's scholarly interest in games had its roots in his fascination with culture in its many varieties, his extensive travel, and his exposure to the work of contemporary anthropologists such as Tylor. As a young man, Culin had lived with a Chinese family in Philadelphia and learned to speak their language. Out of this experience grew a life-long curiosity regarding the art, games, and ceremonies of the Orient. Culin traveled widely and collected artifacts as well as cultural data. During his years as curator at the Brooklyn Museum he often shipped material from his travels back to the museum in boxcar lots. Many of the items he found and obtained were gaming pieces and sporting equipment.

Stewart Culin's contributions to the anthropological study of games and sports were many and varied. The sheer volume of data he collected and published on the subject did much to enrich the literature. His collections of games, toys, and sporting equipment from around the world widened museum holdings and salvaged a rich heritage of such materials for the American public. In the area of theory, Culin's greatest contributions were his classification of games and his participation in the debate over the origin, evolution, and distribution of these. He never treated the fundamental problem of game and sport definition, and some of his theoretical positions have been refuted by modern scholarship (e.g., his notion that Native American games were diffused to Asia, rather than vice versa).

However, Culin still played a vital role in the history of anthropology's treatment of play. He underscored its importance as a component in the study of culture and put many of the fundamental questions into perspective. In his introduction to the twenty-fourth *Annual Report* of the BAE (*Games of the North American Indians*), W. H. Holmes (1907:XL), BAE chief at that time, remarked:

> Mr. Culin's studies...not only afford an understanding of the technology of the games and of their distribution, as well as their bearing on history..., but they contribute in a remarkable manner to an appreciation of native modes of thought and of the motives and impulses that underlie the conduct of primitive peoples generally. [Culin]...creates the science of games and for the first time gives this branch its proper place in the science of man.

During the first five decades of the twentieth century occasional anaylses of sports and games appeared in the anthropological literature. In Germany, Von Karl Weule published a lengthy article, "Ethnologie des Sportes" (Ethnology of Sport), that appeared in a large volume on the history of sport in 1925. Weule approached the subject from the culture-history school perspective, arguing that the primary focus of an ethnology of sport should be twofold: (1) to trace culture, particularly the sport aspect, back to its beginnings, and (2) to put sport as an item of culture into its proper theoretical perspective.

Treating the origin and development of sport in stages comparable to those characteristic of culture in general, Weule contended that there were fundamental differences between the sports of primitive and modern man. In the case of the former, sport activities were more directly related to man's attempt to cope with the immediate problems of adaptation, survival and defense. On the other hand, modern man used sport to perfect the human body, for competition, and simply for pleasure, and was not as practical or ritually oriented in his sport activities.

Weule also described the primary sporting events of many primitive societies around the world, and this is perhaps the greatest contribution of the article. Theoretically, the work is dated and of little value in the process of conceptual development. Also, the material is weakened by the author's total reliance on secondary data sources and the explicit racism that characterizes his view of primitive man.

Anthropologist Elsdon Best gave some special attention to games and sports in his ethnographic research. His 1924, two-volume work, The Maori, contains extensive descriptions of the play activities of this New Zealand group. In turn, these same events were the subjects of a 1925 article that he wrote on "The Games and Pastimes of the Maori."

In 1931, noted British social anthropologist Raymond Firth wrote a thirty-three page article in the professional journal <u>Oceania</u> entitled "A Dart Match in Tikopia: A Study in the Sociology of Primitive Sport." In this he described the competitive dart throwing match of old Polynesia (Firth, 1930/31:65; see Chapter 5 for a more detailed description).

Firth (1930/31:95-96), following a theme established in Culin's work, underscores the important role of sport and its many functions in primitive society:

> From these songs and other data it can be realized how the game of *tika* comes to pass beyond the bounds of simply play for exercise and relaxation, and to attain considerable importance in the general economic and religious life, in addition to its reactions on the social organizaton of the community and on the personality of its component members....
>
> Sport, as an integral feature in the life of many primitive peoples, offers a number of problems for investigation. Some of these are concerned with questions of organization, of the nature of the factors which differentiate a vague play activity from a regularly established game with clearly defined procedure, hemmed in on every side by rules of strong sanction.... The relation of primitive sport to other aspects of the social life, its unique culture value on the one hand, and its interreaction with economics, aesthetic and religious affairs on the other, presents a field of research which merits even more attention than it has already received.

In 1933, Columbia University Press published anthropologist Alexander Lesser's *The Pawnee Ghost Dance Hand Game: A Study of Cultural Change.* This brilliant analysis of the game's role in the total culture process of this particular Plains Indian group is one of the outstanding monographs in twentieth-century American anthropology.

The Ghost Dance, which originated among the Paiute Indians of the Great Basin in the 1880s, was a ceremony designed to affect the ultimate return of the Native Americans' ancestors, who would in turn assist the living in recapturing their land from the white man and reestablishing the more satisfying life styles of tradition. Introduced among the Pawnee in 1891, the Ghost Dance very quickly became a prominent feature of community life.

One of the traditional forms of Pawnee culture affected most dramatically by the advent of the Ghost Dance was the hand game. This guessing game involved two special bones or die that were hidden in the hands with deliberate deception so as to make it difficult for an opponent to determine the location of the counters or pieces. Teams competed against each other, individual members taking turns at hiding and guessing as to the placement of the game pieces, and tallies of the total correct and incorrect guesses were kept. Participants wagered on the outcomes of these contests and took the outcomes seriously.

After the Ghost Dance was introduced among the Pawnee, the hand game became much more highly ritualized and stylized, being transformed in many ways into a vital aspect of the Ghost ceremony itself. The gaming features of tradition were largely overshadowed by the novel ritual dimensions the activity assumed.

On the basis of this analysis, Lesser takes issue with Culin's (1907:109) earlier view that games of the North American Indians were "either instruments of rites or have descended from ceremonial observances of a religious character." Lesser (1933:330) argues that although some Native American games may have evolved from ritual, such is not necessarily the case.

> We may suppose that the relay race, with the associations lent it in the Pueblo area, was received enthusiastically and developed rapidly and fully by the Jicarilla because it was so appropriate to the needs and natures of Jicarilla culture. Not only did the Jicarilla have the social structure to accommodate it (i.e., the two bands), and a long-standing respect for Sun and Moon as important supernaturals but being primarily hunters and gatherers, they were spurred by a profound interest in a dual food supply, an even-handed interest which the more agricultural Pueblos could not match (Opler, 1944:97).

The following year, anthropologist Marvin Opler (1945) published a brief description of Japanese style wrestling. This treatment of a sumo tournament that he observed at the Tule Lake relocation center in California is of little theoretical significance, but does suggest an interest in sport on the part of the anthropological community.

During the period between 1930 and 1960, the social science literature was occasionally graced by contributions from nonanthropologists who addressed sport-related issues of interest to anthropologists. For example, in 1939, Corrado Gini wrote an interesting piece on baseball and shinny as they were played among the Berbers in Libya of North Africa, an article that was published in *Rural Sociology*. Another important contributor to the anthropological understanding of sport and games during this period was folklorist Paul Brewster. Among his many articles on these subjects was a significant one addressing "The Importance of the Collecting and Study of Games" (1956).

Several scholars from the ranks of physical education also added to the limited literature in this area, describing the sport activities of particular primitive peoples (e.g., Dunlap, 1951; Stumpf and Cozens, 1947) and stressing the importance of looking at sport from a cultural perspective (e.g., Frederickson, 1960).

Anthropology and A New Interest in Sport and Games

The year 1959 was a critical one in the history of anthropology's treatment of sport and games. That year, John Roberts, Malcolm Arth, and Robert Bush published their seminal article entitled "Games in Culture" (1959). This publication, one of the first systematic attempts in the discipline to delineate the constant features of "games," served to stimulate productive theoretical debate regarding the general role of play and the special role of sport in human society.

In "Games in Culture," Roberts, Arth, and Bush (1959:597) define game as "a recreational activity characterized by (1) organized play, (2) competition, (3) two or more sides, (4) criteria for determining the winner, and (5) agreed upon rules." In turn, games are classified as those of (1) physical skill, (2) strategy, and (3) chance.

Taking this concept of "games" and applying it to data from 50 tribes treated in the Yale University Human Relations Area Files (HRAF), the authors next attempt to correlate the nature of games with other aspects of culture. As a result of this analysis, they discover that games of strategy are associated with the level of social organization complexity. In other words, the more complex the social system, the greater the likelihood a particular society will have games of strategy. Also, they find that games of chance appear to be associated with religious activities. "It is commonly thought by many peoples that the winners of games of chance have received supernatural or magical aid" (Roberts, Arth, and Bush, 1959:601). Finally, while evidence here is limited, the authors reach the tentative conclusion that there may be a relationship between environmental conditions and the type and number of physical skill games of any group.

While others have since taken issue with the specific findings of this particular research, the article, "Games in Culture" played a significant role in focusing the attention of anthropologists on games and sports.

The 1960s produced a variety of anthropological pieces with sport themes. Typical of the period is anthropologist Robin Fox's classic article on "Pueblo Basball: A New Use for Old Witchcraft" (1961). In this *Journal of American Folklore* publication, Fox describes the introduction of baseball into Cochiti Pueblo in New Mexico, and analyzes the way in which the new sport has provided for the exercise of old forms of witchcraft in new and perhaps therapeutic ways. In his own words:

> Baseball in the Pueblos is a competition intrusion into essen-
> tially noncompetitive social systems. While competition is

between villages, no untoward events occur, as this is in line
with tradition, but within villages, it is... potentially
destructive. Pueblo institutions act as a counter to
aggressive tendencies in the Puebloans and are so
constructed as to eliminate and nullify aggressive conflict
between people by placing them in automatically determined
overlapping role situations. The baseball teams, based on
voluntary recruitment and stressing competition, allow for
the acting out of aggressive and competitive tendencies.
Various steps are taken by the Pueblo to neutralize this
event, but the participants seem bewildered in the face of
the turn of events. Resort to naked authority in the
settlement of interfamilial disputes is a new thing to Cochiti
and in a way a confession of weakness in the social system,
previously so ingeniously adequate to deal with conflict. It
looks for the moment in Cochiti as if the male forces of
authority and order may be able to keep the peace for the
time being. But the women especially have married the old
witch fears to the new sport and thus directed a whole body
of deep-rooted motivations into new and pertinent channels.
When the tension is high and feelings rise, the old cries of
"witch" fly from the women, and the suppressed rages are
given full vent. It may even prove therapeutic (Fox,
1961:15).

In his 1964 presidential address to the American Anthropological
Association, Leslie White gave some credibility to the anthropological
study of sport by suggesting that the discipline provided a viable
model for the analysis of professional sports, in particular baseball,
which he saw as a vital expression of the American cultural system
itself (White, 1965:633-34).
During the mid-sixties, there was a greater tendency for
ethnographic field workers to take notice of sport and play activities
among the people they were studying and include some of this
material in their monographs. Also, at professional meetings of
anthropologists, both regional and national, occasional sessions were
devoted to the reading of papers on sport and sport-related topics.
In a 1973 review of three sociological books on sport,
anthropologist Joyce Reigelhaupt (1973:378) noted that members of
her profession had devoted little attention to sport and games during
the previous twenty-five years. However, she suggested that the time
had arrived for the development of an anthropology of sport and that
Geertz's (1972) essay on the Balinese cockfight would be "a logical
starting point" (Reigelhaupt, 1973:380).
Clifford Geertz is one of the premiere theoreticians among
contemporary American anthropologists. In his "Deep Play: Notes on
the Balinese Cockfight," an article that has already become
something of a classic in the discipline, he describes the process of

the illegal but frequent cockfight in Bali and the betting that surrounds the activity. Detailing the very complicated rules that characterize this betting behavior, he points to what appears to the outside observer to be a irrational "economic behavior" associated with "deep" matches, ones in which the unpredictability of outcomes and the total stakes are increased to their ultimate limits. Using Bentham's concept of "deep play" ("play in which the stakes are so high that it is, from his utilitarian standpoint, irrational for men to engage in [it] at all"), Geertz (1972:432) notes that while money is important to the participants, it is a secondary matter. It is as though there were a moral imperative that demanded wagering in those "deep" matches that overrode basic economic concerns. The author uses the cockfight as a means of illustrating the problems of interpretation encountered by the anthropologist in analyzing any dimension of the cultural experience.

Of equal importance to the coalescence of the anthropological interest in sport during the 1970s was the work of Edward Norbeck. Norbeck, a prominent figure in American anthropology and a well-published authority on a variety of topics, including the anthropology of religion and Japan, has been for many years an advocate of play research. In 1971, he wrote an article, "Man at Play," that was published in a special *Natural History* supplement on play. Norbeck made it clear that play was a subject to be taken seriously, an important dimension of the human experience that anthropologists could not afford to ignore. Then, in 1973, he organized a symposium at the annual meetings of the American Anthropological Association, held in New Orleans, in which several important papers on the anthropology of play were read (Norbeck, 1974).

It was during those 1973 meetings, and partly in conjunction with the Norbeck symposium, that a handful of sport-conscious anthropologists got together. They had been developing their own sport interests independently, in some cases quietly, but used this situation to discuss the feasibility of a special professional organization devoted to the study and dissemination of information about sport and play.

The previous year, Alyce Cheska, working through the American Alliance for Health, Physical Education, Recreation, and Dance (AAHPERD), had organized a group of sport educators interested in the anthropological study of play. Cheska organized a session on the topic for the 1973 AAHPERD meetings, and plans were made to meet the following year with the anthropologists who had begun to make noises about the need for an interdisciplinary organizaton devoted to the study of sport and play behavior.

In the spring of 1974, a group of anthropologists and sport educators met during the North American Society of Sport History (NASSH) annual meetings in London, Ontario. It was at this gathering that The Association for the Anthropological Study of Play (TAASP) was born. In addition to Norbeck and Cheska, other driving forces behind the formation of the organization included Michael Salter of the University of Windsor and B. Allan Tindall, then at the State University of New York in Buffalo.

Since its inception, TAASP has grown to encompass a membership of over 300 as of 1984. These individuals come from a variety of disciplinary backgrounds, in addition to anthropology and physical education: recreation, history, education, sociology, psychology, and others. The proceedings of the organization's annual meetings that are published each year reflect the broad interests of the group and a specialized commitment to the anthropological analysis of sport.

In recent years, the number of anthropologists dealing with sport in their research and writing has increased dramatically; a reality witnessed in the volume of papers, articles, and monographs (e.g., Blanchard, 1981; Azoy, 1982). No longer is sport simply a topic of idle conversation and pastime activity among anthropologists; it has become the legitimate subject of serious study.

THE OBJECTIVES OF THE ANTHROPOLOGY OF SPORT

The Anthropology of sport is tied to the following objectives:
1. the definition and description of sport and leisure behavior from a cross-cultural perspective;
2. the study of sport in primitive, tribal, non-Western, Third World, and underdeveloped societies, as well as in historical and contemporary Western society;
3. analyzing sport as a factor in acculturation, enculturation, and cultural maintenance and adaptation to change;
4. viewing sport as a perspective on other facets of cultural behavior;
5. the analysis of sport behavior in human prehistory;
6. the analysis of sport language;
7. treating the role of sport in a multicultural educational environment;
8. the development and administration of sport/recreation programs for special populations;
9. the application of anthropological methods in the solution of practical problems in sport settings, such as physical education, recreation, and intramural programs;
10. the application of anthropological methods in the development and administration of programs in physical education, recreation, and intramurals;
11. the development of constructive leisure-time activities that utilize the sport model; and
12. the creation of attitudes conducive to cross-cultural understanding. As Cozens and Stumpf (1951:72) have noted, "If

cultural anthropology teaches us anything, it teaches us to look beneath the surface of what we see and to develop our tolerance of the other fellow's pleasures."

In addition to these, the anthropological focus also provides a distinctive framework within which one might address specialized problems such as the role of women in sport, international understanding, the aging process and recreation for the elderly, and sport and violence in human society.

In general, the anthropology of sport is a distinctive social scientific approach to the analysis and understanding of sport and the practical application of the resulting insights to real problems in physical education and recreation programs.

SUMMARY

An effective anthropological approach to sport is grounded in a comprehensive understanding of anthropology as an academic discipline. Anthropology, "the study of man," is one of the social sciences and can be subdivided into four major areas: physical anthropology, archeology, linguistics, and cultural anthropology. While each provides a distinctive window on sport, a particular perspective, the anthropology of sport is primarily a behavioral science and thus more closely tied to cultural anthropology.

During its first one hundred years anthropology gave limited attention to sport and games, the most notable exception being the work of Stewart Culin. With the advent of the 1960s, sport became a more frequent topic in anthropological circles. Anthropologists began to treat conceptual problems in a detailed and systematic fashion. The organization of The Association for the Anthropological Study of Play in 1974 signaled the actual emergence of the anthropology of sport.

This novel subdiscipline is the systematic study of sport from a cross-cultural perspective. The anthropology of sport is an attempt both to understand and apply this understanding in the analysis of sport-related social problems.

Exercises

Discussion questions:

(1)   What are the special features of anthropology that make possible a unique and valuable analysis of sport?

(2)   Imagine you are the coach of a boy's basketball team in a Los Angeles County high school in California. Your team is composed of seven whites, four blacks, two Chicanos, and two Native Americans. On the basis of what you know about the anthropology of sport at this point, how could the

anthropological approach assist you in being a more effective coach?

(3)   Select a contemporary sport-related social issue (e.g., the problem of spectator violence at sporting events). What types of questions would the following social scientists be most likely to ask in the analysis of that issue from their respective professional perspectives: a sociologist, an economist, a geographer, a psychologist, a historian, an anthropologist?

(4)   What are some of the reasons that an anthropologist <u>might not be</u> interested in the serious analysis of sport behavior? On the other hand, what are some of the reasons that this same anthropologist might undertake the study of sport behavior?

Special Projects:

(1)   Select a special population or non-Western group with which you have some familiarity. Go to the literature and read a few short selections about that culture, purposely avoiding or ignoring any specific treatment of sport. On the basis of this reading, what kinds of things can you predict about the sporting activities of these people? For example: What type of games would they enjoy playing? How competitive might they be in athletic events? How serious would they be prone to take their sports? What special elements might they add, delete, or change in typically Western athletic events like basketball and baseball?

(2)   For those who might be interested in the sociology of sport, see the article by Eldon Snyder and Elmer Spreitzer, "Sociology and Sport: An Overview" (1974). Also, see the book by John Loy, Barry McPherson and Gerald Kenyon, *Sport and Social Systems* (1978) or another sociology of sport textbook. After looking through these materials, compare and contrast the sociological and anthropological approaches to the study of sport behavior.

(3)   Thumb through Robert Higgs's (1982) *Sports: A Reference Guide.* Find a sport-related theme that the author addresses that you feel would be appropriately treated in an anthropological context. Defend your choice.

(4)   Many of the significant articles with sport or sport-related themes that have been written by anthropologists have been reprinted in Harris and Park's *Play, Games and Sports* (1983). A serious perusal of this volume and its table of contents will give you an idea of what is distinctive about the anthropological approach to the study of sport. Read one of the articles and write a critique, addressing the issue as to whether or not it is "good anthropology."

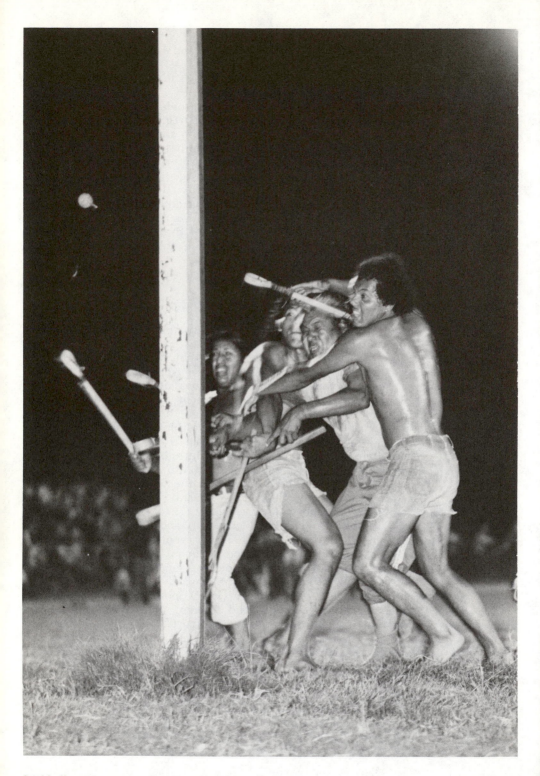

Stickball action among the Mississippi Choctaws

2 The Meaning of Sport: A Cultural Approach

Consider the following activities and situations:

(1)   A demolition derby on a small-town, dirt-track speedway in southeast Georgia on a hot, muggy August night.

(2)   George Blanda walks onto the football field with six seconds left to play, kicks a forty-five-yard field goal, wins the game for the Oakland Raiders, and walks back to the bench.

(3)   A group of dusty farmers, small-time business men, and full-time ne'er-do-wells are crowded into an old barn in backwoods Tennessee watching two specially trained roosters fight to the death.

(4)   A teenager hangs over a Pac Man machine in a suburban Philadelphia convenience store, literally working up a sweat in the attempt to better his own record score.

(5)   A Yugoslavian figure skater does a complicated routine to Ravel's "Bolero" and scores a 9.6 in an international figure skating championship.

(6)   A high school couple in Chico, California, dances a highly stylized version of the "jitterbug" and wins a 1950s dance contest.

Which of these activities would you describe a sport? Can you isolate the rationale that you used in making those decisions? If you are like most, you will find yourself faced with indecision on both counts. Sport is not always easy to recognize. It is sometimes said of "play," that although it is difficult to define, one knows it when he or she sees it. Sport is more specialized than play, and may not afford the same convenience.

Recognizing sport is even more difficult when one is put into a cultural setting other than his or her own. Consider the Eskimos' "song duel."

Among many Eskimo groups in the traditional North American Arctic, an institution called the "song duel" is frequently used to adjudicate criminal offenses or manage potentially dangerous disputes. For example, if a man steals another man's wife, the bereaved husband might challenge the offender to a song duel. If the latter is amenable, a time and place is arranged, and the two meet in head-to-head competition. The rest of the community turns out in force; the spectators will determine a winner, so they are vital to the song duel. Besides, what else is there to do on a long, frigid night in the snow-covered Arctic?

The "song duel" is a battle of words and wit. Combatants mimic, parody, and shout abusive, though often creative, insults at each other. Each puts on a show. The audience is entertained. They laugh with each nasty, cutely phrased accusation and applaud the well-designed, choreographed antics of the duelers. Anderson (1974/75:76-77) has recorded the words of a famous song duel that took place among the Kobuk River Eskimo in the late nineteenth-century as these are recounted in community oral history. The exchange begins with the song of Akausraurak:

> Immok, I wish, I want to use your legs.
> I would like to walk around using them.
> Immok, I wish I could borrow your funny legs,
> The ones you used to go to see your brother's wife, Immok.

Immok sings in response:

> Akausraurak likes to use my legs.
> Real good, respected man shouldn't use my legs because he
>   might become an idiot.
> My legs are not to go to tell my relatives to go away from
>   me,
> My legs are simply good for crossing the creeks without
>   having to use a boat.

The object of the duel from the participants' standpoint is to gain the sympathy and support of the audience. The singer who is successful in working the audience so that it laughs with him and at his opponent is the winner of the competition. So, every effort is made to court the spectators, using both word and dance, with the movement designed to amplify the message of the song as well as to flaunt one's physical prowess. Eventually, the sympathies of the crowd become clear; its laughter suggests that is has decided in favor of one of the two combatants. The reaction eventually makes clear the victory of one and the defeat of the other.

The untrained outsider not familiar with the song duel who is asked to characterize the institution might respond in one of several ways. Like the blind man attempting to describe the elephant, his response is affected by the particular dimension of the song duel that he perceives. One observer might be impressed by the rhythm of the songs, the occasional mention of supernatural figures, and the emotional involvement of the spectators, and call the song duel a "religious ritual." Another might notice the feasting that sometimes takes place in this context and suggest that the song duel is a playful part of a community picnic. An astute student of human behavior might notice the gift giving and interpret the event as an informal market in which reciprocity and the exchange of goods is facilitated. Yet another observer might delve into the events leading up to the song duel and explore the consequences of the event. Such confrontations can have serious repercussions; there have been situations in which defeat has brought with it such chagrin that the losers have committed suicide. Having taken all this into consideration, this latter observer might call the "song duel" a "primitive court" system in which the community acts as jury to determine what is just in a confrontation between litigants. Finally, one observer, the one with the running shoes who plays squash and has season tickets to the Knicks' home games, remarks, "By golly, that's sport, if I ever saw it." And, he could make a good case for his observation. The song duel is playful and competitive, has physical dimensions, involves the eventual declaration of a winner and loser, and has been described by others as sporting. Hoebel (1954:99), for example, has remarked that "as the courtroom joust may become a sporting game between attorneys-at-law, so the juridical song contest is above all things a contest in which pleasurable delight is richly served, so richly that the dispute-settlement function is nearly forgotten."

So, which observer is correct? In one sense, all are right; in another, none. This is the dilemma of behavior definition and classification, a dilemma to which anthropologists are extremely sensitive and one that necessitates a discussion about the concept of "sport" and its definition.

For the most part, key terms such as "play," "game," "leisure," and "recreation," as well as "sport," are yet to be assigned meanings that are generally agreed upon by anthropologists, or for that matter, by any general group of social scientists. Anthropologist-physical educator Allan Tindall (1976:3) has put this problem into perspective for those dealing with sport and recreation on an international level. Noting that such terms are "loaded with a European bias," he suggests that

it is highly unlikely that the terms "sport" or physical education occur in direct parallel in languages of a non-

European origin.

> In the literature with which I am familiar "sport" has no definitive meaning or referent. Many disparate types of activities are labeled "sport." Professional and amateur athletic competition as well as hunting and fishing activities are all labeled sport. As I look across the usages of the term I find neither a consistent use of the word with reference to patterns of human movement or goal orientations (Tindall, 1976:3).

Most of the early literature on sport behavior ignores the conceptual problem and simply assumes that readers know what is meant by terms like "play" or "leisure." For example, in his "Ethnologie des Sports" (1926), Weule discusses at length the evolution of sport and its various expressions among historic primitive peoples, but at no time does he define the term "sport." More recently, similar omissions are obvious in works like Menke's (1947) *Encyclopedia of Sports* and Gipe's (1978) *The Great American Sports Book.* In the Human Relations Area Files (HRAF) a wide range of activities are grouped in section 526, "athletic sports," without any further definitional treatment. Some comparative studies, such as Sipes (1973) "War, Sports and Aggression," have been based on the file materials, and researchers have overlooked conceptual matters, assuming that the HRAF classification was self-explanatory and of legitimate transcultural application.

To the sport sociologists' credit, much of their theoretical writing in recent years has focused on the problem of definition. Important publications on the subject include Caillois's (1969) "The Structure and Classification of Games," Edwards' (1973) *Sociology of Sport,* Kenyon's (1969) "A Conceptual Model for Characterizing Physical Activity, " Loy's (1969) "The Nature of Sport," and Sack's (1977) "Sport: Play or Work?" However, while these works have led to some clarification, many definitional difficulties remain, especially when one approaches the issue from an anthropological perspective.

One of the conceptual problems with which the anthropology of sport must contend is the fact that some of its key terms are without equivalents in many languages. Some groups do not make a clear distinction between work and play, different forms of games, or sport and ritual. Also, physically combative sports are simply nonexistent in some societies (Sipes, 1973:69). In many cases, extenuating circumstances (e.g., climate, work schedules) may obviously prohibit such sport activities, so simple structural explanations, those taking only rules and equipment into account, are often not sufficient to explain the presence or absence of the phenomenon, thus further complicating the analysis.

THE MEANING OF CULTURE

The anthropology of sport approaches the problem of term definition from a cultural perspective. This approach is based on the assumption that sport behavior in any situation is culturally defined; in other words, it is a dimension of the total cultural experience native to and generally shared by a particular society or group of people. As Frederickson (1960:636) has noted, "sport is primarily a cultural product and must be understood as such."

The cultural approach to the analysis of human behavior is rooted in an understanding of "culture," yet the precise meaning of the term remains a controversial subject among members of the discipline. Some argue that culture is purely idea, others contend it is material, while yet another group argues that the complexity of change and modern life has so confused human patterns of relationship that the term has become practically meaningless and of little theoretical value. However, underlying the various controversies there is some agreement.

Webster's *New World Dictionary* (1970) lists six definitions for the noun form of "culture." Of these, only one is appropriate in an anthropological context: "the ideas, customs, skills, arts, etc. of a given people in a given period."

The suggestion that culture is something shared by members of a society and not limited simply to those of a particular breeding or class affiliation dates back to the work of E. B. Tylor and his classic work, *Primitive Culture* (1871:1):

> Culture or civilization, taken in its wide ethnographic sense,
> is that complex whole which includes knowledge, belief, art,
> morals, law, custom, and any other capabilities and habits
> acquired by man as a member of society.

In this same context, Tylor argues for a unique discipline dedicated to the study and analysis of cultural phenomena, specifically, a "science of culture." Although cultural anthropology has only been treated as a science of culture by a few scholars in recent decades (e.g., White, 1949), the concept has never lost the key role assigned it by Tylor.

Since Tylor's day, however, literally hundreds of definitions have been devised by anthropologists for the term "culture." As one would expect, this proliferation of definitional attempts has muddied the conceptual waters, and no one precise meaning of culture has gained general acceptance among theoreticians, despite occasional efforts to resolve the confusion (e.g., see Weiss, 1973). However, some statements may be made about "culture" that most if not all anthropologists who use the term would find acceptable.

1. Culture and Society

In the first place, "culture" and "society" are related concepts, but cannot be used interchangeably. "Society" is generally used to refer directly to a group of people and the relationships among those people that tend to occur on a fairly regular basis. "Culture" is applied to the mode of these relationships. In other words, at a basic level, society is the fact of people and relationship, while culture is the character, quality, and abstract nature of those patterned interrelationships.

2. Universality of Culture

Another commonly accepted characteristic of culture is its universality. Despite the variability of cultural behavior that persists in specific societies, there still is a general tendency for members of a particular group to share broad sets of behavior patterns (e.g., economy, marriage rules, political structure). However, at more specialized levels (e.g., religion, art, values) the actual expression of culture is more varied. Nevertheless, culture, as viewed from an anthropological perspective, is something that affects all members of society. In other words, however one defines the concept, culture is part of every human being's existence; the wealthy aristocrat who reads classics, speaks five languages, likes opera, and spends his summers in Europe, and the beer-drinking truck driver who watches police movies on television, reads only the sports page of the daily paper, bowls, and spends his vacations fishing for bluegill in east Tennessee. Culture is fundamental to human existence and we all participate in it as a prerequisite to living in society.

3. Culture as Learned Behavior

Another important characteristic of culture is that it is learned behavior. An individual is not born the bearer of a particular culture, rather he is raised within a specific cultural setting and by means of enculturation, the process whereby one internalizes a particular tradition, gradually develops behavior patterns consistent with those manifested by the other members of his group. However, to say that culture is learned is not to deny that there are important genetic components underlying the enculturation experience. Certainly, there are many biological, biochemical, and physiological factors that are necessary to the individual human being's capacity to learn culture. These prerequisites are often referred to by the anthropologists as bioculture.

4. Culture As Adaptive Mechanism

Another characteristic of culture is that it is an adaptive mechanism, a means whereby human beings can adjust to and survive in particular environmental niches (econiches).   Humans lack the innate capacities of some animals to get food and defend themselves. They have no large, powerful jaws and teeth, razor sharp claws, powerful forelimbs, exceptional speed, or cripplingly offensive odor that can be released at will.   Instead, these defenseless products of primate evolution are equipped with culture, a learned set of behaviors that compensate for man's physical limitations.   For example, technology is an important part of culture, and technology comprehends all of those special skills, techniques, and tools, which man has developed to hunt, fish, gather, and grow the food on which his survival depends.   For primitive man, a tool kit of stone projectile points, scrapers, burins, knives, and axes was the primary means of adapting to and surviving in the particular environment in which he found himself.   In a more general sense, all phases of culture have adaptive significance.   Even something as specialized as sport behavior can be seen as having such function in a particular cultural setting.   Indeed, the whole process of cultural evolution can be understood as one of an increasingly more efficient adaptation of human beings to their total environment.

5. Culture As an Integrated Whole

Culture also has the quality of being an integrated whole, all of its parts interwoven into a total process so that a change in one affects all others.   For example, in the process of culture change, if the basic technology is altered, it can be predicted that other areas of culture will similarly undergo some significant form of alteration.

6. Componential Nature of Culture

The componential nature of culture is another of its important characteristics.   In other words, culture is comprised of many distinguishable parts or components, as implied in the previous discussion of cultural integration.

The problem of isolating and labeling these components may be approached from several different perspectives.   Some anthropologists have simply broken the entire spectrum of culture into three components.   Julian Steward's three core insitutions include technoeconomical, sociopolitical organization, and ideology (see, Kaplan and Manners, 1972:47).   At the other extreme is Murdock's (1961) *Outline of Cultural Materials*, one of the manuals that accompanies the Human Relations Area Files (HRAF).   In this system culture is divided into 79 major divisions and 631 minor divisions. This scheme is intended to comprehend all the various subsystems or components of culture and includes areas as specialized as "social readjustments to death," number 768 in the system, or "athletic sports," number 526.

In short, there is no comprehensive model of culture that makes explicit all imaginable dimensions of the phenomen.   At best, all one can say is that culture is componential in nature, and that in this context sport must be seen as one of those components.

7. Symbolic Character of Culture

Another feature of culture is its symbolic character. Culture is dependent on the ability of its bearers to use symbols to attach meaning to things arbitrarily. In fact, Leslie White (1949:33) has put it quite succinctly:

> All culture (civilization) depends upon the symbol. It was the exercise of the symbolic faculty that brought culture into existence and it is the use of symbols that makes the perpetuation of culture possible. Without the symbol there would be no culture, and man would be merely an animal, not a human being.

8. Culture As Guide for Behavior

Another important dimension of culture is its function as a guide for behavior or as a blueprint for an individual's actions in society. Clyde Kluckhohn and William Kelly (1945:95), consistent with this focus, devised a definition of culture that has become a popular one in the social sciences: "all the historically created designs for living, explicit or implicit, rational, irrational, and nonrational, which may exist at any given time as potential guides for the behavior of men."

In summary, culture is defined as learned, shared symbolic behavior that functions as an adaptive mechanism as well as a guide for collective and individual human action. Culture is also an integrated whole made up of many interrelated components, each of which is ultimately subject to the same basic laws and general analytic techniques.

THE CULTURAL APPROACH TO SPORT

The basic problem in the cultural approach to the study of sport behavior is that of defining its role within the general cultural framework, and this problem is not so simple as it might seem. By definition culture is componential, but isolating any of its components so that it stands clearly in a distinct category by itself is often difficult if not impossible. For example, even though religion is viewed by anthropologists as one of the universal elements of culture, delineating its boundaries is not always easy, especially in preliterate or nonindustrial societies. In the modern, Western world, what is called "religion" is usually very visible and distinct because of the degree to which the institution has become bureaucratized. Special occupational roles (e.g., preachers, priests, nuns, rabbis), unique languages (both vocabulary and style), patterns of dress peculiar to persons in these occupations, clearly defined hierarchies of religious personnel, special times set aside for performance of their roles (e.g., Sunday, Sabbath), and obvious material manifestations (e.g., church buildings, colleges, publications), make it reasonably simple to distinguish religion from other aspects of cultural behavior. Still, even in this situation, there are areas in which separating religion from other cultural components is problematic. For example, healing services, the matter of the church's tax exempt status, and the use of one's church affiliation as a social or political tool are just some of the gray areas in which clear lines are difficult to draw.

In observing another society from the outside, especially a primitive or preliterate group, it is even more difficult to isolate the religious component. Consider the Navajo situation. When Europeans first encountered these Southwestern Native Americans they witnessed what they thought was a social system absolutely devoid of any religious dimension. The Navajo language lacked words deemed critical, such as expressions comparable to the English "religion" or "God." As late as the mid-nineteenth century, Anglo-Americans frequently commented that the Navajos were an irreligious, totally "pagan" people.

However, nothing could be further from the truth. With a very complex and thorough ceremonial system, the Navajos are among the most religiously conscious people in the world. Kluckholn and Leighton (1974:225), in an analysis of the daily lives of Navajos in the Ramah, New Mexico area, found that

> adult men give one-fourth to one-third of their productive time to activities connected with the "priestly" rites; women, one-fifth to one-sixth. This is undoubtedly a higher proportion of time than most white people give to the church, the theatre, and the doctor combined, and it is excellent evidence of the importance of their religion to the Navahos.

The problem is that Navajo ceremonies and mythologies are so interwoven with other components of the cultural system that it is not easy for an outsider to identify elements that are distinctly "religion." For example, all Navajo ceremonies are curing in nature, all focus on the restoration of health to the being of an individual or group of individuals. This ultimately amounts to bringing the patient back into harmony with the rest of the universe. In a society in which the cause of disease is viewed as spiritual rather than material, drawing a clear line between religion and medicine is difficult.

In many cases, this same problem plagues sport studies in anthropology. Remember the Eskimo song duel. So, in order to define sport, it is necessary to isolate its traits and draw its boundaries as a cultural component. This process of sport definition may be facilitated by analyzing the following topics: the relationship between work and leisure; the nature of play; the work and play dimensions of sport; sport as game; the relationship between sport and ritual; and sport as conflict.

Work and Leisure

Leisure, as a concept, is probably best understood when it is defined in opposition to the idea of "work." Leisure, which DeGrazia (1962:15) defines as "a state of being in which activity is performed for its own sake or as its own end," is generally viewed in an English language context as an antonym for work. The latter is precisely what leisure is not. In other words, it is a state in which activity is performed in order that something else be produced or accomplished.

Nevertheless, this distinction between the two types of activity in question may not be so clear in other cultural settings as it is in the industrialized West. In fact, it appears that in many archaic societies, life was one continuous rhythm of activity, work and leisure being part of one ongoing, daily process.

The rhythmic flow of daily activities has been witnessed by anthropologists among the few remaining primitive peoples of the world. Consistent with such observations, recent studies have altered previous notions that life in simple hunting-and-gathering society is rigorous, demanding, full of hardship, and marked by continued anxiety brought on by the fear of imminent starvation.

In a well-known analysis of subsistence activities among the !Kung Bushman of the African Kalahari Desert, anthropologist Richard Lee (1968:30) claims that the life of a hunting-gathering group is not necessarily "a precarious and arduous struggle for existence." In fact, he discovered that there was clear predictability about the nutritious foodstuffs available to the Bushman on a daily and year-round basis, even in the driest years and the least productive zones of the desert. The ready availability of these items, in particular, the mongongo nuts, limited the amount of time that group members were actively engaged in the quest for food. According to Lee (1968:37), men "spent a maximum of thirty-two hours a week" hunting and/or gathering. although the men, as hunters, "tend to work more frequently than the women," their schedule is uneven, entailing more time spent in food getting activities some weeks than others. However, the time schedule of women is more nearly uniform.

> A woman gathers on one day enough food to feed her family for three days, and spends the rest of her time resting in camp, doing embroidery, visiting other camps, or entertaining visitors from other camps. For each day at home, kitchen routines, such as cooking, nut cracking,

collecting firewood, and fetching water, occupy from one to three hours of her time. This rhythm of steady work and steady leisure is maintained throughout the year (Lee, 1968:37).

If such a continuum of activities, both productive and nonproductive relative to the subsistence base, is characteristic of prehistoric hunting-and-gathering peoples, it is possible that the idea of work and leisure being two distinct phenomena may be a product of agriculture. As man domesticates plants and animals he becomes slave to a calendrical scheme that demands certain strenuous activities at particular times. Whether hoeing, digging, planting, weeding, or harvesting, he is required to perform appropriate tasks during predetermined periods, so that there can be no unbroken rhythm to activities. He must conform to the requirements of the agricultural calendar first, finding leisure only in those moments when the crops are not demanding attention.

However, there is evidence to support the idea that a distinct work-leisure opposition may be an even more recent development, at least in certain areas of the world. DeGrazia (1962:14) has noted that the early Greeks used the word *ascholia* to refer to "work."

In origin the word really denotes the absence of leisure for its root is *schole* [leisure], before which an *a-* is placed to signify a want or a lack. It thus means un-leisure or the state of being busy or occupied. This being at unleisure, though it seems a roundabout way of putting things, may be the closest to our phrase of being occupied or at work.

These same Greeks put a premium on the availability and proper use of leisure time. A thinking man or scholar, in particular, could not be burdened down with work; it only limited his ability to reflect on vital philosophical issues at a leisurely pace. In this sense, work was seen as a temporary aside to the general, overarching leisure process and was to be avoided if at all possible.

With the advent of industrialism, modern capitalism, and the Reformation, however, conceptualizations and values were reversed. Work became a valued human endeavor in and of itself and was viewed as the opposite of leisure. Popular folk sayings, such as "Idle hands are the devil's workshop," reflect this exalting of work and a related degrading of leisure. This polarization of work and leisure as two distinctively different and opposing types of behavior may be a relatively recent and temporarily limited event in Western history.

The twentieth century has seen the gradual reemergence in the Western world of leisure's respectability. Historian Bernard Mergen (1977:55) has studied the rise of leisure among the laboring class in the United States in the early decades of this century and has suggested that although the work ethic "was never as monolithic as history text books make it seem," there was a deliberate attempt by both scholars and industrial leaders alike to combat the more prevalent attitude with a "leisure ethic." The advocates of the latter "hoped that organized recreation would result in a unified and improved national culture" (Mergen, 1977:63).

Despite the fact that the work-leisure distinction is not so clear in some societies as in others, it is probably safe to assume that the dichotomy has universal significance. All peoples experience the two states of existence, one that asks no question of objectives beyond itself, the other that is stimulated and sustained by the goal that exists outside the behavior. While some systems are more deliberate in distinguishing the two processes, work and leisure are transcultural realities.

Play

A definition of play that can be applied cross-culturally is vital to the anthropology of sport. Play is a phenomenon that is not only universal to human beings, but also common among other animals. Most species of mammals, for example, engage in some form of play from time to time, especially during the early years of the life cycle. Many ethologists have studied social play among animals, but satisfactory definitions of such activity are scarce. Typical of the concepts of play generated by ethologists is that of Bekoff (1972:417):

> Social play is that behavior which is performed during social interactions in which there is a decrease in social distance between the interactants, and no evidence of social investigation or of agonistic (offensive or defensive) or passive-submissive behaviors on the part of the members of a dyad (triad, etc.), although these actions may occur as derived acts during play.

Lower primates in particular are inveterate players, especially the preadults. Such play is generally easy to identify, but not so easy to define systematically. For example, at the typical zoo on a warm spring afternoon, the crowd gathered around the monkey island will generally agree on whether and when a particular animal is playing. However, if asked to consider all the observed play behaviors collectively and isolate uniform criteria by which that play can be recognized, the same crowd would find such a task difficult and probably impossible (Miller, 1973:88).

Oakley (1976:173) has attempted to isolate the signals of primate play, its observable characteristics. The most important feature of primate play she labels the "play face."

> This is a facial expression in which the mouth is loosely open, the teeth covered by the lips, and the corners of the

mouth retracted slightly. The eyebrows may be slightly raised.

In addition to the "play face" characteristic which is viewed as baseline, Oakley (1976:173) includes the following elements as observable evidence of play among primates:

1. A reordering of ordinary behavioral sequences;
2. Exaggerating of movements;
3. Repetition of movements or behavioral sequences;
4. Incomplete behavioral sequences;
5. Increased tempo in movements.

Regardless of the conceptual difficulties associated with its analysis, descriptions of primate life are generally replete with reference to play behavior (e.g., Lawick-Goodall, 1971, on chimpanzees; Miller, 1973, on baboons; Dolhinow, 1971, on patas monkeys; Carpenter, 1964, on rhesus monkeys and macaques).

Suomi and Harlow (1971:72) have suggested, "of all monkey behaviors, play is probably the most informative." In this vein, many specialized research projects in primatology have used play as a perspective for understanding other facets of nonhuman primate behavior. In one case, Suomi and Harlow (1971:75) have analyzed the role of play in the socialization process of the rhesus monkey and conclude that it is "one of the most important aspects of social development."

As among monkeys, play is easily recognizable among human beings, even across cultural lines. Most children's play, for example, is readily identified as such regardless of where and within what cultural context it occurs, even by the untrained observer. When the children of the Dani, a group of New Guinea highland people, are shown at play in the classic anthropology film *Dead Birds* (1977), it is not necessary for the narrator to tell the audience what general type of behavior they are watching. It is obvious to all, regardless of particular cultural or linguistic backgrounds.

Although play behavior is easily recognized it is not so easily constrained to conceptual categories. This is witnessed to by the vast amount of literature on the subject and the many definitions of the term proposed by behavioral scientists. One consistency underlying most of these discussions is that they begin by referring to Johan Huizinga and his classic *Homo Ludens*, in which play is defined as

a free activity standing quite consciously outside "ordinary" life as being "not serious," but at the same time absorbing the player intensely and utterly. It is an activity connected with no material interest, and no profit can be gained by it. It proceeds within its own proper boundaries of time and space according to fixed rules and in orderly manner. It promotes the formation of social groupings which tend to surround themselves with secrecy and to stress their difference from the common world by disguise or other means (1950:13).

For Huizinga, then, play is ideally self-contained and provides its own meaning and justification. Also, he develops the notion that play and its various forms are actually the vehicles by which other facets of culture (ritual, law, politics) are acted out. In fact, he argues that civilization itself has developed by means of playlike mechanisms.

It has not been difficult to show that a certain play-factor was extremely active all through the culture process and that it produced many of the fundamental forms of social life. The spirit of playful competition is, as a social impulse, older than culture itself and pervades all life like a cultural ferment...We have to conclude, therefore, that civilization in its earliest phases, played. It does not come from play like a baby detaching itself from the womb; it arises in and as play and never leaves it (Huizinga, 1950:173).

From an anthropological perspective there is a twofold problem with Huizinga's concept of play. In the first place, Huizinga employs a definition of culture that equates it with civilization, a practice consistent with some nineteenth-century anthropology, but unacceptable in the discipline today. In the second place, play is viewed by Huizinga as a form of culture rather than having forms in culture, a novel and interesting idea, but of little value in cross-cultural research. Despite the fact that anthropologists recognize many weaknesses in Huizinga's understanding of play, they are quick to underscore the importance of *Homo Ludens* and its emphasis on play, both as a subject of scholarly analysis and a vital element in modern civilization.

Since Huizinga's work, many social scientists have attempted to create some consensus by offering novel definitions of play. However, no single such definition has captured the fancy of the entire anthropological community. Still, the work of anthropologist Edward Norbeck on the subject of play has gained much attention within the discipline, and many of his colleagues find his understanding of the term useful. Norbeck (1974:1) defines play as

behavior, resting upon a biologically inherited stimulus or proclivity, that is distinguished by a combination of traits: play is voluntary, somehow pleasurable, distinct temporally from other behavior, and distinct in having a make-believe or transcendental quality.

Norbeck (1974:2) views play as taking on explicit cultural form with a broad range of behavioral components:

So defined, play includes games and sports, theatrical performances and other forms of mimicry; painting, music, dance, and the entire range of arts and esthetics; wit and humor; fantasy; and ecstatic psychic states. Ecstasy may be induced by suggestion, auto-suggestion, the ingestion of drugs and other substances, fasting and bodily deprivation of other kinds, and by still other physical means.

Norbeck's (1974:1) definition of play is more appropriate than that of Huizinga in an anthropological discussion. Norbeck recognizes the importance of the inherited (genetic) inclination toward play, he develops the notion that play forms have significant cultural dimensions (though admitting that play can take place in both individual and social contexts), and his model is general enough to be useful in cross-cultural analyses. It is noteworthy, however, that even Norbeck is forced to admit that there is still that intangible element in play that leads to its immediate recognition but that cannot be, or at least has not been to date, verbally articulated. At best it can be said that play is recognized initially by its quality of playfulness, a redundancy to be sure, but a necessary confession of conceptual limitation.

Some of the confusion inherent in the attempt to define play is to be explained by its paradoxical nature. Anthropologist Gregory Bateson (1972) views paradox as the primary feature of play, the complexity that makes play so recognizable on the one hand, but so indefinable on the other. Bateson (1972:179) relates an experience he had in 1952 while at San Francisco's Fleishhacker Zoo:

> What I encountered at the zoo was a phenomenon well known to everybody: I saw two young monkeys playing, i.e., engaged in an interactive sequence of which the unit actions or signals were similar to but not the same as those of combat. It was evident, even to the human observer, that the sequence as a whole was not combat, and evident to the human observer that to the participant monkeys this was "not combat."

Thus, the paradox: what the monkeys seemed to be saying was that they were not doing what they in fact appeared to be doing, fighting. This is the message of play, the message that Bateson (1972:178) classifies as "metacommunication." Metacommunication is communication about communication. Using Bateson's (1972:178) illustration: the statement, "The cat is on the mat" is a simple denotative communication. However, when one subsequently observes "My telling you where to find the cat was friendly," he is engaging in a form of metalanguage or metacommunication. The statement "This is a play" is metacommunicative because it is a message about a message. Bateson (1972:181) suggests that the linguistic complexity of the play act lends credibility to speculation that "the evolution of play may have been an important step in the evolution of communication."

In summary, for purposes of this volume, play is viewed as a behavioral form having both biological and cultural dimensions that is difficult to define at the exclusion of all other behavior, yet is distinguishable by a variety of traits. It is pleasurable, voluntary, set apart by temporal parameters, marked by a make-believe quality, but made real by its unreality (i.e., Bateson's [1972] paradox).

Play, unlike leisure, should not be viewed as an antonym of work. Stevens (1980:318) has suggested in a presentation entitled "Play and Work: A False Dichotomy?" [that] "this is not only a false dichotomy but one which, if its dimensions are not revealed, may stand in the way of meaningful advances in several aspects of our field of study" (i.e., play). If work is to be treated as the polar opposite of play on an activity continuum, work must be consistently involuntary, unpleasurable, and real. Obviously, work is not always characterized by these traits. Work is generally defined as purposeful activity directed toward some goal (For more thorough discussions on the nature of work, see Anderson, 1964, and DeGrazia, 1962). Play, while by definition "not purposeful," can assume some of the characteristics of work in certain situations. Work, on the other hand, can become very playlike in the right context. What this suggests is that the two concepts are related, but certainly not polar opposites.

There is a sense in which it is appropriate to view play and work as compatible elements. In fact, the two can be seen as integrated in some forms of behavior, as persons in effect play at work or work at play. For example, Csikszentmihalyi (1975), in a book entitled *Beyond Boredom and Anxiety,* has analyzed several professions and athletic activities (e.g., surgeons, rock climbers) and attempted to locate and describe the techniques these commitments employ in the achievement of "peak experiences." He suggests that most individuals in these capacities are motivated and rewarded intrinsically, without direct regard or demand for material or extrinsic reinforcement. These intrinsic rewards are defined ultimately in terms of what he calls the "flow experience."

> In the flow state, action follows upon actions according to an internal logic that seems to need no conscious intervention by the actor. He experiences it as a unified flowing, from one moment to the next, in which he is in control of his actions, and in which there is little distinction between self and environment, between stimulus and response, or between past, present, and future (Csikszentmihalyi, (1975:36).

For Csikszentmihalyi (1975:37), "play is the flow experience par excellence" and essential to enjoying work on the one hand and avoiding boredom and anxiety on the other.

In another study, Mergen (1978:8) has described the ways in which the American shipyard worker makes his job more pleasurable and ultimately acceptable, by adding daily doses of play. "The competitive spirit, company sponsored athletics, day dreaming, joking, tricks, gossip, costuming - all have important functions in making shipyard work more like play (Mergen, 1978:197). Implicitly, it is suggested that playfulness can be a productive posture toward work.

In the same sense that one can play at work, he can also work at play; in other words, develop a very serious attitude and commitment relative to recreational and leisure-time activities. In a book entitled *The Mississippi Choctaw at Play: The Serious Side of Leisure,* Blanchard (1981) describes the sport life of this Native American group and attempts to explain the cultural roots and ramifications of the dedication with which these people approach their play. Traditionally, stickball, the parent game of lacrosse, and more recently modern sports like basketball, baseball, and softball that are directed under the auspices of the tribal recreation program, have been viewed as vital elements in community life. A large majority of the Choctaws are involved in these activities, either as spectators or participants, in the respective seasons, and approach them with a seriousness that often surpasses that associated with their jobs. Blanchard (1981) concludes that this worklike attitude toward play is rooted in the very nature of Choctaw culture and is an important adjustment to the economic realities of the twentieth century and yet basic to the maintenance of tradition in the midst of a rapidly changing world. Thus, working at play can be viewed as an important activity pattern among the Choctaws.

Other ethnographic literature provides descriptions of the many ways that work and play activities among primitive peoples are so closely interwoven. Stumpf and Cozens (1947:207), in their analysis of the economic dimensions of Maori culture, have underscored the

> way in which every aspect of their economic life was permeated with a definite element of recreation. Whether engaged in fishing, bird-snaring, cultivation of the fields, or building a house or a canoe, the occasion was marked by activities which we could definitely classify as recreational.

Royce and Murray (1971) have discovered a similar pattern among the Kapingamarangi in Micronesia in which the work and play phenomena are integrated into a single activity. For example, the Kapingamarangi occasionally engage in a four-day event called *ti rauhara* during which all the members of the community participate in a range of fishing, gathering, and food preparation activities. The festive occasion is marked by much laughing, horseplay, singing, and game playing, all in direct conjunction with basic subsistence tasks. Also, *ti rauhara* is circumscribed by special rules, and those members of the community breaking these rules are subjected to "playful" forms of punishment. Some violations are punished by wrestling.

> One of our informants described how on the early mornings when the teams returned from fishing, their canoes had to approach their team's house in a line perpendicular to the beach. Approaching on a slant was considered crossing another team's territorial waters. In case this violation was observed, the violated team raised a shout from the shore and paddled out to wrestle the violators and claim their fish (Royce and Murray, 1971:7).

Such work-play activities are not unlike many events characteristic of rural America. Consider the traditional "husking bee," a festive event in which a necessary economic task (corn husking) was embellished by much singing, dancing, game playing, and eating.

In general, these examples suggest that work and play are not necessary polar opposites. As Denzin (1975:474) suggests, one can work at play and play at play. Therefore, it is probably appropriate to think of work and play as two related concepts with both noun and verb forms that can be used to denote or describe particular kinds of activities. Work and play are initially subjective states, but are generally manifested in behavior in such a way that an observer can identify the activities.

If play and work are not treated in juxtaposition to one another, what type of activity can be opposed to play in order to clarify its meaning? In other words, if work is <u>not</u>, what <u>is</u> the opposite of play? Unfortunately, English does not have an appropriate word to describe the state of non-play, an activity marked by a lack of pleasure, an element of constraint, and a stark realism. Such an activity may be worklike or it may be a form of leisure, but in either case, it is "not-play" (Bateson, 1972:181).

For lack of a better word, therefore, we have chosen to refer to that conceptual counterpart of play as "not-play." This allows us to speak of human behavior as having both work and leisure, and play and not-play dimensions (see Fig. 1). Though play and not-play are defined with reference to several traits (e.g., constraint and freedom, enjoyability, make-believe and real), the continuum between the two is simply a measure of pleasurability. Play is pleasurable, not-play is not, and within each of these categories there exists varying amounts of that quality (i.e., particular play experiences can be more or less pleasurable).

If work is not the polar opposite of play, how does the concept fit into the total range of human activity? As we have done with play, we might suggest that work be juxtaposed to nonwork on a continuum of purposefulness. Work is activity directed toward a specific goal; nonwork is without goal. However, nonwork is comparable to leisure, defined here as "a state of being in which activity is performed for its own sake or as its own end." In this sense leisure is not-work. Work is oriented toward external objectives and never performed for its own sake. For this reason work and not-work or leisure are at opposite ends of the goal continuum (see Fig. 1).

Given this model of human activity, any behavior can be defined in terms of the varying amounts of work, leisure, play, and not-play that it manifests. In quadrant A would fall those activities that are goal-oriented and worklike but that one enjoys (i.e., playing at work). Quadrant B comprehends the many forms of leisurely play, the enjoyable activities that one does, simply to do them. In quadrant C, one finds those forms of work that are not enjoyed, but that are done out of a sense of duty and a commitment to objectives outside the activity itself. Quadrant D defines those activities that ostensibly are leisure, being engaged in purely for the sake of so engaging, but are of no pleasure for participants who might approach them with a sense of boredom or drudgery.

As demonstrated in the following section, this model of activity is a convenient device with which to resolve the sport definition dilemma.

Sport as Work or Play?

One question that is often raised in sport study circles is whether sport should be viewed as worklike or more playlike in nature. Obviously, in some situations, sporting activities are engaged in with leisurely and playful abandon (e.g., a backyard game of "catch"), while in others they are often approached with a seriousness and task-orientation that overrides potential playfulness (e.g., professional football). This work-play variability characteristic of sport is reflected in definitions that social scientists have proposed for the term.

Some scholars have simply called sport a type of play. For example, Huizinga (1950:195-197) views sport as a play form, though he admits that "ever since the last quarter of the nineteenth century games, in the guise of sport, have been taken more and more seriously." Likewise, Caillois (1969:44-45) tends to equate sport, play, and games. Even Loy's (1969:56) definition of sport as "playful competition" suggests that such activities fall under the general rubric "play."

At the other extreme, some writers have chosen to put the emphasis on the serious dimensions of sport. Harry Edwards (1973:55-56), in his popular *Sociology of Sport*, argues that "sports have virtually nothing in common with play," and emphasizes the worklike characteristics of sport behavior: it always involves physical

FIGURE 1...The Dimensions of Human Activity

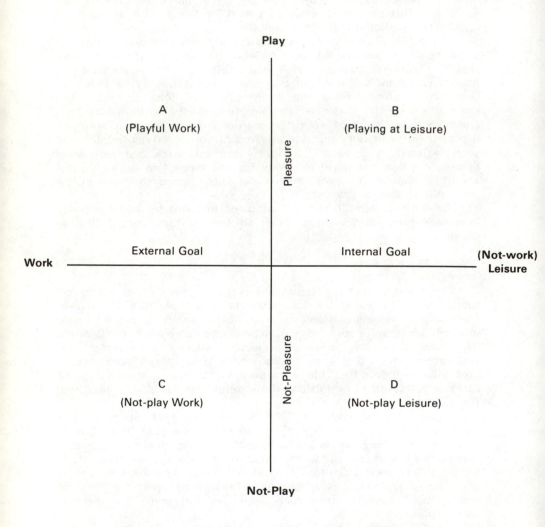

Play

A
(Playful Work)

B
(Playing at Leisure)

Pleasure

Work | External Goal | Internal Goal | (Not-work) Leisure

Not-Pleasure

C
(Not-play Work)

D
(Not-play Leisure)

Not-Play

exertion, has a formal structure and organization, demands an adherence to tradition, has a seriousness of purpose, requires meticulous preparation, and "in sports all roles and positions are explicitly named, defined, and delegated." He then suggests that

> So far from being play, creation, "fun and games," or mere diversion, sports assume the character of occupational endeavors for participants, and of business for coaches, administrators and owners (Edwards, 1973:61).

The problem with Edwards' definition of sport from an anthropological perspective is that the focus is entirely on the modern, industrialized West and the athletic institutions that have developed in the college and professional ranks. As a result, this understanding of the concept has little applicative value in non-Western or primitive situations. It also ignores the fact that certain types of sport are obviously forms of play.

In an attempt to integrate both the work and play aspects of sport into an acceptable definition, sociologist Allen Sack (1977:194) has developed a model in which sport is viewed as "an institution-alized game, dependent on physical prowess," that is characterized by varying amounts of work or play, dependent on the nature of the specific activity. In this context, "Play and work represent ideal types, i.e., mental constructs composed of the most characteristic or essential elements of each phenomenon" (Sack, 1977:194). At the same time, Sack (1977:194) makes a similar distinction between athletic and nonathletic sport, "athletic" referring to the degree of physical effort exerted in a particular game or activity. Thus, any specific sport is viewed in terms of its seriousness on one continuum (work-play) and in terms of its degree of required exertion (athletic-nonathletic) on the other (See Fig. 2).

While the Sack (1977:194) model recognizes the integral nature of work and play in the sport process and provides a workable definition for the term "athletics," it mistakenly assumes that work and play can be defined as states at opposite ends of the same activity continuum. As a result of this one-dimensional work-play juxtaposition, not all forms of sport can be adequately described within the Sack model. The continuum only deals with the inherent seriousness associated with the particular sport in question, so that any given activity has but one possible position on the continuum. For example, professional football will always be seen as more work than play in the Sack model. The approach simply does not allow for varying amounts of work and play in any given sport, a variable necessary for the effective anthropological analysis of actual behavior patterns associated with sport.

A more adequate and comprehensive way to define the various manifestations of sport as a type of human activity is to employ the model suggested in Figure One. Specifically, sport can be viewed as

FIGURE 2...A typology of sport (From Sack, 1977:194)

Nonathletic ←——————————————————————→ **Athletic**

Play

↑

Golf (with friends)   Mountain Climbing

Bowling   Small-time College Football
(with friends for fairly
large sums of money)

                                               Big-time College Football

Professional Pool   Professional Football

↓

Work

assuming several different forms, each reflecting varying combinations of work, leisure, play and not-play.

In quadrant <u>A</u>, the "playful work" category of activity, one might find a sport situation that combines work and play. The goal may be external, but the spirit playful. Consider the professional baseball player, a third baseman standing in the on-deck circle on a cool summer evening, swinging a bat in anticipation of an opportunity to get on base. He is working; he gets paid for this, and his family likes to eat. He wants to win; it's essential if his team is going to make the play-offs. Winning is the external motivation, the goal that qualifies this experience as work. Nevertheless, it's a nice night, he's feeling good, and he's enjoying the game. He is caught up in that experience Csikszentmihalyi (1975:36) calls "flow," but still working.

On the other hand, quadrant <u>B</u>, "playing at leisure," qualifies another type of sport. Here the activity is both playful and leisurely, the utltimate form of play from Huizinga's (1950:13) perspective. As an example, picture the teenager who has a couple of hours to kill after school. While hanging out in the high school gymnasium, she is invited to join a small, informal game of pick-up basketball. She does, and gets lost in the thrill of the movement and the playful interaction with her peers. Similar to the professional third baseman, she feels the flow, but her experience is couched in a not-work environment. The only goal is the self-imposed, internal goal; participation for participation's sake.

Quadrant <u>C</u>, the least playful of possibilities, still comprehends some sport phenomena. Here the athlete sports out of sense of obligation; the only pleasure is the pleasure of knowing that the game will soon be over. Again, the professional athlete can be used to illustrate. This time it's a big center with a National Basketball League team. It's Sunday afternoon, it's play-off time, and the game is being televised nationally. The player's knees are swollen and sore. His doctor has advised him against playing, but a win today is essential, and the team's chances will be seriously endangered without him. The trainer shoots his body full of steroids and cortisone, wraps his knees, and sends him out onto the court. He plays, but the pain taxes the limits of the medication. By the second half, his jaws are cramped from biting against the pain, and his neck is sore from watching the clock. This is not play, nor is it leisure. It is work; working at work. However, it is still sport.

Finally, quadrant <u>D</u> defines those leisurely sport activities that participants might find boring or generally without pleasurable rewards. Take the case of old Uncle Ozzie who's been tucked away in the Oxnard County Nursing Home ever since his kids packed up and left town one night while he was at church. In the midst of watching a good dog fight one afternoon, he gets pulled out of his rocking chair and into a game of shuffleboard by some well-meaning friends. Uncle Oz's lack of enthusiasm is obvious. He has to be reminded every time his turn rolls around: "Come-on Oz. Are you going to shoot or just stand there looking for those dogs?". He peers in the direction of his rocking chair from time to time, wondering if the dogs will still be there when he gets back. The shuffleboard is a leisurely pursuit, but not exactly playful. Ozzie is bored but, nevertheless, engaged in sport.

This four-quadrant model of human activity as applied to sport allows for a greater range of distinctions between various types of sport behaviors than that possible in the Sack (1977) model. It is admitted that these variables are primarily subjective ones and that sport activities vary according to the attitudes of those actually engaging in the activities. However, these attitudes are manifested in actual behavior and are generally observable to the social scientist, even from a cross-cultural perspective. For example, the two major varieties of traditional Mississippi Choctaw stickball fit very nicely into the model. On the one hand, the most highly structured and formal of the many types of traditional racketball matches was that played between two separate Choctaw communities. The classic form of the ballplay was planned well in advance, involved total community participation, and was characterized by extensive wagering, all in an atmosphere of ceremony and festivity. Competition here was fierce, and the game's outcome was viewed as one of ultimate significance. Generally, this type of stickball could be classified as a quadrant A activity, marked by a serious commitment to the object of winning, but still flavored with a persistent playfulness.

The less formal, intracommunity stickball match, however, tended to be more casual and playful in nature than its formal counterpart. Winning was less important than the simple act of playing itself. Therefore, in this context, stickball was more of a quadrant B activity.

The same variability is probably characteristic of most sporting events in any cultural setting, and a comprehensive, cultural approach to the analysis of sport must recognize this variable dimension of sport behavior. Sport has varying quantities of work, play, leisure, and not-play.

Sport and Games

Another aspect of the definitional problem underlying the anthropology of sport is the meaning of "game." When are sport activities to be viewed as "games," and when as something else?

As Sack (1977:189) has noted, the "concept of game is often confused with play," indeed, treated as a synonymous term. The problem with such a conceptual understanding is that many games are often staged for the entertainment of spectators and assume a worklike character for the participants themselves. Therefore, "game" is not always "play."

Sociologist John Loy (1969:56) has defined game as "any form of playful competition whose outcome is determined by physical skill, strategy or chance employed singly or in combination." Implicitly, Loy is suggesting that games are a subcategory of play, but if the "playful" is removed from the definition, it is fully compatible with the cultural analysis outlined herein.

To be more specific, games can be further defined according to categories or types. Perhaps the most popular scheme of this nature is one devised by Caillois (1969:55), in which he classifies games in four categories: *agon* (competition), *alea* (chance), *mimicry* (pretense), and *ilinx* (vertigo) (see Table 1). Within each of these categories, games are then weighted in terms of *paidia*, as uncontrolled freedom, and *ludus*, control by determinate or hindering conventions.

In order for the latter framework to be used in this analysis of sport-related concepts, each of the games listed must be viewed separately as they are observed in actual behavior and evaluated on the work-play continuum suggested earlier. In other words, it is necessary to admit that something like football can be a game, be classified within one of the Caillois categories (i.e., *agon*), and still be more work than play (e.g., the National Football League contest).

In general, then, games are competitive activities that involve physical skills, strategy, and chance, or any combination of these elements. In addition, any game may exhibit variable amounts of constriction (i.e., rules or predetermined patterns) and can be classified as more or less playful or worklike in actual manifestation.

Sports and Ritual

The meaning of sport can also be approached from the perspective of its relationship to ritual. The observation of these two phenomena in human society suggests that they are closely related facets of cultural behavior. The sport and ritual processes manifest similar behavioral patterns. In other words, sport often assumes a ritual-like character. Also, there is evidence to suggest that the evolution of sport behavior has its roots in ritual performance, suggesting further that sport is a relatively recent ritual special-ization in which competition is stressed over and above the proper acting out of the prescribed procedure.

The study of ritual is a popular pursuit in anthropological circles, and though there is great room for debate, theorists are generally agreed as to what they mean by the concept. Ritual is a facet of culture and can be viewed as the symbolic dimension of social activities that are not specifically technical in nature. "Technique has economic consequences which are measurable and predictable; ritual on the other hand is a symbolic statement which 'says' something about the individuals involved in the action" (Leach, 1954:13). In this sense, ritual can be either religious or not, sacred or profane. It is simply a patterned activity that expresses some basic social message of importance to the structure and ongoing

TABLE 1...Types of Games (From, Caillois, 1969:5)

	Agon (Competition)	Alea (Chance)	Mimicry (Pretense)	Ilinx (Vertigo)
Paidia		comptines heads or tails	childish imitation masks costumes	children's swings merry-go-round teeter-totter waltz outdoor sports skiing mountain climbing
	not regulated			
		betting roulette	theatre	
	regulated			
		lotteries compounded or parlayed		
	races combats etc. athletics			
noise agitation laughter dance hoop solitaire games of patience crossword puzzles				
Ludus				

Note: In each vertical column, the games are classified very approximately in such order that the paidia element constantly decreases while the ludus element constantly increases.

cohesiveness of a particular group. As Douglas (1970:42) has suggested, ritual, like language, serves as a "transmitter of culture:" and exercises a "constraining effect on social behavior."

Given this understanding of ritual, it is easy to see the justification for viewing sport as ritual. Even the most sophisticated sporting events of modern society can be interpreted as such. Anthropologist William Arens (1975) has written a colorful essay entitled "The Great American Football Ritual." He claims that

> football, although only a game, tells us much about who and what we Americans are as a people, and if an anthropologist from another planet visited here, he would be struck by the American fixation on this game and would report on it with glee and romantic intoxication anthropologists normally reserve for the exotic rituals of a newly discovered tribe. This assertion is based on the theory that certain significant symbols are the key to understanding a culture; football is such a symbol (Arens, 1975:81).

As a rule, sport always reflects the basic values of the cultural setting within which it is actually performed and thus functions as ritual or as a "transmitter of culture." Even a sport that has been introduced from a foreign source is very quickly redefined and adjusted to fit the norms and values of tradition.

For example, when basketball was introduced among the Ramah Navajos in New Mexico during the 1930s, it was very quickly altered to the point that it became a unique form of "Navajo basketball," something quite different from the game played by their original Anglo Mormon teachers.

> Even from the most nonscholarly perspective, Navajo basketball must be seen as a different game. Behaviorally, it is less aggressive, structured, outwardly enthusiastic, and morally educative; while at the same time it is more individualistic, kin-oriented, and pure good times than that of the town's Anglo Mormon population (Blanchard, 1974:10).

The same phenomenon has been observed among the Utes of the North American Great Basin area subsequent to the introduction of basketball (Tindall, 1975a). Also, after the British introduced cricket into the Trobriand Islands in Melanesia in the early part of the twentieth century, the game was restructured until eventually it had become a culture-bound form of "Trobriand Cricket" (Leach,1976:9).

Ultimately, what is really meant by the assertion that sport is a form of ritual behavior is simply that sport's actual character in any given situation is the result of particular cultural norms. Sport can thus be seen as "saying something significant" about shared values and tradition in any specific society, using the medium of competitive play. At the same time, it is reasonable to assume that if one is going to understand sport behavior in a society he must begin by gaining some insight into the general cultural pattern responsible for the final definition of that behavior.

In a related sense, sport can also be viewed as a setting within which ritual processes, not directly a part of the game, can be acted out. As a case in point, the formal intercommunity stickball match of the eighteenth-century Choctaws was characterized by extensive ritual activity, as the shamans representing both teams went through wide repertoires of ceremonial incantations designed to influence the outcome of the match by extra-ordinary means.

The similarities between ritual and sport make it particularly difficult for some writers to view sport as an element in primitive society. Damm (1970:52), in an article entitled "The So-Called Sport Activities of Primitive Peoples," notes that many of the ceremonial events of primitive societies that are recorded in the ethnographic literature have sportlike characteristics, but lack the competitive element necessary to qualify as sport. As an illustration, he cites a Melanesian tug-of-war game played in conjunction with ceremonial events. One such contest pits male members of the community against the females so that the outcome is virtually predetermined by the uneven distribution of strength. With reference to that situation, Damm (1970:56) reports that the men upon winning "did not only sneer at the losers, but also while howling, rushed onto the opponents laying [sic] on the ground and did publically engage in coitus." Is this sport? Damm (1970:56) implies that it is not and that the sport is only incidental to broader ritual regularities. Competition is secondary to ceremony. In a similar vein, Diem (1971:1) is more direct in arguing that so-called "sports" among primitive peoples were always sacred and consistently part of some form of cultic observance. If this is the case, one must conclude that such societies have no sport, in the contemporary sense of that term.

On the other hand, Guttmann (1978:19) in his popular *From Ritual to Record* takes issue with this conclusion and suggests that while sport may have "entered the lives of primitive adults primarily in conjunction with some form of religious significance, " it is not safe to assume that they had no secular sports. He suggests that it is reasonable to assume that these activities would not of necessity be constrained to the more formal ritual environment, especially as they are participated in by the children.

Nonetheless, even Guttmann recognizes the predominance of the ritual dimension in the sports of the primitive and ancient peoples of the world. Analyzing the history of the Greek games, he concludes,

> To the degree that Greek athletic festivals were religious ritual and artistic expression, they had a purpose beyond themselves and ceased to be sports in our strictest definition of the term. The closer the contest came to the status of

art, the further they departed from that of sport (Guttmann, 1978:23).

Certainly, modern sports are distinguished from primitive ones; the former by its greater emphasis on competition, the latter, by the inescapability of its ritual component. Modern sport often becomes competition for competition's sake, and winning becomes the principal goal of participation. So-called primitive sports on the other hand are more likely to treat the competitive element as a secondary consideration in a highly ritualized activity.

In general, even though sport cannot be understood in primitive or ancient society without one first appreciating its basic ritual orientation, it is still legitimate to use the expression "primitive sport."

Sport as Conflict

From another perspective, sport can be seen as a form of social conflict, "a struggle over values and claims to scarce status, power and resources in which the aims of the opponents are to neutralize, injure, or eliminate their rivals" (Coser, 1956:8). "Competition is a form of conflict in which two or more persons struggle to attain an object," and in which the emphasis rests "entirely on the object itself rather than the persons themselves as antagonists" (Nisbet, 1970:77). Competition is different from other forms of conflict because of the fact that any negative effect that an opponent has on another in this type of social interaction is indirectly rather than directly intended. In this sense, competition may be "thought of as a kind of cooperative conflict" (Popenoe, 1974:52).

Conflict takes many forms in any particular society, and some of these are often defined by sporting events. In the United States, the conflictive dimensions of football are perhaps the most obvious illustration of this fact. As Arens (1975:77) has noted,

> It is hardly surprising...that books by [football] participants are replete with symbolic references to war. Jerry Kramer, a Green Bay Packer during the 1960s and coauthor of *Instant Replay*, divides the book into the following sections: Preliminary Skirmishes, Basic Training, Mock Warfare, Armed Combat, War's End.

The symbolic association of war and sport has been isolated on an even broader scale. Anthropologist Richard Sipes (1973:80) has analyzed the relationship between the frequency of warfare and the existence of physically combative sports in a sample of societies around the world and concludes that these two items "appear to be components of a broader cultural pattern" in any given society. In other words, in those societies with a high frequency of warfare activities there is a great likelihood that there will also be extensive combative sport behavior. Conversely, those people who do not fight generally do not participate in such sport activities.

The ethnographic literature also contains many illustrations of the sportlike character of war in human society. In certain areas of the world, such as the North American Northwest Coast and in the New Guinea Highlands, it is difficult to understand patterns of warfare if they are not allowed that competitive or sport dimension. In other words, some forms of war are too gamelike for the sport scholar to simply write them off as just another form of armed conflict.

In sum, sport is by definition, a type of activity that entails aggressive behavior and some form of competition, and in any given cultural setting it can be viewed as having social conflict dimensions.

SPORT, RECREATION AND PHYSICAL EDUCATION

Recreation can be defined from many different perspectives, and similar to other terms discussed in this chapter, it has obvious cultural dimensions. Although it is difficult to constrict the concept to a universally applicable definition, recreation does have characteristics that set it apart from other related behaviors.

In the first place, recreation, unlike work, is not compulsive or obligatory. Recreation is done in one's leisure time. Nevertheless, it involves activity, actually doing something, a characteristic that distinguishes it from leisure, which may be enjoyed passively (e.g., rest, contemplation). However, any activity may be recreative to the individual or group involved. In other words, the recreation experience is evaluated from a subjective or cultural perspective. What is work to some might be recreation to others. Finally, as Kando (1975:28) has suggested, recreation "frequently refers to sports and outdoor activities and almost never refers to activities that are intellectually strenuous."

Recreation takes many forms, from arts and crafts for some, to sexual intercourse for others. However, the principal type of recreation in many societies involves sports. While such sport participation is not seen as intellectually edifying, it is a constructive way to utilize leisure time. Also, since recreation is a culture-bound category, it is important that the particular sport or sports selected for recreative purposes be viewed by participants as a desired activity. If not, it becomes obligatory, similar to work, and does not qualify as recreational. For this reason, it is vital to appreciate the cultural ramifications of sport and play in the development and implementation of effective recreation programs.

Physical education, unlike recreation, may be normative, prescriptive, or obligatory. By definition, such training places demands on participants, and while some might view the experience as recreational, others may see it as work and simply endure the experience in deference to external pressures.

Physical education is also more inclusive than recreation, involving both mental and physical activities that are designed ultimately to preserve or improve one's health, while at the same time teaching the student to effectively utilize his leisure time. Recreation becomes an important medium for realizing these goals and is thus basic to the physical education curriculum.

All societies subject their youth to types of training that can be called "physical education" in one respect or another. However, the specific nature of that training varies between cultural settings. Among the traditional Mississippi Choctaws, for example, boys at a very early age were taught to play *toli* (stickball), fathers providing their sons with miniature rackets to aid in such education. At the same time, children of both sexes were instructed in the importance of the development of physical skills and the maintenance of good health. This experience is repeated in most human societies and very often involves training in the skills fundamental to participation in particular sporting activities.

By definition, physical education is normative. In other words, participants are subjected to a prescribed regimen or enculturation that someone else has deemed important to their overall well-being and that of the society at large. For this reason, unlike the recreation director, the physical education instructor does not have to conform to the wishes or norms of his clientele. In other words, he can, if he so desires, simply ignore the cultural ramifications of the activities he prescribes. The process will still be physical education. However, by appreciating the cultural backgrounds of his students and developing activities that take these into account, he can more effectively achieve the goals of a successful physical education program. The anthropology of sport provides a perspective and methodology that facilitates the achievement of these very objectives.

SUMMARY

A cultural approach to the study of sport predictably relies on a comprehensive and consistent definition of "culture." Although it is difficult to define the term in a concise fashion that appeals to the entirety of that collective of individuals who call themselves anthropologists, there are some things that can be said about culture that most social scientists would accept as valid.

Culture, unlike society, is learned symbolic behavior. This behavior is adaptive in nature, shared to one extent or another by all members of society, and functions to guide individual human action. Also, culture is an integrated whole, composed of many different parts, including sport.

Sport, as a component of culture, is defined as behavior that can be viewed as related to other behavior such as work, play, leisure, games, recreation, ritual, and conflict.

Play is an inclusive type of activity that is pleasurable, voluntary, marked by boundaries in time, and one that exhibits a certain make-believe quality. Leisure, while related to play, may be passive, and is defined as "a state of being in which activity is performed for its own sake or as its own end" (DeGrazia, 1962:15). Recreation, on the other hand, is an active utilization of leisure time, predominantly in physical ways and within outdoor environments.

Games are competitive activities that involve physical skills, strategy, and chance, or any combination of these elements. Games, like sports, are common in leisure settings.

Sport, then, is a physically exertive activity that is aggressively competitive within constraints imposed by definitions and rules. A component of culture, it is ritually patterned, gamelike and of varying amounts of play, work and leisure. In addition, sport can be viewed as having both athletic and nonathletic variations, <u>athletic</u> referring to those activities requiring the greater amount of physical exertion.

Exercises

Discussion questions:

(1)   Cite examples of sport in your own experience that were more work than leisurelike in actual performance. What type of attitude or attitudes <u>should</u> be manifested through sport in recreation and leisure programs? Can sport participation be as rewarding if it is approached as work rather than as leisure or play activity? Why or why not?

(2)   Cite specific examples of sport activities that could be compared to direct forms of conflict such as fighting. What are the characteristics of sport that make it similar to other forms of conflict? What is the function of the conflict dimension of sport behavior?

(3)   Consider <u>your</u> typical week day. How much time do you spend playing? How much of that time involves sport? Do you make a clear distinction between your play and work, or do you feel you play at your work during parts of the day? What does this say about the importance of sport and play in your life?

(4)   If sport is to be viewed as ritual, and ritual defined as a transmitter of values and guide for behavior, how do sports and your participation in them (as spectator and participant) affect your behavior? In other words, what

lessons do you learn about your culture? What about moral issues?

Special Projects

(1)   Watch the anthropology film *Trobriand Cricket* (Leach, 1976), paying particular attention to the characteristics of the game itself. Analyze the various ways in which the game of cricket, as played by the Trobriand Islanders, reflects the fundamental values and characteristics of Trobriand culture.

(2)   Consider several types of athletic competition that are common in the United States. List the ways that these can be interpreted as war.

A Western Australian boy playing with spear

3   Anthropology of Sport: Theory and Method

The collection and analysis of sport data require a theoretical orientation and a systematic methodology. These two components, theory and method, are essential parts of the research process in the anthropology of sport.

Method and theory have an interdependent relationship. Any methodology, no matter how simple or basic, is linked to some set of theoretical assumptions. For example, the collection of observational data on sport requires at least a definition of sport. Such a definition is in itself a theoretical statement or assumption. Without this conceptual orientation, there would be no parameters, boundaries, or limits. The observer would be forced to note every perceived object and activity, without discrimination. Everything would be sport, and sport everything; the absurdity of a theory-less methodology.

Because theory is essential to methodology, theory makes sense. All too often, students being introduced to the social sciences are given the impression that theories are meaningless abstractions, intellectual exercises, complicated word games, or mental puzzles that have no relationship whatsoever to the real world. Unfortunately, this misconception is sometimes reinforced by the way theory is presented in introductory texts. Sociologists, for example, often make a distinction between theorists and methodologists, implicitly projecting the notion that the two operate independently of each other (e.g., Stewart, 1981:16-23).

Theory is not a difficult concept to understand. In fact, human beings are theoretical by nature. They approach problems with preconceived assumptions about the world and about the general category of phenomenon into which the problem falls. For example, college athletic directors and coaches get together periodically under the auspices of the National Collegiate Athletic Association (NCAA) to make decisions about rules and regulations. In addition to their shaving kits and sweat shirts, these coaches and directors invariably come to these meetings armed with a set of theoretical perspectives that predetermine the way they vote on issues. For example, Paul "Bear" Bryant, former head football coach at Alabama, unabashedly admitted that his ballplayers were athletes first and students second. On the other hand, Frank Ryan, the athletic director at Yale, is inclined to believe that his athletes are scholars who only happen to play ball on the side. These opposing points of view regarding the relative weighting of the two components in the student athlete ideal are in fact theoretical models and they have a direct influence on issues. Bryant's model made athletic scholarships a necessity; Ryan's does not. Therefore, on the issue of whether or not NCAA schools should continue to allow athletic scholarships, it is easy to predict how the two men might have voted.

Actually, theory is just a way of looking at events, activities, or objects; a way of ordering or structuring data. In the social sciences, this generally means that theory is a way of approaching and analyzing human behavior. In anthropology, this often means culture or one of the components of culture.

Although theory is not difficult to understand, it is difficult to define with any precision. However, as Kaplan and Manners (1972:12n) have noted, "while there may be some disagreement about what theory is, there seems to be considerable agreement about what theories may do." And what is that? Theories explain, predict, lead to new avenues of research, or simply open the door to new data or important facts. In this sense, theory is best understood in terms of its function as a methodological tool.

Theory is often confused with law. However, theory and scientific law are radically different from one another. Theory is constructed, while law gives the impression of being discovered. Theory is devised or created by the scientist as a result of observations and generalizations. A law, however, is simply a statement about some seeming regularity or unvarying phenomenon. For example, the law of gravity is a basic "law of nature" that simply describes the fact that under certain conditions gravity will behave in a particular way. There is no exception or variability. Theory, on the other hand, is a generalization that allows for exceptions and variations as well as the testing of that variability's limits.

Actual theory construction takes place within a broader framework provided by models. A model is a general statement about reality that provides a basis for theoretical exploration, but a statement that itself cannot be tested, cannot be proven or disproven. The validity of the model rests on its utility for theory construction and its appropriateness to the objectives of the particular research.

In this book, the expression "theoretical model" is used to refer to the model, that broad statement about behavior or events that serves as a basis for narrowing the focus of the research. Theoretical models are general action plans that point the way to the type of theory to be devised and tested, the type of data to be collected, and the method of analysis to be used. This use of the concept of "theoretical model" is similar to what is referred to in some contexts as "theoretical orientations" (e.g., Kaplan and Manners, 1972:32-33).

The number of possible theoretical models that might be devised is unlimited, but those actually developed and employed by anthropologists are relatively few. The major theoretical schools in the discipline's history have developed around certain theoretical models. These tend to be the most frequently used and include such approaches as evolutionism, functionalism, structuralism, and others to be discussed later in this chapter. In many ways, the history of anthropology can be viewed as a history of its most widely used theoretical models, those comprehensive, macrocosmic generalizations that allow for the construction and implementation of the more specialized, testable theories.

Theory, because it is testable, can be defined as a set of hypotheses, propositions, or intelligent hunches that are phrased in such a way that they can be proved or disproven, accepted or rejected, on the basis of data collected and analyzed. Theory is the testable extension of a theoretical model, and its validity is determined by verifiability rather than by simple utility.

In order to illustrate the relationship between theoretical model and theory, consider the following hypothetical research design. The sport anthropologist is studying modern team sports. She is convinced, for whatever reason, that human behavior is best understood from the perspective of the geographical and spatial dimensions of the context within which that behavior occurs. She develops a theoretical model that she calls "geospatialism," a general proposition that when applied to the sport setting suggests that sport behavior can be better understood if it is analyzed in relationship to the dimensions of the playing field or area where the game is played. This geospatial model cannot be proven or disproven. But it does allow for novel approaches to the study of sport and facilitate the construction and testing of new sport models.

For example, the sport anthropologist decides to use her geospatial model as a basis for studying the relationship between rule structure and playing field dimensions. Her set of hypotheses - in this case a set of one - is operationalized as theory by her construction of the following testable proposition: in modern team sports, the complexity of the rule structure varies in inverse proportion to the size of the playing field. In other words, the smaller the playing area, the more detailed and specific the rules. She then tests this hypothesis by studying the rulebook for each of the major sports and comparing the level or volume of rule complexity with the physical dimensions of the playing areas; either proving or disproving her initial hypothesis. In sum, the geospatial model becomes a blueprint underlying the theory regarding the relationship between rule complexity and space; the theory operationalizes the model; and the data provide the basis for either accepting or rejecting the theory.

THEORETICAL MODELS IN ANTHROPOLOGY

The theoretical models that are used by anthropologists generally fall into one of two types: models that are explanatory and models that are interpretive. Explanatory models are designed as explicitly "scientific" models and suggest cause-effect relationships. Interpretive models simply provide the observer with different perspectives for understanding events or behavior. Cause-and-effect relationships might be implicit in interpretive models, but they are not explicit objectives.

Explanatory models, such as structural-functionalism, though they suggest theoretical casual relationships, do not in reality explain by demonstrating cause and effect. For example, a structural-functional analysis of American football might conclude that football is a ritual conflict that functions to divert the aggressive tendencies in the social system that might otherwise be expressed in more serious forms of conflict, such as war. Implicitly, then, sport is explained as the effect of the system's need for alternatives to war. However, is that really an explanation? Do such models ever really explain social phenomena?

Explanations in the social sciences are similar to those used in everyday life. They may isolate a factor of a cause, but generally it is only one of many causes and by itself does not explain. For example, your older sister - assuming that you have an older sister - and her husband get a divorce. Predictably, those close to the situation are concerned and try to understand the divorce, to explain it. Each has his or her own answer, a cause that he or she believes to be basic to the problem. Your mother believes that the divorce is a result of the couple's not going to church, the way they should. Your father believes that it is happening because the daughter finally realized what he has been trying to tell her for a long time, that the husband is never going to amount to anything. You feel that the cause is your brother-in-law's mistreatment of your sister, while your sister simply suggests that she wants to try it on her own, that marriage is too restrictive and that she "needs space." It is likely that no one of these causes is the only cause. All of them might be causative factors, along with others that remain unexpressed. Therefore, it is ridiculous to look at any of these suggested cause-effect relationships as explanations.

In some way, this is the dilemma of the social sciences. So-called explanatory models suggest ways of looking at social and cultural phenomena in terms of possible causative factors and approach specific problems with explanation as an ideal goal or objective. However, because of the complexity of human behavior, such explanations remain theoretical objectives or ideals, rather than actual accomplishments. In reality, the models employed by social science do not explain.

What do these explanatory models do if they do not explain? They demonstrate significant relationships; they suggest possible causative factors and possible effects; they elaborate on the obvious, and make explicit the less obvious dimensions of social and cultural events. For these reasons they are both important and valuable.

Interpretive models are not as ambitious in their approach to the analysis of social data as are their explanatory counterparts. Interpretive models simply provide alternative ways of understanding, alternatives that do not explain, but do expand and increase knowledge, and raise new questions. For example, symbolic anthropology, applied in the analysis of Brazilian soccer, may not explain that sport, but it will suggest ways in which soccer reflects the regularities of Brazilian social structure and it will demonstrate the sport's integral relationship with the rest of Brazilian culture.

The most popular theoretical models in the history of anthropology have achieved their respective popularity for a variety or reasons, often external to the discipline itself. The intellectual milieu of the period, developments in other disciplines, changing historical circumstances, and general social needs are often the major factors responsible for the emergence and popularity of particular models. The explanatory and interpretive models that are discussed in this chapter are included because of their prominence in anthropology and their utility in the analysis of sport behavior.

Explanatory Models

Evolutionism The anthropological model with the oldest history among those to be treated in this section is evolutionism. Rooted in the intellectual climate of the nineteenth-century Western world, evolutionism suggests that explanation is a matter of placing a culture or a cultural event into an evolutionary framework. Understanding golf, then, becomes a matter of fitting it into a general evolutionary scheme.

Among nineteenth-century anthropologists, such as Edward Burnett Tylor and Lewis Henry Morgan, cultural evolution was a universal, unilineal process that explained the development of human culture, from its simplest level, "savagery," up through the higher stages of "barbarism" and "civilization." Individual cultural phenomena were explained according to the nature of the broader cultural contexts within which they occurred. In all cases, it was assumed that the cultural values and institutions of civilization were superior to those of barbaristic or savage society. Therefore, any aspect of culture, be it technology, religion, or art, was adjudged to be superior or inferior according to its occurrence within the comprehensive, tripartite division of cultural evolution.

The evolutionism of twentieth-century anthropology still explains culture with reference to the evolutionary process. For example, Leslie White, the most prominent name among cultural evolutionists in recent anthropological history, argues that the evolution of culture is a product of the human species' ability to harness energy. The amount of energy that a particular system is capable of producing and using is the variable by which one determines that system's position on an evolutionary scale. Unlike his nineteenth-century predecessors, White does not suggest that the more advanced cultures are superior to the less advanced, in any aspect other than technology. On this basis, he might argue that while the technology of modern America is more complex than that of the contemporary San of Southwest Africa, one cannot assume that America's religious behavior, morals, or sport activities are superior to those charcteristic of San culture.

The evolutionary model is in many respects a historical one in that it implies that the present is to be explained by reference to the past. Scientific explanation is a process of isolating those historical factors that have given rise to a particular social or cultural event. In the study of sport, this means that particular sports or sport-related events can be explained by the explication of their position in an evolutionary process.

Perhaps the best illustration of the application of the evolutionary model to the study of sport is historian Allen Guttmann's *From Ritual to Record: The Nature of Modern Sport* (see p. 179). Guttmann's evolutionary model suggests that the determinative factor underlying the emergence of modern sport is the breakdown of traditional religious systems and the emergence of a pervasive secularity. Sport has evolved through several stages, from an initial "primitive sport" level through that of Greek and Roman civilizations, medieval sport, and eventually modern sport.

The evolution model is of primary importance in understanding the process and history by which sport has developed. It allows the researcher to set up and test theories that explain in terms of antecedents or past developments, to make predictions based on the facts of history, and to use historical data in the testing of hypotheses. For example, Blanchard (1980) has suggested that modern team sports in America can be better understood by means of more detailed analyses of early European peasant sport behaviors. He theorized that the fundamental charcteristics of modern sport competition developed within the context of medieval peasant sport and games; then he tested a series of hypotheses, using historical and anthropological data.

The evolution model is also useful as a means of structuring sport data from around the world. The various stages or levels of cultural evolution provide distinct categories into which the data can be grouped. This is the model employed in the discussion of world sport behavior patterns that follows in Chapters 5 and 6 of this book.

In general, the evolution model, though it has a long and sometimes controversial history in anthropology, is a useful tool for the analysis of sport behavior either in general cross-cultural contexts or within particular histories.

Functionalism The functionalism theoretical model rests on the premise that cultural phenomena are best understood in relationship to their roles in meeting individual human needs. Institutions are "explained" in terms of their function or functions within the total human need-serving system.

A name often associated with functionalism in anthropology is that of Bronislaw Malinowski, the British-trained, Polish anthropologist who did most of his fieldwork among the Trobriand Islanders of Melanesia. Malinowski suggested that there were three levels of individual human needs and that cultural institutions were to be explained by reference to the way they addressed and met those needs. The three levels of individual human need included the primary needs (e.g., the need for food and water), secondary needs (e.g., the cultural definition of particular foods as acceptable or unacceptable), and integrative needs (e.g., religion). Human culture, for Malinowski, was a set of institutions which existed to facilitate the meeting of these basically biological needs and to guide human adaptation to particular natural environments.

In the Malinowski scheme, an institution such as sport has to be explained in terms of its relationship to some human need or group of human needs. It might be argued, for example, that team sports in a particular society are ritualistic in nature, and like religion, serve an integrative function. In other words, sport functions in a cultural system to integrate a range of more basic institutions, such as the technology and the economy, and thus improves their efficiency in meeting the basic biological needs that are most evident in the adaptive process.

The functionalist model, like all theoretical models, cannot be proven or disproven. However, it can be used as a basis of theory construction and testing. A good example of the model's application to sport is George Gmelch's (1972) analysis of the role of magic in American professional baseball. Gmelch employs the functionalism model to define the parameters of his problem and sets up a specific testable theory. That theory, stated in its simplest terms, proposes that in baseball the lower the chances of success associated with a playing role, the greater the likelihood that magic is used by the player.

As a means of establishing the initial logic of this proposition, Gmelch (1972:128) cites a brief excerpt from Malinowski's *Magic, Science and Religion* (1948):

> We find magic wherever the elements of chance and accident, and the emotional play between hope and fear

have a wide and extensive range. We do not find magic wherever the pursuit is certain, reliable and well under the control of rational methods.

Gmelch then proceeds to discuss the various playing roles in a baseball game (e.g., hitter, pitcher, fielder) in terms of the chance factors involved, noting that the batter's chances for success are less than those of the pitcher, and even more so relative to the outfielder. Predictably, the amount and complexity of magic employed by the batter is greater than that used by those in any of the other roles, giving credence to Gmelch's theory.

The functionalism model has a variety of other potential applications in the anthropological study of sport. Suggesting a relationship between institution and human need, it allows for the construction and testing of a variety of interesting theories about sport participation. For example, one might wish to explore the notion that sport participation is associated with positive self-concept. In other words, sport serves to fulfill a specific psychological need. This proposition, consistent with the constraints of functionalism, could be structured as a hypothesis. One possibility is that within a given population, those participating in sport activities have a stronger self-concept than those not participating. The hypothesis could be tested in a sample population (e.g., a high school) and a conclusion reached about sport participation and self-concept in that particular group.

Structural-Functionalism   Structural-functionalism is a theoretical model that parallels functionalism. Like functionalism it is founded on the premise that social institutions are to be understood in terms of their essential functions (i.e., what they do). Unlike functionalism, however, structural-functionalism explains institutions in terms of their contribution to other parts or aspects of the system rather than in relationship to individual human needs.

British anthropologist A. R. Radcliffe-Brown, a colleague of Malinowski's at the London School of Economics, is often seen as the principal directing force behind the development of strucutural-functionalism. Radcliffe-Brown's model of a social system is analogous to a living organism. Similar to that organism, the social system is made up of parts that fit together with a type of integrated interdependence. Each part has an important role to play in the maintenance of the total system. Ideally, the operation of a social system parallels the life of a healthy organism, and each of the parts of the system, the institutions, is explained according to the contribution it makes toward the maintenance of the system. Thus, from a structural-functionalism perspective, religion as a social institution is treated as a complement to other dimensions of the system (e.g., as a theoretical or ultimate rationalization for law) rather than as an integrator of individual needs, as is the case in functionalism.

When the structural-functional model is used in the anthropological analysis of sport, the basic assumption is that sport as a social institution is to be understood in terms of its relationship to other components or institutions in the system. Sport may be seen as reinforcing or supporting other dimensions of the system, such as law, politics, or religion. It may be viewed as an outlet for aggressive tendencies, reducing conflict in other areas of the system, or it may be interpreted as ritual. But, in all cases, the *raison d'etre* is its interdependence with the other institutions in the system.

A good example of the application of the structural-functional model in the sport setting is Robin Fox's (1961) "Pueblo Baseball: A New Use for Old Witchcraft." (see p. 22). Fox describes the role of baseball in the contemporary Cochiti Pueblo community and explains its form and popularity by suggesting that the sport functons as a means of "acting out...aggressive and competitive tendencies" in a system that traditionally has been noncompetitive.

Structural-functionalism is a popular model among those who do sport studies. Sport in America, as in many other cultures, is tied to such a wide variety of institutions and behaviors that many structural-functional questions emerge almost automatically from the simple observation of sport activities. Perhaps the greatest utility of structural-functionalism in this context is in its focus on the general yet very important question of the role of sport in society.

Cultural Materialism Cultural materialism, made popular in anthropology by Marvin Harris (1979), is a theoretical model that treats human culture as though adaptation were its primary reason for existence. It is assumed that human beings are concerned, first and foremost, with the basic problems of surviving, getting something to eat, having water, keeping warm, and satisfying the other biological needs. Culture in any given social system is designed to address those problems and can only be understood in relationship to its resulting adaptive function.

According to the cultural materialism model, culture is a tripartite phenomenon made up of techno-economic, sociopolitical, and ideological components (see Kaplan and Manners, 1972:47). In the process of adaptation, it is most directly interfaced with the environment and thus most directly responsible for human survival. Thus, culture change is essentially techno-economic change. The other components of culture, the sociopolitical and the ideological, are likewise adaptive, but are secondary and tertiary adaptations. In this sense, the sociopolitical institutions are viewed as products of the techno-economic base, while ideologies are also products of that same material component with additional molding resulting from its being filtered through the sociopolitical component. In this sense, culture is determined by the material, adaptive needs of society. Social institutions, such as kinship and marriage, law and political behavior, as well as sport, are the direct result of determinative pressures emanating from the technology and the economy. Religion, values and philosophies are created by a multiplicity of materialistic forces that have worked their way through the sociopolitical level of culture to find theoretical justification and legitimation in ideology. When the technology changes, the social system and the ideology change. If a hunting-and-gathering group depends on the buffalo as their primary source of meat, cultural materialism predicts that their ideology will reflect a variety of buffalo-related themes. But, when the buffalo disappears and is replaced by sheep herds and wage labor, the old buffalo focus quickly becomes obsolete.

The cultural materialism model has been used as a means of demonstrating the adaptive significance of many interesting and often hard to understand cultural practices from around the world. Harris, in his *Pigs, Cows, Wars and Witches: The Riddles of Culture* (1974), explains everything from the Islamic pork taboo to the Hindu sacred cow complex. With reference to the latter, Harris argues that the Hindu's refusal to kill cows for the simple purpose of having meat makes sense. The cattle play an essential part in the agricultural process. They are valuable work animals, and their dung is used as fertilizer. These latter functions ensure the continuing importance of the cow and explain the sacred cow complex as an adaptive mechanism.

The cultural materialism model treats sport as an aspect of the sociopolitical component of culture. As such, it is viewed as a product of the materialistic base. In other words, sport is only to be understood with reference to the technology and economy of the system within which it occurs. American football, from its elaborate equipment to its complicated rule structure, is explained by the primary materialistic forces that have fostered its development. Conversely, sport and its various accouterments can be treated as adaptive mechanisms.

In an application of the cultural materialism model to the sport institution, Blanchard (1979a) has attempted to demonstrate that the betting associated with the traditional racket game of the Mississippi Choctaws functioned as an important redistributive device. The formal ball game among the Choctaws pitted community against community, and each game saw the two sides wager masses of material wealth on outcomes. Individuals bet only on their own community teams, there were no odds, betting was more important than the relative values of items wagered, and nothing was con- sidered too sacred to wager. Horses, cows, goats, chickens, produce, guns, tools, knives, clothes, baskets and blankets were part of the total package of wagered items accumulated and placed on large, specially built scaffolds at opposite ends of the field. The first team to strike the ball against the goal an agreed-upon number of times was declared the winner, subsequently laying claim to all wagered materials.

It is significant that during the eighteenth and nineteenth centuries, the years during which stickball was king among Choctaw sports, the game tended to be played most frequently during those times of the year marked by economic inequities among communities, in the weeks before and after the early fall harvest. It also appears that no one community tended to dominate the racket game so that wins and losses tended to be reasonably distributed among the various competitors. This in effect created a redistributive network, a collection of wagered items, a pool of resources, that circulated through the various communities and made important tools, food-stuffs, and other materials available to those in need while at the same time providing a useful means for the redistribution of surplus in other communities. The data thus support the theory, suggested by the cultural materialism model, that stickball wagering acted as a redistributive device among traditional Choctaws in Mississippi.

The cultural materialism model has a variety of potential applications in the analysis of sport behavior, historical, ethnological, and futuristic. One might use the model to better understand the emergence and popularity of soccer in South America, explain the relationship between spectator behavior at professional athletic performances and social class, or make predictions about particular sporting events. For example, with reference to the latter, it might be theorized that with the growing sophistication of football technology will come more elaborate and effective protective gear. While this portends greater player safety and fewer injuries, it could be argued that it will also bring with it a decline in spectator interest. The more elaborate the gear, the greater the impersonalizaton of the player; the fans under such conditions are less likely to establish personal identifications with particular athletes, identifications basic to spectator support.

Interpretive Models

Unlike the explanatory theoretical model, the interpretive model does not purport to isolate cause-and-effect or explain. It merely provides a perspective for understanding. In many cases, this means providing the observer with insights that he or she would never have achieved without the direction provided by the model. The interpretive theorist is less likely than his explanatory counterpart to worry about whether or not his research is labeled "scientific." Most interpretive models do not generate easily testable theories, so it could be argued that those employing such models are not doing science but something else (e.g., art). However, in defense of interpretive models, they often lead to important new insights about culture and social structure, raise important questions for future research, and generate information that had predictive value. Interpretive theoretical models are important to anthropology in general and sport studies in particular.

Symbolic Anthropology The model that is being defined here as "symbolic anthropology" is actually a composite, simplification of models used by several prominent anthropological theoreticians such as Mary Douglas, Clifford Geertz, and Victor Turner. The symbolic anthropology model described here is based on the assumption that many group activities can be interpreted as symbolic messages about the social structure, the fundamental nature of the system being investigated. Geertz's (1972) "Deep Play: Notes on a Balinese Cockfight" illustrates the way that the symbolic anthropology model works. In describing the theoretical framework within which the Balinese cockfight is analyzed, Geertz (1972:452) suggests that "the culture of a people is an ensemble of texts, themselves ensembles, which the anthropologist strains to read over the shoulders of those to whom they properly belong." The cockfight in Bali is such a text, and Geertz details the events of the cockfight, noting the various ways in which the behavior and relationships parallel and reflect the fundamentals of Balinese social structure. For example, betting styles are predicated more on the social relationship of the parties to the wager than on predicted outcomes. The Balinese cockfight, as a form of play or spectator sport, is a symbolic message or story about Balinese social life, related or told in a metaphorical and different way. The message is a means by which both participants and the researcher learn the norms and values of Balinese culture.

In a recent application of the symbolic model to the sport setting, anthropologist Frank Manning (1981:616) has described the cricket festival in Bermuda, the country's "major public celebration...aside from Christmas." Arguing that the cricket festival is a symbolic or "metaphorical map of the political system" of Bermuda, he concludes that the events surrounding the formal cricket matches reflect the "dramatic tension" characteristic of Bermuda political organization, a tension resulting from the assertion of black culture on the one hand, and on the other, the awareness among blacks of their economic dependence on whites. Illustrating this dilemma or tension, the festival cricket is characterized by what Manning (1981:626) calls "racial inversion."

> Blacks dress up in "white" (white uniforms) to play a white game that they have transformed into a celebration of black culture. Blacks take a white gambling game and make it the setting for a hyperbolic performance of their social personality. Whites enter a black milieu and baldly demonstrate their superordinate position.

In the application of the symbolic model there is generally no positing of theories that one proves or disproves. The application of the model rings with a sense of "givenness" as though the data, like music or poetry, are simply there. The symbolic model guides the researcher in recognizing and isolating the message.

The use of the symbolic anthropology model in the analysis of sport behavior raises many interesting possibilities. In every situation in which sport and play forms become public performances, there are many opportunities to apply the symbolic anthropology model. The circumstances often raise questions about social organization, social class, political behavior, national character, religion, because all of these aspects of culture are potentially symbolized in sport activities. The objective of the researcher is to analyze exactly what the symbolic messages are, how they are communicated, and what they teach us about the system from which they have emerged.

Ethnoscience Ethnoscience is explicitly both method and theoretical model. It is both a conception of human culture and a way of analyzing specific cultural systems. It is based on the assumption that culture is knowledge, knowledge shared by members of a particular society. The knowledge provides a structure whereby the individual culture bearer is able to organize and interpret the raw data of sense experience. In other words, culture--or the knowledge that is culture--structures, classifies, and makes real the unstructured, unclassified, and otherwise unknowable stuff of experience.

This cultural knowledge not only structures, but is itself structured; structured hierarchically, from general to specific. This means that in the process of knowing, one approaches an experience with a set of categories that have been learned as a result of enculturation. In the actual perception or realization of that experience, the information is subjected to those categories; a process that takes the mind from the most general to the most specific. Actual knowing occurs only as the information has been fitted conveniently into one of the specific categories. The many areas of knowledge that constitute a particular cultural system or framework are known as "cognitive domains," subsets of knowledge specific to and structured consistently with a particular culture.

The objective for the ethnoscientist, in studying a culture, is to elicit and record as many of these cognitive domains as possible and come to an understanding as to how members of the subject society know--structure--reality or any part of reality (e.g., sport). This process, which is largely one of recording language, involves the reconstruction of that knowledge that is culture.

One method of cognitive domain reconstruction is the isolation of componential definitions. These definitions describe the hierarchies of knowledge that are included in the domain, the terms in the native language that make up the components of the domain. For example, a componential definition of "sport," elicited from a group of English speakers from Terre Haute, Indiana, might begin at the most general level by distinguishing between individual and team sport, and then move down through several levels before arriving at the most specialized categories, including all the various types of sports (e.g., basketball, tennis, golf, football) that are included (i.e., are components) in the general term "sport."

FIGURE 3...Componential definition of "football player" (hypothetical)

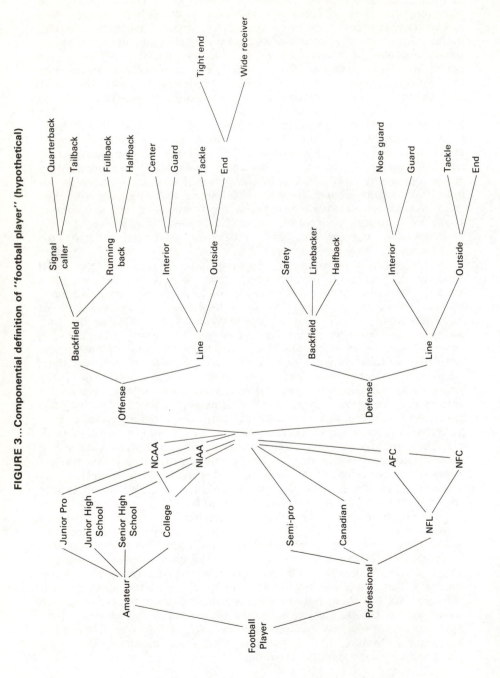

The eventual reconstruction achieved by the ethnoscientist is called an "emic" reconstruction, because it represents the native's point of view, the inside view of a culture. The outsider or scientific point of view is called the "etic" perspective. In the first case, the explanations given for particular events or behaviors are those of the subjects themselves, the emic explanation. In the second case, the explanations are provided by the anthropologist. These etic explanations are predicated on the theoretical models that are employed in the research.

As a means of illustrating how the ethnoscience model works, assume that an anthropologist from Pakistan comes to the United States to study American football. Among the many cognitive domains she chooses to explore is the domain "football player." Working with several informants, natives who are familiar with and who adequately represent American culture, the Pakistani anthropologist asks a variety of questions as to how these informants conceptualize the category "football player." Eventually, she arrives at a componential definition, a reconstruction of that domain that begins with a very general level distinction between "professional" and "amateur," and moves through several levels of generalization within each of these categories until the level of specialized distinctions between positions is described (see Fig. 3). What emerges in this reconstructed domain is an insider or emic understanding of "football player" that is specific to the variety of American culture being explored.

In addition, if the Pakistani ethnoscientist wishes to know why her American informants are so interested in football, why the sport is so popular in America (i.e., she wants an explanation), she asks them. The answer they provide is sufficient, without academic embellishment or translation into anthropological jargon. For example, if the natives claim that football is popular because it allows players and spectators alike opportunities to get out into the fall weather, that is a legitimate emic explanation in itself. No other explanation (e.g., structural-functional) is necessary.

Blanchard (1974) has used the ethnoscience model in an analysis of Navajo basketball behavior as mentioned earlier (see p. 55). Playing basketball with the Navajos in the early 1970s, he noticed that despite their having learned the game from local whites, the Ramah Navajos played a distinctively Navajo type of basketball. As a means of describing those characteristics of the game that made it distinctive, he employed an ethnoscience model and elicited several cognitive domains relative to the Navajo's perception of basketball, basketball players, and the meaning and ideal strategy of the game. The cognitive domain "the good basketball player" was elicited and a componential definition constructed. Several interesting tendencies emerged. For example, the Navajo basketball player, as opposed to his Anglo-American counterpart in the same area, was likely to consider kinship regularities in on-court decision making as more significant than position, talent, or strategy. In other words, in most cases, the Ramah Navajo basketball player with control of the ball was more likely to throw the ball to a kinsman, regardless of position or scoring potential, than to a nonkinsman in a strategically ideal situation. In this particular case, then, ethnoscience, as a theoretical model and methodology, has provided a basis for understanding basketball from a Navajo perspective.

THEORETICAL MODELS: GENERAL SUMMARY

Summarizing what has been suggested about theoretical models in anthropology, the following major points require reiteration:

1.   Theoretical models are ways of drawing lines around and focusing on particular areas of experience. They suggest and provide a context for the construction of testable theories, but cannot themselves be tested.

2.   Theories are testable propositions that can be proven or disproven, accepted or rejected, affirmed or refuted by collected information or data.   Theories are frequently tested by the construction and testing of theoretical subsets called hypotheses.

3.   Theoretical models in anthropology can be divided into two groups or categories: explanatory and interpretive.

4.   The ease with which the researcher can construct testable theories within the parameters provided by the model varies from one theoretical model to another.

5.   The ultimate measure of a theoretical model's value is its utility in explaining or interpreting particular cultural patterns or sets of patterns.

GENERAL ETHNOGRAPHIC DESCRIPTION

Not all anthropological research is tied to or defined by a major theoretical model. Some basic ethnography, cultural description, is guided by only a few assumptions or definitions. Ethnographic description is the essential raw data of anthropological analysis and cross-cultural research (i.e., ethnology). For this reason, the fact that it is less theoretically sophisticated or specialized than some ethnological research does not limit its importance.

The ethnographic description of sport activities is an important part of the anthropology of sport. Such description is based on a few assumptions about the nature of culture, the definition of sport as an aspect of that culture, and the way in which the elements of culture are interrelated. A good example of this type of description is Mooney's (1890) analysis of the classic Cherokee ballgame.

The straightforward ethnographic description of sport activities in the various societies from around the world is especially important. So little of that has been done in the past, and cultures are changing so rapidly in the modern era that if the data is not recorded now, in many cases it will be lost forever, leaving gaps in our future understanding of human sport and play.

METHODOLOGY

As suggested earlier, there is an underlying logic to the relationship between theory and method. Ideally, the former leads naturally into the latter. Theoretical models suggest, both implicitly and explicitly, the types of data to be collected and in some cases actually prescribe method (e.g., ethnoscience): In any case, methodology only makes sense when developed within a specific theoretical framework.

Research Design

The research design is an important preliminary exercise in the process of doing sport research. The research design assists the researcher in putting the research process into perspective and in working through that process before doing any actual data collection.. It also serves to keep the central problem in focus so that the energies of the researcher are not wasted.

The first step in the writing of the research design is that of problem definition and description. The researcher is as specific as possible in discussing the issue or issues central to her project. Background information concerning her selection of this particular problem and some general observations about the geographic and ethnographic setting for the research are also useful.

The next step in the construction of the research design is the listing of project objectives followed by a description of the procedure or "plan of action." The latter includes a discussion of the theoretical model to be employed, the theory and its hypotheses to be tested, the methods of data collection and analysis techniques to be used, and the mode to be employed in presenting the results of the research (e.g., paper, article, book). Finally, the research design includes a discussion of expected results and the significance of the research and its conclusions (see Fig. 4).

Data Collection

The heart of the methodological process in anthropological

FIGURE 4...The research design

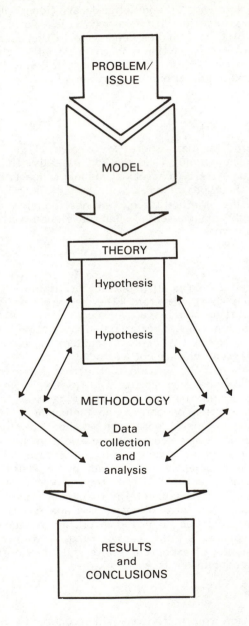

research is data collection. In most cases, the data collection means fieldwork, an activity as fundamental to anthropology as kicking is to soccer. Fieldwork generally means participant observation, a process in which the researcher participates in the lives of the people being studied while at the same time maintaining a scientific objectivity as observer. Malinowski's extended stay among the Trobriand Islanders during the early part of the century (1915-16, 1917-18) set a precedent for subsequent anthropological fieldwork, and over the years participant observation has remained a distinguishing characteristic of the discipline. Ideally, the anthropologist moves into the lives of the subject people, learns their language, experiences what it is like to be a member of that culture, and at the same time collects data relevant to other research problems. Often this takes several years to accomplish.

Classic participant observation is an ideal but not an essential part of anthropological research. Many variables limit the research-er's ability to do this type of fieldwork. One may not have the time, the resources, or adequate access to subjects to accomplish the objectives of traditional participant observation. Nevertheless, the method remains an ideal, and every fieldwork experience, no matter how small or specialized the problem can be structured in terms of that ideal.

The fieldwork experience begins at the level of passive research, a stage during which the researcher moves into the community that is to be the subject of the investigation and begins to develop some general understanding of the people and the situation. At this level, the anthropologist is interested in establishing relationships and developing a comfortable role for herself in the community. The anthropologist studying sport will find herself spending a lot of time hanging around ballfields and gymnasiums. If possible she will become involved in the play itself. The athletic arena is an innocuous setting within which the anthropologist can develop relationships and create for herself a nonthreatening role that is acceptable to members of the subject community. In many cases, it is difficult for an anthro-pologist to explain what she is and why she has suddenly moved into town. She has no job, no visible means of support, and no obvious reason for being there, and the explanation, "I have come to study your culture and your way of life" is often the basis for suspicion. But in many cases, anyone (anthropologist or otherwise) who likes to play ball does not have to justify her presence.

One technique that is frequently used at this passive research stage of anthropological fieldwork is a method that has been called "lurking" (Strickland and Schlesinger, 1969). Lurking is a process whereby the researcher simply "hangs out" in a public place, watching and listening without intruding. It is valuable in helping the anthropologist to perceive a sense of community life, the nature of social relationships, and issues and values of greatest importance to the subject people. For an anthropologist studying sport, the ballfield, festive activities that involve athletic events, or public places where ballplayers gather subsequent to a ballgame make ideal settings in which to lurk.

The active stage of research is initiated when the anthropologist feels comfortable moving around in the community, has made some contacts, and knows something about the nature of political alignments among her subject group. Active research involves the direct and specialized collection of data relevant to the problem being investigated and the theory being tested.

One of the principal techniques of data collection among anthropologists is the informant interview. The informant is selected from among the membership of the subject community because he or she is viewed as knowledgeable about the topic being explored, is a representative of the culture being studied, and is available to work with the anthropologist. The anthropologist may choose to pay the informant, present a gift, or offer compensatory services (e.g., transportation). The interviews are generally unstructured. The anthropologist raises a few basic questions and then lets the conversation take its own course. Interviews are often tape recorded, the fieldworker transcribing the tapes at some later time.

If the researcher is interested in getting a broad, representative sample of the community, she may wish to interview many individuals, combining and comparing their responses to her questions. In order to facilitate this comparison, she may find it profitable to standardize and structure the interview format, asking her subjects or informants a limited number of specific questions.

The questionnaire is also a popular data collecting tool in anthropology. In many ways, the questionnaire can be viewed as a way of structuring an interview. The questionnaire presents special problems when used in an anthropological context. The design of questionnaires is a complex art, even when they are developed and used in the researcher's own community. However, when the problem of translation is added to the variables to be considered in developing and administering the questionnaire, the margin of possible error increases dramatically. Therefore, any questionnaires used in an anthropological field setting should be well-thought out before they are used, and the results considered only in light of all the possible extraneous factors affecting responses.

Psychologists have developed many methodological devices that have been employed by anthropologists. Standard psychological tests such as the Rorschach Ink Blot, the Draw-A-Man, and the analysis of life history data are frequently useful in the attempt to uncover some less than obvious cultural tendencies or patterns. Likewise, anthropologists borrow from sociologists, since many of their data collecting techniques have obvious anthropological applications. (For a description of available tests, see Buros, 1974).

Another legitimate source of anthropological data is the literature, the vast resources of published and unpublished material available in libraries, special collections, agencies, information services, and government offices. Very often, newspapers and other community information media provide invaluable data for the anthropologist studying sport.

The recording of anthropological data has traditionally been done with field notes and journals. Field notes are often done on small sheets of paper or cards (e.g., five-by-eight-inch index cards) and filed according to subject matter, with identifying information regarding the source and the date on which the material was obtained. One handy device for numbering and filing field notes according to subject matter is the Human Relations Area Files (HRAF) system described in *The Outline of Cultural Materials* (Murdock et al, 1961).

The journal is a less formal mechanism for the recording of data significant to the research process. Ideally, the anthropologist keeps a daily log or journal in which he records observations or information not directly appropriate to field notes. Throughout the fieldwork experience, the researcher keeps a daily account of his activities, significant events, personal observations and feelings, possible explanations or interpretations of collected data, additional questions raised by the day's events, and directions to be taken in the subsequent stages of the research process. These can be extremely valuable in assisting the researcher in keeping the project on target and pulling the collected data together in the final stages of the process. Journal entries can also be very personal and often reveal much about the nature of the anthropologist himself. Malinowski's (1967) journals, published posthumously, exposed a side of the famous anthropologist that appears incongruous with the humanistic sensitivity that flavors his other writing but they illustrate the value of the journal. It is important that the anthropologist keep his own personality under scrutiny during his fieldwork to make sure that his problems do not affect or become a part of his research. The journal helps one avoid such problems.

The active research stage of the data collection process in anthropology involves not only the gathering of verbal data, but also visual and auditory records. The camera has long been an important part of the cultural anthropologist's tool kit, be it an Instamatic, a Polaroid, a thirty-five millimeter, a twin lens, or an expensive movie or video camera. In the analysis of sporting events, pictures and the interpretation of those pictures can be invaluable sources of information. Tape recorders are also useful in the field and can be used to record the sounds associated with sport, especially those songs, chants, and cheers that are important ritual dimensions of the sport event. These recordings are important descriptions that cannot be reproduced in any other medium.

Data Analysis

Ideally, some analysis of the data collected during the anthropological fieldwork experience is done during the fieldwork session itself. However, the logical order of the research design suggests that the analysis is undertaken after the data collection has been completed.

Data analysis is essentially theory testing. The anthropologist organizes his data and weighs their various implications over against the hypotheses posited in the initial research design. The data may be verbal, statistical, pictorial, or auditory. In all cases, they may be used to build a case either in support of or in opposition to the theory being tested.

Statistical or quantitative data add a valuable perspective to the anthropological research process. Wherever possible, the researcher should collect quantifiable data, subjecting it to statistical procedures appropriate to the sample, type of data, and problem being investigated. A variety of handbooks are available to assist the researcher in the collection and analysis of social statistics (e.g., Loether and McTavish, 1974). Also, there are now several computer programs available that require minimal effort on the part of the anthropological fieldworker but yield maximum statistical computations and results (e.g., Statistical Package for the Social Sciences -- SPSS).

Good anthropology is good description. Therefore, any data, qualitative or quantitative, can be important to problem analysis in anthropological research if it adds to the understanding of a particular culture, problem, or area of behavior. The anthropological study of sport is thus a descriptive process, but descriptive within the constraints imposed by theoretical models and systematic methods of data collection.

THE ANTHROPOLOGY OF SPORT RESEARCH PROJECT:
AN ILLUSTRATION

In 1974, Blanchard heard about the Mississippi Choctaws and their passion for sports, from the traditional stickball to contemporary baseball, softball, and basketball. Interested in the anthropological study of sport, he determined that the Choctaw community offered an excellent opportunity for sport research. After a few preliminary trips (passive research) to the pine and kudzu-covered, red-clay hills of east-central Mississippi that spring, he moved down for an extended summer field session. Having had coaching experience, Blanchard volunteered his services to the Choctaw recreation program and worked for the tribe as a "recreation consultant" while actively conducting anthropological research among the Choctaw people.

Blanchard was particularly interested in the nature of sport competition among the Choctaws. His preliminary research suggested that Choctaws, while competitive, were less physically aggressive in their sport activities than were their southern white counterparts. It suggested that the Choctaws in Mississippi had a notion of sport competition that was distinctive, different from that of non- Choctaws in the same area. Eliciting and describing that model of sport competition became the essential problem in the summer's research.

Theoretically, the model most appropriate to such a problem was the ethnoscience model, providing as it does both a perspective and a method for isolating cultural knowledge specific to particular areas of behavior. Given the problem and the model, Blanchard's primary objective then was the description of a Choctaw "emic model" of sport competition. The theory to be tested in this context was simply that the Choctaw view of sport competition differed sharply from that of comparable non-Choctaw groups, reflecting some fundamental values in traditional Choctaw culture.

During the early phases of Blanchard's research he observed a variety of athletic contests pitting Choctaws against Choctaws. He was particularly interested in the signs of aggression and conflict. As he moved into the active stage of research, Blanchard began a series of loosely structured interviews with Choctaw athletes, male and female. The questions asked included queries about the conception of particular games and their importance, notions about competition, and feelings about opponents. Later, the anthropologist devised a series of nonstandardized projective plates roughly depicting action at a typical football game. He then met individually with a sample of Choctaw sport enthusiasts and asked them to respond to the plates, specifically to the general question, "What do you think is going on here?" After several of these interviews were conducted, it was obvious that the format was going to have to be revised. The subjects were not volunteering enough information to make the excercise worthwhile. So Blanchard designed a list of direct questions for each of the five plates. The more specialized questions forced the respondents to deal with a range of issues and make chioces that they might not have made under the less-structured arrangement.

This same projective test was administered to a comparable group of non-Choctaws later that year, and the results of the comparison provided an interesting insight into the Choctaw conception of athletic competition. For example, in the interpretation of those plates involving physical contact between players of opposing teams (e.g., a tackler and a runner in open field), Choctaws were less likely than the non-Choctaws to read malicious intent into the motives of the players. Non-Choctaws were more prone to assume in these cases that someone was 'trying to hurt' an opponent. Similarly, there were significant differences between the two samples in the way they viewed the nature of spectator response, intrateam disagreement, the role of the officials in conflict situations, and coaching styles.

These data, coupled with the results of the unstructured interviews, led to the following observations regarding a Choctaw emic model of sport competition:

1.   The Mississippi Choctaws have a less complex repertoire of conflict terms applicable to the athletic context than do speakers of English.

2.   The Choctaws are less likely than their non-Choctaw neighbors to use these conflict terms in a sport context, whether they are players or simply spectators.

3.   The Choctaws are less likely to read violence or malicious intent into the physical confrontations characteristic of sport than are their Anglo-American counterparts.

4.   The Choctaws dislike physical coerciveness and both distrust and dislike any player, official, or coach, whose mode of operation is characterized by frequent attempts to coerce.

5.   Among the Mississippi Choctaws having fun is more important than winning in any athletic event. Sport outcomes are not to be taken very seriously, thus violent forms of conflict are generally avoided.

The data collected and analyzed in the active research stage of the project confirmed the initial proposition, that the Mississippi Choctaws exhibited a distinctive conception of sport competition, one that is consistent with traditional norms and values in Choctaw culture.

SUMMARY

Theory and method are essential components in the anthropological research process and must be viewed as interdependent. Theoretical models outline and define the limits of the research and suggest theories, theories that can be tested. The history of anthropology can be viewed as the history of theoretical model development and application. Some of the models that have been developed have been more popular than others. These can be divided into explanatory and interpretive types. The explanatory models include evolutionism, functionalism, structural-functionalism, and cultural-materialism. Two important interpretive models are ethnoscience and symbolic anthropology.

Evolutionism suggests that explanation is a matter of putting events or behaviors into a chronological sequence. Functionalism explains by relating institutions to individual need fulfillment while structural-functionalism sees causation in the inner-workings of the social system, individual institutions working together for the well-being of the total system. Cultural materialism is based on the premise that culture is an adaptive response to the physical environment and is to be understood as essentially technological and economic in nature. Social organization and ideology are also components in the adaptive system, but are viewed as by-products of the techno-economic base.

As an interpretive model, ethnoscience does not isolate cause-and-effect, but it does suggest that culture is a knowledge that can be elicited and structured in such a way that it is possible for the anthropologist to understand directly the native's perception of reality. The methodology by which this knowledge is retrieved and interpreted is implicit in the model itself. Symbolic anthropology, a generic title encompassing several specialized theoretical models in anthropology, is based on the assumption that cultural behavior symbolically manifests social structure.

All of these models have possible applications in the anthropological study of sport. Evolutionism explains sport as the product of a long process of prehistoric and historical development. Functionalism looks at sport behavior in terms of its contribution to individual need fulfillment. Structural-functionalism treats sport as an institution having reciprocal ties with many other institutions in the social system. Cultural-materialism treats sport as an adaptive mechanism whose essential characteristics are determined by the technological and economic components of the cultural system in which the sport developed. Ethnoscience provides a method for understanding sport(s) as viewed from the perspective of a particular cultural framework. Symbolic anthropology interprets sport as a setting within which relationships are symbolic reenactments of the social system itself.

Straightforward ethnographic description is an important research strategy in anthropology and does not require the use of a formal theoretical model nor the testing of a particular theoretical proposition. Ethnography can be viewed as a model and as an implicit method for doing research. The collection of ethnographic data relative to the sport process in societies around the world is an important dimension of sport studies in anthropology.

The research design is the preliminary blueprint of the proposed research. The anthropologist outlines and elaborates on the issue or problem to be explored, lists his objectives, discusses the theoretical model to be employed, and suggests a theory (or theories) to be tested. He then specifies the methodology to be used, the data to be collected, and the analysis technique to which the data will eventually be subjected. Possible results and the significance of the research are also discussed.

The anthropological research process itself is generally understood in terms of fieldwork and participant observation. However, there are many varieties of data-collecting techniques and styles in anthropology so that actual methods to be employed in any research project are legitimately selected with the demands of the objectives and practicality as the primary considerations. From passive research to informant interviews, questionnaire administration, and the use of sociological and psychological testing devices, the possibilities are myriad.

Data analysis is essentially theory testing. Verbal, statistical, visual, and auditory data are employed either to make a case for or reject the hypothesis or hypotheses that the anthropologist has chosen to test. The actual presentation of the data is governed by the simple premise that good anthropology is good description.

Exercises

Discussion questions:

1.   Consider your normal daily routine. What implicit theoretical models guide your behavior? (For example, what general model do you use in making a decision as to where to eat lunch on any given weekday?)

2.   Again, with reference to that same daily routine, what theories have you tested lately? In other words, what assumptions have you made that you then tested? (For example, when you enrolled in a class, you were given information about where and when it was to meet. You got that information from the schedule, but you also realized that such schedules can be wrong. Nevertheless, you began with that assumption as a hypothesis and tested it each time you came to class during that first week or two of the semester. Your initial hunch about when and where the class was to meet may or may not have been proven by your subsequent testing.)

3.   Describe one the of most popular sporting activities of your local community or region of the country (e.g., girls' state basketball tournament; city league softball championships). What questions would one ask if he or she were analyzing this activity from a structural-functional perspective? From an evolutionary perspective?

4.   It is suggested that professional sports in the country reflect the basic values of the American system. Using a symbolic anthropology approach, isolate some of those values and discuss ways in which one or more major professional sports reflect those (i.e., isolate and describe the symbols).

5.   Using your own experience in a particular sport as data, construct a componential definition that reflects the way you structure that sport. Do you think the persons with whom you

compete would structure it the same way? What about participants in other parts of the country or other parts of the world?

6.   Comedian George Carlin does a routine in which he compares the respective languages of football and baseball. Describe some of the terminologies and expressions common to particular sports in American society. What does the language tell us about these sports?

7.   Consider each of the following sport-related social problems from the perspectives of cultural materialism, structural-functionalism, and symbolic anthropology: (1) drug use in sport, (2) excessive bureaucratic control of scholastic sports, (3) the unionization of professional athletes, (4) the responsibilities of professional athletic organizations relative to college athletic programs (e.g., the recent case involving Herschel Walker, the University of Georgia and the United States Football League).

Special Projects:

1.   In a grill, bar, lounge, hallway, or other informal atmosphere where one might pick up on interesting, sport-related conversations, spend a brief period lurking. Record the information, especially what you overhear concerning the myths and recollections of particular sporting events. Analyze the information as a source of data about a particular sport.

2.   Attend a local sporting event and describe the events of the game. Using a structural-functional model, isolate particular behaviors that have cultural significance. Analyze the game from both the players' and spectators' perspectives.

3.   You are interested in the student-athlete role and the controversy surrounding the issue of the college or university's obligation to its athletes. Assuming you were going to study the problem in your particular institution and that you had access to all the necessary information, set up an appropriate research design. Include a model and at least two theories that you might test. Discuss expected results.

George Catlin's "Ball Play of the Choctaw—Ball Up"

4 Prehistory and Early History of Sport

One of the most interesting issues addressed by the anthropology of sport is the question of sport origin and development. How and where did sport first become an institutionalized human activity? What are the forces underlying the evolutionary development of sport behavior? What were the earliest forms of human sport? These are archeological questions, and one might wish for simple answers: the excitement of a Howard Carter discovering King Tutankhamen's tomb; the riddle-solving insight of a Rosetta Stone. If only it were just a matter of finding a stack of Stone Age baseball bats piled around a prehistoric homeplate, a carving depicting Neanderthal Man picking up a wooden club and hitting a round rock over an ancient scoreboard, or a message painted on a cave wall announcing "baseball is born." But, sadly, it is never that easy.

Archeologists have uncovered some information about sport and play in prehistoric society. However, faulty definitions, a paucity of sport and game artifacts, and a hesitation to use play as an interpretive model have limited archeology's contribution to the discussion of sport prehistory (Fox, 1977). Nevertheless, as archeological models become scientifically more sophisticated and archeologists more sensitized to the significance of play and games, sport-related findings will become a more regular feature of the archeological site report.

Archeology is the study of prehistoric culture and shares with cultural anthropology the notion that culture is componential. Archeological models of culture can include sport as one of those components, with the assumption that sport behavior develops, changes, and evolves just as do other facets of culture (e.g., the economy, social organization, religion, law). This suggests that sport is a dimension of the human cultural experience at all levels or periods of archeological time, from the Lower Paleolithic, to the Middle and Upper Paleolithic, Mesolithic, Neolithic, Chalcolithic, Bronze, and Iron Ages. Over time, sport behavior has evolved from simple to complex in rule structure, nature of competition, and equipment. Ideally, this process is reflected in the archeological record, and archeologists are able to reconstruct that process and describe the nature of sport in prehistoric culture.

SPORT IN STONE AGE SOCIETY

The Paleolithic tradition of human prehistory, the Old Stone Age, comprises the great bulk of human cultural time. Assuming that human culture has existed for approximately two million years, it is safe to suggest that for over 99 percent of that time human beings have lived in Stone Age conditions. They have hunted wild game and gathered plants, used stone tools, and lived in small band societies in which population levels are predicated directly on the availability of natural resources (see Service, 1963, for a description of band level society). Throughout the Lower, Middle, and Upper Paleolithic periods, the total human population remained fairly constant. Technological change, while significant, occurred only slowly, and individual cultures manifested minimal elaboration.

The presence of play throughout the thousands of years of human Paleolithic existence is taken for granted by the archeologist, given the nature of play and its ubiquity among primates. However, games and sports are less likely to be so rapidly presumed. In fact, some scholars suggest that sport is a characteristic of recent human history and that the archeologist should not expect to find evidence of sport in the Paleolithic record because it did not exist (e.g., Diem 1971). Early man acted out a variety of ritual dramas, engaged in physical activities, and played, but did not sport. Only in the past few centuries have some competitive rituals evolved into sport. Such a model yields the concept of prehistoric sport an empty set and makes it a virtual misnomer. Small-scale, hunting-and-collecting cultural systems simply "lack the necessary free time on a predictable, regular basis to develop and maintain structured, institutionalized, sporting and recreational pastimes" (Fox, 1977:67).

If one dismisses the idea of prehistoric sport or suggests that Paleolithic band society was not structured to accommodate institutionalized sport or recreation, then the obvious implication is that archeology should abandon the quest. This is precisely the problem. If the archeologist too hastily discards prehistoric sport as a possibility, he limits his ability to develop sport-related hypotheses and interpretive models. The argument against so-called primitive sport (as in Diem 1971) has not been conclusive enough to warrant taking such a risk. Many of the differences between the competitive activities of peoples are quantitative rather than qualitative. The idea that sport is the youthful descendant of ritual is largely speculative. In fact, it has been demonstrated that sport has the potential for developing into ritual, as easily as ritual into sport (Lesser, 1933). Also, contrary to earlier notions, anthropologists are now generally agreed that people in small-scale hunting societies traditionally have had ample free time for leisurely pursuits (Lee, 1968). As Sahlins (1972:34) has suggested , "hunters keep bankers' hours." For Paleolithic man, leisure was likely the expected norm, and free time at a surplus.

It is reasonable to suggest that for early humans sport activities made sense. They would have provided recreational alternatives in a leisure-rich environment, promoted physical exercise, fostered skill development in techniques vital to the hunt (e.g., running, throwing, dodging), served as socialization mechanisms, and reinforced cultural norms and values. The case for prehistoric sport is a viable one. Archeologists will continue to pursue evidence for sport, game, and play.

THE ARCHEOLOGICAL RECORD

What evidence has been unearthed by archeologists so far that attests to the reality of sport in prehistoric hunting-and-gathering, band societies? As Fox (1977:66) has noted, very little; "there are few direct references to sport and recreation behaviors in the archeological literature." Much of the material archeologists have found suggesting sport has been game-related paraphernalia: game counters, gaming sticks, dice, gaming boards. One type of sport artifact found in the American Southeast is the chunkey stone. Chunkey is a game played among Southeastern tribes (e.g., Choctaws, Creeks) in which a player rolls the large stone along the ground, and participants compete by throwing wooden poles in the path of the stone. The object is to throw the pole as closely as possible to the point at which the chunkey stone will eventually come to rest.

When the archeologist finds items such as the chunkey stone, their prehistoric function is not always evident. How does he determine that they were used for sport or game purposes? In some cases, interpretation is based on contextual information. In other words, the data associated with the particular find creates a total picture within which the sport significance of the artifact makes sense. For example, if a future archeologist were to excavate a twentieth-century American site and discover a leather football, he might not recognize it as a sport device. But, if that football were to be found in association with a stadium, playing field, goal posts, and kicking tee, it might seem obvious that the artifact was a sport object.

In other archeological settings, interpretation is based on ethnographic analogy, a technique in which the archeologist reasons from information that he has about a living group of people to interpret the activities of a similar but extinct group. The problem of the chunkey stone is a good illustration of how ethnographic analogy works. The archeologist is familiar with the ethnography of the Southeast and assumes a continuity between prehistory and history in the area. Knowing that chunkey is common among the historic tribes and being familiar with descriptions of the game that appear in the ethnographic literature, he concludes that the large round stones were used for similar purposes in analogous situations in the past.

In other situations, the interpretation of archeological materials as gaming objects or sport paraphernalia is the result of a combination of interpretive techniques. One such interpretation came out of the analysis of the materials from the Eva Site, an Archaic occupation in west Tennessee. An interesting bone implement found in a stratum dated to over 7,000 years ago presented an interpretational problem to the archeologists (Lewis and Lewis, 1961:101). The object was a portion of the occipital bone surrounding the foramen magnum of a deer skull that had been cut and smoothed, then placed over the end of a section of deer antler (see Fig. 5). The smoothing suggested to the archelogists that the combination had a purpose. In their words,

> The only idea that comes to mind is that this was a ring and pin game, many variations of which existed among American Indians. If that is what is represented, it carries the existence of the game well back into the early Archaic. This might be expected, considering how wide-spread and how variable the game was (Lewis and Lewis, 1961:101).

SPORT AND THE URBAN STATE

Sport historians Denise Palmer and Maxwell Howell (1973b:22) have argued that the "earliest archaeological evidence of sport and games is found in the Early Dynastic Period of the Sumerian Civilization (3000-1500 B.C.)." While the evidence uncovered at earlier sites, such as the Eva Site in Tennessee, predates the Sumerian evidence, Palmer and Howell are probably correct in their assertion that the first clear, graphic representations of sport come from the early phases of Sumerian Civilization.

Looking at the reproductions in Eva Strommenger's *5000 Years of the Art of Mesopotamia,* one is struck by the frequent representation of sports and games. For example, Figure 46 is a photograph of a limestone votive plaque from the Mesilim Period, dated between the third and fourth millenia B.C. Approximately nine and one-half inches long and three inches high, the plaque depicts three pairs of wrestlers. Each pair is engaged in different wrestling

FIGURE 5. Gaming Device (?) from Eva (Tennessee) Site dated to Early Archaic Phase of Southeastern Prehistory (Lewis and Lewis, 1961)

holds, and an implicit animation threatens to send all the combatants tumbling to the ground, but with an athletic rhythm. No barroom brawl or awkward mauling, this prehistoric contest; the deliberate moves, the skills, and style all speak of sport. The heads on the thick, muscular bodies appear to be those of mythical creatures, but the wrestling that is depicted is not the result of an artist's imagination, a fictional athletic encounter between supernaturals. It is obvious that the sculptor has seen mortals wrestle; mortals who had mastered the sport and whose skills invited admiring spectators.

Sport is an obvious element in the archeological ruins of all the primary civilizations around the world; in Mesopotamia, Egypt, India, China, and Mesoamerica, as well as in the later secondary civilizations; Etruscan, Minoan, Greek, and Roman. What are the factors leading to this sudden clarity of sport and athletic event in the archeological record?

With the evolution of the Neolithic phase of human prehistory and the concomitant development of agriculture came larger and denser populations. The domestication of plants and animals made it possible for a few to produce food for many. With the larger populations came new forms of social and political organization, and eventually the urban state emerged. In Mesopotamia, and later in other areas of the world, urban civilization evolved and brought with it new technology, writing systems, complex legal and political institutions, elaborate architecture, and multiple artistic media. In the new world created by urbanity, sport and games became more complex, sophisticated, and institutionalized than in their previous Paleolithic existence. The new technology led to an elaboration of equipment, from ivory gaming boards to special protective gear. Sporting events often became spectacles, competition acted out before large crowds in amphitheaters and massive arenas. Sport competition reflected the complexity of the new social system and was expressed at various levels: individual versus individual, team versus team, family versus family, town versus town, or state versus state. And, frequently, sport was a subject for the artist or the craftsman.

The sporting activities characteristic of the early urban states are myriad, but seem to cluster around several basic themes: track and field, combative events, outdoor skills, gymnastics, water sports, and ball games (see Table 2). The earliest clues to the existence of sport in the urban state, those from the ruins at Sumer, suggest not only wrestling, but boxing and sport hunting and board games as well. The evidence of sport in prehistoric Egypt is more detailed than that for Sumer. Materials found in graves--specifically, playing equipment, dated to the predynastic period in Egypt, (ca. 3000 B.C.)--betray the presence of various games and sports: marbles, ninepins, board games, and several games employing balls (Abdou, 1973:59). Later archeological remains from the Egyptian Pharaonic dynasties point to both athletic event and spectacle: hunting, fowling, fishing, dancing, stick fighting, archery, competitive swimming, running, and bull fighting. Apparently, some of the sports and games from this era were restricted to elite or upper class participation: acrobatics, tumbling, tug-of-war, ball games, hoop games, and various throwing games (Palmer and Howell, 1973b:23), although it is likely that most of these phenomena had their lower class counterparts. Egypt is the source of the earliest evidence for the ballgame, according to Uriel Simri (1973:94): "The wall paintings from the tombs of Beni-Hassan, dating back to the beginning of the second millennium B.C. depict a series of activities...performed by women" involving small spherical objects.

Among the Etruscans, archeological data from 600 B.C. reveal the presence of acrobatics, ball games, track and field competition (e.g., javelin and discus), running, jumping, boxing, wrestling, chariot racing, and gladiatorial contests (Howell and Sawula, 1973).

Sport was also a prominent and complex institution during the Minoan period of ancient Crete, according to archeological reports from the era. Sir Arthur Evans' voluminous account of his excavations in the Palace of Minos at Knossos is replete with descriptions of sports and games, both the activities and the equipment. The sports of the Minoans included tumbling, boxing, wrestling, running, ball games, bull fighting, hunting, and fishing. Evans (1921:689), in describing a carving found in the palace ruins, refers to one of the participants in a boxing match as the "highly athletic figure of a pugilist who has just knocked out his opponent."

Archeologists have reported little in the way of sport activity in prehistoric China. However, by the time of the Chou Dynasty (1100-800 B.C.), it is obvious that games (e.g., competitive archery) were important elements in Chinese daily life (Sasajima, 1973:36). Also, according to Giles (1906:510), as early as the Han Dynasty (206 B.C.-25 A.D.) the Chinese were playing "football" (i.e., soccer).

From the Neolithic era of prehistory in India, archeologists have retrieved marbles apparently used in games (Rajagopalan, 1973:47). A 12,000 square feet public bath at the ancient city of Mohenjo-daro has been labeled a "swimming pool" (Rajagopalan, 1973:47). Terra-cotta toys, rattles, whistles, animals, and dice have also been found in association with this period of Indian prehistory. With the subsequent Aryan invasion, wrestling, riding, boxing, and javelin throwing become part of the Indian sport institution.

By the time the Greek and Roman states emerged, the so-called "civilized" Western world had developed large-scale sport and spectacle institutions. Archery, boxing, wrestling, rowing, swimming, hoop bowling, javelin and discus throwing were popular among the Greeks. The ball was used in a variety of games, but play with the ball was never very popular with the Greeks (Harris, 1972:75-111).

Although the Romans adopted most of the Greek sports, they seemed to be less enthusiastic about track-and-field events than were the Greeks. However, "though they were lukewarm about Greek

TABLE 2...Sport in Prehistory: Selected Archeological Evidence by Area and General Time Period

DATE	Mesopotamia	Egypt	India	China	Mesoamerica	North America	Crete	Etruria
4,000 B.C.	Gaming devices					Gaming devices (?)		
3,500 B.C.	Wrestling Boxing							
3,000 B.C.	Acrobatics	Nine-pins Ball games						
2,500 B.C.								
2,000 B.C.	Horse riding Archery Hunting Swimming	Stick fighting Hunting Archery Swimming Tumbling Bull fighting Horse riding					Tumbling Boxing Wrestling Ballgames Running Bull-vaulting	
1,500 B.C.			Marbles Gaming devices Swimming Wrestling Boxing Javelin Jumping Ball games	Gaming devices Archery Horse riding	Olmec ballgame			
1,000 B.C.			Bull-chasing	Soccer	Mayan ballgame			Ballgames Running Track/field Boxing Wrestling
500 B.C.					Aztec ballgame			
—								
500 A.D.						"Rubber" ballgame		
1,000 A.D.						Chunkey		
1,500 A.D.						Hoop-and-pole Racket game		

98

athletics, the Romans appear to have adopted Greek ball-play with enthusiasm" (Harris, 1972:85).

Actually, by the time the Greek and Roman civilizations came into being, a plethora of writing systems had been developed and Western history was a *fait accompli*. From that point, sport was a frequent subject in written records as well as in art and artifact. However, the subject of sport in history is more a matter for the historian than for the prehistoric archeologist.

MESOAMERICA AND THE BALLGAME

The prehistoric sporting event best known and most frequently discussed by anthropologists and archeologists is the Mesoamerican ballgame, known to the Maya as *Pok-ta-pok* and the Aztecs as *Tlachtli.* No other prehistoric sporting event has received as much attention or has been the subject of so much controversy, but no other game has been so well represented in the archeological record. With its broad geographical distribution, hundreds of ballcourts, many artistic depictions, stone yokes and other paraphernalia, as well as ethnohistorical references, the classic rubber ballgame of Mesoamerica literally demands attention.

Despite the volume of archeological data, many questions about the ballgame remain unanswered. Perhaps the situation illustrates the old adage that the more one knows, the more one realizes how much he does not know. Although the reality of a rubber ballgame in Middle America during as much as 2,000 years of prehistory is generally taken for granted, many issues remain unresolved: the time and place of origin; the process and meaning of the game; the pattern of diffusion; the social, political, and religious dimensions of competition; and the bases of its popularity and importance. 229315

The Mesoamerican ballgame has taken a variety of forms, as reflected in court size and shape, equipment, and artistic depiction. Also, it has been played in many locations throughout Middle America, the American Southwest, and, perhaps, the upper tip of South America. Ballcourts have been located as far north as Arizona and New Mexico, as far south as Honduras, as far east as Puerto Rico, and as far west as the Pacific coast of Mexico. The game was being played as early as 1500 B.C., and modern variations of the sport are still being played in certain parts of northern Mexico today.

In all of these situations, the ballgames shared certain essential features: the use of a rubber ball; a court of variable dimensions; and goals through or against which the ball was to be propelled with hips or feet (or in some cases, hands) in order to score points. The ultimate objective was to accumulate more points than an opponent. Simple enough, perhaps, but the range of variation, the complexity of ritual meaning associated with game performance, and the many possible outcomes, make the analysis of the classic ballgame a multifaceted problem.

One of the more fascinating ballgame-related archeological problems is the issue of origins. The earliest ballcourts have been dated to the early Classic period of Mayan prehistory (i.e., 200 - 300 A.D.). One of the earliest of these courts is found at Copan in what is now southwestern Honduras. A rectangular, stone-paved playing floor flanked by parallel platforms and sloping sides, with three stone slabs set in the floor as markers, the structure is typical of the I-shaped Mayan ballcourt (See Fig. 6). The ballcourt evidence is one of the reasons that Blom (1932:487) argues that "the game which played so great a role in the life of the Middle American peoples was of Maya origin."

However, other archeologists have contended that the ballgame is older than the Mayans. Coe (1962:75), for example, argues that it dates back to the Olmec period, perhaps as early as 1000 B.C. Is it possible that clay mounds at the Olmec site of San Lorenzo on the Mexican Gulf Coast may be the remains of ball courts? Also, early ballplaying figurines have been found in several Olmec sites. Coe (1962:88) suggests that the helmetlike headpieces of the colossal Olmec carved heads may be ballgame headgear, evidence that the Olmec people may have been playing the game over three thousand years ago. Olsen (1974:210) uses language data to argue for a similar provenience for the ballgame. The word "Olmec" itself is usually interpreted to mean "rubber people" (from the Mayan word *olli*). Also, *uol* or *uolol* in Mayan refers to a "round thing" or "ball." Olsen (1974:210) suggests that "perhaps the Olmecs had a round thing--the rubber ball for playing a game."

Humphrey (1981:134) accepts Coe's (1962) dates and points to archeological evidence from other areas of Mesoamerica, such as Teotihuacan and Oaxaca, that argues for a pre-Mayan ballgame. Carved stones and frescoes depict ballplayers in full regalia and actual ballgame combat. It is obvious that the ballgame is more than just a Mayan institution.

Whether or not the Mayans were initially responsible for the intervention and institutionalization of the rubber ballgame, they took more seriously the business of building elaborate courts than did any of the other prehistoric Mesoamerican populations. Most of the major Mayan sites--Copan, Palenque, Tikal, Uxmal, and Kaminaljuyú --include several courts among their ruins, as many as seven or eight in some cases.

The largest among known prehistoric ballcourts is that at the Mayan site of Chichen Itza. This immense arena is 492 feet in length, and though it is clearly marked by a Toltec influence, it is an expression of the importance the Mayans attached to the insitution of *pok-ta-pok*.

Although archeological data are not as plentiful as they are for

FIGURE 6. Mayan ball-court at Yaxchilan[1]

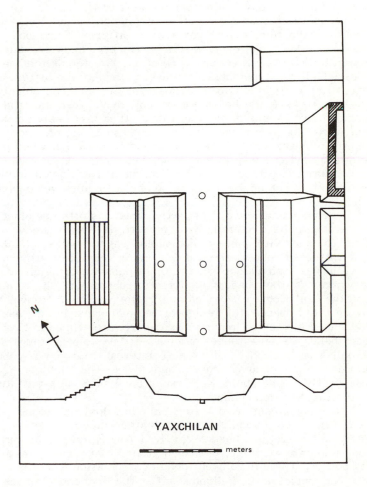

YAXCHILAN

meters

[1]From Blom, 1932:518

the Mayan period, it is clear that the rubber ballgame was an important factor in Toltec, Tenochtitlán, and Aztec life, as well as in the American Southwest.

Although the ballcourts ranged in size from the smallest two-man variety of approximately thirty feet in length to the large court at Chichen Itza, the design was fairly consistent from one area to another. The basic construction included the I shape, sloping side walls, and plastered stone floors (see Fig. 6). In addition, there were often large stone rings in the center of the wall on either side of the court, and occasionally inlaid stone markers on the floor.

Just as the features of court construction varied from one area to another, the rules of the game were different from one time or place to another. However, several basic principles prevailed. The game pitted two teams against each other, two teams that had to be composed of equal numbers of players, though the actual number ranged from as few as two to as many as eleven. The object of the game was to keep the heavy rubber ball moving without the use of hands or feet. Hips, elbows, knees, and other less likely parts of the torso were legitimate propulsion mechanisms. Points were scored when the ball was driven into the opponent's end-zone, when it fell to the ground and the enemy was unable to return it, or when it was knocked through a stone ring or against one of the floor markers. The first team to reach an agreed-upon number of points was declared the winner.

The equipment used by the participants was often as elaborate as the paraphernalia required by a modern-day professional football team. The most vital piece of equipment was the ball itself. Made of solid, untreated rubber, the ball varied in diameter--from eight to twelve inches--and weight--five to eight pounds. Originally collected and worked in the Amazonian forests, rubber was later harvested along the Gulf Coast of Mexico and in the Yucatan. Rubber did not grow in the Toltec-Aztec region of Mesoamerica, but it was traded into Central Mexico or imported as tribute, sometimes in the form of rubber balls. Because rubber had not yet been discovered in Europe, the ball was frequently of greater interest to the early Spaniard explorers and conquistadors than was the ballgame itself. Subsequently, rubber balls were taken back to Spain and introduced into existing European games.

Other equipment used in the ballgame included stone yokes or belts, hand-stones, padlock stones, leather gloves, knee pads, chin pieces, half-masks and headgear. The yokes (*yugos*, in Spanish) were large, elaborately carved, U-shaped stones that weighed as much as sixty pounds. These have been found in association with the ballcourt ruins and depicted in ballgame art. The evidence suggests that despite their bulk they were worn by the players for protection as well as for striking the ball. Humphrey (1981:140) argues that "the yokes are representations in stone of leather or rubber protective belts." However, Ekholm (1961:361) has experimented with some of the stone collars found in Puerto Rican ballcourt sites and defends the idea that these cumbersome stone rings are not just artistic representations, but were actually worn by players. The hand-stones and the padlock stones were used for striking or fending off the ball, although in the latter case they may have been used as stomach protectors.

The ballcourts and the gear were made even more elaborate by the artistic stylization that added both beauty and ritual meaning to ballgame accouterments. Frequently the stone rings, yokes, and hand-stones were eloquently carved, depicting cosmic forces, the gods, or various symbols of fertility. The material culture of the ballgame suggests that it was more than athletic competition.

This extra dimension of the classic Mesoamerican ballgame was expressed in its intensity, its ritual celebration, and the attendant gambling. The pace of the competition was fast and brutal. The heavy, hard-rubber ball pounding against unprotected flesh, careening off stone walls to slam into flashing limbs and brittle bones, created a hazard that compounded the ever-present danger of body crashing against body. The results were predictably bloody. Duran's (1971:315-16) frequently quoted description of the Aztec ballgame captures that sense of frantic, bonejarring combat:

> All those who played this game were stripped except for their usual breechcloths, on top of which they wore coverings of deerskin to defend their thighs, which were continually being scratched on the floor. They wore gloves so as not to injure their hands, which they constantly set down firmly, supporting themselves against the floor....
>
> Some of these men [the players] were taken out dead from that place for the following reason. Tired and without having rested, they ran after the ball from end to end, seeing it descending from above, in haste and hurry to reach it first, but the ball on the rebound hit them in the mouth or the stomach or the intestines, so that they fell to the floor instantly. Some died of that blow on the spot because they had been too eager to touch the ball before anyone else. Some took a special pride in this game and peformed so many feats in it that it was truly amazing.... They employed a bounce or curious hit. On seeing the ball come at them, at the moment that it was about to touch the floor, they were so quick in turning their knees or buttocks to the ball that they returned it with extraordinary swiftness. With this bouncing back and forth they suffered terrible injuries on their knees or thighs so that the haunches of those who made use of these tricks were frequently so bruised that these spots had to be opened with a small blade, whereupon the blood which had clotted there because of the blows of the ball squeezed out.

The essential message of the ballgame was in its complex ritual component. The competition was an event of cosmic significance. The courts were consecrated to the deities. At Tenochtitlan, for example, the playing arenas were dedicated to the Sun and the Moon. The movement of the ball symbolized the movement of heavenly bodies across the skies, and the mythology surrounding the game was filled with struggles between gods. As Humphrey (1981:147) has noted, "the game enabled the individual to test his powers against those of the universe in a profound game of chance."

It was the element of chance that kept the ballgame above the mundane. One struggled with an opponent, but the ultimate competition was with fate. The ballplayer worked at preparing himself for a match. There were skills to be mastered and physical stamina to be fostered. But, more importantly, there were the ritual preparations, the magical rites, incantations and prayers, that aided the player in his attempt to manipulate fate and affect outcomes. And always he was confident of victory; so sure if he properly attended to spiritual prerequisites of combat preparation he would win that he bet on his presumed success with abandon. Among the nobility who played, the items wagered included turquoise, gold, emeralds, jade, corn fields, slaves, women, and children; in some cases, whole kingdoms. In one famous contest, the Mexican priest-king Axayacatl is reported to have played

> against the lord of Xochimilco and laid the marketplace of Mexico against a garden belonging to this lord. He lost. The next day, Mexican soldiers appeared at the palace of the fortunate winner and "while they saluted him and made him presents they threw a garland of flowers about his neck with a thong hidden in it and so it killed him" (Soustelle, 1961:160).

The commoners and the peasants--either as players or spectators--also gambled on the outcome of the ballgames. They invested in the game results with an enthusiasm similar to that of their more fortunate counterparts. Craft items, produce, wives, children, personal services, and their own personal freedoms were likely stakes.

The forces of fate brought in their wake more than capital gains and losses. Personal pride, political power, social status, and the honor of victory were also part of the complex stakes that rode on the outcome of the competition. The social and political importance of the ballgame is illustrated in Aztec history. Montezuma II and Texcoco chief Nezahualpilli once attempted to resolve a personal argument on the ballcourt. Nezahualpilli wagered the kingdom of Acolhua against three turkeys, eventually winning three out of five games, a turn of events that contributed to an erosion of public confidence in Montezuma and his ability to rule.

The honor that accrued to athletic skill and success was not unlike the esteem accorded the modern athlete. However, in the Mesoamerican ballgame that honor was expressed in a distinctive style. Today's typical sport fan envisions unruly throngs erupting out of crowded stands along the prehistoric ballcourts, screaming themselves into hoarseness in their enthusiasm, stomping their feet, and chanting out the names of their heroes. However, available evidence suggests that even though the ballgame provided entertainment and suspense for its spectators, crowd behavior was more likely marked by reverential silence than by boisterous cheering.

The stone rings also provided an opportunity for player reward. Among the Aztecs, the player putting the ball through the ring could claim the clothing and possessions of the spectators. The other members of the team assisted the victor in retrieving his rightful prize.

Another possible result of the ballgame competition was human sacrifice. In sorting out the winners and the losers, fate may have sentenced one group to die. Although it is not certain that such sacrifice followed in the wake of victory, not clear as to whether victors or vanquished were slaughtered, the archeological and historical data raise some provoking questions. For example, at Chichen Itza, a bas relief on a wall of the large ballcourt includes a carving that depicts what appears to be the captain of a losing team being sacrificed, though by exactly what means is not clear: decapitation or the removal of the heart. At Chichen Izta, a long platform has been decorated with carved human skulls skewered on stakes. According to Coe (1966:125-26), such platforms supported the great racks upon which the heads of victims were displayed and that "it is entirely possible that the game was played 'for keeps,'" the losers ending up on the rack along with the skeletal remains of other unfortunate victims of earlier ballgames.

Olsen (1974:202-05) proposes an alternative interpretation of these artistic suggestions of human sacrifice. According to Olsen's model, the depicted players are gods rather than mortals, portrayed as fertilizing the earth by the symbolic shedding of their own life blood. However, even Olsen (1974:204) admits that human sacrifice was common among Mesoamericans, especially the Aztec, and that special games may have been staged as a means of providing sacrificial victims.

If decapitation and instant open-heart surgery were common to the ballgame finale, it is not to be assumed that the losers were necessarily the players falling under the knife. The giving of one's life in ritual sacrifice was an honorable deed and insured the victim a glorious afterlife and his surviving family added social status. Under such conditions, it is possible that two teams might have competed for the honor of being ceremoniously beheaded for the glory of the gods.

While the ballgame was not the exclusive property of any particular social class or rank, it appears that the most colorful matches pitted nobles, princes, priest-kings, or other notables, against each other. And, as expected, these are the games most frequently recounted in history and folklore (e.g., the game between Nezahualpilli and Montezuma). According to Duran's account (1971:316), these matches were staged primarily for the recreation and enjoyment of the players. On the other hand, the games of the common people often involved so-called "professional" players or "gamblers," attracted great crowds, and if Duran's appraisal is accurate, were motivated by the lust for gambling and related vices (Duran, 1971:316). One might also expect that variants of the ballgame were played at other, less formal levels, in backyards, open fields, or abandoned ballcourts. However, these less-structured events are not accounted for in the archeological record and can only be assumed.

Nevertheless, it is the less formal varieties of the ballgame that appear to have survived into the twentieth century. Humphrey (1981:146) witnessed a variety of the ballgame being played in Oaxaca in 1976 and 1977, a game he claims contains "some elements of ancient *Tlachtli.*" Two teams of five to nine men each competed on an elongated court with three chalk floor markers. A solid rubber ball, six inches in diameter and some six to eight pounds in weight, was driven back and forth across the court by fists in leather gloves covered with nail-head studs.

Over the past three thousand years, at all levels of the social system, under various playing conditions, and in many geographical areas, the ballgame has been an important Mesoamerican institution. Not only the great civilizations--Olmec, Mayan, Toltec, Aztec--but also many of the smaller and more obscure states in the American Southwest, the Carribean, and the valley of Mexico have embraced the ballgame and given it special meaning. Why this importance, the popularity, and persistence? Surely, the ballgame's longevity cannot be explained purely on the basis of its recreational qualities. Several possibilities have been suggested.

The ballgame was a form of physical combat, a mock war. Thus, it could be argued that the ballgame, with all of its brutality, intentisy, and pain, was a substitute for war. It functioned as an alternative to war. This idea seems to be implicit in myths about the gods and their athletic confrontations with each other as well as in accounts of ballgames between rulers.

It could also be argued that the ballgame was an important preparation for war. The physical conditioning, the intensity, the strategy, and the skill development; all of these served to make the soldier battle-ready. Recognizing that the great Mesoamerican states, in particular the Toltecs and the Aztecs, had developed economic systems that depended on military might for their sustenance, it is reasonable to assume that they were war-conscious peoples, and that the model of the athlete as warrior would have been appropriate. This is also consistent with Sipes' (1973) thesis that warlike societies also tend to institutionalize physically combative sports.

Another possible factor in the long life of the Mesoamerican ballgame was its significance as ritual. The ballgame symbolized man against nature, man against the gods, man against fate, and man against himself. It provided an opportunity for agricultural peoples to pit themselves in mock combat against those forces over which they had little direct control. And, in their dramatic enactment of cosmic-level struggles, they made less tedious the demands of the fields and less anxious the uncertainties of the harvest.

According to Humphrey (1981:136), Coe (1968) underscores the ritual importance of the ballgame by his speculation that a significant relationship existed between the marine toad (*Bufo marinus*) and the Olmec version of the sport. The toad, though inedible, was the source of bufotenine, a hallucinogenic that was used by the Olmec people on various ritual occasions. The symbol of the toad has been found in association with ballgame-related artifacts and has led Coe to the conclusion that the Olmec game was an integral component in a broader, more comprehensive ritual event, and was perhaps a vehicle for the diffusion of Olmec religious symbolism.

Some might suggest that the clue to understanding the ballgame's success lies in the sport's ecological significance. If indeed human sacrifice was a normal complement of games, then it could be argued that the institution served as a population control device. Sherburne Cook (1946) has proposed that among the Aztecs both war and sacrifice were unconscious checks on population growth in a state where resources were strained by excessive numbers.

Michael Harner (1977) has taken the ecological explanation of Aztec sacrifice one step further and suggested that not only were these Mesoamerican theocrats ritually slaughtering people, but that they were also eating the flesh of their victims. He argues that the reason for this practice has to be seen in the serious protein deficiency characteristic of the Aztec diet. The meat, blood, and fat garnered from those hapless captives or willing volunteers whose sliced and still warm bodies were symbolically offered to the gods were instrumental in addressing that shortage. Now, if it could be demonstrated that both human sacrifice and cannibalism followed in the wake of ballgame activities, one might use Harner's model as a means of understanding the sport's continued vitality. However, as Harner himself (personal communication, October 1982) admits, there is neither historical nor archeological evidence to support the idea of a postgame cannibalism.

It is likely that a combination of factors, economic, social, and religious, have been at work in the development, elaboration, and survival of the Mesoamerican ballgame. Perhaps more important than an explanation for its popularity is the awareness of its importance, its centrality in the Mesoamerican state, and its eventual impact on Native North America.

THE BALLGAME IN NORTH AMERICA

The rubber ballgame, apparently a Mesoamerican invention, eventually worked its way up into the American Southwest. Archeologists have identified over ninety ballcourts in this area. They have also found at least two rubber balls. These small, mishapen spheres (one measured 3.4 inches in diameter) have been subjected to chemical analysis with the conclusion that they were made of rubber extracted from *guayule*, a local desert shrub. These balls were not found in asociation with any of the ballcourts, but it is speculated that they were used for playing purposes and that, in addition, others were manufactured and traded in from the south.

The ballcourts in the American Southwest have been found in Arizona and New Mexico, and are geographically isolated from the ballgame centers of Mesoamerica, some 1100 miles to the south. As Schroeder (1955:156) points out, no ballcourts have been "observed elsewhere in the United States nor have any been definitely identified between the Mexico City area...and the Arizona-northern Sonora region." Does this mean that the North American ballgame developed independently of those in the Olmec, Mayan, and Aztec regions of Mexico? The two types of ballcourts identified in the Southwest, the Snaketown and Case Grande, are different than any further south. However, they do share the basic features of the latter: the long playing floor, side walls that slope toward the floor, floor markers, and, if Haury's (1968:678) speculation is correct, side rings. It is also interesting that in several areas of Northern Mexico where no prehistoric ballcourts have been located, the ballgame itself has survived into the historic period, but without courts. Therefore, diffusion from south to north appears likely. However, the mechanics of that diffusion are still not understood. It is speculated by Schroeder (1955:161) that the ballgame may have been part of a broader ceremonial complex that "stretched unbroken from Middle American to Arizona," but was not essential to that complex in the intervening area among those groups unable to sustain the total institution. In other words, it may have been that the cultures in the area between Middle Mexico and the American Southwest simply lacked sufficient concentrations of population and social structures adequate to maintain the material and organization requisites of the ballgame. So, in these areas, the ritual was preserved, but without the ballcourts and the other ballgame paraphernalia. To have done otherwise and constructed large ballcourts would have been analogous to building a superdome in Dodge City, Kansas, or a mammoth cathedral in Tupelo, Mississippi.

Typical of the prehistoric culture in which the ballgame and all of its violence and grandeur apparently thrived in the Southwest was the Hohokam. The Hohokam peoples, descendants of the Archaic Cochise culture, were concentrated in the desertlike region of the Salt and Gila River Valleys in southern Arizona. During the Hohokam period, which dates from 100 A.D., these industrious agricultural people raised beans, squash, and maize, lived in pole-framed, mud-plastered houses built in pits, and developed an elaborate ceramic industry, featuring a beautiful red-on-buff pottery. Perhaps their greatest accomplishment was the development, sometime after 800 A.D., of a complex irrigation system through which they diverted waters from the Salt and Gila Rivers into their gardens and fields. Another prominent feature of Hohokam culture was the presence of a strong Mexican influence: rings, bracelets, pyrite and slate-backed mirrors, copper bells, turquoise beads, zoomorphic forms, stepped pyramids, and ballcourts.

Ballcourts have been identified at several of the Hohokam sites. The ballcourt at Snaketown is perhaps the best known. Now only a large, oval-shaped earthen depression, it once was the scene of boisterous athletic competition. In Haury's (1968:678) words:

> More battle than sport, a Snaketown ball game may have resembled ancient Mexican contests described by the Spaniards. Forbidden to throw or kick the rubbery ball--probably made from *guayule,* a desert bush--players tried to knock it through rings on the walls with hips, knees, or elbows. So rarely did a goal occur that the scorer could claim the clothing and jewelry of the spectators. Thus when a goal was scored, the contest ended; viewers took to their heels, pursued by friends of the victor.

The Hohokam ballgame, like other elements of its complex culture, faded into obscurity after the fourteenth century, although many archeologists speculate that the Hohokam peoples are the ancestors of the contemporary Pima and Papago of the desert Southwest. Again, it might be argued that with the demise of a strong economic and political base, the formal ballgame could no longer be maintained, so the ballcourts disappeared. This apparently happened throughout the Southwest, so that by the advent of the historic period (ca. 1500 A.D.), the big, elaborate courts were only archeological features. However, did the ballgame itself become extinct?

Similar to the way in which variants of the original ballgame appear to have survived into recent Mesoamerican history, various offspring of the formal Southwestern game may have kept the athletic tradition alive among the Native North American communities. In other words, a selection of sports involving the use of a ball may have evolved out of the classic ballgame and diffused into other areas of the Southwest as well as into more distant regions of the North American continent. Although limited archeological data are available, the direct historical approach might be more useful as a perspective for analyzing this possibility of a continuous ballgame tradition.

The direct historical approach is "a method of reconstructing prehistoric societies by progressive extension of analogies back through time" (Sharer and Ashmore, 1979:462). This technique, which is similar to ethnographic analogy, suggests that if one had sufficient ethnographic data about ballgames among Native North Americans, a person might successfully tie these bits of information together and eventually link them historically to the classical ballcourt game. In this way, one might test the theory that most, if not all, of the ballgames played by the Indians of North America can be traced to the Southwest and ultimately Mesoamerican influence.

Much of what is known about ballgames among traditional Native North American societies is a result of the work of Stewart Culin, in particular, his *Games of the North American Indians* (1907). In this survey of Indian games and sports, Culin (1907:561) developed the following system for classifying ballgames:

> First, racket, in which the ball is tossed with a racket; second, shinny, in which the ball is struck with a club or bat; third, double ball, a game chiefly confined to women, played with two balls or billets tied together, tossed with a stick; fourth the ball race, in which a ball or stick is kicked. In addition, subsidiary to the preceding and not general, being confined to a few tribes, we have:...football...hand-and-football...tossed ball...juggling, and...hot ball.

Culin's (1907) description of the games and sports of the 221 tribes treated in his analysis suggests that 38 (17 percent) played the racket game, 57 (26 percent) shinny, 20 (13 percent) double ball, 19 (8.6 percent) ball race, and 19 (8.6 percent) football, with smaller percentage occurrences of the others. Some of the tribes treated included several of the ball sports in their repertoire of activities, but many played no ballgames whatsoever.

The geographical distribution of these ballgames among Native North Americans is broad. Also, many of the conditions and equipment of the games vary from one culture to another. Nevertheless, all of these ballgames tend to share a set of common features. As Cheska (1981c:57-8) notes, these include:

> (1) A smoothed or cleared area of play was made ready with goal post(s) at the midpoint on the end lines. No side lines were designated. (2) Two opposing sides, ranging from six to one thousand players on a team, contended for victory. (3) The games were started by placing the ball in the midfield spot or dug hole or, at ceremonial and intertribal matches, by the tossing in the game ball by a highly esteemed tribe

member or visiting dignitary. (4) The ball was advanced toward the opponents' goal by the use of sticks, baskets, or feet. (5) The use of hands on the ball was usually prohibited. (6) A goal was scored by passing the ball through or over the goal or by wrapping a double-ball around the goal post. (7) Crude differentiation of play responsibility was made by assigning persons to the central area of action while others protected the goal. (8) Referees were used in important matches. (9) The game concluded when one team had scored the agreed-upon numbers of goals....

These are the same features that are common to the classic rubber ballgame of Mesoamerica and give credence to the idea that the various ballgames of historic Native North America are related to the game once acted out on the prehistoric ballcourts to the south. Stern (1949:93) has proposed that the competitive ballgame of North America (e.g. racket, shinny, and kicking race) "presents a continuous distribution...which overlaps the northern limits of the rubber-ball game in Mexico and the Southwest." He explains this continuity by reference to a historical relationship. The Indian ballgames of North America "represent diversified, widespread descendants of a ball-and-stick game that was ancestral as well to the competitive rubber-ball game" (Stern, 1949:93). Smith (1972:349) takes a similar position and notes that it is not a question of if, but rather one of how and when the ball-play concept first reached North America.

Therefore, the question to be addressed by the direct historical approach is that having to do with the mechanics rather than with the fact of the development of aboriginal North American ballgames out of a complex that took shape initially in prehistoric Middle America. Although much of the intervening data necessary to fill the gap between the present and the prehistoric past are currently unavailable, there are some observations that shed light on the process.

In the first place, it is significant that types of ballgames among Native Americans tend to be correlated with subsistence bases. In particular, shinny is more likely to be played by those tribes who hunt and forage for a living. Smith (1972:353) has opined that there may be a relationship between the digging stick that is ubiquitous among the root-and-tuber-gathering aboriginals (e.g., Shoshone) of the Great Basin area of the American West and the simple playing-stick used in shinny. On the other hand, the racket game is more frequent among agricultural peoples, the complexity of team structure and equipment being consistent with the greater sophistication of the technology and the higher level of social organization characteristic of people who subsist by farming.

Despite fundamental physical, linguistic, and historical differences, the aboriginal peoples throughout Middle and North America tended to share many common religious themes and symbols (e.g., the centrality of the Sun, the little people). This similarity itself may have been exaggerated by diffusion, but as Smith (1972:350) has observed, it facilitated the movement of the ballplay concept from one cultural setting to another. In other words, the shared ritual became a medium for the dispersal of ballgames, themselves important complements of that ritual.

Predictably, the various ballgames among Native North American tribes have developed regional specializations. As a particular game has diffused into a North American culture area, it has taken on a distinctive set of attributes that identify it with the area while at the same time maintaining the fundamentals. For example, a comparison of the varieties of the racket games for which Culin (1907) has provided detailed descriptive data reveals at least four regional specializations: Northeast, Southeast, Plains, and Far West (see Table 3). The variables that tend to cluster by area include the number of rackets, the position of the racket pocket, the shape of the racket shaft, and the type of goal.

Given the availability of sufficient ethnographic detail, such comparisons assist the archeologist in understanding the evolution of particular game forms. They also aid in the reconstruction of ballgame histories and isolation of ecological and ritual forces that have helped shape these histories.

Another method of use to the archeologist is ethnohistory. Ethnohistory is the study of history among nonliterate peoples in which the anthropologist relies on oral traditions, genealogies, relevant documents, and written accounts. It can be viewed as a valuable complement to the direct historical approach, providing data with which to fill the gap between prehistory and history.

Such a gap exists in the history of many sport activities, especially those that appear to have developed initially among preliterate peoples before their adoption into societies with writing systems. Often these activities burst onto the pages of history as though they had emerged fully developed, *ex nihilo.* "In the beginning, there was basketball..." In an attempt to correct such distortions, the ethnohistorical complements the historical by reconstructing many of the ambiguities of sport's development, describing roots for what otherwise seems adrift in time.

The question of lacrosse origins illustrates the importance of ethnohistory's potential contribution to sport studies. Euphemistically referred to as "the Indian ballgame" and "the granddaddy of American sports," lacrosse is assumed by most of its historians and officiandos alike to be the direct descendant of the Native North American racket game. Menke (1947:669), in his sport encyclopedia, sums up the popular notion of lacrosse origins:

The Indians played baggataway, under rules somewhat different from those which govern lacrosse today. But they

TABLE 3. Four racket game traits by culture area[1]

Culture area	Tribal group	No. of Sticks	Type racket pockets	Stick shape	Type of goal
Northeast (n = 6)	Chippewa	1	Sinew/Side	Round	Strike post
	Menominee	1	Sinew/Side	Round	Strike post
	Passamaquoddy	1	Net	Round	Hole-in-ground
	Mohawk	1	Net	Round	Strike post
	Seneca	1	Net	Round	Strike post
	Winnebago	1	Sinew/Side	Angular	n/a
Southeast (n = 4)	Cherokee	2	Sinew/End	Round	Between posts
	Choctaw	2	Sinew/End	Angular	Strike post
	Muskogee	2	Sinew/End	Angular	Strike post
	Seminole	2	Sinew/End	Angular	Strike post
Plains (n = 2)	Sauk/Fox	1	Sinew/Side	Round	Between posts
	Oto	1	Sinew/End	Round	Between posts
California (n = 6)	Pomo	1	Sinew/End and Side	Round	Base line
	Yokuts	1	Sinew/End	Round	n/a
	Miwok	1	Basket	n/a	n/a
	Topinagugin	1	Basket	n/a	Base line
	Nishinan	1	n/a	Round	Between posts
	Thompson Indian	1	n/a	Round	Between posts

1. Based on descriptions of racket games available in Culin's (1907) *Games of the North American Indian.*

113

had the original idea, and the Canadians merely made some betterments.

The name lacrosse, "the stick," the story goes, was given the name because of the web at the end of the racket. It "reminded them [the French Canadians] of a bishop's crozier--or cross" (Menke, 1947:669).

Only a few have challenged the reliability of this version of lacrosse origins. Clapin (cited in Culin, 1907:563) argues that lacrosse is only a variation of *soule,* a game played by the Ardennes mountaineers in France and introduced into America by the first French colonists. Henderson (1947:40) points to the use of the phrase *chouler a la crosse* in the fourteenth century to describe *la soule* and is unequivocal in his assertion that this sport was the forerunner of modern lacrosse. Though dissenting views such as these are in a distinct minority among sport historians, the arguments are not entirely without merit. The origins of lacrosse are not sufficiently understood at this point to justify the perfunctory dismissal of all who would question the traditional view of the sport's history.

Is it possible that the racket game is a relatively recent development in the Native American community, especially in the Southeast? It is curious that the earliest historical reference of the game was recorded in 1636 (de Brebeuf, 1636:185). The first note regarding ball play in the Southeast was Father Pierre Francois Charlevoix's reference to the racket game of the Creek in 1721. As popular as the racket game has been among the Northeastern and Southeastern tribes in the past two centuries, it is strange that so many of the early writers, from Biedman and the Gentleman of Elvas to Jonathan Dickinson, failed to mention it even though they described so many other dimensions of Indian life.

On the other hand, there are earlier references to ballgames among the aboriginal Americans (e.g., de Paina, 1676; Laudonniere, 1562), but ballgames that do not involve the use of rackets. Could it be that the racket was a recent introduction and only came into the Southeast subsequent to European contact?

Hoffman (1896:130) has argued that

the game of lacrosse originated without doubt among some one of the eastern Algonquian tribes, possibly in the valley of the Saint Lawrence river, and from there was carried down along the Huron-Iroquois, and later on into the country of the more southern members of the Iroquoian linguistic stock, as the Cherokee.

This conclusion is reinforced by what is known about the movement of the racket game across cultural lines and the reality of a general Iroquoian influence on the Southeast.

Hoffman's (1896) thesis gives some credibility to the notion that the Indian ballgame was altered significantly as a result of French contact. The area described by Hoffman (1896:130) as the point of lacrosse origins is the area most heavily infiltrated and influenced by the French. Is it possible that the medieval game of *la soule,* with its *lacrosse,* was transplanted in early history America and reordered the traditional Native American ballgame by the addition of a racket?

Data at this point are insufficient to leap to conclusions, to paint pictures of invading Frenchmen waving sticks and screaming at the Indians, "With the racket! Not your feet!" And whether or not historians eventually give the French credit for the invention of lacrosse, the lacrosse played in North America today will remain "the Indians' game." For at least two hundred years, after European contact, the Native American community refined the equipment, skills, and mechanics of the game, before it became a white man's sport. Its roots lie intertwined with those of the ancient Mesoamerican ball game. It is as much a part of the continent as cactus and buffalo grass.

THE FUTURE OF SPORT AND ARCHEOLOGY

Perhaps the most visible development in the past two decades of archeological history has been the emergence of the so-called "new archeology." Born in the idealistic sixties, the decade in which every college student majored in anthropology at least once, the new archeology exuded the enthusiasm of its parent discipline and threatened to revolutionize the study of prehistory. No more would archeology be limited to observations about material culture. No longer would it be only the science of the obvious. Archeology was to be the anthropology of extinct culture, approaching its data with a perspective analogous to that of the cultural anthropologist. No bit of data would be left unexposed nor any behavior unreconstructed. Politics, law, social organization, even religion became legitimate foci of archeological investigation and would not escape the excavator's trowel. And how was this to be accomplished? Archeology was reconceptionalizing itself as a science, breaking away from earlier definitions as merely art or one of the humanities. It would become a science by using theoretical models, some of which it would borrow from cultural anthropology, and by testing theories. Every problem would be cast in scientific language, every dig operationalized as a set of hypotheses, and every analysis approached as a quest for validity.

The "new archeology" has had almost twenty years to affect its revolution. Its approach is no longer "new," and the ambitious theoretical archeologists of the sixties have yet to stand the academic community on its ear, but prehistoric archeology has changed. The scientific approach to archeology has broadened the understanding of prehistory, increased the reliability of data collection and interpretation, and expanded the areas of possible investigation.

One of these possibilities is the deliberate collection of prehistoric sport and games material. By constructing sport-sensitive theories, the archeologist is less likely to disregard the clues of prehistory that tell the story of people at play. As anthropologists in general open up to the importance of sport as an element of human culture, it will become increasingly difficult for the archeologist to ingore the phenomenon. Inevitably, hypothesis construction and data collection will be affected.

SPORT ORIGINS AND DEVELOPMENT REVISITED

Until archeology undertakes this deliberate quest for answers to the sport prehistory question, science's understanding of sport origins and development will remain largely speculative. However, anthropologists know enough about sport, play, human culture, and prehistory to speculate about that issue with some degree of confidence.

One way of approaching the problem is by means of a cultural evolution model. The basic premise underlying such a model is that sport behavior is a component of culture and that it evolves in conjunction with the lineal development of the total system. In other words, just as there is a religious, political, or technological evolution, there is a sport evolution.

Several anthropologists have pointed to a similarity between sport and games and their cultural contexts (e.g., Roberts, Arth, and Bush, 1959; Sipes, 1973). In this particular analysis, it is proposed that the nature of sport at any level of the cultural evolution process is primarily a product of three major variables.

> 1. *The type of subsistence.* Subsistence, the institutionalized method for procuring food in any cultural system, is a key element in that system's distinctiveness, affecting, directly or indirectly, all of the other institutions. Therefore, it is reasonable to assume that whether a group survives by hunting-and-gathering or produces its groceries on large corporate farms, subsistence is vital to its definition of sport. More productive and resourceful subsistence systems entail more complex material cultures and technologies, which in turn make possible more elaborate sport institutions.
>
> 2. *Sociopolitical structure.* The nature of social organization and political life in any culture is reflected in its sport activities. Larger populations tend to sport on grander scales than do small band societies. Also, sport competition often occurs along political lines.

3. *Geographical and ecological variables.* The nature of
sport is also affected by the type of environment in which it
occurs and the special problems of adaptation faced by the
subject population. Population pressures, topographical
features, floral and faunal patterns, climate, availability of
land, and other factors may enter into the definition of sport
at any level of the evolution process.

These variables are expressed at the several stages of the
evolutionary process, and sport is a reflection of subsistence, social
organization, and adaptation; from its simplest forms among
hunting-and-gathering band peoples to its most complex varieties in
the agriculturally based urban state (see Chapter 5 for more details
regarding levels I-V in the evolutionary process). These variables,
while they assist in the interpretation and classification of sport
activities, do not explain sport origins.

The prehistoric roots of sport as they are manifested at the
simplest levels of human society from the beginnings of cultural time
are to be found in play. Despite the uneasy relationship between
certain types of athletics and the model of pure play (as in Huizinga,
1950) sport and play are members of the same family. Play, a
universal feature of mammalian life, is older, but may be viewed as
both parent and sibling of the sport phenomenon. As suggested in
Chapter 2, sport can be viewed as a form of play. This is of
particular importance in the discussion of sport origins.

The Bateson (1972) paradox, play as metalanguage, is
fundamental to the development of sport. Sport, like play, is a
communicative act. Unlike play, its message is not simply paradox.
It is the actualization of the paradox, the making real of the unreal,
indeed, *meta-play.* Bateson's (1972:181) monkeys play by pretending
to fight, and he recognizes the play because of the implicit message:
despite giving the impression of being serious conflict on the surface,
it is not. It is play, and the monkeys are both doing what they are not
doing, and not doing what they are doing. Such is the nature of play.

Sport takes the act of "playing at" one step further. Two boxers
pounding away at each other's heads in a formal bout, like the
monkeys, are communicating that message of fighting but
not-fighting, the paradox of play. However, the boxing match is more
than just play. It goes one step beyond the paradox by saying "this is
not simply play; this is play with a purpose, a "playing for" as opposed
to a "playing at." The paradox is objectified, and play is
reinstitutionalized.

The principal objective of sport, the key to understanding this
metaplay, is competition. One sports in order to compete, although
other motives, exceptions to the rule, may affect particular contests
(e.g., gambling, prizes). The boxer "plays for" a reason. He plays for
the purpose of competing.

Competition is a fact of existence; it is the nature of

participation in the food chain. Therefore, despite the fact that some societies are more aggressive or value competition more highly than others does not mean that there are competitive and noncompetitive cultures. All peoples are competitive. Part of the process of cultural adaptation is the adjusting of competitive and cooperative behaviors. Different adaptive needs elicit different competitive and cooperative responses. For example, one group might conceptualize its world as the pitting of human beings against their animal resources. Such a group encourages cooperation between humans in a struggle against their faunal environment. Another group might define its world as one in which humans compete against humans in pursuit of limited resources, thus encouraging a different type of competition. However, in both groups, there is competition.

The Semai of Malaysia are often cited as an example of a nonviolent, passive, cooperative group. A strong food-sharing ethic prevails among these Southeast Asian horticulturalists. Survival is tied to generalized reciprocity, giving without thought of return. Children are socialized to believe that injuring, insulting, or denying requests of others is wrong. Nevertheless, the Semai inevitably are forced to compete, albeit nonviolently. There is competition for sexual favors, as young men compete for the attention of attractive age mates. Semai headmen compete for public support. And, implicitly, there is the ongoing competition with nature. Even among the most cooperative of people, competition is a way of life.

Ruth Benedict, in her classic monograph, *Patterns of Culture* (1934), portrayed the Zuni Indians of the American Southwest as passive, nonaggressive, and cooperative. According to Benedict, competitive impulses were often squelched. Even the attainment of political office among the Zunis was made difficult by the public pressure against ambition.

> The ideal man of the Pueblos is another order of being. Personal authority is perhaps the most vigorously disparaged trait in Zuni. "A man who thirsts for power or knowledge, who wishes to be as they scornfully phrase it 'a leader of his people,' receives nothing but censure and will very likely be persecuted for sorcery," and he often has been (Benedict, 1934:99).

However, several years later, an anthropologist named Li An-che (1937) visited Zuni Pueblo and came away with a different understanding. He was particularly unhappy with Benedict's (1934:99) description of the Zuni as noncompetitive. Noting deception and manipulation among Zuni elders, An-che (1937:69) generalized about the competitive spirit:

> A healthy amount of ambition is in existence in any living society. Only the means of acquiring prestige and realizing

ambitions are different, being culturally conditioned. Once agreed to play the game, it must be played according to the rules of the game. The rules are different in different societies, but their existence is universal. With reference to the Zuni in particular, not only do ordinary forms of struggle for individual supremacy exist, but violent forms also occur once in a while.

An explicit set of rules is essential to sport competition (i.e., playing for). Unlike play, sport specifies its objectives and the procedures for attaining those objectives. In this way, it makes real or concretizes the "playing at." It resolves the paradox. Sport takes play beyond itself by ordering and systematizing specific play forms. Like play, sport conveys the message "this is not real," yet unlike play, it adds "but it has its own reality." The rules and objectives create that reality.

From the beginning, primates have played but their playing has been only playing at. They have also competed, but that competition has been for food, for mates, or for dominance. When competition among monkeys and apes has been playful, it has been "playing at" not "playing for" competition. Only humans have played for competition. Sport is a uniquely human form of behavior.

With the expansion and specialization of the human brain came the development of language, the ability to communicate symbolically, to conceptualize; in essence, to talk and to think about thinking. These new skills made it possible for humans to reflect and elaborate on all their behavior, including play, so that the metalanguage of play could be taken to new levels of abstraction. Humans verbalized about play, and in so doing selected out and regularized specific play forms that eventually evolved into something other than play. These play forms became sport.

Imagine the following scenario. The setting is the open savannah of the southeastern interior of the African continent. The time is approximately one and one-half million years ago. The actors are a small group of *Homo erectus* adolescent males. In their leisure hours, the young men frequently resort to play: running, chasing each other, throwing sticks and dried bones out across the grassy plains, and engaging in a variety of mock combat. Gradually, the running begins to follow a consistent pattern, and the prehistoric teenagers find themselves running a regular route. They run, and act on a natural urge to excel. Soon they are competing, though nothing has been said, pushing themselves toward some loosely defined goal along the route: a tree, a large rock, a clump of grass. There is laughing amidst the heavy breathing and slapping of bare feet against the trail worn hard by repeated use. Then, one of the players breaks off the beaten path and streaks across a grassy short-cut and races to the goal several yards ahead of his closest competitor. At that moment, an unexpected crisis develops. Something is wrong, and the losers begin to protest. A heated discussion ensues, and the rules for the running game that had evolved unconsciously are made explicit. The running is no longer simply play; under the conditions prescribed by the competition, it has become sport.

Human social organization is built around a different set of principles from that characterizing other primate societies. Nonhuman primates are organized into groups to facilitate mutual defense and mate selection. Humans, on the other hand, organize themselves into social units so that they may cooperate in the food quest. They band together in order to get something to eat. This unique form of cooperation and food sharing is a vital element in human culture and may be viewed as a factor underlying sport evolution and maintenance. Sport participation demands adherence to rules, and rules are necessary to the social order and the corporate quest for food. Sport regulations are arbitrary, often having no logical relationship to the natural order. (For example, why is a football field 100 instead of 110 yards long?) Adherence to social norms often requires the same unquestioning allegiance. In this sense, sport teaches one to abide by the rules without asking why. Sport competition facilitates cooperation. Team sports promote a sense of cooperation between teammates, and participants learn to put group interests ahead of their own. Competition assists one in conceptualizing cooperation. In the competition-cooperation dichotomy, the one is pitted against and clarified by the other. The competitor better understands cooperation by virtue of his engaging in a contrary behavior. In these several different ways, sport is useful in a social system based on cooperation.

Human technology, the material means by which social groups adapt to their particular environment, is complex and multifaceted. It is essentially tool-making and tool-using. Although other primates use tools, and in a few cases alter natural objects for use as tools, only man depends so explicitly on technology for his survival. Man must invent and improve tools, develop strategies, and perfect tool-using skills. Sport is of particular use in strategy and skill development. It is at this point that the adaptive function of sport behavior is most obvious.

The human brain makes sport possible. Human technology and social organization make it practical. Eventually, sport evolves as an important component of human culture. People play at hunting, play at running, play at ritual, play at sex, play at war, play at parenting, and play at building. They play at every imaginable activity in their total life experience. In some of the cases, however, the "playing at" becomes "playing for," and humans create a new reality, a form of metaplay. Special rules and objectives are created. Sport lives.

This model of sport origin and development is speculative. It offers no immediate solutions to the archeological problem. Sport as an element in the earliest stages of human culture remains difficult to document. However, the archeologist should be alert to the evidence for play, particularly, evidence of regularity. Patterned or repetitious play may suggest sport. Also, the technology of sport, those material means devised specifically for sport and games, as before, will continue to be an important clue to the presence and evolutionary development of sport. In addition, as archeologists begin to develop a more thorough understanding of sport evolution, the process itself will provide clues and suggest hypotheses. Important to a reconstruction of this process is a knowledge of the ethnography of sport, and that is what the next chapter is about.

SUMMARY

The issue of sport origins and development is a question for prehistoric archeology, a question that remains a riddle with minimal clues. Little is known about the sports and games of stone age or Paleolithic peoples. Some artifacts have been interpreted as gaming or sport objects; others might have been had the excavator been more sensitive to the reality of play in prehistoric society. The so-called "new archeology" and its more explictly scientific approach, a new openness to the possibility of sport and play, and new theoretical approaches to play, have increased the likelihood that archeologists of the future will tell us more about the playful dimensions of the past.

What do we know about sport in prehistory? The data for the period previous to the rise of primary urban civilization is limited. But, with the emergence of the city, the archeological record is unequivocal in its indications of complex sport institutions. In Mesopotamia, Egypt, India, and China, records dating back several thousand years point to such activities as wrestling, boxing, racing, swimming, and various ballgames. Later, secondary civilizations, such as Crete, Greece, and Rome, elaborate on the earlier sport themes and lay the groundwork for the eventual development of modern sport.

The best-documented example of prehistoric sport is the rubber ballgame of Mesoamerica. With its roots in the Olmec experience almost three thousand years ago, the game was a complex institution that overlapped several civilizations. It eventually influenced the development of other ballgames throughout Native North America. The nature of this influence is amplified by the use of the direct historical approach, an important archeological method.

It is suggested that sport can be viewed as an evolving institution, an important component in the development of human culture. The basic forces underlying sport evolution include subsistence, sociopolitical, and geographical variables. Treating sport as metaplay, a case is made for the institution as a factor in the evolution of human social organization.

Exercises

Discussion questions:

1.   Why is archeology important in the analysis of human sport behavior? What are the fundamental questions that the prehistoric archeologist should be asking relative to sport and play?

2.   If an archeologist 5,000 years into the future were to excavate the remains of a small 1980s town in your part of the country, what material evidence would he or she uncover (other than any written record) that could be interpreted as sport related? What nonmaterial evidence could be used in the interpretation? Could the archeologist determine the times or seasons of the year during which particular sports were played in the 1980s?

3.   Compare the formal rubber ballgame of prehistoric Mesoamerica with modern-day professional soccer. What are the major differences? Can you isolate economic or technological variables that might explain these differences?

4.   Given the data provided relative to the Mesoamerican ballgame, do a structural-functional analysis of that sport. What insights might a structural-functional approach to the problem provide that the use of an evolution model would not?

Projects:

1.   Find a detailed archeological site report and look for drawings or photographs of artifacts that have possible sport or game significance. What additional archeological evidence could you use to support you in your interpretation?

2.   Watch *The Hunters,* (1977) a classic anthropology film about the San (Bushmen) of the Kalahari Desert in Southwest Africa. Imagine that the life style depicted is similar to that of prehistoric, hunting-and-gathering band society (i.e., living prehistory). Describe the examples of play and other leisure-time activities treated. Does the film depict any sport activities? What sport activities not covered in the film would make sense in the San situation (i.e., would have adaptive significance or other important leisure-time applications and be possible given San technology)?

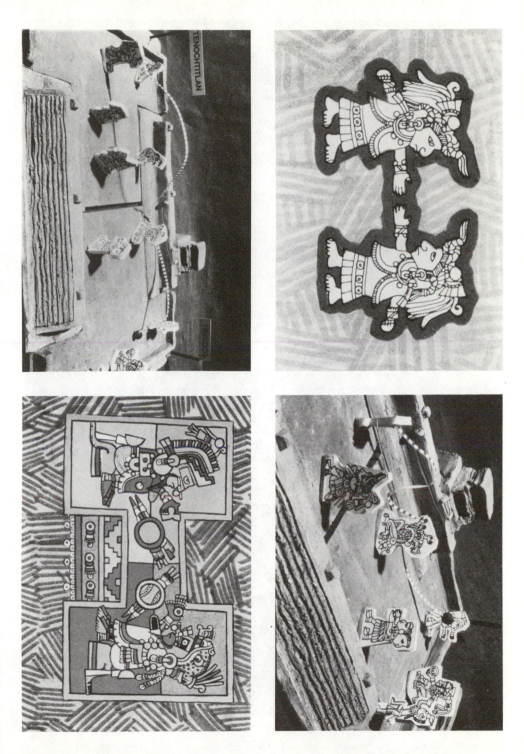

The Rubber Ballgame at Tenochtitlan; drawings and clay models depict the action

Buzkashi horsemen in Afghanistan struggle for control over a calf carcass across an unbounded field.

5 Sport in Culture: An Evolutionary Perspective

Part I: Band Society

On Pentecost Island, part of the New Hebrides chain in the South Pacific off the southwest corner of New Guinea, the Melanesian inhabitants participate in one of the most daring sports in the world, land diving. Standing on a flimsy tower, a shaky melange of timbers, branches, and vines reaching uncertainly into the sky some eighty feet above the ground, divers plunge headlong toward a patch of loose soil at the base of the platform. The impacts of the dives, from distances of some twenty-five to almost eighty feet, are mitigated by long liana ropes tied around the divers' ankles and anchored to the upper frame of the platform. The vines are adjusted to fit the height of the particular dive, and the objective is for the diver's head to touch the prepared dirt without breaking his neck. Ideally, the diver keeps his hands to his side, and just as his body hurtles downard at speeds up to forty-five miles an hour and threatens to crash with fatal force into the ground, the safety vines snap taut. The competitor's soaring frame is snapped back up into the air by the resilency of the vine and the shaky tower. Seconds later, the Pentecost Island sportsmen, his brains somewhat scrambled by the abrupt termination of his downward flight, and his hair matted with bits of dirt from the jump pit, dangles by his ankles a few inches above the ground. After checking his jolted chassis for loose joints and massaging his sore ankles, the diver stands back to watch the performances of his peers and to wait for his next opportunity to take the plunge.

The land diving competition is a combination of ritual, drama, and community entertainment often associated with the coming-

125

of-age of young men. Spectators dance and sing in preparation for the event and cheer with enthusiasm as the divers leap into the void beside the tower. The ceremony and pageantry does not overshadow the fact that land diving is also sport. A man's proficiency in diving off the platform is a measure of his courage and manliness; he competes against himself, the forces of nature, and his fellow tribesmen. To dive from greater heights, to soar without sign of fright, and to resist the urge to break the fall with one's arms are the basic goals of the competition; success brings prestige and honor.

What does this colorful sporting event tell us about the culture of Pentecost Islanders? Like all sports, it provides insight into the activity itself as well as manifesting much about the social lives of the participants. The construction of the tower and safety equipment suggests a certain level of technology. To their credit, as of 1955 no diver had been killed in competition, though there had been broken bones and lacerations (Johnson and Johnson, 1955:92). The objectives of the contest reveal Hebridean values: the manhood ideal, the relationship between risk and ritual, the importance of ceremony. Political norms are illustrated in the way the land diving spectacle is managed. Also, local myth and legend are reiterated. Typical of such legend is the etiology of the sport itself. According to Pentecost natives, "the land dive originated when a runaway wife leaped from a tall palm tree to escape her avenging husband" (Johnson and Johnson, 1955:80). As Hildebrand (1919:90) has observed "sports and games ever were magic touchstones to geography and to those allied sciences which provide the surest clues to how peoples live, and work, and think."

Land diving and the attendant community enthusiasm also suggest something about sport and human nature in general. The daring and bravado is not unlike that witnessed so often in our own culture: the thrill of climbing treacherous mountain peaks, racing automobiles at velocities exceeding 200 miles an hour, or skiing at breakneck speeds down icy, snow-packed slopes. The enthusiasm of the New Hebridean spectator reminds us of the boisterous professional baseball fan of the American summer. And, seeing the message of Pentecost Island culture so clearly outlined in the ritual of land diving competition, we are inclined to look more clearly at our own athletic pursuits as a means of better understanding the culture that is us.

The high-risk free fall of the Pentecost athlete is also a perspective on the past. The New Hebrides experience, a virtual living prehistory, is a comment on the evolution of sport. It also raises questions about history. The land dive may have its roots in a general Melanesian diving behavior that is broader than the athletic arena. Among the Trobriand Islanders, for example, climbing into a tall tree and leaping to one's death is a legitimate form of suicide when a man is guilty of incest (e.g., having sexual intercourse with a sister). The plunge in this context is viewed as an appropriate punishment for the crime. Is it possible that the underlying structure of a form of punishment among the Trobriands has its roots in the same phenomenon that gave rise to the land diving sport of the New Hebridean natives?

The understanding of sport as an element in other cultures is thus a potential source of ethnographic, ethnological, archeological, and ethnohistorical data. Also, it has futuristic applications, for by studying the play of others we develop new and more entertaining ways of playing for ourselves. It is not unlikely that some enterprising, thrill-seeking American, on hearing of the Pentecost Island spectacle, will take up land diving. Perhaps less likely, but not impossible, is the eventual formalization of American land diving, with official rules, elaborate equipment, and various leagues. Already some courageous (or foolhardy) thrill seekers have taken to diving off high bridges (e.g., Golden Gate) with long bungee cords tied to their ankles. The study of sport in those societies of traditional interest to cultural anthropologists has unlimited possibilities.

THE PROBLEM OF SPORT CLASSIFICATION

Due to the apparent universality of sport and games, there are literally thousands of these activities that the anthropologist would need to treat were he or she to attempt to describe all the sports that are played in the many societies of the culturally complex world. However, such a task would be a mammoth, encyclopedic enterprise. Even if one were to limit the coverage to the material on "athletic sports" contained in the Human Relations Area Files, the project would be voluminous. Two hundred and fifty-two (82 percent) of the 306 societies treated in the HRAF files (Memphis State University library microfiche, summer 1982) include at least one entry under the category 526 ("athletic sports"). Many of these are extensive and include chapter-long citations. The compilation of these data would be informative, but largely unmanageable, frequently repetitious, and cumbersome.

In order to make a general sport enthnography more useful as well as palatable, an appropriate system of classification must be employed. There are a variety of techniques that might be used in such a classification. One might create a typology of sports and illustrate these by simply describing examples from around the world. Such typologies include those developed by Roger Caillois (1959) and by Roberts, Arth and Bush (1959), described in Chapter 3 of this work. However, both are game typologies and treat sport only incidentally.

On the other hand, one might devise one's own componential classification, such as the one provided in Figure 7. Then, this scheme then might be used to group the major sport activities from around the world and describe examples for each type. Although this information would be valuable, the end result would be more akin to a cookbook than an anthropology text.

Sports can and have been classified geographically. Perhaps the best known geography of sport is John Rooney's *A Geography of American Sport* (1974). Other scholars have described sports according to nationality. Riordan (1977), for example, has provided an interesting analysis of sport in the U.S.S.R. This orientation to national boundaries as a mode of sport classification is also employed by Johnson in his edited collection of articles titled *Physical Education and Sport around the World* (1980). Even though the focus of the latter work is on the history and development of physical education, the individual authors manage to provide the reader with descriptions of many sports and games.

Unfortunately, all of the existing sport classification schemes are of limited value from an anthropological perspective. They employ categories that have little social or cultural value, they are tied to geographical or political boundaries that do not allow for the treatment of sport in small-scale society, or they are simply too general and cumbersome to provide a constructive anthropological framework.

What options are appropriate to sport ethnography? The anthropologist might select an approach that singles out the most interesting or unusual sports played by peoples of the world. These sports might be viewed as the essential body of knowledge in the discipline. Just as all students of cultural anthropology are expected to know about the *kula* ring of the Trobriand Islands or the potlatch of the Native American Northwest Coast, sport anthropology classes would remember certain "unusual" activities.

One such sport is the Afghanistan game of *buskashki* in which two teams of men on horseback struggle to capture and gain control of a dead calf or goat. The game is played on a specially prepared field. A large circle is drawn on the ground in the center the playing area, the calf or goat is placed inside the circle, and on a signal from the game official, the players (*chapandaz*) rush into the circle. In the subsequent melee, riders push, lean into the action, grab, and spur their animals. Horses snort, shove, and struggle in concert with their riders' commands. Dust flies, the air rings with the slaps, grunts, and shouts of the competition, and the combatants pull at the unresisting carcass as though they would rip it too shreds. Eventually, a rider breaks free of the pack, the lifeless animal in tow, and gallops through an imaginary plane and out into the area beyond the circle. He is declared the winner, given a reward (e.g., money, handkerchief), and praised for his strength and horsemanship. His team is awarded a point.

After the praise, the strutting and hoopla, the slightly abused calf or goat is returned to the center of the circle, and play is resumed. The action is repeated, another *chapandaz* eventually gains

FIGURE 7...Sport: A Componential Definition

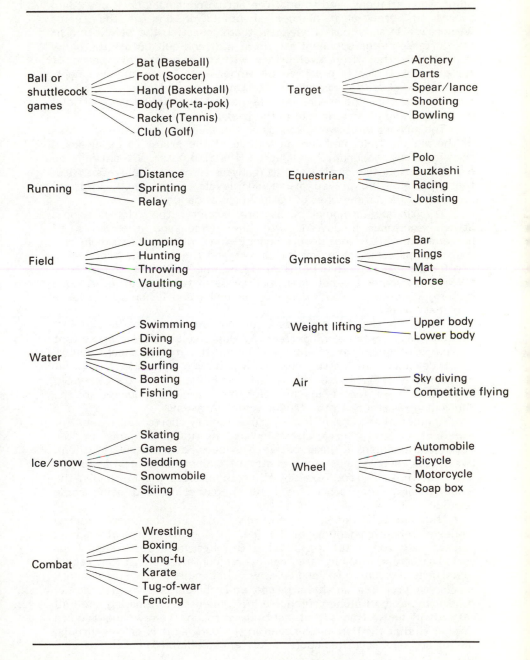

control of the increasingly tattered carcass, there is another prize, point, and ceremony, and so on. The action continues until one team scores an agreed-upon number of points or one of the teams withdraws. In some cases, *buzkashi* teams question the officiating or take offense at the opponent's style of play and quit before the game is finished. The withdrawal brings with it a defeat by reason of forfeit, but it also is a source of embarrassment to the opponent, especially if it is the host team. For this reason, efforts are made to minimize conflict and ensure fair play, a task that falls to the official (*tooi-bashi*), an important role in the *buzkashi* contest.

The number of players depends on the level of formality, the size of the playing field, and the magnitude of the prizes to be awarded the victorious *chapandaz*. As Dupree (1966:20) notes, a team may be composed of as few as five and as many as a thousand players. Also, the game may be played at various levels, from small, informal contests to formal matches of national significance.

Traditionally a nomadic, pastoral society, the Afghan people attach enormous importance to the horse and the skills of horsemanship. It is thus understandable that winning at *buzkashi* is a source of prestige, both for the player and the team he represents, and for the *khan* or other political figure who fields the team. Azoy (1981) underscores the political importance of *buzkashi* in the Afghan system, a system in which winning can make and losing can break a political career.

The game also functions as a mechanism by which the skills of waging war are refined and perfected. Dupree (1966:22) observes that the game provided "excellent training for the mobile shock cavalry which developed in Central Asia and which even Alexander the Great could not defeat." One might also speculate that the *buzkashi* experience is a factor in the Afghanis' frequent success in the continuing resistance to the recent Soviet invasion.

Another of those well-known tribal society sports that makes for excellent cocktail party discussion is the kickball game of the Tarahumara Indians. These native Mexicans, over 40,000 of them, live in the mountainous high country of Chihuahua State, some 300 miles south of El Paso, Texas. Calling themselves the *Raramuri,* the "foot-runners," they subsist by hunting, gathering, and doing some farming.

The kickball game, called *rarajipari* in the Tarahumaran language, requires phenomenal stamina. During the course of a game, players may run a total of over 200 miles in a forty-eight-hour period. Running in their bare feet over mountain trails, often rocky, sometimes treacherous, and always challenging, the Tarahumara sportsmen propel a small hardwood ball comparable in size to an American baseball along the course in front of them, passing the ball with their feet. Races that continue through the evening require torches so that the ball can be seen in the dark as it is driven through the air around a specified course. As Kennedy (n.d.:89) notes,

It [the ball] is lifted into the air so swiftly and rapidly by foot that it appears to be kicked. Great skill is required to stop running temporarily and scoop the ball into the air. The Tarahumara are so adept at this that they appear to be in continuous motion.

On most occasions, two teams, representing their respective pueblos or communities, compete against each other. The teams may vary in size from three or four to thirty or forty players. The teams bunch together at the finish line, and on a signal the two balls, often painted in different colors to distinguish the teams, are tossed into play, and the race beings. The two teams

remain in two main groups but slower runners plod along behind. The air is filled with shouts, as those behind warn the runners ahead that the ball is coming down. It seems a miracle that someone is not killed. Old men from both sides are stationed at various places along the course to make sure no fouls are committed, such as short cutting, touching the ball with the hands, or interference with other players. They shout encouragement to their runners. In a large race many runners help as long as they can and then drop out. A very common sight is to see an eliminated runner hobbling along with a toe bleeding from kicking stones or cacti (Kennedy, n.d.:94).

The winning team is the team that is the first to push its game ball across the finish line of the course after completing the required number of circuits (*vueltas*). These circuits may be trails of several miles, and teams may be required to complete as many as twenty of these, making the total race some twenty to thirty-five miles in distance, although much longer ones are reported.

The race is marked by elaborate physical preparations, ceremony, betting, and festivity. Important to the ritual and celebration phases of the game is the drinking of large quantities of *tesquino*, the Tarahumaran beer. After the race is over, bets are collected and participants gather at prearranged households for a *tesquinada* (drinking party). Great volumes of beer may be consumed in the ensuing celebration.

More incredible than the gallons of homemade brew quaffed down by the celebrating runners is their ability to run the long and difficult courses without the expected signs of physical exhaustion and collapse. The Tarahumara have a capacity for physical stress that while bordering on the unbelievable illustrates the potential of the human body to endure. Adapted as they are to the high altitudes, over 8,000 feet above sea level in some cases, the cardio-vascular systems of the Tarahumara runners are virtual wonders of the world. Norman (1976:703) reports that even under the stress of mountain climbing, the pulse rate of the Tarahumaran athlete rises only slowly. Heart ailments are unknown. Physical endurance appears unlimited.

In the 1928 Amsterdam Olympics, two Tarahumara men represented Mexico in the marathon. Their reputation as runners of unequaled capacities for distance having preceded them, the Indians disappointed many by their failure to place. However, both turned in respectable times, crossing the finish line with their typical unharried composure and running on until they were stopped and informed they had covered the distance. They were nonplussed by the relative shortness of the race. Twenty-six miles was "too short." They were surprised and offended by the distance, having expected a challenge, a real race.

The endurance of the Tarahumara can be viewed as an adaptation to the rough Chihuahuan terrain. Travel, predominantly a matter of moving on foot, requires running or walking over hills and valleys with radical variations in altitude. It is not unusual for the Tarahumaran traveler to climb 4,000 feet during the course of a short walk, a feat made more difficult by heavy loads of cargo strapped across the back. A forty-mile trip under these conditions is a normal, single day's accomplishment.

Traditionally, the Tarahumara hunted deer by pursuing them on foot, relentlessly chasing a single animal until it fell over in exhaustion. Also, many daily activities were structured to tax the limits of one's endurance, the prevailing maxim in all cases: "Why walk when you can run?" It is no wonder that the Tarahumara runner has become a symbol for being in shape and is an inspiration to fitness buffs everywhere.

SPORT: AN EVOLUTIONARY MODEL

Perhaps the most instructive approach to the description of human sport activity from an anthropological perspective is that provided by the evolutionary model. This theoretical model is predicated on the assumption that culture evolves just as the physical or biological dimension of life evolves. And, different cultures, similar to different forms of animal and plant life, represents different levels or stages of evolution (see Chapter 4). It is assumed in this application that sport is a component of culture and that it evolves in concert with the other components of the cultural system. This approach offers insight into the issue of sport development and prehistory and it also provides an informative classification scheme.

Perhaps the most widely known among available culture evolution models is that of Elman Service (e.g., 1963). This model assumes that in the course of change and adaptation, human societies have made various adjustments, adjustments that over time can be viewed as an evolutionary process. In the attempt to segment and analyze this process, Service (1963:xvi-xxiv) isolates five stages or levels of cultural evolution: band, tribe, chiefdom, primitive state, and archaic civilization. This model provides a mechanism for understanding the chronological development of human culture as well as a means of categorizing the various cultures still extant in recent history. Its application to the study of sport suggests a parallel development in the area of physically competitive activities so that one may think of band sports, tribal sports, chiefdom sports, primitive state sports, and those of archaic civilizations as well as of modern society. The implication then is that a widespread sport such as wrestling is initially an element in its host culture, so that band-level wrestling and state-level wrestling, though similar in many respects, are actually two different sports. The differences are largely those characteristic of their respective total cultural frameworks. In other words, band-level wrestling is to state-level wrestling as the band is to the state.

Morton Fried (1975:65) has taken issue with Service's understanding of cultural evolution, particularly the concept of "tribe." According to Fried (1975:114), "tribe" is not a necessary stage in the evolution of prehistoric culture, rather it is the product of the urban state, a historical phenomenon. As a means of facilitating the administration of the small outlying bands under its jurisdiction, the state found it convenient to lump together those small isolated groups that shared certain linguistic and cultural traits. Thus, many bands with no previous formal ties or political unity were combined into "tribes" and given names. As Fried (1975:114) concludes, these tribes are really "secondary tribes" and cannot be viewed as illustrative of a stage in the evolution process.

Although Service (1968:167) himself has acknowledged the wisdom of the Fried critique and essentially eliminated the "tribe" concept from his cultural evolution framework, we are suggesting that a supraband organization is an important stage in the evolution record. Thus, the model employed here is characterized by five levels (see Fig. 8). Level I is defined in a way consistent with Service's (1963) original understanding of band. Level II, however, is viewed as a collection of bands that are socially and politically more complex as well as larger than level I bands. At the same time, the fact of secondary tribalism cannot be ignored. So, for purposes of classification, level II culture as it is treated in the evolution model employed here, includes both the primary and secondary tribe. It is assumed that the distinction between level I and level II bands is reflected in their respective sport activities.

LEVEL I BAND

The typical level I band is characterized by a small population, some sixteen to twenty-five persons, and subsists by hunting-and-gathering or hunting-and-foraging. Actual size is controlled

FIGURE 8...Levels of Sociocultural Adaptation

LEVELS	I	II	III	IV	V
Population density	2-5/100²km	+	+	+	200/100²km
Subsistence	Hunting and foraging	Hunting/gathering pastoralism	Horticulture, hunting, fishing, gathering	Horticulture, pastoralism	Irrigation agriculture
Productivity	1	2	3	4	5
Technology	1	2	3	4	5
Resource allocation	Intra-band reciprocity	Inter-band reciprocity	Informal redistribution networks	Formal redistribution networks	Institutionalized redistribution networks
Political definition	Band	Band	Chiefdom	Emerging or primitive state	Urban, developed or civil state
Status	Ascribed	Ascribed	Ascribed/achieved	Ascribed/achieved	Ascribed/achieved
Political authority	Familial	Familial	Familial/non-kin	Familial/non-kin	Familial/non-kin
Settlement pattern	Nomadic	Nomadic Semi-nomadic	Sedentary	Sedentary	Sedentary
Division of labor	Natural	Natural	Natural with some specialization	Greater occupational specialization	True
Material culture	Simple	Simple	Some accumulation	Architecture, conspicuous wealth	Extensive
Fried EPS[1]	Egalitarian	Egalitarian	Rank	"Stratified"	Stratified
Service POE[2]	Band	"Tribe"	Chiefdom	Primitive state	Archaic civilization
Examples	Eskimo Australian aborigine Yahgan	Navajo Chukchi Dani	Choctaw Maori Samoa Tikopia	Ashanti Zulu Maya	Aztec Sumer Egypt Inca

1. Fried, 1967.
2. Service, 1963.

directly by resource availability, and households are economically independent. Relationships within the group are defined exclusively by kinship regularities, statuses are largely familial, and leadership is legitimized by the leader's position in the kinship system. Sport and games in level I societies reflect the simplicity of band technology and sociopolitical organization. Equipment is limited, competition generally occurs at small, localized levels, and the nature of games played directly parallels basic economic activities in most instances. Typical level I bands include those of the aboriginal Australians, the Eskimo, and the Yahgan.

Aborigines: Australia

Australian Aborigines: Background The small island continent of Australia was inhabited by human life for the first time somewhere between 25 and 20,000 years ago. The descendants of those original settlers, the Australian aborigines, are physically distinct from other peoples of the world and often classified racially as Australoid. The difficult Australian environment presents a challenge to human survival, and those hunters-and-gathers who manage to eke out an existence under these conditions do so only in the most meager terms. The technology of the Australian aborigine is one of the most basic and least complex among historic peoples of the world. There is no agriculture, no bow-and-arrow, no pottery, no basketry, no cooking utensils, or iron tools, and the only domesticated animal is the dog (dingo). The boomerang, the spear, the wooden spear thrower, the digging stick, and crude stone tools for cutting, scraping, and chopping, are the major items of the simple Australian tool kit. Living in small isolated bands, the Australians represent a part of prehistory that has persisted, an example of cultural time standing still. As Spencer and Gillen (1927:vii) have noted:

> Australia is the present home and refuge of creatures, often crude and quaint, that have elsewhere passed away and given place to higher forms. This applies equally to the aboriginal as to the platypus and kangaroo. Just as the platypus, laying its eggs and feebly suckling its young, reveals a mammal in the making, so does the Aboriginal show us, at least in broad outline, what early man must have been like before he learned to read and write, domesticate animals, cultivate crops, and use a metal tool. It has been possible to study in Australia human beings that still remain on the culture level of men of the Stone Age.

Although the many bands and language groups that characterize the aboriginal Australians manifest extensive cultural similarities, it is difficult to generalize about some of the more specialized regional and local traits. Nevertheless, the Arunta, the largest dialect division in central Australia, may be used to illustrate the typical aboriginal culture.

The Arunta, made famous among anthropologists by the publication of Spencer and Gillen's monograph, *The Arunta: A Study of a Stone Age People* (1927), numbered about 2,000 at the end of the last century, a little more than one percent of the total aboriginal population. A few of the Arunta have survived into the modern era, but much of their traditional culture has been squeezed out with the adoption of European technology and custom.

The Arunta of tradition are typical among Australian hunters-and-foragers. Employing the simple technology discussed above, they rummage through their environment taking advantage of almost every edible resource: seeds, bulb roots, snails, ants, beetles, caterpillars, birds, bird eggs, reptile eggs, rodents, grubs, and other insects. In addition, they hunt the wallaby, emu, and kangaroo. Hunting techniques are simple but physically demanding. For example, the kangaroo is often stalked by groups of hunters and either ambushed or run into exhaustion.

Similar to their technology, the material culture of the Arunta is anything but elaborate. Few, if any clothes are worn, despite the frequently cold nights of the outback wasteland. Often body decoration of paint and feathers constitute the only alteration of the *au naturel.* Arunta shelters, basic grass covered frames, are likewise simple, and provide limited protection against the cold.

The basic social unit of the Arunta is the economically self-sufficient nuclear family. Descent is patrilineal, and residence, patrilocal. One of the most complex elements of Arunta social organization is the marriage exchange system, which ideally results in the marriage of second cousins and the development of bonds between individual families and local groups.

The basic political unit of the Arunta is the band, local group, or horde; a collection of related families who migrate en masse over a large geographical area perceived to be a territory belonging to that group alone. Leadership in the band is generally informal and predicated on kinship roles, so that male heads of household are those with the most authority in the system.

A complex ceremonial life characterizes the religion of the Arunta. Spiritual life among this group is tied to the totem, a particular plant or animal that symbolizes the unity of the local group. Much of Arunta ritual is associated with the socialization of the young and the several rites of passage. One of the most complex rites is that surrounding the initiation of boys into manhood. Initiates are painted, tossed into the air, bled, subjected to fire ordeals, circumcized and subincised. Becoming a man among the Arunta is both an important and a painful process.

Despite the hardness of life in the barren wilds of Australia, the Arunta are not starved for spare time. According to Service (1963:9)

Much of the time...the Arunta are inactive. This is not laziness, of course, but a response to external circumstances. The size of the social unit, the limit of its possible growth, is set by the recurrent seasons of relative scarcity. When times are good, there is little to do in order to acquire sufficient food, and little <u>is</u> done except for visiting and the observance of the great seasonal ceremonial occasions, for in the absence of storage facilities, excess products of fruitful seasons cannot be carried over into the lean periods.... The Arunta, because of their undeveloped technology, are literally one of the most leisured peoples in the world.

In this latter characterization as leisure rich, the Arunta characterize Australian aboriginal populations generally. The band-level hunters-and-foragers of Australia have ample time for sport and play.

Australian Aborigines: Sport   Many sport and game activities have been witnessed among aboriginal groups in Australia. Ethnographers have recorded some of these in detail. Although not all of these are engaged in by the Arunta, they are generally typical of native Australian populations.

One of the sports noted by Harney (1952:377) among the aborigines of the Northern Territory in Australia was what he labeled "spearing the disc:"

A disc of soft wood or bark is made, generally about eighteen inches in diameter, and as it is thrown along the ground the players, generally the old men and youths in groups, throw reed-spears at it from a distance of fifteen feet. When the disc is struck, it is knocked upright to the accompaniment of the shouts of the players, who generally have a good deal of joyful argument as to the owner of the winning spear.

This sport is similar to what Roth (1902:18) calls the "bowl-ball" game.

Another sport observed by Harney (1952:377) was a game the Wargite tribe called *mungan-mungan,* that pits the old men against the young. On most occasions the old men prepare a hibiscus limb of about two feet in length, paint it white and call it the *wormar* (i.e., "young girl"). Having prepared the *wormar,* the men send out an announcement that a *mungan-mungan* contest is to be staged.

On the appropriate day, males from several local groups assemble, bodies painted in special preparation for the event. Standing in a large circle with the old men in the middle, the participants began to play when the maker of the stick issues the challenge to the young men to "Come and get the young girl."

> This challenge is immediately accepted by the youths, who try to take the *Wormar* from the challengers. The old men hold the *Wormar* behind their backs as they play, but the youths hold it under their armpit when they get it, a means of identification as to the different sides (Harney 1952:378).

Resembling a type of "no holds barred" keep-away, the game revolves around the attempt to maintain possession of the hibiscus stick, the "young girl." The stick is thrown through the air, men are tripped and tackled, and spectators boisterously shout and encourage both sides. The game goes on until one side becomes so exhausted that it surrenders. The winner is the team holding the stick at that moment. The *wormar* is hidden until the losers have had an opportunity to recruit additional players to strengthen their team and issue a new challenge.

> This game was always played with much laughter, but sometimes a brawl would begin when some old fellow--realizing that he was not as good a man as he once was--will claim he has been hit or insulted and the row begins (Harney, 1952:378).

A variety of ballgames are played by the Australians. Roth (1902:18) describes a "spin-ball" game played in the northwest central districts of the continent. The basic equipment is a small round ball (one to one and one-half inches in diameter) made of "lime, ashes, sand, clay, and sometimes hair, rolled into shape, either between the hands or the folds of a blanket, and subsequently baked, thus making it smooth and hard" (Roth, 1902:18). The object of the game is to spin the ball with the fore and middle fingers on a specially prepared, smooth surface (e.g., a pitch of hard ground) so that it continues to spin longer than that of any competitor. Played by both men and women, the game has several variations, one involving team competition that pits one group of spinners against another.

Another Australian ball game is referred to simply as "catch-ball." Roth (1902:17) claims that

> in the North West Central districts [catch-ball] is played everywhere by both sexes, and either singly or with sides: in the latter case, the ball is thrown from the one to the other, the participants trying to intercept it while still off the ground. From the fact of the players jumping to catch it resembling the movements of a kangaroo, the Kalkadun blacks sometimes describe this game as the "kangaroo play." The ball itself is made of a piece of opposum, wallaby, or kangaroo hide, etc., tied up with twine.

Moncrieff (1966:6) noted several variations of this ball play, including a game played by the Kurnai using a kangaroo scrotum stuffed with grass in which local groups competed against each other. "Each side had a leader and the object was to keep the ball away from the other side as long as possible by throwing it from one to the other. The game might last for hours" (Moncrieff, 1966:6).

A sport called "football" by Moncrieff (1966:7) is described by Harney (1952:378) as the "ball game of the Djinghali tribe:"

> A ball, similar to the one used in cricket but made of grass tied up tightly with string and then covered with beeswax, is used for the game, where men of different moieties took sides as in football, and the game was started by kicking the ball into the air.
>
> Once kicked off, however, the hands could not touch the ball again, only the feet were used for this purpose, and the side who kept it in the air and away from the others were looked upon as the winners.

Moncrieff (1966:7) also reports that the natives of Bathurst Island, just off the north coast of Australia, played a handball game in which the seeds of the zamia *cycas* tree were used as small balls.

> Two lads faced each other and hit the seeds to and fro with their palms somewhat like tennis. Further refinement was used by the natives of the Meda district in North West Australia. Here the players used flat pieces of wood resembling cricket-bats, and balls fashioned out of the woody fruits of the Pandanus (Moncrieff, 1966:7).

Wrestling, one of the most widespread of human sports, has also been observed among the so-called Australian bushmen. In November of 1898, Walter Roth watched an aborigine wrestling match at a camp near Princess Charlotte Bay on the northeast coast of the continent. In his words,

> the combatants were all collected on a cleared circular space, about eight yards in diameter--a disused initiation ground--where I watched them playing one morning for quite a couple of hours. Any individual who happens to pride himself on his skill in the game will open proceedings by challenging another, while the bystanders, egging them both on, and barracking for their respective favorites, will sing away and clap their hands in accompaniment. The wrestling itself takes place somewhat on the following lines. Bend- ing forwards, the challenger will grip his adversary with both hands round the loins where he interlocks his fingers so

as to maintain a very firm hold: the latter, with arms raised, remains passive, and in this position is lifted from off the ground on to which he is next thrown. Honors are divided so long as he touches ground with this feet, i.e., not thrown off his balance. The individual who is temporarily gripped may, however, steady himself with his arms on the other's shoulders, and usually prepares himself for a fall on his feet by keeping his lower limbs strongly flexed, thus rendering them springy on whichever side he may be thrown. There is no mutual clutching, or both combatants falling: strictly speaking, it is a throwing, rather than a wrestling match. Only males engage in this sport: as soon as one proves himself victorious, another challenges him, and so on (Roth 1902:17).

Roth (1902:17) later discovered that what he had assumed to be a rare occurrence was an amusement common to other parts of native Australia. Wrestling was a sport well-known around the Princess Charlotte Bay district, and frequently took place in connection with initiation ceremonies (Roth, 1902:17).

Although large-scale warfare is not common among Australian bands, intergroup fighting does occur. As a result, some of the sport activities of the region manifest a basic combat model. Of these mock war contests, some of the most frequently encountered are listed by Salter (1974:12): sham weapon battles, mud-ball fights, stick dueling, and weapon throwing for accuracy and distance.

Another interesting sport activity among the traditional bush people of Australia is the tournament, known as the *prun* among the Mallanpara. Meeting at various times during the year on the *puya* or *prun* ground, competing local groups may use the event as an opportunity to settle disputes, to entertain themselves, or simply show off their respective skills. As Roth (1902:15) notes, the *prun* "gives the men a chance of showing off their prowess and courage before the women."

The several groups represented assemble on the *prun* ground on the scheduled day, appropriately dressed and decorated for the occasion in fighting costumes and with shields, swords, spears, and boomerangs. The competition begins when the host group challenges one of the visiting bands by throwing a boomerang into their number or taunting them with verbal abuse in the attempt to provoke a fight.

When the challenging team is finally successful in goading one of the visiting groups into fighting, the action shifts to the center of the *puya*, where either individuals or groups of individuals square off and the combat ensues. Spears and boomerangs are thrown, shields are clashed together, and a volley of abusive language is hurled between competitors. Despite the confusion and the use of potentially deadly weapons, serious or fatal injuries are rare, although many minor wounds occur. Both men and women enter the melee.

Women come into the circle and egg their husbands and relatives on: they bite their spears and sticks, strike and throw them on the ground, and will fight with members (female) of the opposite faction. They are using their tongues all the time and with far greater effect than the men. The din is something terrible while the tournament lasts (Roth, 1902:16).

Every ten or fifteen minutes, participants relax the fighting for a brief rest. Spears and boomerangs are collected and returned to their owners. In this fashion, the *prun* may go on all day long. Darkness brings an end to the mock hostilities, but the next morning may see a commencement of the action. Throughout the event, a sense of fair play and willingness to abide by the rules (e.g., fighting only in the *puya* circle) prevail. Winning is occasional and limited to individual confrontations. When the tournament is over, participants generally depart on good terms, old scores settled and a good time having been had by all.

Salter (1974) has noted several general functions of the sport and play forms among Australian aborigines. They assist in the acquisition of skills that permit the young "to ultimately become effective tribal providers" and reinforce these abilities among the adults (Salter, 1974:5). Other games, such as the *prun*, provide a forum for justice and a first-hand involvement in the judicial system (Salter, 1974:10). Sport provides a means of both planning and preparing for warfare (Salter, 1974:12), although games such as the *prun* also function to avoid more serious forms of conflict. Finally, play among the Australians serves as a means of recording and disseminating tribal lore (Salter, 1974:16). Sport and games are integral parts of traditional Australian aborigine life.

Eskimos: the Arctic

Eskimo: Background   One of the classic hunting groups among primitive peoples of the world is the Eskimo. Sparsely settled over a huge expanse of the Arctic that stretches from the Asian coast of the Bering Straits to Greenland, a distance of over 3,000 miles, a small population of Eskimos (100,000 in the mid-eighteenth century) manifests a surprising degree of cultural, linguistic, and physical uniformity. This uniformity suggests that the Eskimos have moved into the North American Arctic only in the recent prehistoric past. Archeological evidence suggests that they may have been in Alaska as early as 4,000 B.P. (Before Present), migrating gradually eastward and reaching Greenland as recently as 1500 years ago.

For the most part, Eskimos survive by hunting and fishing, though economies and subsistence techniques may vary slightly from one group to another. The technology is simple, though often ingenious, and there is neither agriculture nor domesticated animals, with the exception of the dog. Perhaps the real wonder of Eskimo life is their ability to adapt to such a difficult environment. The long winters that extend for nine months bring mountains of ice and snow and temperatures to minus fifty degrees Fahrenheit. The short summers bring relief from the cold but dampen the pleasures of the thaw with swarms of hungry mosquitos and sand flies. Life under these conditions is a constant competition with the environment. Some lose, and there are the suicides, senicides, infanticides, mercy killings, periodic bouts with hunger, and a psychological condition called "arctic hysteria." But, despite the hazards of an Arctic existence, Eskimo life is marked with a characteristic playfulness, a pervasive good humor, and an elaborate complement of leisure time activities.

The Copper Eskimo

Despite the many similarities of the Eskimo bands across the Arctic, the variety of microenvironments and historical circumstances have resulted in regional variations. Not all Eskimos are alike. However, one culture that can be said to be typically Eskimo is that of the Copper Eskimo, a small group of hunters and fishers located in the North-central Canadian Coastal area, distinguished by their use of copper in recent generations. According to Service (1963:67), there were between 700 and 800 Copper Eskimos in the period around 1915. This population was divided into fourteen individual bands of about fifty persons each.

The Copper Eskimo hunt the seal using the ingenious *maupok* method, which involves waiting beside a breathing hole in the ice until the seal swims up to fill its lungs, at which point the hunter harpoons the unwary mammal and pulls it through the ice. During the spring the Eskimo hunts the caribou, and in the summer he fishes (e.g., salmon trout, lake trout). Like most Eskimos, the Copper bands do not eat much in the way of fruits and vegetables. They gather a few berries from the tundra and occasionally eat the contents of a slain caribou's stomach, but these items make up a very small percentage of their diet.

The technology of the Copper Eskimo features the bow-and-arrow, various lances, fish spears, and harpoons. Their typically Eskimo material culture includes the dog-sled, igloo, rotary bow drill, and the *kayak*, but not the *umiak*, the woman's boat common to other coastal settlements. The Copper Eskimo wear caribou skin clothing and boots made from seal skin tanned by the saliva and mastication of the female cobblers.

Descent among the Copper group is bilateral, and the kinship terminology is similar to that of English-speaking peoples. For example, brothers and sisters are distinguished from cousins, who are lumped together much as is done in Anglo and other European communities. Unlike the pattern in some Eskimo societies, male and female relationships are predicated in many cases on a sense of equality. Though wife-swapping is customary and the woman's primary economic responsibilities are in the home, the female is not as likely to be viewed as property belonging to a male as she is in some other Eskimo groups.

Marriage and divorce among the Copper bands are characterized by little ceremony, freedom, and frequency. Sexual behavior is regulated only in the vaguest sense, illegitimacy is a concept foreign to the Copper experience, and postmarital residence rules are nonexistent. A married couple lives where and with whom it is most convenient.

Politically, there is no pattern of formal leadership among the Copper Eskimo, but the individual bands are jural societies. Legal norms, though unwritten, guide behavior, and various primary social control mechanisms function to ensure conformity. One of the most effective forms of social control is the supernatural sanction, and perhaps the most important figure in Copper society is the shaman who mediates between supernatural and natural worlds.

Though the ceremony surrounding life's passages (e.g., puberty, marriage) in Copper Eskimo culture is minimal, the religious life of the group is characterized by a complexity of gods, taboos, and spirit figures, the best known of these being Sedna, the female spirit of the sea who protects sea life and punishes humans for violating ritual regulations and social norms.

With the coming of the white man, the Eskimo world has changed. Guns, a cash economy, alcohol, diesase, and most recently oil, are just a few of the forces eroding the bases of traditional Eskimo culture. Nevertheless, the Eskimo has survived.

Eskimo: Sport   The leisure hours of the Eskimo people are spent in singing, story-telling, sport, games, and other forms of play. The most detailed description of Eskimo sport available is that contained in Gerald Glassford's *Application of a Theory of Games to the Transitional Eskimo Culture* (1976), in which he analyzes the broad spectrum of Canadian Eskimo games, including the physically competitive ones.

One sport common to several Eskimo groups as well as to many Indian groups throughout the North American continent is the ring-and-pin game, referred to by various Eskimo terms (e.g., *ajagak, ayagak, ajaquktuk*). The ring varies in its construction, from the skull of a small animal to an elaborately carved ivory object.

> The pin was made from a stick, sharpened bone or ivory which was then attached to the ring by means of a thong of leather or *babiche*. The pin was held in the hand (most frequently the right) with the point obliquely upward while the ring was swung in a half revolution which had a high trajectory so as to prevent a maximum opportunity for the player to impale it on the pin (Glassford, 1976:276).

The rules vary from one area to another, but are always specific. The game is most clearly "sport" in those cases where points are accumulated by totaling the number of successes in a predetermined number of tries. In some instances, ring-and-pin becomes a team sport, and two groups compete against each other, sometimes wagering on the outcome.

Harpoon throwing is a sport in some areas of Eskimo land, men competing in contests that require both strength and skill. One such contest is reported among the Eskimos of Baffin Land.

> The spear-throwing competition calls for a high degree of skill. From the top of a fixed, inclined pole, a line is carried to the earth, having an ivory ring tied in it half way down. This ring is carefully concealed by fringes of hide, and the spear throwers stationed at a recognized distance away, have to cast their weapons deftly through it. The attempt demands the greatest accuracy of vision and training of the hand (Bilby, 1923:241).

Eskimos are also known to engage in a form of ring toss they call *kipotuk.* Two stakes are driven into the ground approximately six inches apart. Seal humerus bones are tossed from a distance of twelve to fifteen feet. The object is to throw the bone ring so that it falls between the uprights. The winner is the first to achieve this feat. Glassford (1976:282-3) describes a variation of the game in which points are accumulated in a fashion similar to horseshoes, but suggests that this activity is of "relatively recent Arctic vintage."

Also included in the Eskimo sport repertoire are such common favorites as foot races, a dart game, archery, and tug-of-war. Boas (1888:197) has described the latter as it occurs among the Central Eskimo in conjunction with a festival conducted to drive away Sedna and other evil spirits:

> The crowd...divides itself into two parties, the ptarmigans (*axigirn*) those who were born in the winter, and the ducks (*aggirn*), or the children of summer, a large rope of sealskin is stretched out. One party takes one end of it and tries with all its might to drag the opposite party over to its side. The others hold fast to the rope and try as hard to make ground for themselves. If the ptarmigans give way the summer has won the game and fine weather may be expected to prevail through the winter (*nussueraqtung*).

Of some similarity to the tug-of-war is the mouth pull (*iqiruktuk*):

Two contestants faced each other and wrapped their right arms around the opponent's neck in such a way as to permit them to insert their forefinger into the corner of the opponent's mouth. On a signal both would pull as hard as possible. The player who permitted his head to turn in the direction of the pull was declared the loser. The winner often challenged another to such a contest and so the game proceeded (Glassford, 1976:287).

Although there is no evidence to suggest that boxing is a traditional Eskimo sport, some of the bands do engage in a hitting contest called *ungatanguarneg*. Two men face each other and take turns striking each other with closed fist or open hand. The blows are directed toward the side of the head, the shoulder or chest, and the recipient of the blow offers no resistance. The contest continues until one of the combatants collapses or simply surrenders. Boas (1888:201) describes a situation in which this activity is part of a greeting ceremony:

If a stranger unknown to the inhabitants of a settlement arrives on a visit he is welcomed by the celebration of a great feast. Among the southeastern tribes the natives arrange themselves in a row, one man standing in front of it. The stranger approaches slowly, his arms folded and his head inclined toward the right side. Then the native strikes him with all his strength on the right cheek and in his turn inclines his head awaiting the stranger's blow.... While this is going on the other men are playing at ball and singing.... This they continue until one of the combatants is vanquished.

This practice is not unlike the chest beating of the Yanamamo in Venezuela in which two men exchange blows to the chest until one is too battered and bruised to return the punches. In both the Eskimo and Yanamamo cases, the slugging matches are viewed as endurance contests and measures of one's courage and manliness. Hoebel (1954:93) notes that among the Eskimos, both boxing and head-butting contests may be used as "means of settling all disputes except homicide."

The Eskimo are also football players. The game is called *akraurak* and is played with balls of various sizes and shapes, usually hides stitched into spheres and stuffed with hair, feathers, moss, shavings, or whalebone. The goals are markings on the snow at unspecified distances from each other. Teams kick the ball up and down the field, the object being to drive it across the goal line of the opponent. The game is played predominantly in the spring and summer months, and everyone, regardless of sex or age, may participate.

In some cases two participants acted as leaders with each

alternately choosing teammates from among those present until the group was evenly divided... Players stood beside their goals and, when the ball was tossed onto the ground midway between them, both sides rushed toward the ball and attempted to drive it across the opposing team's goal line. The first team to do so was the winner (Glassford, 1976:304-5).

Glassford (1976:306) suggests that while it is conceivable that these various football or soccer games (*akraurak*) are the result of contact with Euro-American society, the games are mentioned in Eskimo myths. It is possible they are traditional.

The Eskimo do not sing "Take Me Out to the Ballgame" or collect bubble gum cards, but they do play a game similar to modern baseball. *Anauligatuk* or *mukpaun* is played on a court composed of two wooden bases, approximately ten feet in length, spaced from 70 to 100 feet apart. A single batter stands at one of the bases and faces a pitcher and group of fielders. The ball is thrown, the batter hits the ball and tries to run to the opposite base and back before the ball can be fielded and returned. If the runner is hit with the ball before he reaches "home" he is out and is replaced by the fielder making the successful throw. The game is not limited to sex or age group and is played in some contexts so that one team is pitted against another.

Other Eskimo ball games include hand-ball, a type of keep-away often pitting the men against the women, and whip-ball. Boas (1888:162) reports on the latter suggesting that it is played by the men only:

A leather ball filled with hard clay is propelled with a whip, the lash of which is tied up in a coil. Every man has his whip and is to hit the ball and so prevent his fellow players from getting at it.

Wrestling (*unatartoat*) is a popular sporting activity among the Eskimo men that is engaged in as ceremony in the celebration of a successful hunt or as simply an entertaining way to spend an evening.

Methods of defeating an opponent apparently varied from region to region. Among the Copper Eskimo a match ended when a wrestler was thrown off his feet; the Ungava Eskimo wrestling match ended when the head of a competitor touched the floor; and the western Arctic Eskimos stated that the match ended when the buttocks of either man made contact with the floor (Glassford, 1976:318).

The Yahgan: South America
Yahgan: Background   The Yahgan were a small group of hunters and

gatherers who inhabited the southernmost extremity of South America,the wet, chilly, and generally unpleasant environs of Tierra del Fuego. Despite the unfriendly climate, the Yahgan traditionally went unclothed, swam in the icy waters of the South Atlantic, and lived in simple shelters made of grass, bark, or skins draped over light frames of flexible sticks.

The Yahgan economy was predominantly a maritime one, and much of their time was spent on or near the water. The *Yamani,* as they called themselves, were also referred to as the "canoe Indians" because of their manufacture and navigation of small, beechbark vessels. The most valued game animal of the Yahgan was the seal, important as a source of meat and for its workable hide. Although the whale also figured in Yahgan subsistence, these hardy Teirra del Fuegians did not have a highly developed whaling industry. In most cases, they simply used the carcasses of the dead whales that happened to wash up on the shore. Despite the maritime orientation of their economy, the Yahgan had a simple fishing technology, using only the spear and the bare hand for procuring fish.

The Yahgan also hunted and gathered on land, using bows-and-arrows, slings, and clubs to hunt various birds. They collected some plant foods as a supplement to their meat, fish, and fowl diet. Despite the diversity of economic activity, it is suggested that the Yahgan culture was among the most primitive among historically known peoples. Service (1963:30) has noted, "These Indians lack agriculture and domestic animal (except the dog, which may have been a late acquisition) and, of course, the host of appurtenances associated with a sedentary life.... A commensurate simplicity exists in social organization, ceremony and ritual, art, and games."

Yahgan social organization was built around the local group or band, a collection of nuclear families. Though polygyny was permissible, it was rare. Descent was reckoned bilaterally, and residence was patrilocal (i.e., the couple resided in the area of the groom's family subsequent to marriage). Although women played an active role in Yahgan social and economic life, the system tended toward male dominance. Leadership was largely informal, male, and predicated on one's position in the family.

Typical of most hunting-and-gathering societies, religious ceremonies were central to Yahgan community life, and puberty rites tended to be the most elaborate of these. both girls and boys were ushered into adulthood with great pomp and circumstance marked by feasting, dancing, and celebration in addition to ordeal. Despite the elaborate nature of ritual events, such as these initiation ceremonies, the only ritual practitioner was the male shaman, a part-time medicine man who specialized in treating illness, divining, predicting the future, and controlling the weather.

In the mid-1800s, there were approximately 3,000 Yahgan living in a variety of small bands having linguistic and cultural similarities but without significant political ties. The advent of European diseases proved devastating, and by the turn of the century fewer than 200 were left. This number fell to 40 by 1933, and today the Yahgan are extinct, one of many New World groups wiped out by the deadly germs imported from the Old World.

Yaghan: Sport   As Service (1963:30) has noted, Yahgan games were simple, reflecting the nature of Yahgan culture. However, this does not mean that the Yahgan were apathetic about sport and play. Indeed, the opposite is true. Both children and adults spent much of their daily lives engaged in playful activity and recreation. As suggested earlier about primitive people in general (Chapter 4), the Yahgan had plenty of time for leisure activities, devoting only about 20 percent of the time that modern man spends in earning a livelihood (Service, 1963:40). That left ample room for sport and games.

The most popular sport among the Yahgan was wrestling. Called *kalaka mulaka,* Yahgan wrestling pitted two men against each other; it was not open to female participation.

> Before the match begins, a person chooses his opponent from the audience and challenges him by placing a little ball, *kalaka,* at his feet. This man must accept if he does not want to be called a coward, and with the other man he immediately steps inside the large circle of spectators. At once they seize each other and wrestle until one of them is held down by the other in such a way that his entire back is on the ground. The spectators follow the match with loud cries and enthusiastically acclaim the victor. Tripping a person is not permitted, but one man can use his knee to kick the shank of the other so hard that he sways and is more easily knocked over. The one who is defeated suffers a considerable affront to his own honor and that of his best friends. One of the latter immediately steps inside the circle of spectators, grasps the ball, and places it at the feet of the winner who has no choice but to prove his skill with the new opponent, and the two grapple (Gusinde, 1937:1422).

Being a successful wrestler was important to the Yahgan male, especially the young men. It not only vindicated his honor, but also made him more desirable as a possible marriage partner. Because of the importance of this competition, a loser was given several opportunities to save face, his friends and fellow community members challenging his successful opponent. Should the opponent continue winning, the match could evolve into a general melee with no one being the clear winner, so that everyone's reputation was salvaged.

The importance of wrestling in Yahgan life is reflected in mythology. For example, in the explanation of the origin of the finch and starling:

> Ceip and Siika were two strong men, constantly quarreling.

One day they again came close to each other, immediately took to violence, and started to wrestle. In their mutual rage they seized each other firmly. With his left hand Siika grabbed Ceip by the throat; with the right hand he pulled out a tuft of his hair. The result was a white spot on Ceip's throat, and sticking upon the back of his head, a bump with a tuft of feathers.

Ceip was somewhat smaller than his opponent. From below he gave him a strong cuff on the nose so that much blood gushed forth. The bleeding never stopped. Even today one can still see the big red spot on the breast of this bird (Gusinde, 1975:142-43).

The Yahgan also enjoyed several varieties of ballgame. The most popular ballgame was played in a circle. The ball, *kalaka,* was the size of an American softball and was made of an albatross web, blown up, stuffed with goose feathers, and sewn together. The ball was tossed into the air with the flat palm of the hand, each player attempting to throw it exactly perpendicular to the ground so that it stayed within the circle. Before the ball fell to the ground, it was caught by the next player and tossed again into the air. The object of the game was to keep the ball in the circle and not allow it to hit the ground. Both men and women took part in the ballgame.

Another variation of the Yahgan ballgame involved the use of an inflated, dried seal stomach. Because the ball was larger and more irregular in shape than that made from the albatross tissue, the flight of the ball was less predictable and more apt to fall outside the circle, increasing the difficulty of the game.

Bridges (1947:97) mentions a Yahgan activity in which one participant dragged a basket on a string; "this basket would be about the circumference of a steel helmet, but much deeper." The other players threw spears at the moving target. The skill developed in the context of playing this game was useful in fish spearing, a basic subsistence technique among the Yahgan.

In addition, to these physically competitive activities, the Yahgan engaged in many nonathletic games during their leisurely hours in their cold and clammy yet resourceful environment. Imitative games appear to have been the most popular of these, and the players frequently displayed outstanding acting abilities, reproducing "the movements and the calls of certain kinds of animals with amazing accuracy" (Gusinde, 1937:142-43). These animals included the sea lion, blue whale, kite, hawk, great gerfalcon, great albatross, loud gull, Molinas goose, oyster catcher, and Vigua cormorant.

In general, Yahgan sports and games functioned to improve their hunting and fishing skills, develop their understanding of the behavior of those animals important to their subsistence, increase band interaction, provide opportunities for marriageable young adults to mingle, and socialize the young, as well as entertain. At the same time, these activities manifested the basic values of Yahgan culture, the mechanics of social organization (e.g., male-female relationships), and the ritual order.

LEVEL II BAND

Level II bands are essentially collections of level I bands. However, the population is larger and concomitantly, denser. Subsistence techniques include hunting-and-gathering as well as occasional pastoralism and horticulture, and the economy is characterized by greater interband exchange and reciprocity. Statuses are still largely ascribed and familial, though leadership roles may cross-cut kin lines, as in the case of voluntary organizations.

Sports and games in level II societies are a bit more complex than those at level I, but are in many cases similar in structure and function.

Examples of level II band societies include the Navajo, the Chukchi, and the Dani.

Navajos: American Southwest
Navajo: Background The Navajo of the American Southwest are an Athabascan-speaking group that migrated out of what is now central Canada and into their present location during the fourteenth or fifteenth centures, not many years before European contact. Originally, the Navajos were part of a large, undifferentiated Apachean group and are still classified as Western Apache. However, shortly after their migration into the Southwest, the Navajos came in contact with the Pueblo peoples. As a result of that contact, a distinctively Navajo culture emerged. They shifted from an exclusively hunting-and-gathering subsistence base to one including some dry farming. They adopted a clan system and matrilineal descent, in contrast to the Apachean bilateral pattern. Their traditional nomadism was modified and a semi-sedentary life style emerged. Therefore, by the time the Spanish arrived on the scene, the Navajos, while speaking a similar language, had fashioned a culture for themselves that was distinctively Navajo.

With the Spanish came a variety of domesticated animals. The Navajos, long known for their pragmatism, quickly learned to ride the horse, "borrowed on a permanent basis" a virtual barnyard of sheep, goats, and horses, and developed a new economic base, one marked by a combination of pastoralism and raiding. The Navajos, unlike the settled Pueblo peoples of the Southwest, were successful in avoiding much of the violent suppression of the Spaniards, and thrived throughout the sixteenth, seventeenth, and eighteenth centuries, raising sheep and goats and attacking various Native American and Spanish communities on horseback to supplement their domestic animal production with agricultural produce and other capital goods. Spanish troops made periodic forays into the rugged basalt flats and rocky mesas of Navajoland in an effort to put an end to the frequent Navajo raids, but these efforts were of limited success.

Navajos remained relatively aloof from outside control until the mid-1800s subsequent to the Treaty of Hildago Guadalupe (1848) and the beginning of an American presence in the Southwest. By the 1950s, the United States Government was aware of the seriousness of the "Navajo problem" that it had inherited as a result of its victory in the Mexican War. White settlers protested frequent interference from Navajos, and the Pueblo peoples made repeated appeals to Washington to bring a halt to the continuing Navajo raids.

The United States Cavalry began a series of systematic invasions of Navajo territory in an attempt to quell the Navajo bellocosity and make the area safe for settlers, Indian and non-Indian alike. By 1964, a series of treaties with isolated Navajo bands had proven ineffective, so Washington ordered all Navajos to report to Fort Wingate, near Window Rock, Arizona, the current capital of the Navajo Nation, and surrender. To help speed up the process, Kit Carson and his cavalrymen were sent into Navajo territory later that same year to round up every man, woman, and child and drive them to Fort Wingate. Orchards were burned, fields destroyed, animal herds wiped out, and in some cases Navajos were killed. Eventually, Carson succeeded in forcing the Navajos to assemble at Fort Wingate. From Wingate, the Navajos were forced to walk to Fort Sumner some 300 miles to the southeast, where they were imprisoned with the Mescalero Apache for four years. During that time many of the original Navajos died of disease and starvation before the government realized that its plan for Navajo resettlement had been a mistake. A treaty was drafted, a new reservation was created, and the Navajos were allowed to walk back home.

Since the return to their original homeland, the Navajo population has increased to over 170,000, making it the largest among contemporary American Indian tribes. It has developed a constitution, its own form of tribal government, and an economic base that is now more directly tied to an industrialized, cash economy than to pastoralism, though some Navajos continue to do dry farming and raise sheep, goats, and cattle.

The "Navajo tribe" is a clear illustration of Fried's concept of secondary tribalism. Initially a group of isolated bands with similar physical, linguistic, and cultural patterns, the Navajo tribe emerged as a unified political entity only after the Fort Sumner experience. Previous to that event, Navajo bands were politically independent, local authority being in the hands of the *nataani* or local headman. The *nataani*, usually designated as either a war or peace *nataani*, led by example rather than coercion, and exercised only limited authority over his own people. He had no voice in the decision of other bands. This was a cause of confusion among the Americans in the 1850s and

1860s who negotiated many unsuccessful treaties with the Navajos. In most cases, the *nataani* who entered into the agreement did so knowing he could make a commitment only for his own small band, while the government officials assumed he was speaking on behalf of all Navajos. As a result, the American negotiators were consistently puzzled by the assumed failure of the Navajos to abide by treaty agreements. The Fort Sumner captivity and the subsequent treaty was the American government's way of imposing political unity and thus creating the "Navajo tribe."

Despite the fact of its secondary tribal status, it is nevertheless important that the Navajo tribe be viewed as something larger and culturally more complex than the bands of level I. The increased complexity of Navajo culture is manifested in its clan system (there are over fifty Navajo clans), its mixed economy of dry farming and pastoralism, and its elaborate religious life. Navajo religion is characterized by a long list of lengthy ceremonies designed to reestablish one's spiritual relationship with the rest of the universe and thereby bring healing. Navajo ceremonies such as Blessing Way, Yeibichai, Enemy Way, and Ghost Way, are just a few of the many liturgical events that last from two to three to nine days and provide entertainment, opportunities for social exchange, and a political forum, as well as renewed health.

Although Navajos have been described as exceptionally anxious about the supernatural, serious, and distrustful of outsiders (Kluckhohn and Leighton, 1974:303-06), it is also suggested that they have a "keen sense of humor."

> They appreciate ridiculous or incongruous situations, either accidental or prepared, at least as much as do whites. However, their practical jokes are seldom cruel, and individuals are not often satirized in their presence. All types of humor are about equally indulged in and reacted to by all classes of persons. There is much less difference due to age, sex, and social position than there is in white society. A respected older man who is usually quite dignified does not feel that there is anything out of the way in acting the buffoon for a few minutes (Kluckhohn and Leighton, 1974:97).

Navajo: Sport   That keen sense of humor is a factor in Navajo recreational life, and having a good time is a priority. While that portion of the daily activities that can be described as leisure time is more limited than it is in a typical level I band society, Navajos have ample time for playing. There are the games played in the hogan (the Navajo house) at night, the folktales told around open campfires, hunting parties, rodeos, chicken pulls, and social drinking. Ceremonial occasions, such as the ubiquitous "squaw dance," are frequently the setting for racing, roping, and other forms of sport activities. In recent decades, the Navajos have adopted American sports, such as baseball and basketball, so that both traditionally and in the 1980s, Navajo society can be described as both play-sensitive and sport-conscious.

One of the most popular of traditional Navajo sports is the hoop and pole game (*na'azhozh*). A hoop wrapped in sheephide and measuring some six to seven inches in diameter is rolled along the ground, and a decorated stick or pole of variable length is thrown in an attempt to penetrate the hoop while it is in motion. Participants take turns throwing at the moving target, and score points with each successful toss. The first to reach an agreed-upon total is declared the winner. The Navajo players frequently bet on the outcome of a match.

The Navajos have been excellent horsemen ever since they began confiscating Spanish horses back in the sixteenth century. Ironically, the Navajo male emulates the cowboy model; his blue jeans, colorful shirt, hat, boots, kerchief, and pony are important symbols. The rodeo is a significant sporting event. Horse racing, calf roping, bulldogging, bull riding, and bronco busting are the key activities of the rodeo. The rodeo is a major community event, and often lasts for an entire day, surrounded by feasting, gambling, and other forms of gaiety. Children play in small groups, sometimes pretending to be cowboys. Women sit huddled beside the arena fence or in the back of pick-up trucks, talking quietly, nursing babies, eating pieces of fry-bread or smoking, and watching. The men and older boys are the rodeo: the cowboys who fly out of gates on the backs of snorting broncs or half-crazed steers, chase terrorized calves on horseback, and wrestle uncooperative longhorns to the dusty turf. Then they strut, saunter among the women and children, joke with each other, and lean against fence posts with a deliberate posturing, and watch. It is all part of the sport.

Navajos also enjoy foot racing. The race is usually staged on a prepared course, often one used for horse racing. The participants run in their bare feet, dressed only in a traditional loin cloth. In some cases, the contestants are given a running start so that they hit the starting line in full stride. Races vary in length from short distances of less than half a mile to long ones of several miles. Reagan (1932:69) contends that the ability to run long distances is the result of their "cantering" pace.

Another traditional Navajo sport was a shinny game called *ndashdilka'l*. The ball is a buckskin bag filled with seeds and closed with a draw string. The bat is "a peeled sapling curved at the striking end with bark at the handle" (Culin, 1907:623). A playing field is marked off by drawing two goal lines, usually at a great distance from each other. As in field hockey, the ball is knocked along the ground, the object being to hit the ball across the goal line of the opposite team. The first team to do so is the winner.

The Navajos also wrestle. According to Reagan (1932:69-70):

Wrestling matches usually take place wherever there is a

gathering of Navajos, such as at feasts, daytime dances, and other daylight gatherings. On these occasions the Navajos surround a central space, which might be termed the arena. Into this, one or more sets of contestants, of two men each, enter and walk about, as the two of each set spar for a strategic hold. Often they endeavor to seize each other by the hair of the head or by the thighs; but if both of these holds fail, they seize each other wherever they can. They then wrestle, while those present often sing and dance or loudly talk and shout. The only dexterity they make use of is in the first seizing each other. After that it is all decided by main strength; and woe unto the clothing they wear, if they are not nude, for before the contest closes it will probably be torn to bits. Around the arena they wrench and twist each other till one or the other is thrown on his back. Should it happen, as it sometimes does, that neither can throw his antagonist, they part by mutual agreement, or are parted by others.

The chicken pull game of the Navajos has some resemblance to the Afghan *buzkashi* contest. The chicken pull is held in conjunction with other important community activities or feast days. The event begins with the burying of a live rooster so that only the head is left protruding up out of the ground. Participants in the contest strip to their loin cloths and mount saddleless horses. On the signal from an official, the riders race toward the bewildered bird and lean to grab the head and jerk the animal from the ground. After several unsuccessful tries, the rooster has been worked gradually out of the ground, and one of the riders manages to grab its neck and ride clear of the other riders. Subsequently, the rider with the chicken becomes the focus of the action, as his opponents attempt to tear the squawking, ruffled bird from his grasp. Contestants pull at the bird, eventually ripping off legs, wings, and feathers until there is nothing left but bits and pieces, too small for serious competition.

After the rooster has been sufficiently demolished, another is placed in the ground and the event repeated until "the roosters in the immediate camps have been mutilated in the sport, and all the men are bloodier than a butcher in a slaughter house" (Reagan, 1932:71). A prize is awarded the winner, the rider judged most successful in retrieving and controlling the rooster. The Navajo chicken pull is perhaps the only game in which the winner is the player drawing the most "fowls."

In recent decades the Navajos have adopted a variety of typically American sports. Baseball, basketball, and softball are popular on the reservation both as participant and spectator sports. Most of the traditional games, including the chicken pull, have been abandoned. The rodeo and various horseback contests (e.g., racing) survive, but the school teams and adult basketball or baseball leagues have become the most visible aspects of Navajo sport behavior.

Traditionally, Navajo sport functioned to hone the skills necessary to a pastoral existence. Horsemanship was a valuable skill. Foot racing helped to keep one "fast on his feet" and in condition to sustain long treks on horseback or on foot. Wrestling was important to agility and hand-to-hand combat, an occasional activity during a Navajo raid. Also, sport was a community activity, providing not only entertainment for participants and spectators, but also an opportunity for social interaction. Navajo households live in relative isolation from each other, often several miles apart, making extrafamilial activities rare delights.

Modern sports among the Navajos also serve to facilitate community interaction. In addition, they have been refined so that they reflect some of the basic values of Navajo tradition. Individual performance takes precedence over team success, having fun is more important than winning, and kinship is a factor in game interactions. The meaning of sport still goes beyond the basketball court, the corral, or the baseball diamond in Navajo society.

The Chukchi: Northern Europe and Siberia
Chukchi: Background   The Chukchi, another level II band society, are part of a large population of reindeer-herding peoples that extends from Northern Europe across the top of the Asian Continent all the way to the Arctic Coast of Siberia. The Chukchi inhabit the easternmost extreme of that expanse.

The name Chukchi is derived from a native word, *chau' chu,* which means "rich in reindeer," a term more appropriate to the so-called Reindeer Chukchi than the Maritime Chukchi. The latter are adapted to a coastal environment and subsist largely by exploiting sea life. The Reindeer Chukchi, the subject of this description, are more nomadic, moving their camps from 100 to 150 miles each year over territory that includes coastal as well as interior environments.

Life in the cold extremities of northern Siberia is difficult. Temperatures range from eighty degrees above to over fifty degrees below zero (Fahrenheit). Noxious insects and soggy tundra make even the warmer months uncomfortable. Yet, the Chukchi survive, largely because of a technology appropriate to the conditions. The reindeer is the center of Chukchi life, and there are various ingenious devices for managing and exploiting the herds: traces, halters, sleds, packs. The Chukchi also have developed an elaborate arsenal for the hunting of sea life (e.g., seal, walrus) and small game from the forest (e.g., marmot, ermine, ground squirrel). The hunting technology includes the harpoon, cross-bow, and various traps and snares. In addition, the Chukchi have domesticated dogs and methods for water travel, including the reindeer-skin sailboat.

Similar to that of the Eskimo, the Chukchi diet is largely meat. Most meat is boiled, rather than broiled or roasted, and vegetable foods make up only a very small portion of the diet. Some roots are gathered, rodent nests robbed, and the soft green moss extracted from the butchered reindeer's stomach is prepared and eaten.

The Chukchi have developed several different types of living shelters, but the most common are the large, round skin tents that range from fifteen to twenty-five feet in diameter and ten to fifteen feet in height.

Descent among the Chukchi is reckoned through the paternal line, paternal relatives called "those of the same blood" (Bogoras, 1904-9:537). Although there are no patrilineages or clans, the Chukchi are organized in kin units they call *va'rat*, a "collection of those who are together" (Bogoras, 1904-9:541). The *va'rat* is a residental group composed of brothers and their families.

Some first cousin marriage is allowed, polygyny is an alternative, and couples generally move into the *va'rat* of the groom (i.e., patrilocal residence pattern). Also, the levirate is practiced, meaning that when a man dies, his younger brother is expected to assume the responsibility for his wife and family.

The camp is the basic social unit above the joint family or the *va'rat*. The camp is relatively unstable, but normally includes at least two or three families. Shortly after 1900, there were 650 Chukchi camps with a total population of between 7,500 and 9,000, camps ranging in size from 15 to 100 individuals with herds of from 200 to 5,000 animals.

Political authority is exercised by the "oldest brother" in the prominent family groups. Total reindeer herd size is a factor in social rank in a Chukchi community so that those families with larger herds may be more likely to exercise authority, although that authority is largely informal and of limited coercive potential. Legal matters such as the determination of guilt in a criminal case (e.g., theft) are handled by a "council of the family group."

Religion among the Chukchi is tied to a cosmology that views all things as embued with spirits, in most cases, benevolent supernatural beings. Religious practitioners among the Chukchi include family as well as community shamans, male and female, each with a collection of talents that range from ventriloquism, prestidigitation, drumming, and various forms of sleight of hand. Chukchi life is surrounded with magic, amulets, charms, and ceremonies. In fact, even the slaughtering of a reindeer is viewed as a sacrifice and a ritual occasion.

Russian contact with the Chukchi dates back to the seventeenth century. There have been skirmishes, but the superiority of Russian firearms has limited the effectiveness of the Chukchi resistance, although the Chukchi have had ample experience at war, fighting each other and the Eskimos. The Russians, in the attempt to control the nomadic Chukchi, imposed an artificial clan system designed to unify the Chukchi in a way convenient to administration by the Russian state. The system remained largely artificial and ineffective, but the Russians were influential in changing Chukchi lives in other ways. Iron tools, guns, beads, calico, and alcohol have had more lasting effects on Chukchi society than the Russians' unsuccessful administrative ploy.

Chukchi: Sport   According to ethnographer Waldemar Bogoras (1904-9:264), "the Chukchee are fond of all kinds of sports and indulge in them whenever opportunity is offered." Despite the harshness of the environment and the varied nature of subsistence demands, the Chukchi still find ample time for play.

Reindeer racing is viewed as the major sport among the Chukchi. Almost every camp arranges a race every year, and in such a way that its time does not interfere with that of another camp. This leads to a veritable circuit, maximizing participation and spectatorism.

The host of each race, usually the principal man or eldest brother of the camp, furnishes a prize (e.g., tobacco, beaver skins). The length of the race track, which can extend for more than ten miles, usually varies with the value of the prize.

Contestants saddle their reindeer, mount their animals, and gather around the point at which the prize has been deposited. On a signal from the host, the riders spur their animals toward the goal. There is no stipulation requiring racers to stick to a particular course. They must ride to a point selected by the host and return. Some stay on the road; others gallop through the woods or snow. Most riders do not push their mounts until the last leg of the race, and the competition does not really heat up until the participants begin closing in on the prize. Spectators along the course hoot enthusiasticalliy. Then, the first rider grasps the prize and is declared the winner. The race is over. Prizes for second or third place finishes are sometimes furnished by visitors from other communities, and in some cases, the man placing last is given a small stake, partly in jest, but also to assuage his despondency. The host may participate in the race, but is careful not to finish first since it would be improper for the host to claim his own prize. The competition is taken seriously, and any irregularity may lead to fighting. Bogoras (1904-9:264-5) describes a race he observed in 1896:

> Two rivals of several years standing met in a race. When one had almost reached the goal, one of his reindeer suddenly stumbled and fell, thus allowing the other man to capture the prize. A quarrel ensued; and the winner, who had the reputation of being a shaman, was accused of laming the reindeer by means of secret incantations. The quarrel was quieted down by the other guests. After two days the loser suddenly died. Of course, the other one was accused of using further incantations to kill his rival. He fled in the night to his native country, about five hundred miles away. Two brothers of the dead man followed his tracks in the morning, but were unable to overtake him. It was understood, however, that one of them would seek the

supposed criminal the next fall in order to settle the blood score.

The Chukchi also enjoy foot racing, and often these contests follow in the wake of a reindeer race. Generally, endurance is more important than speed, the races sometimes covering several miles. Nevertheless, swiftness is a consideration, and the Chukchi pride themselves in their ability to run even through deep snow at a reasonably fast pace. Some of the men have claimed that they could overtake a reindeer running at full speed or keep pace with a dog team for ten or fifteen miles. Bogoras (1904-9:265) reports having seen a "man run behind a dog-sled for forty miles. At the end the dogs were only half an hour ahead of him." The women and girls have competitive races of their own, as do young boys.

Each contest pits an "attacker" and a "passive subject." The former attempts to throw the latter. If he proves unsuccessful, the roles are reversed and the action repeated. Subsequent to this initial stage of the contest, a free-style form of wrestling ensues, each attempting to pin the other's back to the ground. These three phases of the match are considered as sufficient, but often the loser insists on continuing, as a means of saving face. The excitement can lead to excess, and often violent scuffles result. However, the wrestling matches continue until one man emerges as the winner, having defeated all his opponents in a round-robin style tournament. Occasionally there is a prize for the winning wrestler.

The Chukchi male prides himself on his fierceness, and often assumes a personal style that mirrors the cultural ideal of masculinity. Even their table manners reflect this image. Bogoras (1904-9:34) observed

a peculiarly fierce and hasty method of eating accompanied by sounds reminding one of the snarling of a hungry dog. One of the young herdsmen whom I saw on the Anui River acquired so much skill in this respect, that he could strip a whole joint of its reindeer flesh by taking hold of it with his teeth and pulling off first one side, then the other--"like a wolf," his companions remarked admiringly.

In keeping with this image of manliness, endurance is tested and strained in the foot race, and wrestling matches often are made more dangerous by introducing hazards. "Several Chukchee tales describe a peculiar wrestling match that takes place on a spread walrus-skin, slippery with blubber and made dangerous by having sharp splinters of bone or wood stuck around its edge (Bogoras, 1904-9:266). In all of these events, violence and feuding are possible aftermaths. The will to be fierce and the desire to win make a volatile combination. The women also wrestle but face the same problem. Their contests often degenerate into screaming, scratching, and hair pulling.

In guarding against the possibility that sporting events mightexplode into more serious forms of conflict, the Chukchi are careful not to provoke violence. For example, outsiders and members of distant camps or other tribes participating in formal competition are usually careful about winning and taking the best prize or prizes. It is feared that the host community might resent the loss of the prize in this fashion and eventually take retaliatory action. Also, most wrestling matches do not include prizes for the winner. Wrestling is a passion-provoking sport. A prize is not needed to pique participant enthusiasm and might only serve to heighten emotions beyond what is appropriate to the competition itself.

The Chukchi are conscious of their physical fitness and engage in sport activities and exercises designed to increase their upper body strength, endurance and coordination. They lift large rocks or tree trunks often weighing more than 200 pounds and carry these for long distances. They practice fighting with the lance. They participate in jumping matches, competing in a modified form of the long jump that involves placing the heels together and jumping several times until the starting line is reached, from which they leap for distance. Men, and sometimes women, also compete in a crawling race. All of these activities, although frequently competitive in nature, are designed initially to increase the strength and physical capabilities of participants.

The Chukchi also play ball, although ballgames are more common among Maritime than Reindeer Chukchi. According to Bogoras (1904-9:271), "there are no particular rules for ball-playing." Balls of various sizes and shapes, made of decorated reindeer hide and stuffed with appropriate fillers (e.g., feathers), are kicked or hit with the hands, back and forth, from one team to another.

A variation of the hoop-and-pole game is played by the Chukchi. The game is called *o'kkal* and is played with a stick and several small wooden hoops. The hoops are thrown into the air, and the player attempts to catch as many of these on the stick as he possibly can before they hit the ground.

Just as the sports described in connection with the other societies treated in this chapter, the physically competitive games of the Chukchi function in many ways to reinforce and refine the skills required to survive in their particular econiche. The importance of these activities is illustrated in Chukchi myth and sacred formulae. For example, the following is an incantation used to insure victory in a foot race:

I get the line of the Spider-Woman supernatural figure, and make of it my lasso. This I throw on the person "doomed to anger." His whole body becomes wound around and around with it, and then he soon tires, loses his strength, and wants to sit down. If he does not, he becomes heated quickly, is covered with sweat, and blood spurts from his nose. He spits out blood, and cannot keep up with his rival (Bogoras, 1904-9:508).

The Dani: New Guinea

Dani: Background   Another interesting level II band culture is that of the Dani in the highlands of western New Guinea in what is now West Irian. A population of over 50,000 Dani live in the area called the Grand Valley in a series of small compounds or communities that are in turn part of larger alliances and confederations. This complex sociopolitical arrangement is based on a stone-tool technology and an economy in which sweet potatoes and domesticated pigs are the main staples.

Social life in the Grand Valley is built around a system of patrilineal descent, clans, and moieties. One inherits his or her clan membership from father and is thus automatically affiliated with the moiety to which that clan belongs. Political organization among the Dani centers on the role of the "big man," an individual who by virtue of his charisma, largess, and good nature is accorded a position of leadership. He leads by example, and is more likely to persuade with reason than with force.

The Dani have an elaborate and often ostentatious ritual life. The Dani supernatural world is filled with various ghosts and spirits, and the management of one's life is a process of propitiating, appeasing, and guarding against the unwanted intrusion of those otherwordly beings. The concern for the ghosts of dead relatives is reflected in the lengthy funeral ceremony of the Dani. The death of a community member sets in motion a series of ritual observances that extend over a period of several years.

It is the preoccupation with death and the ghosts of the ancestors that lie at the root of one of the most visible features of traditional Dani life, war. The Dani are fighters, and time is an ongoing series of battles between the various alliances and confederations. Battles are generally staged on the open plains of the valley floor, fought with wooden spears, bows-and-arrows, and are central to Dani community life. Beneath it all is the notion of revenge. The Dani fight to avenge the death of an ancestor; the spirit of that ancestor demands it. For every person killed, someone must pay. A life must be taken to balance the account. But the account is never balanced, and the battles go on. To leave a death unavenged is to invite the wrath of the ghosts; one's peace of mind demands it.

The Question of Dani Sport   The Dani fight a lot, but do they play? They play, but as though something is lacking. According to Heider (1979:60-61):

> The Dani children play a lot. One might expect this of a culture with so much free time, where younger people are not drawn into full-time work. But what is most interesting about Dani play is that it is quite casual and unorganized.

Children run about in groups, sometimes just exploring, sometimes having mock battles with grass stems as spears, sometimes making model houses. If we follow the classic definition of games (see Roberts, Arth, and Bush, 1959:597) as organized play with rules, in which there is competition resulting in a winner, then the Dani have no games, for none of Dani play fits these criteria. In fact, the Dani seem to be one of the cultures in the world which do lack games.

Thus, one might conclude that the Dani do not play games nor do they possess that sense of competition essential to sport. For example, when the Indonesians introduced a game Heider (1977:75) describes as "Flip-a-Stick" among the Dani (in 1969), the children adopted it with enthusiasm. They played in small groups, frequently, and for long periods at a time. However, the original mechanism for determining the winner was dropped. The Dani children simply played, taking turns hitting and catching the stick. No attempt was made to keep score. Heider (1977:79) concludes: "Not only do the Dani lack true games, but certainly as late as 1970 their traditional culture was strong enough to resist games by altering one introduced game into a more compatible form of play."

If this is a valid observation, then the Dani system is one that might be used to question the assumption that games and sports are universal. Having not worked among the Dani we have no reason to doubt Heider's assertion that the Dani are without games. However, what we do know about the Dani raises an interesting question: cannot Dani warfare be described as sport? And if that war is sport, are not the Dani among some of the most sport-conscious people in the world?

The intratribal warfare of the Dani was made famous by the anthropology film *Dead Birds* (1977), in which there is lengthy footage of an actual battle as well as other activities surrounding the fighting. The battle which occurs as a result of an earlier killing appears sport-like in nature; is surrounded with much pomp and circumstance, shouting, and enthusiasm; is fought according to a set of understood rules; and is marked by a playful or sporting attitude that seems to take precedence over the idea that eventually someone must be killed.

Dani warfare is an example of what Wright (1942:546) calls "social warfare." Social wars, unlike economic wars, are fought for purposes other than for taking over territory, capturing resources, or subjugating people. In the social war, the objectives of the combatants tend to be more ephemeral and include such goals as prestige, honor, revenge, supernatural reward, and entertainment. To suggest that wars are waged at least partly for the purpose of having a good time does not mean that other motivations are absent or that the consequences are not serious. Heider (1979:106) in analyzing the sample of remembered deaths (n=551) among the Dani, discovered that over 28 percent of the male and two percent of the female

deaths were the result of warfare. Although he admits that the
tendency for the Dani to remember "war deaths" longer than others
may have skewed the results of this analysis, it still underscores the
serious consequences of war.

Nevertheless, it appears that the Dani enjoy the fight.

> Battles are exhilarating. There is danger, of course. Many
> men walk away with painful arrow wounds and some must be
> carried home to spend weeks recovering. But for most, a
> battle is full of excitement. There is a tremendous amount
> of shouting, whooping, and joking. Most men know the
> individuals on the other side, and the words which fly back
> and forth can be quite personal. One time, late in the
> afternoon, a battle had more or less run out of steam. No
> one was really interested in fighting anymore and some men
> began to head for home. Others sat around on rocks and
> took turns shouting taunts and insults back and forth across
> the lines, and connoisseurs on both sides would laugh heartily
> when a particularly witty line hit home (Heider, 1979:98).

Heider (1979:96-97), who admits that the battle has gamelike
qualities, also suggests that it is not just a game or "welcome change
from the routine life of sweet potato farming and pig herding." While
this may be true, it does not negate the analogy between Dani war
and sport. Indeed, Dani warfare has many sportlike characteristics,
as these have been isolated and described in the first chapter of this
book. The battles are playful, competitive, gamelike, and are
conducted with a set of agreed-upon rules. Even the injuries or
deaths resulting from Dani war do not mean that this conflict is not
sport. How do these injuries and deaths differ from those occurring in
boxing matches and football games in the United States in the 1980s?

It is also interesting that the dominant forms of Dani child's play
discussed by Heider (1970:193-99) are what he calls war games or war
play. Boys play at "grass-spear battles," practice throwing their
spears at targets, and play "kill the hoop."

> This is played by two groups, standing fifteen to thirty
> meters apart. One group throws a hoop about four
> centimeters in diameter, made of intertwined vine, at the
> ground, and as it rolls and bounces past, the other group tries
> to throw spears through it, pinning it to the ground. The
> spears are simple sticks sharpened at the end (Heider,
> 1979:196).

Another game called "kill the berry" is a "miniature war game" in
which boys, and sometimes girls, use berries as warriors and stage
battles in competition with each other (Heider, 1979:196). Heider

(1979:193) admits that while "there is almost complete lack of competition" in many of the Dani children play activities, the war games are exceptions, although even in those he claims there are no scores or winners.

The suggestion that Dani warfare can be analyzed from the perspective of a sport model is not to be interpreted as a definitive classification. In other words, we are not asserting that fighting among the Dani is sport. The available evidence does not allow for such a categorical conclusion. However, the data are sufficient to justify raising the question. And, for the sake of future research, the possibility that such social warfare is sport should not be disregarded. This approach may prove to be a valuable perspective on the eventual understanding of both human sport and warfare.

SUMMARY

People the world over have devised numerous forms of competitive play. Sport behavior is a veritable kaleidoscope of movement, risks, physical skills, technological imagination, and ritual elaboration. From land diving on Pentecost Island to *buzkashi* among the Afghans and the kickball of the Tarahumara Indians, there seems to be no end to the possibilities. How then does one classify, structure, and comprehend this sport collage? Although other means of classification have been used by sport and game scientists, the most appropriate anthropological scheme is an evolution model.

Evolution as a way of understanding human culture provides a model for explaining prehistoric changes and development. But, it also serves as a system of classification, a system that makes available categories for structuring the myriad cultural and social experiences treated in the ethnographic literature. It is assumed here that sport, as a component of culture and as a transmitter of other cultural values, evolves in concert with the broader cultural framework of which it is a part. Therefore, societies at different levels of the evolution scheme define sport behaviors so that they in turn reflect the features characteristic of their respective degree of evolutionary development. What results is a system that distinguishes between level I and level II sport, for example, rather than between specific games or activities (e.g., baseball and boxing). In this scheme, baseball may be a different sport in two different cultural contexts because the actual style of play varies, specifically, as a direct reflection of the cultural differences. Level I baseball is different from level II baseball because level I culture is different than level II culture.

The evolution model used in this analysis is a modified version of the original Elman Service (1963) system. It is suggested that those cultures of greatest interest to anthropologists can be grouped into five categories or levels of adaptation: level I bands, level II bands, level III chiefdoms, level IV primitive states, and level V archaic civilizations.

The first two stages of the evolution model are described, and sport activities common to each of the cultures are illustrated. Level I bands include the Australian aborigines, Eskimos, and Yahgan. These primary level systems have ample leisure time and fill that time with a wide variety of skill games and other forms of competition. These activities are indicative of the nature of sport in hunting-and-gathering societies generally. In some ways, sport ethnography at this level constitutes a living prehistory of sport.

Level II bands are a bit larger and more complex than those at level I and include the Navajo, Chukchi, and Dani. It is suggested that level II sport reflects a quantitative advance over the competitive play of level I. Questions are raised about Dani warfare and whether or not one might interpret that as sport.

Exercises

Discussion questions:

1.   In what ways do Eskimo sports serve important social control and political ends in Eskimo society? Develop your response within a structural-functionalism theoretical framework.

2.   Salter (see p. 141) has suggested that the sporting activities of the aboriginal Australians have important adaptive significance. Using the Australian relationship between game and economy as a model, identify the adaptive characteristics of some typically American sports.

3.   What is the most "unusual" sport engaged in by any of the band society peoples treated in this chapter? What are the features that make it "unusual?" How do you think that someone from a level I or level II band society would react to professional tennis as it is played in America in the 1980s?

4.   Isolate and discuss some of the ways in which sport ethnography can be used to better understand and reshape sport behavior in contemporary American society.

Special Projects:

1.   Do some additional reading/research on the history of the American rodeo. Analyze that phenomenon from a cultural materialism perspective, focusing on its adaptive features. Why do you think the rodeo has such a broad appeal among particular Indian groups such as the Navajo?

2. Watch the anthropology film *Dead Birds* (1977), paying particular attention to the intertribal warfare. Analyze the characteristics of the fighting that are sportlike in nature. Do you think that the Dani "play at war?" What are the similarities between Dani fighting and sport? The differences?

3. Select a band society that has not been described in this chapter and do some additional reading/research. What sports are traditional among this group? How do these activities reflect the values of the cultural base?

A Trukese Race Day event; in this case some members of the team race forwards and others backwards

6 Sport in Culture: An Evolutionary Perspective

Part II: Supraband Society

The evolution of sport does not end with band society. As culture becomes more complex, technologically sophisticated, and segmented, sport reflects those changes. Levels III through V are more localized in time than levels I and II; they are more fleeting in their occurrence. Band society is a feature of human existence that dates from the beginning of genus *Homo* and spills over into the few tiny pockets of primitive life that remain in the 1980s. The chiefdom, the primitive state, and archaic civilization are abbreviated comments on cultural evolution. They are significant phases of the evolutionary process, but must be understood as transitional; always going somewhere else. Because of the temporary nature of these levels of human prehistory, they are more difficult to illustrate than levels I and II. Likewise, the sport institutions of these supraband societies can be more elusive, making it difficult to pinpoint the mechanics of sport change characterizing the transition from primitive band to modern sport. However, the data can be pieced together sufficiently so that the process is illustrated. That is what this chapter is about.

LEVEL III: CHIEFDOM

Level III cultures are chiefdoms. The chiefdom tends to be sedentary and more densely populated than levels I and II. Subsistence is based on productive horticultural systems, supplemented by hunting, gathering, and in some cases, fishing.

Individual households are economically interdependent, and social life is characterized by both ascribed and achieved statuses, though relationships remain largely familial. Ranking systems emerge, so that everyone has equal access to goods and services but not equal access to positions of prestige. Political leadership is inherited; the chief is the member of a particular clan or family. From an evolutionary perspective, level III society is transitional between the band and primitive state.

Sport in the chiefdom involves more elaborate equipment, more complicated rule structures, and wider units of competition than that of levels I and II. Examples of level III societies include the Choctaws, Maori, and Samoans.

Choctaws: American Southeast

Choctaws: Background The Choctaws of Native North America are descendants of the prehistoric Mississippian peoples, a complex archeological culture that flourished throughout the southeast and much of the midwest in the period between 500 and 1500 A.D. Prior to the 1930s, the Choctaws lived in an area covering many square miles of what are now the states of Mississippi, Alabama and Louisiana. However, with the passage of the Indian Removal bill and the subsequent signing of the Treaty of Dancing Rabbit Creek (1831), most of the Choctaws were forced to move west and settle in the Oklahoma Territory. Nevertheless, some stayed behind. Those were the ancestors of the Mississippi Band of Choctaw Indians, a group of some 5,000 Native Americans who now live on reservation lands in the east-central part of Mississippi.

Traditionally, the Choctaws were horticulturalists, growing maize, squash, pumpkins, and a variety of beans. They also hunted deer and small game such as rabbits. Descent among the Choctaws was matrilineal, and a system of four clans served to regulate marriage. By the late 1700s, there were over 100 Choctaw communities. Each of these communities was under the jurisdiction of a local headman or chief, one of three district chiefs or subchiefs, and the titular head of the Choctaw system, the Choctaw chief. Political authority was tied to family and clan position and was minimal. The Choctaw chief had limited powers and at best led by example, often acting as mediator in the resolution of intercommunity disputes.

Religion among the Choctaws was tied to a cosmology that treated the sun as the basic source of supernatural power. The most visible aspects of Choctaw ideology were the religious practioners. There were medicine men (*alikchi*), herb doctors, rainmakers, prophets, and witches of various types. Each of these possessed a variety of powers that allowed them to cure, divine, and work magic.

By the time the dust of removal had settled, the nature of Choctaw social organization had changed. Among those remaining in Mississippi, the clan system had disappeared, and the local community had become the basic unit of social life. By 1980, there were seven major Choctaw communities managed by an elected tribal council and chief. The traditional cosmology had been replaced by a Judeo-Christian conception of ultimate reality, although many of the traditional religious practitioner roles remained reasonably intact.

Choctaws: Sport   The Choctaws have long been noted for the enthusiasm they bring to their sport activities. Traditionally it was the racket game (*toli*) and chunkey. More recently, modern sports such as softball, baseball, and basketball have assumed central roles in their serious approach to leisure (Blanchard, 1981).

The most important traditional sport among the Mississippi Choctaws was the game of *toli*, referred to in various ways, as the two-racket game, stickball, or the parent game of lacrosse. A fast-moving, physical, and often dangerous sport, *toli*, pitted two teams against each other; two teams armed with specially constructed rackets (*kapocha*) and strong desires to win at any cost. Winning required that the golf-ball-sized *towa* (racketball) be moved down the field and tossed against or through a goal a predetermined number of times. Twelve is a frequently mentioned total, and in this case, the first team to score twelve points was declared the winner.

The rules of the game were minimal. Of primary importance was the stipulation that players were not to touch the ball with the hands. Any other means of propulsion was legitimate, but ideally the ball was either thrown or carried toward the goal using the netting of the *kapocha*. Defensive tactics were varied and often brutal. Preventing the opponent from scoring often meant tripping, tackling, or striking the head or body of a foe with the hand or an unyielding hickory racket. As a result, injuries were frequent, and some games were actually terminated before a winner was determined owing to casualties that decimated one or both team ranks.

The *toli* playing field was variable in length, marked at both ends by large wooden posts. In some cases, the posts were to be struck with the ball; in others, two posts were planted side-by-side, and the object was to toss the game ball through the space between them. In all cases, there were no boundaries left and right. The flow of play often moved into the ranks of the spectators, sending racket game fans scurrying out of the way to avoid being trampled by stampeding players in pursuit of the elusive game ball.

The number of players on a team was variable. The only stipulation was that both sides had to field equal numbers of players. Most formal matches began with a face-off, a pairing of players. Each player squared off against an opposing player. If one team had more players than the others, the players without paired opponents had to sit out the match, though they were allowed to play as substitutes for injured or exhausted teammates. As a result of the flexible team size regulation, a team could be composed of as few as ten or as many as several hundred players.

The game began when an official tossed the ball into the air at the center of the playing field. Players scrambled after the ball, their sticks flashing through the air and penetrating into the tight spaces between the bodies of scrambling teammates and opponents. The action was furious. Cushman (1899:127-28) has described a match he witnessed during the late nineteenth century:

> Like a herd of stampeded buffaloes upon the western plains, they ran against and over each other, or anything else, man or beast, that stood in their way, and thus in wild confusion and crazed excitement they scrambled and tumbled, each player straining every nerve and muscle to its utmost tension, to get the ball or prevent his opponent, who held it firmly grasped between the cups of his trusty *kapucha,* from making a successful throw.
> ...a scene of wild confusion was seen--scuffling, pulling, pushing, butting--unsurpassed in any game ever engaged in by man.

Choctaw stickball, like many other sports, was played at several levels, from very formal to informal. The classic matches, however, were the formal intercommunity contests. These were arranged by the local headmen or chiefs, often as means of preventing other more serious forms of conflict. The Choctaws were not strangers in the art of war, and Choctaw history is replete with instances of intra- as well as intertribal battles. Often conflict was resolved on the *toli* field.

The formal *toli* game involved entire communities. The preparations were extensive, the ritual practitioners played central roles, and the players went through a strict regimen to ready themselves for the big match. There were special medicines, self-imposed deprivations (e.g., sexual activity was curtailed), singing, and dancing. The match itself was part of a large ceremony with feasting, socializing, and ritual. Everyone participated. The men played, the women and children cheered, and the religious functionaries prevailed on supernatural forces to bring victory. The *alikchi* treated arms and legs to make players invincible. The witches looked for opportunities to invoke the powers of the sun, often using small mirrors to direct its rays so that they reflected on the bodies of and gave strength to players. Witches also used magic to harm or bring bad luck to the outstanding ball players on opposing teams. Even the rainmakers got into the act, using their powers to provoke precipitation if defeat for their team was imminent. In many ways, the formal match involved more competition between religious personnel than between players.

The formal match was characterized by large-scale betting. It was as though there were a moral obligation for an individual to wager something on the outcome of a match, and everyone did. The parity of wagered items was incidental; one might bet a new gun against a three-legged coon dog. Value was not the primary issue. There were no odds, and Choctaws always bet on their own teams. Before each match, large scaffolds were constructed at both ends of the field to hold the many wagered items: articles of clothing, food, hardware, animals, and jewelry. In addition, players might bet their services or those of their wives. In some cases, children were used as stakes. When the game was over, that final point scored, the winning team and members of its home community swooped down on the scaffolds, collected their booty, and headed home.

During the latter decades of the nineteenth century, the Mississippi Choctaw racket game was the focus of some missionary concern. Local whites frequented the "Indian ballgames" and with the whites came a new type of betting, whiskey, and threat to the safety of Choctaw women. New forms of violence, including gunplay, emerged. Finally, in the 1980s, missionary H. S. Halbert (1897:25) appealed to the Mississippi legislature to enact legislation against betting on the Choctaw ballgame with the assumption that "the institution will soon die out, for hundreds of Indians would not go to a ball play if they were not permitted to bet or gamble there."

In 1898, the State of Mississippi followed Halbert's advice, and outlawed gambling at all Indian ballgames. In a few years, the formal intercommunity match had disappeared. In some cases, this has been interpreted as a validation of Halbert's prediction (Blanchard, 1981:42). However, more recent evidence suggests that while the formal match itself ceased to be a major event in Mississippi Choctaw life, small-scale matches continued into the early decades of the twentieth century. And, rather than the oulawing of betting, the principal factor underlying the demise of the formal matches was the Choctaw Removal of 1903. Under pressure from Choctaws in Oklahoma and on terms worked out by the Dawes commission, many of the Mississippi group immigrated West in the years just prior to 1910. As a result, the local community populations were decimated in most cases, so that the demographic basis for the traditional intercommunity game was eliminated.

For several decades after 1900, the Choctaw stickball game was an informal, recreational activity. Games were played with small teams, and the thrill of victory was subordinated to the joy of playing. It was not until the advent of the Choctaw Fair (1949) that Choctaw stickball once again became a serious intercommunity event. Now, several of the Choctaw communities in Mississippi have stickball clubs and compete on a regular basis, with the big championship games reserved for the summer fair. Although the game that is played today is restricted by new time and boundary constraints, it is still an important part of the Choctaw sport institution and a symbol of what it means to be Choctaw.

In addition to *toli*, the traditional Choctaw sport complex included games like chunkey (see p. 93) and a type of handball game in which opposing teams threw a large ball made of woolen rags up and down a field of some 150 feet in length. The object of the contest was to throw the ball through the opponent's goal and score points. This game was more open to female participation than was the formal stickball match.

The twentieth century has seen the Mississippi Choctaws embrace a variety of so-called "modern sports." Baseball became a Choctaw pastime in the early part of the century; then it was basketball, and finally softball. As is the case with the Navajos, the Choctaws have redefined these activities to fit the norms and values of their own tradition. Recreation league ballgames are strongly influenced by community and family regularities. In fact, in some cases, whole teams are composed of close kin: brothers, sisters, fathers, sons, daughters, mothers, uncles, aunts, cousins, etc. Implicitly, social relationships become an important factor in actual play. Even the nature of sport competition among the Choctaws is affected by kinship. In many contests, the will to win is less evident than in others. For example, in intracommunity events, winning does not appear to be as important as having a good time. Similarly, games between Choctaw and non-Choctaw teams appear to be predicated more on player enjoyment and the athlete's sense of having played a good game (i.e., looking good). However, when teams from two Choctaw communities compete against each other, the desire to win takes precedence over all other motivation. The Choctaw athlete's sense of competition in many ways can be viewed as a product of the social setting (see Fig. 9).

Choctaw ideology and religious practice also affect the nature of contemporary Choctaw game playing. The *alikchi* treats athletes, marking their arms to make them invincible pitchers or batters, protecting them against black magic, or divining the nature of a sport-related ailment. The witch still looms as a threat, especially to the successful athlete. If one is too good, he or she runs the risk of having a jealous opponent hire a witch who in turn will cause some crippling event to befall the athlete. Also, the logic of witchcraft still provides an explanation for otherwise inexplicable sport outcomes. If a women's softball team from community A beats an obviously superior team from community B, it is reasonable to assume that the visitors overcame their talent deficit by enlisting the aid of a witch. It is not fair, but it happens, and one protests only in the quiet of a personal conversation.

Another interesting feature of Choctaw sport is the central role played by women. In a society not marked by a significant emphasis on male and female equality, it is interesting to note the importance attached to the sport activities of women. High school girls who excel at basketball or softball are accorded social status equal to that of their male counterparts. It is normal that the most popular female students are ballplayers. Likewise, adult women with athletic

FIGURE 9. Importance of team competition and individual performance factors in Mississippi Choctaw sport behavior, defined by intensity of expression in each of the four basic kinship-residential sectors.[1]

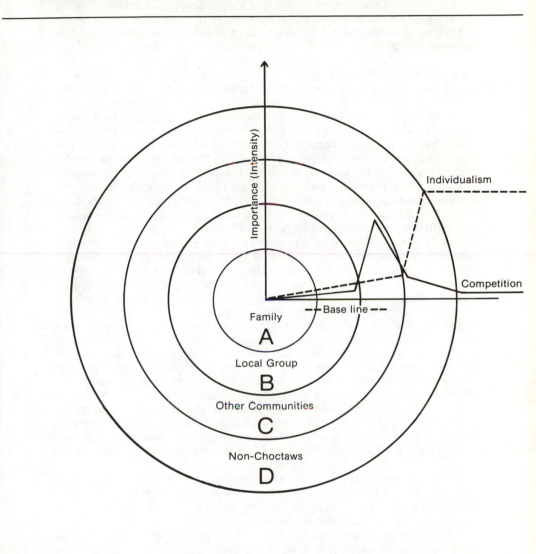

1. Concept adopted from Sahlins, 1972:199

skills are often community leaders and women's recreation league activities are as well attended as those of men. Being an athlete has been a legitimate source of power and status among Choctaw females for decades. In this sense, the Mississippi Choctaws are years ahead of their Anglo-American neighbors and the latter's treatment of the female athlete.

Maori: Polynesia (New Zealand)

Maori: Background   Another level III society is that of the Maori, the original inhabitants of New Zealand. The Maori were contacted in 1642 by Abel Janszoon Tasman, a captain of the Dutch East India Company, and again in 1769 by the great English explorer, James Cook. However, it was not until the early nineteenth century that the Maori began to feel the real effects of British influence: trade, technology, missionaries, and disease. The introduction of the musket and European maladies led to the significant decimation of the original Maori population within four or five decades. By 1840, only 100,000 of a population that before contact "may have been near the half million mark" remained (Oliver, 1960:30).

It is difficult to generalize about the Maori, owing to some diversity of adaptive strategies and political organization between different segments of the population, nevertheless, classic Maori culture is described by Raymond Firth in his *Primitive Economics of the New Zealand Maori* (1929).

The Maori were farmers, specializing in the cultivation of sweet potatoes and other root crops. Agricultural produce was supplemented by fishing (e.g., grouper, snapper, crayfish) and small-game hunting and trapping. The Maori village was composed of numerous rectangular, thatched dwelling huts, some ten feet by twelve feet in dimensions. Maori society within the village was built around the extended family unit. Descent was reckoned ambilaterally, meaning that one chose to identify with the most important or influential side of his or her family, either the mother's or father's line. The Maori had no clan system, but the *hapu*, an ambilateral, nonexogamous group, functioned like a clan, as a large kin unit.

Maori society was ranked, meaning that not every member had equal access to prestige. The three ranks included the chiefs, the commoners, and the slaves, with varying levels of prestige within these three general categories.

Marriage among low-ranking men in Maori society was monogamous, although chiefs were allowed a plurality of wives. In the majority of cases, residence was patrilocal, wives living with the husband's family subsequent to marriage.

Political authority in Maori society was in the hands of the chiefs, the highest ranking chief being the dominant figure in the system. His rank was marked by the number of wives and slaves he had, and his position resulted from his having descended through a particular family line. However, his personality and executive capabilities were also factors in his legitimacy as chief, and his largess and continued generosity were essential to the maintenance of his authority. Intercommunity wars were common, and the Maori were capable fighters.

Basic to Maori cosmology was the concept of *tapu* (the same as *tabu* in other Polynesian settings). *Tapu* was the sacred essence of reality, the focus of Maori magic and religious life. "Any person or thing was regarded as *tapu* was only to be approached or handled with caution, and under certain rigidly delimited conditions" (Firth, 1929:235). *Tapu* was manifested as power in *mana*, a quality manifested in persons of esteem. *Mana* was the symbol of the chief's power and the rationale underlying the deference accorded the position.

The Maori have survived the Anglicization of New Zealand. Although their traditional cultural system has undergone extensive change, the Maori now have a population of over 200,000.

Maori: Sport The major sporting activities of the Maori functioned to prepare participants for war. Firth (1929:36-7) has suggested:

> Physically the Maori was of a type which enabled him to cope vigorously with exigencies of a somewhat rough life. Fairly tall, and well built, he cultivated by war, games, and manly exercises the qualities of strength, speed, quickness, and endurance.... The Maori may be said to have had a cult of fitness, but such an expression must not be pushed too far. By social approval, the young man strove to render himself strong and agile.

Despite the emphasis on exercise and fitness, the Maori referred to the games as *nga mahi a te rehia*, "the arts of pleasure" (Best, 1952:137). Among the arts of pleasure, one category of games was called *kaipara* (i.e., "athletic games"). Of these, the most desirable and beneficial were those involving training in the use of military weapons. The young boys, for example, played with light reeds, using them as swords in mock competition.

The spear-throwing game was another Maori sport with obvious military ramifications. Using spears made of flower stalks some six feet in length with blunted ends, "opponents stood some distance apart, and one threw while the other avoided the missiles by dodging, parrying with a stick, or, as they became expert, by catching occasionally with the hand" (Buck, 1949:238). The mechanisms for score keeping are not clear in the literature.

A related game called *ti rakau* or *touretua* was played with thicker sticks, between two and three feet in length.

> ...the players knelt in a circle with two sticks each. In time

to a chant, they beat the sticks together and then threw first one and then the other to the neighbour on the right, sticks being thrown in a vertical position. Each threw the first stick in the right hand, caught the incoming stick with the empty hand, threw the second stick with the left hand and caught the incoming stick with that hand. The passing of sticks, first right then left, continued for some beats and then the two sticks were beaten together. The tempo of the chant was quickened and great dexterity in catching and passing had to be displayed to remain in the game. Those who dropped a stick fell out and the circle lessened until the last one left in was declared the winner (Buck 1949:239).

Wrestling (*mamau*) was also a popular sport among the Maori. Typically, a wrestling match would pit two men against each other. According to Best (1952:140), before each match the wrestlers "would recite a charm" and spit into their respective hands and close them, "presumably for luck." A variety of holds and tricks were used, including "catch-as-catch-can, holding by the arms alone, and holding around the body" (Buck, 1949:240). Occasionally, two women would wrestle one man. The physical competition of the two sexes was not unusual in light of the fact that the women were known to carry weapons and fight alongside the male warriors of their villages.

Boxing, though not practiced frequently, was also a Maori sport. Buck (1949:240) reports that boxing was done with bare fists and usually in the context of resolving "private quarrels when no weapon was handy." This boxing was done in one of two ways. Either the opponents hit each other with the front of a clenched fist, as is typical of modern boxing, or the "blow was delivered with the side of the fist" so that "the edge of the palm and the little finger would come into contact with one's opponent" (Best, 1924:82).

The Maori also raced. Sprints were generally not known, but long distance runs were common. Best (1952:140) has noted that the Maori ran with a "bent-knee jog-trot peculiar to bare-footed people." The Maori raced in the water as well as on land. They were noted for their mastery of water sport skills: swimming, surf-riding, and jumping (as opposed to diving) from great heights. In addition to swimming races, the Maori competed in their canoes, competition

...running on family and tribal lines. With large canoes with a double row of paddlers, the space between was so close that perfect time had to be observed in the dipping of the paddles. The fugleman who gave the time with various canoe chants was important and he quickened the time of his chant to quicken the stroke of the paddles (Buck, 1949:241).

Dart throwing, a sport found throughout Polynesia (see Firth, 1930/31; Davidson, 1936), was a traditional Maori activity that appears to have been abandoned after the arrival of the Europeans. According to Best (1952:143):

> That was not the form of dart-throwing that might be viewed as a military exercise or training for spear-throwing. The dart (*teka* or *neti*) was merely a light reed, and was cast underhand so as to glance off the smooth surface of a small earthen mound. No mark was aimed at, but the longest cast marked the winner. Dart-throwing contests were sometimes quite large meetings, social gatherings of the people. Prior to casting his dart, a player would expectorate upon it and recite over it a charm to cause it to make a good flight.

The following example of such a charm is provided by Best (1924:94): "Fly forward, my dart, like a meteor in the heavens. A dart of Tuhuruhuru cannot be passed. Fly directly forward, arise and descend beyond yon mountain range. May this dart be lucky."

The dart match is an important element in Maori myth. The magic dart in particular is often a factor in stories about missing persons and faraway places. In each case, the hero of the story throws the magic dart, the dart travels through the air, often for miles, the hero locates the dart, throws it again, and follows it; eventually the dart lands near the sought-after goal. Best (1924: 95-97) relates a Maori legend about the son of a famed chief who had been separated from his father since infancy. Knowing nothing about the father he had never seen, he found him by throwing and following a magic dart until it fell purposely at the front of the chief's home.

The Maori also competed at stilt walking. Using stilts made from *aristotelia*, "a light wood when dry," the young men raced against one another, across rivers or ponds (Best, 1952:152). Using their *waewae rakau* ("wooden legs"), they also engaged in a form of wrestling in which participants attempted to throw their respective opponents to the ground.

The Maori children played a variety of games, many of which were both physical and competitive. As Firth (1929:170) has noted, "the games and pursuits of children were often in mimicry of the activities of parents or, again, were of a competitive sporting nature."

As a result of the British influence in New Zealand, the Maori have adopted a variety of English sports. Tennis, rugby football, and cricket are popular, although Buck (1949:251) remarks that cricket has never attained the same popularity as rugby for one simple reason:

> Cricket requires a pitch, a good ground, and special gear that make the preliminary preparations too much of a bother to the country village, whereas a football ground is readily marked off in a neighbouring paddock, goal posts erected and a football purchased without any strain on finances.

Samoans: Polynesia

Samoa: Background The people of Samoa live on a group of islands located in southwest Polynesia, approximately 1,000 miles northeast of New Zealand. The level III Samoan chiefdom is similar to but slightly more complex than that of the Maori. Although the Samoans live on islands separated in some cases by great distances, they view themselves as all belonging to a single political unit, a corporate entity that is administered by an all-Samoan Council, the great *Fono*, which in turn is sanctioned by the hierarchy of gods that inhabit the complex Samoan cosmos.

Traditionally, the Samoans were horticulturalists, growing a variety of plants including taro, sweet potatoes, yams, and bananas. A thriving fishing industry complemented the garden crops with such items as shellfish, crabs, bonito, and shark. The Samaons were excellent wood workers and made seaworthy canoes that were basic to interisland trade and communication. According to Mead (1937:287), "Samoan life is based upon an economy of plenty."

The basic unit of Samoan social organization was the extended household. Descent was reckoned patrilineally, but the postmarital residence pattern is most appropriately described as ambilocal, a couple choosing to live in the household offering them more in the way of material goods and status. Household size ranged from as few as eight to as many as fifty individuals. Each was under the control of head men called *matai*. On a larger scale, each village or collection of households viewed itself as a large bilateral family of the resident chief.

This local chief was the village head, the prominent figure in a hierarchy of ranks and political personages including talking priests, princesses, and princes. The complex system of ranks in Samoan society provided a prestige category for everyone and figured into all relationships and social situations. The village chiefs and the great chief assumed their respective roles on the basis of heredity, although one's individual personality and character as well as his lineage membership was a factor in his legitimacy and authority. In addition to the local chief, each village had a council that acted only on special occasions, to plan some important ceremony or to arrange for war.

Samoan religious life was limited, despite the complexity of their supernatural world. Mead (1937:304) argues that "religion played a very slight role in Samoa; the gods were conceived as having resigned their sacredness to the chiefs."

War, on the other hand, was a significant institution in traditional Samoan culture. According to Mead (1937:302) "war in Samoa was part of the ceremonial rivalry between villages and was fought for no gains other than prestige, nor were there any important rewards for individual warriors."

As a result of 150 years of European influence, Samoan culture has changed. Nevertheless, the Samoan people themselves have survived. In the 1920s, there were approximately 60,000 Samoans; today that figure is over 150,000.

Samoa: Sport It has been said, with reference to the Samoans:

> Time is plentiful in the South Seas, and cares are few...there are great slices of time for which there are no pressing engagements...life has no engagement so important that the islander will not cancel it at once on the plea of sport (Churchill, 1899:562-63).

Not only do they have the time, the Samoans have the spirit and the will to compete. The issue of Samoan competitiveness has become part of the controversy prepetrated by the recent publication of Derek Freeman's *Margaret Mead and Samoa: The Making and Unmaking of An Anthropological Myth* (1983). Freeman takes Margaret Mead to task for her description of Samoan life and the conclusions of her *Coming of Age in Samoa* (1928). One of the things that Mead suggests in that first volume of her famous trilogy is that there is a pervasive cooperativeness in Samoan society. Freeman argues that the Samoans are fiercely competitive and that violence is much more characteristic of Samoan life than Mead's (1928) analysis would have us believe. In Mead's defense, her short piece on Samoa that appeared in *Cooperation and Competition among Primitive People,* a collection she edited in 1937, underscores the continuing dialectic between cooperation and competition among the Samoans. Certainly, she was aware of the competition for prestige and the strong sense of rivalry that colored intercommunity and interisland relationships (Mead, 1937:302). It was this same rivalry that tempered Samoan sport behavior.

Additional credence is given to the idea of an overriding competitiveness by the observation that Samoan sports were more likely to be viewed as individual rather than team or cooperative efforts. According to Churchill (1899:563):

> It is foreign to island custom to engage in individual contests for a championship. Two villages may meet to settle a rivalry in any one of several games; the event will be decided by the result of a large number of simultaneous contests of individuals, but the result sought is the victory of the community and not of the individual. Thus if each town had an individual who was known to be exceptionally skillful at whatever game was being played, the aim would be to prevent these two individuals from coming into a decisive contest, and rather to use each for the purpose of rolling up as many victories as possible against inferior opponents. But it should be stated that the idea of teamwork seems never to have occurred to any Samoan community in its games.

One of the most popular of Samoan sports is wrestling. The object of the matches between adult males is to throw the opponent to the ground and stand clear. Any hold above the waist is permissible, but since the wrestlers normally oiled their bodies, all holds were difficult. Traditional Samoan wrestling was perilous, the falls often violent, and accident frequent.

The great sport of Samoa was the dart match (*tika*), essentially the same dart match played by the Maori (*teka*). Major contests pitting one village against another were real events; there was feasting, drinking, gift exchange, speeches, and ceremony. The gala affairs sometimes lasted for several days.

The game itself was played on a long, flat stretch of grass-covered ground across which combatants attempted to throw their darts as far as they could. The object was distance; the player tossing his dart beyond all the others was declared the winner.

The dart was actually a small stick about the thickness of a man's finger and approximately four feet in length. The darts were made from the wood of *fau* (hibiscus). Cut while the wood was still green, the darts were peeled, washed in sweet water, and soaked in salt water for two days. They they were scraped with a piece of coral, dried over a coconut husk fire, and scraped with shell and straightened. The resulting sticks weighed between one and two ounces. Each player had his own special dart, and it was assumed that luck was a property that varied from one dart to another so that a lucky dart was a winner; an unlucky one was not.

The Samoan athlete tossed the dart from his hips, actually running a few steps before whipping the stick down the alley. Ideally, the dart glanced off the ground some thirty feet from the launch and sailed an additional 200 feet or more.

As Churchill (1899:566) described the match, there was no limit to the number of players on the two competing teams.

> In match-playing there is no limit to the number of contestants on each side. One side puts in all its players in succession; the stick thrown farthest from the crease is left on the green as a mark, while all which fall short of the mark are picked up. The opposing side next comes into play. The sticks which fall short of the mark are picked up without affecting a score. At the end the playing side counts as many sticks as may lie beyond the mark set by the other side. The most distant stick of this side sets a new distance mark, and the first side comes again into play. The game is commonly ten, and that is long enough in getting when the players are well matched; it is not to be had short of several days of playing.

Another popular sport among the Samoans is a game that Churchill (1899:567) describes as "a sort of shuffle-board on a small scale." A short woven mat, made especially for this game, was stretched across a flat surface. Two players, one from each team, sat on opposite sides of the mat facing each other and took turns tossing small disks made from coconut shell and Tahita chestnut. The object was to toss the disks so that they came to rest as close as possible to the opposite edge of the mat. As in the American game of horseshoes, points were scored for all of those disks of one player that fell closer to the opposite edge than did all those of his opponent.

The Samoans also engaged in a variety of water sports, including surf-riding with canoes, and war games such as kick matches, club fighting and spear parrying. In addition, competitive fishing and the netting of doves are traditional activities that may be viewed as sport.

Cricket was introduced among the Samoans by the English in 1884. Subsequent to its enthusiastic adoption by the Samoans, the game underwent several dramatic changes. Both men and women played. Team size was variable; in some cases, a team might field as many as two-hundred players. Games consisted of single innings and were only finished when every player had had a chance to bat. As a result, some games took as long as twelve days to complete. By the 1940s, most Samoan villages had their own cement cricket pitches, and the opening of a new pitch was the cause for major celebration:

> ...large teams from all over the country compete. Heavy entrance fees are charged and the prizes take the form of cash, banners, cattle, pigs, beef or tinned biscuits, the losers being required to pay a forfeit in the nature of singing and dancing items for the entertainment of the victors. More than one thousand pounds may change hands at a large gathering, for defeated teams are not debarred from paying further entrance fees and competing a second or even a third time (Grattan, 1948:124).

Cricket became such a passion that it began to interfere with economic productivity, many of the Samoans working only as long as it took to meet their immediate needs. At one point, "cricket matches were forbidden except by special permit from May until February," and then the courts were generally "filled with cases concerning the playing of cricket without permission" (Dunlap, 1951:307).

Baseball, boxing, and rugby are other sports that have been introduced into Samoan society and undergone modifications similar to those affecting cricket. The new sports continue to be refined and adapted to the continuing realities of Samoan culture.

Sport in Level III Society: some General Observations

The social intricacies of sport in level III societies are well illustrated in Firth's (1930/31) detailed description of the Tikopian dart match. The Island of Tikopia is located north of the New

Hebrides chain, some 600 miles west of Samoa. The Tikopians, like their fellow Polynesians, the Maori and Samoans, have a system or ranks, a chiefdom, and an elaborate dart match (*tiak*). But, the Tikopian dart game has its distinctive characteristics. The dart pitch or playing area is more carefully prepared than that of the Samoans, the dart (*tika*) has a heavy point attached to the end of the shaft, and players throw their respective darts at distances approaching 150 yards. A complex system of scoring makes the Tikopian dart match a time-consuming and complicated event, yet it is without equal among local ceremonial and festive occasions.

The nature of Tikopian social organization is directly reflected in the dart match. Teams are rigidly defined; one's membership on a given side is predicated on his family memberhip. Also, rank figures into match play. The team captains, for example, are men of rank or chiefly status. The strong will-to-win, the competitive edge to the Tikopian dart match, is related to inter-group rivalry, as is the case in Samoa. However, Firth (1930:95) suggests that the real motivation is the players' "sensitiveness to public opinion." Winning gains approval; losing nets approbation. Therefore, every possible effort is made to win, if for nothing else than to save face. It is interesting that after the match, the winners provide refreshments for the losers, in the way of coconuts. "It helps to restore the equilibrium of the losers, to take the keen edge off their bitter emotions, to prevent their defeat from rankling, and to give them time to assume a natural manner in social intercourse (Firth, 1930/31:71).

The *tika* match also has a strong religious flavor. Preparations for important contests include the use of various magical techniques for treating the darts and bodies of the players. Ritual practitioners appeal to the supernatural for assistance as a means of affecting game outcomes. As was the case in Choctaw stickball, Tikopian dart matches are settings for competitive ritual. At the same time, *tika* is ritual; it goes "beyond the bounds of simple play for exercise and relaxation" and "attains considerable importance in the general economic and religious life, in addition to its reactions on the social organization of the community and on the personality of its component members" (Firth, 1930/31:95).

In an analysis of Samoan recreation activities, Dunlap (1951:308-09) described the basic functions of Samoan sport. It "provided social intercourse," socially approved outlets for feelings of rivalry," "the opportunity for groups of individuals to gain prestige and honor," and "an outlet for excessive emotions connected with the life crises of birth, marriage and death." Also, "the skills of war were perfected through the specific amusements of disc and stick throwing for distance, spear throwing for accuracy, spear parrying and club fighting." This observation could be generalized to describe the function of most chiefdom society sport.

LEVEL IV: THE PRIMITIVE STATE

Level IV primitive state societies are built on agricultural bases and are different from chiefdoms in two principal ways: the state is socially stratified and it monopolizes force. Stratification entails the existence of social classes. Unlike the ranks typical of chiefdoms, different social classes have different and unequal access to goods and services as well as to positions of prestige. In other words, stratified societies are characterized by "haves" and "have-nots." At the same time, the primitive state reserves for itself the right to determine what is legitimate force. It also decides who has the right to use that physical force. In Service's (1963:xxvi) words, a "state constitutes itself legally."

Leadership in the state is formal and the result of either ascription or achievement. Formal markets facilitate exchange, and occupational specializations are part of increased economic diversity and productivity. State populations are larger than those of chiefdoms, and law tends to be defined in terms of geographical boundaries rather than familial relationships (i.e., territory as opposed to kinship). Unlike the more advanced urban state, the primitive state does not have cities or urban centers, nor does it have a writing system. Examples of the primitive state include the Zulu and Ashanti states of East and West Africa, respectively, as well as the prehistoric Mayan state.

Zulus: South Africa
Zulu: Background   The Zulu are a group of over two million Bantu-speaking peoples who today inhabit a large region of Natal, South Africa. The Zulu state was a nineteenth-century phenomenon, a system that evolved in the period between 1816 and 1828 under the leadership of a tribal chief named Shaka. The Zulu state, the product of military conquest and consolidation, encompassed a territory of over 80,000 square miles, boasted a population of almost half a million people, and maintained its independence for approximately seventy years until the British conquest of the area in the 1800s.

Traditionally, the Zulus were pastoralists who raised cattle, largely for the by-products, in addition to other animals such as goats, sheep and chickens. They also farmed, growing maize, sorghum, pumpkins, and sweet potatoes. Hunting-and-gathering supplemented domesticate production.

Zulu material culture was marked by the products of a sophisticated iron-working technology and dwelling structures called *kraals*, beehive-shaped grass huts.

Zulu social life was built around the household (*kraal*) unit. Descent was patrilineal and residence patrilocal. Lineages, groups of persons related through the paternal line, tended to reside together in family units under the jurisdiction of senior males. A complex system of exogamous clans integrated the entire social system.

At the head of the Zulu state was the king, a member of the royal family, which was composed of the descendants of Mpande, Shaka's brother and successor. The king exercised authority through a system of district chiefs and a standing army. All land was considered the property of the king, and members of the royal family formed a distinct ruling or upper class.

Religion among the Zulu centered on the worship of important patrilineal ancestors, gods (e.g., *Unkulunkulu*, the Creator), and other spirit figures. A complex ritual life was managed by a potpourri of specialist shamans and magicians (for more detail, see Service, 1963:293-314).

Zulu: Sport   The formal hunt of Zulu tradition can be viewed as sport. The "public hunt" as Bryant (1970:682) calls it, was a "systematically and scientifically arranged 'battle' with the beasts." During the heyday of the independent Zulu state, the plains of Zululand were a hunter's paradise. Big game was abundant, from elephants and rhinos to zebras, elands, kudu, hartebeest, and antelope. "Perpetual sport was there for commoner and king to revel in; and thrilling too, when all had to be tackled at close quarters with naught by a spear" (Bryant, 1970:682).

Any district chief had the authority to call a public hunt, and on doing so sent his messengers out to announce the time and place. In preparation for the hunt, the men slept on one side of the body only for fear that any moving about might provoke restlessness among their prey. They ate a special breakfast, prayed to the ancestors for protection and good luck, and danced before the spirits. Then each man gathered his gear--a small bundle of spears, a hunting shield and a short stick with a knob at the end for administering a heavy blow--and assembled at the announced location.

The hunters gathered in parties defined according to district wards. The pattern was prearranged and the host ward assumed the central location. Each party was managed by a master hunter, selected because of his luck and expertise in hunting. After a series of songs and dances, the director of the hunt gave the several parties directions as to where each was to go, the group moved into one large semicircle prior to their dispersal.

Having taken their appropriate stations, the parties moved out across the plains. Each kill was surrounded by team effort, shouting, and celebrating. At the end of the hunt, the parties reassembled at the starting place. "There the leaders of the several parties sat down, while each party in turn marched past them bearing its own kill, and singing its own hunting-song, the while it constantly clattered its weapons" (Bryant, 1970:685). The meat was eventually divided and the hunters returned to their respective *kraals.*

Other hunts, including the royal hunts that were reserved for the pleasure of the king and his family, were sporting events among the

Zulu. One of the most sinister versions of the hunt was the "treacherous or conspiracy hunt." This was designed not as a competition between hunting parties but as a method for getting rid of disagreeable persons. On these occasions, "the only game intended to be killed" were those unfortunate individuals deemed obnoxious and expendable (Bryant, 1970:687). The definition of this Zulu version of "snipe hunting" as sport is questionable.

Young boys among the Zulu engaged in a rolling target game. Small, sharp-pointed sticks were used as spears and a large spherical root the size of a small melon as a target. Players stood in two lines down the side of a slope and tried to hit the ball as it rolled down the hill between the two columns of spear throwers. With each successful throw, a player made a notch on his stick or simply moved up the hill to the head of the column. The "winners" of the match were those players at the head of the line or those with the most notches on their spears at the conclusion of the contest. This game was similar to the many rolling target games that have been found throughout Africa (see Raum, 1953).

> As most people already know, the Zulus used to be an essentially "fighting race," and nothing was more enjoyed by the boys than sham-fighting (*uku Qakulisana*) with the quarter-staves. Every boy, like every man, when away from the home *kraal,* always carried with him a couple of strong sticks; and, fist or hand-fighting being utterly unknown to the Zulus, their fights were always with these sticks. One stick, held about the middle in his left hand, was used for parrying; the other, held near its end in the right, was for striking. This exercise in a way resembled our own fencing, and the boys became great adepts both at parrying and at striking, the aim being practically always for the head (Bryant, 1970:691).

From available enthnographic accounts, it appears that Zulu sport was largely a matter of exercising and refining those skills necessary to war. In some ways, sport among the Zulu can be viewed as an extension of the battle.

In recent decades, soccer has become the dominant sport of Zululand. Called "football" by the natives, the game has become the major leisure time activity; endless hours are spent playing, watching, planning, and talking about the sport and the many complex rivalries that have developed. These rivalries have become bitter in many cases, leading Scotch (1961:71) to suggest that

> Interpersonal and intergroup hostility and aggression are much greater in an urban setting than in the more traditional rural Zulu community. Unnaturally crowded conditions and competition for scarce employment opportunities lead to

more frequent accusations of sorcery in the city. Football, it may be hypothesized, serves a dual function in this context: first, it is one of the few opportunities open to the Zulu for release from the anxiety and tensions of anomic urban life; and more specifically, it allows the expression of the increased aggression and hostility that arises in the city between Africans, within the framework of a modern, acceptable form.

The various Zulu football teams employ their own witch doctors, who, as is the case with traditional Choctaw sport ritual figures, serve a dual purpose. On the one hand they do magic designed to increase the abilities of their own team, while casting spells that debilitate opponents. Although the latter practice is not admitted, fear of sorcery is so rife in the football leagues in Durban that players suspected of being the object of sorcery may not be recruited despite their reputed talents or in some cases they "may be dropped from the team for fear that the spell might generalize to include the teammates of the unfortunate victim" (Scotch, 1961:471).

The regularities of traditional warfare and political authority among the Zulu have also colored the new football craze that has swept the urban center of Zululand. Strict discipline is maintained, the teams "camp-out" on the nights preceding matches, purification rites similar to those once performed before battle are carried out, and the teams move into the playing field in military formation.

Ashanti: West Africa

Ashanti: Background   Another level IV African state is that of the Ashanti. A collection of chiefdoms that united in response to European intervention in West Africa during the eighteenth century, the Ashanti developed one of the "most complex civilizations ever attained by nonliterate peoples" (Service, 1963:366). Part of what became the Gold Coast nation in 1957 and later Ghana, the Ashanti number over 200,000 and speak a language called Twi, a member of the Niger-Congo family. Like the Zulu state, that of the Ashanti flourished in the nineteenth century prior to its defeat by the British in 1874.

Ashanti subsistence is built around an extensive horticultural system. Plaintains, maize, yams, manioc, sweet potatoes, millet, peanuts, and beans are the major domesticates raised. Garden produce is supplemented with a few fish, but hunting is of limited importance in the economy. Like the Zulu, the Ashanti are accomplished iron workers and weavers. Another interesting feature of the Ashanti technology is the role of the "talking drum," a communication system that allows messages to be sent over long distances and unites the many villages of the Ashanti network.

The villages of the Ashanti are of variable size, some with populations of more than 1,000. The house types range in size and style from small mud huts to large elaborate structures that Service (1963:369) calls "veritable palaces," a reflection of stratification in Ashanti society.

Social organization among the Ashanti centers on the individual household, frequently a polygynous household. A man has the freedom to take as many wives as he can afford, and the resulting household arrangement is basic to daily life. Nevertheless, descent is reckoned through the maternal line, and a complex system of matrilineages and matrilineal clans provides the basis for Ashanti political life.

A council of elders represents the various lineages and elects regional chiefs from the appropriate lineages, in other words, those lineages of prominence and appropriate social status. The king, *Ashantihene* ("King of all Ashanti"), is the "first among chiefs" and assumes his role as a result of his position within the royal family. Indicative of the king's power is the fact that one of the most heinous of crimes among the Ashanti is "cursing the king," that is, "calling upon a supernatural power to cause the death of the king." This offense is punishable by death.

Ashanti religion combines a reverence for the ancestors with a complex pantheon of gods and spirit figures. The complexity of Ashanti religious life is manifested in multiplicity of ritual practitioners and complicated ceremonies. The most frequent of these are the ceremonies the Ashanti call *Adae*, observances designed to recall the spirits of former rulers and request favors.

The first contact between the Ashanti and Europeans occurred in the fifteenth century. Since that time, Ashanti society, specifically the Ashanti state, has become a prominent force in West African politics, and continues to be a major faction in contemporary Ghana.

Ashanti: Sport   The literature about Ashanti tradition gives one the impression that games of strategy were more popular than games of physical skill or sport. For example, Cardinall (1927:253) suggests that the widespread West African game of *wari* is the most serious of all Ashanti games. *Wari* is a board game that has several variations, but in all cases players attempt to "capture" the pieces of their opponents by a series of strategic moves.

Despite the greater visibility of traditional games like *wari*, the Ashanti also have a developed sport institution. The young boys, for example, play a variety of war games, some in which they actually engage in "bloodthirsty" fighting (Cardinall, 1927:250). Other less physical contests include a type of badminton game. Using "an old corn-cob wrapped in leaves all carefully tied together" as a shuttlecock, two teams hit it back and forth over a vine rope stretched between them about eight feet above the ground. "Each player has a racket..., a running noose made of a very strong, almost wirelike liane" (Cardinall, 1927:251). The object of the game is to catch the shuttlecock as it is thrown over the rope before it touches the ground. The first team to catch the corn-cob seven times is declared the winner. In all cases, the losers must then pay a forfeit.

Each member of the losing team is dealt a blow with a stick. The anticipation of this painful degradation provides strong incentive for winning.

Cardinall (1927:251-52) describes another game that is played in the street with a noose of fine twine and some sand:

> This latter is heaped up and one of the players buries the noose under the heaped-up sand. Then each player in turn takes a small stick--a thorn from a lime tree is usual--and sticks it into the heap of sand where he expects the noose to be, the hider being the last to play. The end of the string is then uncovered and pulled, and if a thorn is inside the noose, that thorn's player wins.

As in the badminton game, the loser is punished. If the noose is pricked, the hider must hold out his arm and allow each of the other players to slap him. However, if no one finds the noose and he does, "he is entitled to throw a lime at each of the others" (Cardinall, 1927:252).

Like so many other African peoples, the Ashanti also wrestle. As Danquah (1928:229) describes it:

> Two opponents meet to wrestle arm to arm, leg to leg, and body against body, in a rather violent but artful manner. Until one of them succeeds in conquering the other by sending him down or getting his opponent exhausted, the contest is a draw. This game is somewhat similar to the Japanese *"Ju-jitsu,"* at least in principle.

The twentieth century has seen the emergence of Western sports in Ashanti society. Soccer, cricket, volleyball, basketball, boxing, and other so-called modern sports have supplanted traditional activities. As early as the 1920s, Danquah (1928:229) was lamenting the transition.

> Our regret...is that with the growth of English schools this healthy and muscle-developing pastime (wrestling) is being gradually given up for the more attractive games of cricket and football [soccer]. Cricket and football are good games; nobody doubts that. The fear is not that we are discarding the good for the bad, but that we are dispensing with the essential for the convenient. Our national character as a race of people having endurance and capable of prolonged exertion involving determination to see a thing through to its end, stands the risk of being modified, and in time altogether lost, if we give up our national games, pastimes, and customary practices. Cricket and football games help to make good conservatives. But if the Akans [in this case,

Ashanti] have to acquire or enrich these qualities, should they do so at the risk of losing their national character?

Despite such concerns, modern sports have become a craze in contemporary Ghana, affecting the Ashanti as well as the other tribal groups represented in that country. Soccer, basketball, boxing, table tennis, lawn tennis, field hockey, and swimming are just some of the many sports that have been imported by the Ghanaians. These activities have become the basic form of entertainment. There are associations, organizations, leagues, festivals, and competition of all types. Soccer, for example, is played at various levels, including that of the National Soccer League. This league includes such teams as the Ekuw Volta United, All Blacks, and the Ashanti team, *Kumasi Asante Kotoko.*

Sports in Ghana are also serious business. Professionals play for money, sport-related gambling is big business, and players are expected to give their all for team and country. One official of the National Redemption Council, the wing of the Ghanaian government responsible for the administration of sport organizations and activities, has remarked that "Sportsmen and women would find it duty bound to perform even at the risk of their lives to the glory of the nation" (*Ghanaian Times,* July 15, 1975:11).

The gravity of sport in contemporary Ghana is also indicated in the weight assigned to the institution as a socializing agent and educative tool. It is viewed as an instrument for the development of physical skills and the maintenance of personal health. It breeds sportsmanship, an important quality in Ghanaian society. It also breeds patriotism and national unity. In some cases, sporting events are designed with these goals in mind, specifically, "to break tribal, religious and ethnic barriers among the youth and inculcate in them the spirit of oneness as enshrined in the Charter of Redemption" (*Ghanaian Times,* July 17, 1975:10). Consistent with national objectives, sport activities do appear to function as "important integrating factors" in Ghana and throughout West Africa (Little, 1965:149).

Prehistoric Mayan Sport

Prehistoric Mayan society can also be classed as a primitive state. The Mayan ballgame discussed in the previous chapter is thus an example of a sport institution in a level IV society.

LEVEL V : THE ARCHAIC CIVILIZATION

Level V is that of the archaic or primary urban state. Primary urban civilization is characterized by the emergence of true cities, large-scale agriculture, complex military technologies, science, writing systems, plow and irrigation agriculture, codified law, true government, and bureaucracy. Sport in the primary urban state features elaborate playing fields and equipment, professionalism, sport art, extensive spectator involvement, and class distinctions between sport institutions. Examples of archaic civilizations include the Mesopotamian (e.g., Sumer), Egyptian, Chinese, Indian, and Mesoamerican states (e.g., Teotihuacan). The sport activities of level V societies are largely a subject for ancient history scholars, but are treated briefly in Chapter Four.

Sport Evolution: General Observations

The evolution of sport does not end with its elaboration at the level of archaic civilization. With the unraveling of subsequent history, sport continues to change, reflecting the norms and values of its various cultural contexts. Thus, with the emergence of modern society, modern sport is born. As Guttmann (1978) has suggested, this modern sport is different from that of early historical periods. An evolutionary model of sport classification cannot ignore the last several thousand years of human history and the forces that have led to the development of the contemporary sport institution.

Having considered the nature of cultural evolution and treated the issue of sport in several sample societies at each of these levels, it is appropriate that we make the following cautionary observations:

1.   It is difficult to make qualitative distinctions between the sport institutions characteristic of the several evolutionary levels; most differences are only quantitative. This is consistent with our initial contention that sport is a universal institution.

2.   Because so few detailed analyses of particular sport or sport complexes have been undertaken by anthropologists, one must be careful in generalizing about the characteristics of sport at the various levels of the evolutionary scale.

3.   Nevertheless, the fact that sport is a part and reflection of the total cultural system means that societal-wide characteristics should be manifested in sport. This suggests that differences may exist even though they may not be evident in the available literature. In other words, it is safe to assume that if the total cultural systems of two groups of people vary, their respective sport institutions will vary in similar ways.

What then can one say about the sport evolution process and the differences that exist between the various levels or social system types? The process is best characterized by a description of the changes as these occur along a series of eight continua or axes: secularity, bureaucracy, social identity, social distance, special-ization, equipment, ecological meaning, and quantification (see Table 4).

Table 4...The Major Continua or Axes of Sport Evolution

	Level I	Level II	Level III	Level IV	Level V (Modern)
Secularity	Necessary ritual meaning		*(increasing secularity)*		Incidental ritual meaning
Bureaucracy	No formal organizations		*(increasing bureaucratization)*		Many formal organizations
Social Identity	Limited social contexts		*(increasing social setting options)*		Many social contexts
Social Distance	Limited competition variables		*(increasing social spheres)*		Many competition variables
Specialization	Limited sport options		*(increasing number of institutional components/ activities)*		Many sport options
Equipment	Simple		*(technological evolution)*		Complex
Ecological Meaning	Direct adaptive significance		*(increasing subtlety of culture-environment relationships)*		Ambiguous adaptive significance
Quantification	Little concern for numbers		*(increasing quantification)*		Record setting and breaking

1. *Secularity.* In the movement from level I through level V and up
to mid-twentieth century, sport has become increasingly secular.
Similar to Guttmann (1978:16-26), we see this as a major component
underlying sport change. Varying amounts of both religious and
profane elements affect sport at all levels of the evolutionary
process, but as populations become more complex and pluralistic,
sport activities become less ritualistic. Games like basketball and
football in the contemporary postindustrialized world reflect the
secularity of the social system that sustains them. Yet, they are not
completely devoid of religious meaning.

2. *Bureaucracy.* As Guttmann (1978:45) has noted, "primitive
societies are not characterized by bureaucratic organizations of any
kind." Thus, one would not expect the sport institutions in simple
society to be burdened down with the trappings of bureaucracy (e.g.,
team owners, leagues, captains, officials, boards). This is generally
true of the simplest nonstate societies, although with the increased
complexity of political organization, hierarchical arrangement of
institutional roles can occur even in prestate systems. In a chiefdom,
for example, the levels of rank society may manifest themselves in
sporting events (e.g., the Tikopian dart match) in a regularized
management pattern that can be viewed as an incipient if not actual
bureaucracy.

With the emergence of the state and true government,
bureaucracy is a feature of practically all institutions in social
systems. This obviously affects organized sport. Notice the Zulu
soccer situation and the authoritarianism characteristic of managerial
roles, reflecting in many ways the nature of traditional Zulu political
behavior. At the bureaucratic extreme, sport in the modern state is a
virtual potpourri of hierarchically arranged decision-making roles:
from players' unions, league associations, support groups, and owners,
to various governing boards. The complex and often contradictory or
competing roles of organizations such as the National Collegiate
Athletic Association (NCAA) and the Amateur Athletic Union (AAU)
illustrate the furthest reaches of sport bureaucracy evolution.

The evolution of sport, then, is characterized by an increasing
bureaucratization, from little or no formal organization to one of
elaborate complexity.

One correlate of the level of bureaucratic development in sport
is the complexity of rule structures. The more managers and boards,
the more rules that attach to particular sports. And, the more rules,
the more they become ends in themselves. Bureaucracies breed
commitment to procedure. In sport this means that adherence to
rules can become a primary objective in sport participation. It has
been observed in some societies (e.g., among the Mississippi
Choctaws) that rules and officiating are components of the game that
are tolerated. "Good" sport is that in which players are allowed to
play and officials intervene only when the most flagrant rule
violations occur (e.g., a player hits an opponent over the head with an

empty wine bottle). On the other hand, there are some situations in which the rules seem to become the reasons for the game. Consider the college basketball game in which fouls and rule violations determine the outcome of the contest. In the latter situation, the official becomes a principal actor in the sport drama.

3. *Social identity* As cultural systems become more complex in the evolutionary process, sport organizations likewise become more complex. As a result, the more highly developed the social system, the more likely that intrateam relationships will be extrakin or even impersonal. In other words, in prestate contexts, teams or other playing units are generally composed of persons related to one another. As has been noted among groups such as the Choctaws and Navajos, this affects style of play. On the other hand, in more modern pluralistic societies, teams are more likely to be composed of persons both unrelated and only casually acquainted with each other. The general trend appears to be from a primary to secondary group team orientation.

4. *Social distance* As spheres of social distance become more complex in the evolutionary process, so too does the nature of sport competition. Social distance is a measure of perceived relatedness between two groups or two individuals. In the simplest of social systems, such distance is limited to several categories or spheres. There is the closest sphere, the individual's immediate family; there is a larger sphere, the kin group; there are other nonkin who are members of one's society but not kin; and finally, there are all of those persons that do not fit into one's immediate social world, the "everyone else" category. In more complex societies, there are often myriad social distance spheres, many of which overlap. A lifelong resident of Baltimore may have hundreds of such spheres: family, friends, associations, church, work, neighborhood, and so on. He or she moves in and out of many of these spheres every day. In both cases, sport competition can be affected by intersphere relationships. Among the Mississippi Choctaws, the character of sport competition is tied directly to the social distance factor (see Fig. 9). When Choctaws play intracommunity ballgames (e.g., stickball, baseball, basketball, softball), the simple joy of the game overrides competition considerations. Everyone is more intent on having fun than winning. But, when Choctaw teams from two different communities compete against each other, winning is viewed as the principal objective of everyone involved, spectators and participants alike. On the other hand, when a Choctaw team competes against a non-Choctaw team (e.g., recreation league, high school games), the sense of competition is minimized once again; instead there is a premium on individual performance (i.e., "looking good").

Most athletes and sports fan know how the will-to-win can be tempered by the social setting. In everyone's high school experience, there was that cross-town or other community opponent, the "arch-rival." And in any competition with that rival, be it football or tiddlywinks, emotion ran high; so high that just the thought of losing was unbearable. Yet, there were other games with schools, far away or new to the schedule, that inspired so little enthusiasm that the cheerleaders had to throw tennis shoes at the fans to keep them from falling asleep. Why the difference? It is the social distance factor; the differential meanings attached to different types of relationships.

To reiterate, it is reasonable to assume that the greater the variety of social distance spheres the greater the range of sport competition possibilities in a society.

5. *Specialization* Sport evolution is characterized by an increasing specialization of rules, games, playing roles, social contexts, and meanings. In the simplest of societies, the number of activities is limited by ecological and demographic factors. The relative uniformity of the social system is reflected in playing roles; in such situations it is not unusual for everyone to compete at everything. However, in state systems, especially those of recent centuries, there is a tendency for athletes to specialize. Some wrestle, some box, some play football, and some play basketball. Although it is still possible for an American teenager to be a three-letter athlete in some high schools, this is rare, and even a three-letter career does not span the total range of sport possibilities in the high school. As Guttmann (1978:36) has noted, some specialization occurs in the most primitive of sport institutions, but modern sport is specialized to the point that the difference is almost qualitative. Consider the specializations that occur within sport, the place-kicker on a National Football League team, for example. He is an athlete, but one whose role is so specialized that all he does is run out on the field several times during each of sixteen games in the season and kick the ball from under the hand of a holder. When a blocked kick or fumbled snap from center forces him to run with the ball or tackle an opponent, he must move outside that role. The results generally demonstrate that he is of professional quality only as long as he sticks to his specialization. The "football" players among the Djinghali of aboriginal Australia know nothing of such specialization.

6. *Equipment* With the evolution of human culture, technology becomes more sophisticated and concomitantly the sport equipment more elaborate. This is a facet of the process that perhaps does not need mentioning. The differences between an inflated reindeer bladder and an official NBA basketball; between a grassy dart pitch in Tikopia and a bowling alley in a St. Louis suburb; between a Navajo hoop-and-pole and Jack Nicklaus' bag full of golf clubs; and between counting sticks and an electronic scoreboard are obvious. Nevertheless, the fact that technology affects sport should still be underscored.

7. *Ecological Meaning* The ethnographic literature on sport in society suggests that in simple society the adaptive significance of particular sport activities is more directly evident than in complex state societies. For example, the adaptive functions of sport among

the Australian aborigines (see Salter, 1974:5) are more obvious than those of modern sport. A spear-throwing contest in a society where the food supply is a function of the hunter's ability to spear wild game serves an immediately evident adaptive purpose. The link between play and economy is clear. But what can one say about the adaptive features of modern volleyball? Such functions exist, but they are less direct and more diffuse. Thus, it is suggested that the ecological meaning of sport becomes less immediately evident as the institution becomes more complex.

8.   *Quantification* Quantification is basic to record-keeping and a fundamental factor in Guttmann's (1978:47-51) evolution scheme. As he admits, counting and quantification are factors in some of the simplest activities and in nonstate sport activities (Guttmann, 1978:47). Nevertheless, with the development of notational and writing systems, the ability of human beings to make permanent records of their sport statistics changes the nature of sport quantification. With the additional invention of more sophisticated measuring devices (e.g., clocks) the range of quantification possibilities increases. As a result, "the minute discriminations between the batting average of the .308 hitter and .307 hitter" have become significant considerations in the world of modern sport (Guttmann, 1978:55). The East African cattle nomads tossing bean-filled bull scrota through a woven reed hoop are oblivious to such distinctions; today's outcome may be tomorrow's history, but the actual numbers, like the makeshift target, will be abandoned, lost, and quickly forgotten.

SUMMARY

Sport has evolved beyond the level of band society. The supraband levels, those of chiefdom, primitive state, and archaic civilization, have molded sport institutions commensurate with the basic designs of their more complex cultures.

Level III, the chiefdom, is characterized by the emergence of rank systems and inherited leadership roles. And, consistent with the greater complexity of its cultural framework, chiefdom-level sport is more elaborate than band sport. This is illustrated by descriptions of sport activities among the Choctaws, Maori, Samoans, and Tikopians. The dart game, one of the most widespread of South Pacific sports, is discussed in detail. It is suggested that its social functions are indicative of the general function of sport in chiefdom level societies.

Level IV, the primitive state, is a transitional phase with few examples in the ethnographic literature. The Zulu and Ashanti states of Africa are two of the primitive states described by Service (1963). These level IV systems are marked by territorial law, social class, and the monopolization of force by the state itself. In both the Zulu and Ashanti cases, statehood emerged as a result of consolidation in the face of nineteenth-century British imperialism. The Mayan state is cited as an example of a prehistoric primitive state.

Descriptions of sport behavior at the primitive state level are limited, but sufficient to support the thesis that there is a continuity between cultural context and sport. For example, the sport activities of the primitive state manifest patterns of management and authority typical of that level, as was noted in Zulu football. Among the Mayans, the realities of social stratification and religion are made obvious in the rubber ballgame.

Level V archaic civilization is marked by the appearance of the city and all of the novelty that entails: occupational specialization, true government, large-scale architecture, elaborate military technology, and perhaps most importantly, writing. The sport of level V groups is illustrated in Chapter Four. More elaborate equipment, a greater tendency toward class-defined sport, large-scale sport spectacles, and the specialization of sport roles are some of the major distinguishing characteristics of the sport institution in primary urban civilization. The Sumerians, the early Egyptians, and the Aztecs, are just some of the groups engaging in sport typical of this stage of cultural evolution.

Reiterating the theoretical assumptions underlying the chapter, it is concluded that sport can be viewed as evolving from simple to complex, in accordance with the development of human culture in general and along a series of continua or axes. The eight most obvious of these axes include secularity, bureaucracy, social identity, social distance, specialization, equipment, ecological meaning, and quantification.

Exercises

Discussion questions:

1. Assuming that you have seen the film *Trobriand Cricket* (Leach, 1976) by now, what typical chiefdom (level III) cultural characteristics are manifested in the game and the activities surrounding the game? (Note: The Trobriand system is a classic example of chiefdom-level culture.)
2. What impact does inherited leadership in a society have on its sport? Is this necessarily the case? In what ways does sport tend to ease the informality of normal respect relationships? Cite examples in your own society.
3. In what general ways do supraband sports prepare participants for waging war? What sport activities in modern America serve similar functions? Are these functions obvious (i.e., manifest) to the participant?
4. Assume that the Tikopian-Maori-Samoan dart match were to be introduced into American society. What adjustments to the sport do you predict would be made in the process of adaptation?

5. On the basis of the discussion provided in this chapter, compare the enthusiasm for sport displayed in contemporary Ghana and that evident in America. What are the differences? Assuming there are differences, what are the reasons for those differences?

6. Social class as a factor in sport has been manifested in American society in many ways. Perhaps the most obvious difference, however, has been in the types of games played at the several socioeconomic levels of the society. For example, tennis and golf have tended to be more "upper class," while bowling and professional wrestling are associated with the other end of the social spectrum. Still, social class can be manifested within as well as between sports. In other words, two groups can play the same game but play it in different ways--ways that reflect social class values. Can you think of situations in American sport where social differences are reflected in style of play? What does this mean about social consciousness in this country? How is this similar to the situation in the sport institutions of other supraband societies?

Special projects:

1. Analyze the sports section of a large daily newspaper, looking for evidence of the several characteristics of modern sport (i.e., secularity, bureaucracy, social identity, social distance, specialization, equipment, ecological meaning, and quantification). Compare the results with the same characteristics as these are seen in band society (levels I and II) sport.

2. Select a type of sport (e.g., wrestling) that is widespread and common to many cultural settings. Using your imagination where data are not available, construct an evolutionary model of that sport at each of those levels.

Women's collegiate basketball

7 The Anthropology of Sport: Applications

The description and analysis of culture change is the central task of applied cultural anthropology. Change is a basic premise of human existence in the individual and in the group. That a culture and its many features, including sports, are constantly being modified is inevitable, whether we are talking about the Trobriand Island villagers' adaptation of British cricket or about the remarkable invention and development of basketball in the United States. A review of any people's history, without exception, reveals change. Unfortunately, continual observation and analysis of all the subtle--and not so subtle--changes of a society is unrealistic, so anthropologists have settled for intermittent participant observation. This can be on site "fieldwork" with its descriptive written, graphic, and film record, called "ethnography," or its analytic interpretation called "ethnology," which extracts general guiding principles and their application in a society.

Since human behavior is active, directional, and purposeful, the observational analysis which summarizes such past sequences (hindsight) can identify logical pathways. However, when hindsight and "current-sight" are used to predict future behavior, only broad interpretations can be made. A major reason is that within and between societies humans have the capacity to direct and redirect, accelerate and/or decelerate change, but it will occur unceasingly, variantly, and for the most part--unpredictably. So with this caveat in mind, this chapter addresses the processes of change which can be enacted in society and reflected in the sport context, processes such as societal maintenance, enculturation, conflict management, program development, and cross-cultural relations. Within this operational approach, generalities can be applied to specific sport settings, which may in turn facilitate understanding of change and the human element in that process. In other words, theory is practice generalized, and practice is applied theory.

Inherent in this discussion is the assertion that anthropology can be an applied science, such as medical, educational, developmental, or legal anthropology, to name a few. Now we propose to add sport anthropology to that list.

Applied sport anthropology addresses the primary change issues, including societal maintenance, enculturation, and acculturation. The first topic refers to an inherent balancing or equilibrial process of a society, the manuvering for societal consistency, constancy, and existence. However, maintenance is not static, but a dynamic and bounded flux in which persistent adjustments are being made. A change in culture may be identified as discovery, invention, or transmission of something new or perceived as new by a certain segment in a society. For example, the newborn's introduction to and consequent development in relationships, behavior and beliefs of its parents' culture, is called enculturation or socialization. Paralleling enculturation is acculturation, introducing into a society's patterns those from another society. Both enculturation and acculturation introduce something different or variant, the former to new group members and the latter to members of another cultural group.

The innovative forces underlying culture change include discovery and invention. Discovery is the perception of the existence of something which has existed before but has not previously been observed. Invention is considered a change or adjustment in objects, beliefs, or practices so that a new kind emerges--and it may be unique combinations of previously known parts or processes. Every deliberate and designed change in human activity is an invention, whether in material or nonmaterial culture, although conditions for pure discovery are opportunity, observation, and the combined ability to appreciate and imagine. For example, it is surmised that the discovery of the cohesive property for heated latex from its natural liquid state after being scorched in a fire led to the shaping of the first rubber ball by South American Indians. The native(s) who observed and appreciated the rubber plant sap's unique property deliberately manipulated the material by throwing, kicking, or maybe pulling. The actual moment is not recorded, but we do know that the South Americans were the first peoples of the world to play games with a rubber ball (Stern, 1949). Curiosity and need are often factors in both discovery and invention. The invention of the game of basketball by James Naismith in 1891 grew out of a college class assignment which was to "invent" a game that could be played safely by middle-aged members of the Springfield, Massachusetts Y.M.C.A. Naismith deliberately designed a ballgame within the specifications of the indoor gymnasium for the aging participants with limited energy levels and as an activity to be used during the winter. History proved he should have received a grade of "A" for his efforts. By the way, the first modification of Naismith's original game was the replacement of the football used during the first week by a more predictable soccer ball. It was several years before this type of ball was replaced by a manufactured basketball. The intriguing history of the game of basketball reveals a development based on felt need--Naismith's week-end assignment!

In examining the development of modern sports, some scholars contend that there is an historic intermediate step or transition between kinetic play/games and sport called the sporting phenomenon. Ibrahim (1975:40-41) suggests two basic differences between sporting and sport activities. The first concerns the nature of the act. He thinks that a sporting activity is composed of a number of acts, the meanings of which are to a great extent detached from the activity and are symbolically related to another social order, thus having a communally motivated and socially imperative reason for striving for excellence. For example, an esteemed athlete in some primitive societies usually excels in sporting events that pertain to hunting and war activities, such as running after an animal and throwing the spear. In feudal European society, excellence in sporting events such as horsemanship, fencing, and jousting was used by men to reach a certain preferred status in the political order, such as squire or even knight. Participating in the pageantry of the Tournament or Lists celebrated this status.

Ibrahim's second difference involves minimal role differentiation between and among players and spectators in sporting activities. In traditional tribal societies the whole population is actively involved in the production of a community-wide celebration, festival, and ritual, of which a sporting event is a part. To a great extent an individual's role behavior is legitimized as part of the general identity attributed to gender, age, and kinship. (See examples given in societal maintenance later in this chapter.) Thus, assignments are made by ascription, such as belonging to a certain social status or family membership, rather than by personal merit or recognized competency. Even today, ascription helps define sports opportunities and conditions under which these opportunities are enacted (Guttmann, 1978:26-36).

In the modern sense, societal approval is needed for sport to evolve from a general activity of the total community endeavor to a separate category of leisure distinct from work. For such approval, conditions or antecedents are necessary: (1) an endorsement of the activity is shown in some fashion by the dominant central authority (i.e., sports needs to be accepted and approved by one or more leading political, social, educational, or religious structures in the society), (2) such endorsement allows the activity to emerge as a form of leisure activity (e.g. the condemnation of the early American colonists' ballplaying by the leaders of the Puritan colony in Massachusetts prevented the endorsement of ballplaying as a proper activity, while the opposite was true in the Virginia colony), (3) the permeation of the activity to the level "below" that of the leisure, the privileged, or upper class (e.g. the democratization of tennis participation occurred in the United States in the second two-thirds of the twentieth century; previously, tennis was generally a private social club activity for members only, and court tennis is still an elite sport [Nickerson, 1982]), and (4) the establishment of a sport order which necessitates crystallization of roles and statuses (e.g., today sports governing organizations determine "official" rules of a sport [Ibrahim, 1975:40]). When the preceding four conditions are met, the sporting activity is recognized as significant in society through its own autonomous subsystem on one hand and through its support of other societal structures on the other.

SPORT IN CULTURE CHANGE

Sport contributes to culture change in many ways. One way is through expressive behavior which reinforces social norms in a process called social maintenance. Another method, referred to here as enculturaton, is by means of the integration of new persons into the ways or customs of society. A third type of sport change is acculturation, the borrowing of cultural traits or complexes between members of different societies.

Societal Maintenance

Maintenance can be considered the condition of continuity and consistency of a culture. This does not mean unchanging stability, but the dynamic flow of relationships within the limitations of existence (Cheska, 1979:227).

The issue of societal maintenance has been hotly debated in anthropological circles over the last century. One side of the issue contends that s society's prime reason for existence is to survive by retaining its basic structural integrity through adjustive interrelationships of the structure's parts. This is sometimes referred to as a static model of culture. Each society is considered a functionally interrelated system, and the purpose of all behavior is to maintain the society's social structure (see Cheska, 1978a:17-35). The total network of social relationships is directed toward maintaining consistency or equilibrium, developing institutions for reinforcement of the structure and necessary social roles (see Radcliffe-Brown, 1952). However, the cultural traits involved in maintaining the system must also satisfy basic and/or derived needs of the individuals in a society (see Malinowski, 1939). Of course, the conflict between the individual and societal needs is a major point of contention. Which one proves to be more important is the grist of the dynamic balance between the individual needs and the societal structure. We recognize that the communal good has been and still is a viable belief in many societies, so that in action the ultimate welfare of the individual is closely tied with that of the society.

The other side of the issue holds that a society's prime reason for existence or survival is not by maintenance of a structure, but by adaptation of that structure through and toward change. This is sometimes referred to as a dynamic model of culture. Its essential premise is the continual interaction and flow of existence. The joining of human life to the nonmaterial and material environment surrounding man is assured by adaptation to change. The themes of cultural materialism (see Harris, 1979) and sociobiology (see Wilson, 1980; Lumsden and Wilson, 1981; Wilson and Lumsden, 1983), highlight other evolutionary and environmental selective processes through which man attempts to adapt to external or imposed change by material, neural-psychological, and cultural modification. In other words, change, as variation, deviation, or transformation is inevitable; thus the agenda of society is always amended. In the drama of a society, its past is prologue; its present is being written; its future is creative.

Sport exists in a more than chance relationship with other social processes iden.ified with cultural maintenance. As earlier indicated, there has been a progression from informal play and games as pastimes to what Ibrahim (1975:40-41) calls sporting behavior in preliterate societies, and then to the sport behavior prevalent in modern societies. Sport activities and functions become increasingly complex. However, Hans Damm (1970:65) argues not necessarily for increased complexity, but for concurrent presence of ritual (cultic) games and sportive activities. He claims that in primitive societies sportive (sporting) activities existed parallel to ritual games and were indeed very much like them. He argued that the exotic people knew and celebrated sportive physical activities in the best recreative meaning of the word, while similar games during cultic events were derived from magic (religious) motives.

Damm related Kauffman's (1941) account of the Thadou-Kuki, the Assam people of northeastern India, among whom wrestling was a pure and highly regarded sport of youth. This was especially so during weddings, where the male kin of the groom and those of the bride engaged in a big wrestling match. Rewards were not distributed; the contest was only for joy and honor. He who won during seven weddings received an honorary degree (Kauffman, 1941). Each of Ibrahim's antecedents for the existence of sport were fulfilled here, yet the traditional wrestling contests continued without substantial change over centuries. The custom provided a vehicle of kinship unity as well as having faint vestiges of past bride capturing by show of strength, a method of obtaining wives in preliterate tribes. It also showed that sportive activities not necessarily related to religious practice did exist in preliterate tribal societies. In such groups, sport became an activity in which physical competition and the individual's will to excel overrode practical and/or religious significance. Thus, for individuals in tribal society, the sporting event provided access to and legitimization within the larger, dominant social system without requiring the wholesale rejection of tradition (Blanchard, 1974).

Gunther Lüschen (1970:96) contends that sport helps in pattern maintenance, integration, adaptation, and goal attainment of a culture:

> On the level of primitive cultures, sport's function is universal, often religious, collectively oriented, and in the training of skills, representative and related to adult and warfare skills; while modern sport's functions may be called specific for pattern maintenance and integration, is individual-oriented, and nonrepresentative in the training of skills.

The following accounts of two similar sports events highlight the above characteristics. The running race of the Tewa (Pueblo) Indian farmers of the southwestern United States is an example of sport being used to reorder community groupings during times of potential conflict, thus preventing different factions from solidifying. The nineteenth-century ceremonial kick race of the Tewas was held at the summer solstice to "give the sun strength" for the start of its journey to its winter home (Ortiz, 1969:108-10). June 21 and December 22 were the two times a year when the sun was at its greatest distance from the celestial equator. For the contest, runners, who as a team completed a two-mile cross-country run while kicking a two to three inch wooden cylinder before them, were chosen from the "winter" and "summer" moieties. If the "summer" team won, there would be a long and productive summer; if the "winter" team won, there would be a long, hard winter. These divisions for the kick race represented social groupings different from which the shinny teams were chosen for the spring planting ritual ballgame. The crossing and overlapping of moieties in team memberships and the total village realignment for these events helped to cancel or override divisive influences in the Tewa dual social organization structure (Ortiz, 1969:111). Thus, the total Tewa population collectively addressed an issue of universal importance: their food supply, which was directly tied to the length of the growing season. For the total tribal good, the overriding need for the summer team's success was to overcome the winter team's desire to win. This was clearly understood by both sides. The contest was one of "quality" rather than "quantity" performance, because the preferred outcome was already known. The principle of societal continuity was symbolically enacted in the kick race.

In the 1980 pan-Pueblo running race commemorating the three-hundredth year of the Pueblo Revolt of 1680 against the Spaniards, the selection procedures were different from the above

described ceremonial Tewa kick race. The runners were self-selected
and they prepared for the event individually, if at all. Running was
not considered essential to their livelihood and was peripheral to their
survival. By participating, each represented his village, but the
villages prepared little for the event or for "their" team's
participation. However, during the event its purpose gradually
became clear as the runners of the six-day race passed through each
Pueblo village--to maintain the overarching concept of Pueblo
identity (Nabokov, 1981). Thus, the total tribal good was indeed
served through another "ritual" race, one in which the quality was not
paramount, but the fact of participation was significant to the
individual and later to the village. This situation provides the
appealing proposition that sport event participation by both
performers and spectators can stimulate cultural maintenance. An
additional observation is that in the midst of other changes--one only
needs to mention the major changes of the North American Indian
tribes between the mid-1800s and the late 1900s--sport can be used to
preserve tradition. In this case the revival of an ancient foot race
served to rekindle the meaning of tribal identity. The character of a
society can alter measurably, but the perception of continuance must
be present. We shall see in considering enculturation that this
perception helps explain much of the behavior attributed to that
process.

Enculturation

Enculturation is the way in which a society integrates its
members and the process by which individuals adapt to and assimilate
the values of their society. Thus the human being learns to fulfill the
functions of humanhood through position, such as status, role,
responsibility, and privilege; production (creation) and consumption of
products, people, knowledge, and ideas; structure, such as economic,
social, political, religious and family organization; belief systems,
such as philosophy, values, environmental adaptation, and
cosmological harmony; and aesthetics, such as art, drama, dance,
games and sport, literature, and music.

The individual and society are for the most part in bipolar
tension. The enculturation process, according to Goodman (1967), is
no more a matter of tribalism than it is of individualism. A child
learning the culture of his or her society conforms in response to
more or less insistent and forceful pressures, but also resists, evades,
selects and experiments. She or he becomes a member of society, but
the process is a creative becoming (Goodman, 1976).

Within this malleable view of human behavior, play assists as (1)
preparation, (2) remediation, and (3) innovation (potentiation).
Between and within societies, the relative importance of these
dynamic processes vary over time; therefore, no single one can be
declared the "right way" to enculturate or educate new members into
any society. Within each society and its subsystems are pools of

allowable normative behavior. These are bordered by limitations, such as mores, authoritative edicts, sanctions, and laws, which "fence in" and define for the novices the acceptable range of preparative and innovative behavior. Remediative behavior consists of error adjustment by individuals or groups as a result of negative cultural feedback.

Preparation

Inherent in enculturation is the principle of learning by formal and informal modeling and imitation. From birth--and even during the mother's pregnancy--the human is bombarded with information about the behavior of others in that society. Cultural transmission is literally at the fingertips, for to a great extent the older persons point the way to the younger.

> Playthings, usually miniature copies of familiar things, animals, people, play a very important role in a child's world. These playthings are made by adults and represent adult ideas, tastes and values. Whether consciously or unconsciously, the objects a parent gives a child are indicative of the way the adult perceives of the world, and are instrumental in developing the child's societal awareness (Zibro, 1970:6-7).

A gift of a calculator by an American father or a hand-carved *wari* board game by a African Ashanti father both represent adult values of computation. Further, a society's perception of preferred adult models is transmitted to its young.

> Every society must sort its children according to the traits it values .... Ancient Sparta needed warriors, Athens needed a sense of the hero, the ancient Hebrews needed knowledge of the Testament, nineteenth-century Americans needed managers and technicians (Kagan, 1973:41-42).

Thus, within major child-training methods, society tends to negotiate with its novices the basic cognitive modes of that society. The relationship between the individual and society seems to be reinforced by such play theories as Roberts and Sutton-Smith's (1962) "conflict enculturation," Piaget's (1962) "cognitive development," and George Mead's (1934) "social role."

Using child training data collected in 111 societies by Barry, Bacon, and Child (1957), Roberts and Sutton-Smith (1962) compared the relative severity and degree of anxiety associated with particular child-training values, (e.g., responsibility, obedience, self-reliance, achievement, nurturance, and independence) with kinds of games in which children of these societies participated. They noted that games of physical skill were played extensively in societies rewarding achievement and in societies in which children showed anxiety about nonperformance of achievement. Games of chance were associated with societies that stressed responsibility (i.e., routine chores which allow little scope for personal initiative or autonomy); and games of strategy were associated with societies that stressed obedience to commands and management by others. They concluded that games are microcosmic structures of the culture to which the individual in conflict is attracted because games model the emotional and cognitive aspects of his or her conflict that are unavailable to that individual in full-scale cultural participation. Basically, games are cognitive operations involved in competitive success; the child learns in simple direct form how to show skill, take chances, and deceive. Thus, through this buffered learning, the child makes progress toward adult behavior. This explanation became known as the conflict enculturation theory (Roberts and Sutton-Smith, 1962; Sutton-Smith, 1973).

Jean Piaget's "cognitive development" theory (1962) is popular among Euro-American educationalists. Piaget coupled children's age/stage of intellectual development with three sequential game stages. In the first stage (zero to two years), the child engages in sensory-motor practice play which is the imitative exercise of functions or activities simply for the intrinsic pleasure that exercise gives; such as the joy of repeatedly kicking the legs. In the second stage (two to seven years), the child engages in symbolic games in which absent objects are mentally recalled and manipulated to represent something else. These objects are organized into action sequences by using concrete props; for instance, pretending that the pencil is a gymnast and acting out a scenario with it. In this second stage both action and objects are combined and symbolically transposed. In the third stage (seven to eleven years), the child learns the rules of social relationships by playing games-with-rules or constructive games in which procedures and regulations are imposed by agreement and violation carries sanction. Most of us have been youngsters negotiating a game of Tag, a pick-up game of basketball, or even Four Square (see Hughes, 1983). Piaget concludes,

> Just as the symbol replaced mere practice as soon as thought makes its appearance, so the rule replaces the symbol and integrates practice as soon as certain social relationships are formed, and the question is to discover these relationships (1962:142).

In the adult stage, according to Piaget (1962:142), although examples of practice games (e.g., playing with one's wireless set) and symbolic games (e.g. telling oneself a story) are rare, games with rules remain and even develop throughout life (e.g. sports, cards, chess). These are the ludic activities of the socialized being. In games with rules there is subtle equilibrium between assimilation to the ego (i.e., bending the reality of the world to one's own mentalschema) and accommodation to the demands of social reciprocity(i.e., bending one's own mental schema to fit the reality of the world). He concludes:

> There is still sensory-motor or intellectual satisfaction, and there is also the chance of individual victory over others, but these satisfactions are as it were made "legitimate" by the rules of the game, through which competition is controlled by a collective discipline, with a code of honour and fair play (Piaget, 1962:168).

Piaget has been criticized because he utilizes only a southern European child population to test his theory, therefore, cross-cultural consistency is doubtful. However, a major contribution of Piaget to our understanding of enculturation is the recognition that intellectual development unfolds in an orderly sequence which appears to be universal. For example, some societies will accelerate and stress practice games to a higher success level than others. The accurate throwing of a projectile would be very important in a hunting society and of less value in an industrialized society. The skill training would probably start earlier and continue through adulthood. The proportional weighting of Piaget's cognitive components would vary in timing, intensity, and quality between societies, but they would all be present.

Sociologist George Mead (1934) proposes that the human personality develops only in a social context. Using a baseball team analogy, he notes how the child, through social role rehearsal, tries on various positions. By imitation, copying, matching, and role-taking, the individual presents himself as he thinks others present themselves, thus reflecting consciousness of self as part of the social group to which one belongs. This part of the self as a public personality is the social self of "me," whose attitudes, meanings, pressures, and values are revealed and displayed for others' consumption. The other part is the unrevealed "private self" or "I" made up of impulse, freedom, creativity, and subjectivity (Pfuetze, 1954:84-96). Self and society are thus mutually conditioned and exist only in and through each other.

Remediation

Remediation is the return or change from an unnatural to a natural condition. Synonyms are correction, restoration, rehabilitation, or reestablishment, each implying that something has gone amiss and a return to the former or previous condition is desirable. Assuming that the condition in which the person finds himself or herself is seen as harmful, then techniques of recovery must be called upon to change the present behavior or situation. Remediation necessitates change in action and attitude; one vehicle to achieve this is play or games.

Freud (1922) considers play a form of catharsis that allows the individual to overcome fear by seeking more control over threatening experiences and to eventually satisfy the basic drive for pleasure. He contends that the supremacy of the pleasure principle in the psychic life of the human is achieved by keeping the quantity of disruptive excitement as low as possible or at least constant. An attempt at repression of the source of pain as well as simulated practice of the painful situation enables the individual to reduce anxiety to a manageable level. In this process play and games provide a relatively safe context for manipulative practice of the various elements in the threatening situation. Active involvement changes the person from a passive recipient or reactor in the situation to an active agent or actor. He or she actually plays out the situation as the individual wants it to be, thus learning how to handle the various parts, including those that cause stress and/or pain. By positive acts of the player, reducing negative impact, and readjusting the stress level of the situation, the player turns a sense of failure into a sense of mastery.

Piaget (1962) defines "compensatory combinations" of behavior in which the individual corrects reality rather than reproduces it. This is associated with neutralizing a fear through play or doing in play what one would not dare do in reality; thus, compensation becomes cathartic. The "liquidation of combinations" allows one to face a difficult or unpleasant situation by either substituting or reliving it through symbolism. The stress is reduced to a manageable level by reconstituting the instance in play. Piaget's young daughter was impressed by the sight of a dead duck which had been plucked and put on the kitchen table. The next day Piaget found his daughter lying motionless on the sofa in his study, her arms pressed against her body and her legs bent. "What are you doing? Have you a pain? Are you ill?" queried the father, to which the answer came, "No, I'm a dead duck" (Piaget, 1962:133).

A major criticism of repression, simulated practice, or substitution is that the player may be retreating to a fantasy of wish fulfillment in feeling mastery over a minimized or substitute situation. When the original situation must be faced, the individual can only partially cope with reality. In remediation, the appropriate balance between ego assimilation and reality accommodation must be negotiated.

Psychoanalyst Erik Erikson (1963) argues that the development of a person's ego is the synthesis of the body and social process with the self. Play contributes in sequential stages to this ego-systhesis. The three stages in which this occurs are termed *autosphere, microsphere,* and *macrosphere.*

Autosphere or autocosmic play begins and centers in the child's own body. The autocosmic play includes exploration by repetition of sensual perceptions, kinesthetic sensations, vocalizations, etc. Getting accustomed to one's own bodily capabilities and developing psychomotor skills is primary to the progression. The joy of actual movement, manipulation, and function includes the delight of "being the cause" of something happening, such as dropping a spoon to thefloor from a highchair or kicking a ball away from oneself to watch it roll (Buhler, 1928).

Microsphere or microcosmic play involves play with people or things. The microsphere may seduce the child into unguarded expression of dangerous themes and attitudes which arouse anxiety and lead to sudden play disruption. The child finds that the thing-world has its own laws, and that it may resist manipulation and reconstruction or may simply break to pieces. It may belong to someone else, be subject to parental confiscation, or be taken away by a superior. The small world of manageable toys is the haven which the child establishes and returns to when bruised, for an overhaul of his or her ego. The successful mastering of toy things gives pleasure to the child.

Macrosphere or macrocosmic play involves sharing the world with other persons. At first the child treats other things to be inspected, manipulated, and forced to be used. Learning what is restricted to fantasy or autocosmic play, what content can be repeated in the microcosmic world of toys and things, and what content can be shared with and forced upon others is the essence of macrocosmic play.

In the autosphere, play is similar to Piaget's practice play in which sensory-motor skills are discovered, repeated, and extended as the child expands its physical world. Within the microsphere, compensatory and liquidating behavior is remedial through substituting and/or eliminating unpleasant involvement with other persons and things. Retreating from pain and unpleasantness and regrouping one's ego help the child to overcome the situation. The macrosphere, similar to Piaget's constructive games stage, is truly the interactive, negotiating stage where there is reciprocal adjustment to others without undue sacrifice of one's ego.

Remediation is also implemented through reversing access routes to success, routes not necessarily available under normal conditions (Sutton-Smith, 1975; Sutton-Smith and Roberts, 1981). Both children and adults who are normally not permitted success in certain situations are allowed such luxury. The handicap is an example used in sports; one opponent or team who is known to be better than the other is assessed penalities prior to competition. In golf, the better player may have additional strokes or a handicap added to his or her score card; this reversal gives the poorer golfer an increased chance for success.

Eifermann (1973) has identified this process as evoking a metarule, one of four kinds of regulations or game rules. The metarule enforces a rule drawn from an available frozen or spare repertoire which can be called upon by consensus to help equate players' abilities. In use, it modifies or even cancels any of the other rule categories: (1) requirements which dictate action a player will take and how it will be executed; (2) prohibitions which disallow certain actions that if committed carry penalities; and (3) <u>rules of</u> <u>permission</u>, which allow various choices between action and nonaction. In general the metarules raise or lower the level of the game challenge, thus allowing for a greater range of participation. The less skilled and/or younger players can join with the more skilled and/or older players. For example, in a softball game, the poorer batters may be allowed four strikes instead of the usual three, thus setting aside a rule requirement by a metarule modification. This subtle device is a powerful enculturation tool.

Innovative Potentiation

Potentiation is based on experiental modification of action that results in new combinations. It is sometimes called creativity or protostructure. This may be accomplished by readjusting the importance of the means and the ends of action (Miller, 1973). An acitivity can be changed in part by elaboration, exaggeration, deletion, reordering, reversal, and differing temporal and/or spatial sequences of repetition which Miller (1973) calls "galumphing" or play. Millar (1968) proposes that this kind of exploratory play or repeated playful manipulation of familiar objects and/or humans may seem unnecessary, but it provides opportunities to code, classify, and assimilate information; master skills; and reduce or arouse excitement.

Berlyne (1960) cites two types of exploration, specific and diversive. Their difference lies in the person's motivation for dealing with objects and settings. Specific exploration examines the characteristics of a stimulus, looking for useful information about its functions. Diversive exploration is aimed at stimulation providing variety, regardless of content (Berlyne, 1971), and can be described as activity directed toward generating new and different sources of stimulation (Barnett, 1976). Diversive exploration in this context is defined as play, but is usually preceded by specific exploration. In other words, useful skills resulting from specific information seeking are basic to immediate necessary response. "Playing," on the other hand, generates additional and varied behaviors which increase flexibility and novel responses. Hutt (1966:79) explains that specific exploration seeks to answer the question "What does this object do?" while diverse exploraton or play seeks an answer to the question "What can I do with this object?" It may be that when mastery is achieved by familiarity, the object no longer possesses uncertainty, so the "player" then creates his or her own controlled uncertainty through varying, creative behavior toward the object or other person.

On the surface such playful flexibility seems minimized in formalized competitive sports. However, the same principle of orchestration is utilized. Innovative behavior in sports is founded in performer competency; the ability to vary and elaborate actions as sources of stimulation are in delicate balance with goal-oriented behavior. The expressive behavior of the highly skilled player beyond base-line performance is his or her signature or style.

Csikszentmihalyi's (1975) "flow" theory (i.e., performer's competence equal to the task's environmental requirements as a state of euphoric equilibrium) falls short of explaining the performer who goes beyond the task requirements. The authors of this text feel that this performer on another level of innovation may "play" with task fulfillment by creating obstacles to his or her own achievement. An example is goal shooting in basketball. A skilled player precedes a dunk, the two-handed downward thrust of the basketball into the hoop, with self-imposed bodily gyrations during the jump, making the shot an inordinately difficult execution. One reason that discriminating spectators, who have perhaps participated in the sport themselves, so thoroughly enjoy the dunk is that they recognize the player's challenge of personal fulfillment. But when the performer substitutes theatrics of impression management of the audience, then play has vanished and with it the mutual recognition of playing by both the individual and the observers.

In some sense, innovation appears to be a potent integrative mechanism. Inversion of the ordinary, by its very existence and termination, accentuates the previous normal structure. In another sense, the variability or flexibility in innovation which offers new ways of doing things may be of equal cultural significance. It has been suggested by Sutton-Smith (1972:20):

> If play is the learning of variability...then perhaps all forms of inversion involve experimentation with variable repertoires. All involve the development of flexible competencies in role taking and in the development of variable repertoires with respect to these roles.... In this view the anti-structural phenomena (reversal in games of order/disorder) not only make the system tolerable as it exists, they keep its members in a more flexible state with respect to that system, and therefore, with respect to possible change. Each system has different structural and antistructural functions. The normative structure represents the working equilibrium, the antistructure represents the latent system of potential alternatives from which novelty will arise when contingencies in the normative system require it.... We might more correctly call this second system the protostructural system because it is the precursor of innovative normative forms. It is the source of a new culture.

It would appear that games and sports may serve dual functions in innovation. On one side they provide acceptable vehicles for experimenting with a variety of behaviors in order to enhance the normative patterns of life; while on the other side, through novel alternative patterning, they may provide a protostructure for a new culture.

In summary, Roberts and Sutton-Smith's conflict enculturaton theory, Piaget's cognitive development theory, and Mead's social role theory all offer explanations of preparation techniques used by novices and other members of a society. Freud's catharsis theory, Erikson's ego-synthesis theory, and Sutton-Smith's reversal hypotheses all help explain the role remediation plays in assisting the novice to adapt to society's expectations. Miller's "galumphing" observation, Millar's and Hutt's diversive exploration theses, and Sutton-Smith's potentiation hypothesis help clarify the role of innovation in enculturation. Without innovation in each generation there would be cultural stagnation, robbing humans of their creative uniqueness among the animals of the world.

Thus, through sport behavior, the continuance of a society can be served by the enculturaton of the new members into acceptable ways of behaving, by providing remediative, adaptive mechanisms to mollify the conflict between the individual's anxiety and societal demands, and by providing new combinations of behavior as possible prototypes for the future.

Acculturation

Acculturation parallels enculturaton. However, acculturation is considered the process by which culture is transmitted through contact between groups with different cultures, while enculturation involves the internal transmission of a single culture to its newly born members. Simply put, when two cultures meet and exercise influence over one another, acculturation occurs.

In summarizing anthropological studies of acculturation, Ogawa (1978:10) points out three approaches:

> They focus: (1) on the situation under which acculturation takes place--for example, whether it is voluntary or imposed, and the degree of social and political inequality between the two groups concerned; (2) on the process of selection, integration and acceptance; and (3) on subjective experience of people whose culture is undergiong change, or discrepancy between the objective social order and people's subjective feeling.

Focusing on situation or context, Redfield, Linton, and Herskovits (1936:149-50) say that acculturation comes about through firsthand contact, as in colonization, commerce, evangelical endeavors, migration, militarism, and travel. For example, eighteenth-century British administrators introduced several games to the Indian princes with whom they negotiated trade agreements, among them cricket and badminton. In turn, the Indians exposed the British to polo and the popular board game of pachisi. Through this voluntary exchange, these activities proved over time to be extremely popular in their adoptive lands. Another such situation is exemplified by missionaries who spend extended periods of time in foreign cultures and often impose their own game patterns on the natives. In the South Pacific islands of Tonga, Hide and Seek or *Langtoi,* Cat and Mouse of *Pani,* Drop the Handkerchief or *Putini moe Pulini,* and Rachel and Jacob or *Ngali ngali 'a toke,* still persist from their introduction by nineteenth-century European and American missionaries (Miller, 1983). These ambassadors of Western Christianity also discouraged adult Tongan women from active sports and dance participation. Bulky, full-length dresses suitable to northern climes were substituted for the more revealing yet functional clothing of tradition. Thus, even in the 1980s, the women remain heavily clothed, making swimming almost impossible (Miller, 1983).

Other acculturation studies focus on the acculturation of members of another culture--such as prisoners, war refugees, or immigrants--who are brought into a more powerful culture group. Vietnamese war refugees brought into the United States after the Vietnam conflict are a case in point. Robinson (1978) studied the acculturation of the Vietnamese children into the American elementary school playground groups. According to her, the refugees needed to show certain physical and verbal skills in game play before being accepted. The Vietnamese boys quickly adapted to this requirement because their native play groups also stressed similar physical skill prerequisites. The Vietnamese girls had a more difficult time because their socialization depended more on verbal skills than physical prowess. Also, the lack of language facility was a barrier to their acceptance by the American girls. In this instance, differential skills were associated with acculturation into the dominant culture. It is important to understand the weighting of values in both cultures and their compatibility in the process of acculturation.

As Ogawa (1978) suggests, acculturation is the process of the "superior" or more advanced society imposing its cultural traits upon the "subordinate" or weaker society, the weaker eventually becoming more like the stronger. It is further assumed that acculturaton of a foreign culture into the local one leads to disintegration and breakdown of tradition with its replacement by the new ways. Presumably the tension is set up between the process of change and the continuity of traditional past, sometimes creating an either/or dilemma rather than a synthesis. This mode of resistance is well illustrated by Maccoby, Modiana, and Lander's (1964) cultural experiment in which an alteration in the social character of Mexican village chilrden was planned through the introduction of a new American-style game, Red Rover Come Over. Instead of stimulating cooperation and independence as experimenters hoped, "both boys and girls distorted the game to conform to their attitudes toward authority and the formal structure of the central-person games they normally played" (Maccoby, Modiana, and Lander, 1964:162). As soon as the experimenters left the village, the children stopped playing the game.

A less extreme way to resist a foreign feature is to modify its elements and interpretation to fit the ongoing culture. This process is called syncretism. The traditional culture does not vary, but the original aspects of the game do. Heider (1977) described the maintenance of traditional patterns by a New Guinea highland people, the Dani, in the face of attempted cultural change by the Indonesian government. One instance was the Javanese teachers' introduction of "Tip-Cat" to the Dani school children who proceeded to change this competitive game into the noncompetitive amusement, "Flip-a-Stick." an activity more consistent with the nature of Dani games than was the original "Tip Cat" (see p. 161).

The second approach to acculturation, according to Ogawa (1978), carries the mark of societal maintenance through selecting foreign culture traits compatible with the receiving culture. This process, in fact, is implicit in all acculturation. For instance, the Japanese enthusiastic acceptance of baseball, which was introduced in 1873 by an American missionary (Whiting, 1982:10), and later of volleyball and skiing is predicated on the Japanese respect for personal space. These adopted sports reinforce this cultural value because they do not involve body contact with another person. Another example is seen in the overwhelming preference by Southwestern American Indian youth of Anglo team sports, basketball, baseball, football, which were introduced through the federal government's Bureau of Indian Affairs school system. These team-oriented games are popular because they provided game elements--two opposing teams attempting to obtain goals--similar to traditional games of shinny, lacrosse/stick ball (Cheska, 1981a). More importantly, they furnish vehicles for expressing or "playing out" tribal values such as group cohesion, loyalty, social exchange, and egalitarianism (Allison and Lüschen, 1979; Blanchard, 1974; Cheska, 1979).

Some change can be regarded as an opportunity for transition and as being useful in adjusting the discrepancy between the imposed objective social order and people's subjective feelings. This is Ogawa's (1978) third focus, stressing cultural construction. An example of this is the Trobriand Islanders' reaction to the introduction of cricket in 1903 by the British Methodist missionary, William Gilmore. This event followed closely on the heels of the British administrative edict outlawing warfare between villages and the natives' harvest celebrations which featured erotic Kalibom and Bisila dances. Intervillage cricket matches provided a viable mechansim with which to reconstruct intervillage wars ritually and offered alternative forms of expressing the sexual symbolism. The competing villages' team members and spectators painted their bodies in war colors (black and white). Teams used military marching formations. They chanted witty, rude, and sexually-suggestive rhymes as they performed erotic dance steps in team entrances, exits, and when an opponent was declared "out." The reciprocal exchange ceremony of food gifts climaxed the cricket event just as had been done at the traditional *"Kayasa"* (competitive activity) which ended with its obligatory food exchange. Thus, traditional Trobriand customs were creatively incorporated into the cricket contest. Through a foreign cultural event, Trobriand society was in part constructed and reconstructed. By the 1970s and 1980s the unique Trobriand version of cricket was being exported by the Trobriand Islanders to their surrounding island neighbors.

The above examples of acculturation illustrate the ability of societies to redefine a sport or game diffused from another society so that they fit local norms and values. This syncretism by the Mexican and the Dani children, the Southwest American youth, and the Trobriand Island villagers suggest that physical activities can contribute to the preservation of cultural tradition in the midst of other change.

However, there is another side of acculturation. In many instances, the diffusion and adoption of "modern" sports from the industrialized world by the small-scaled societies of the world seem to parallel the flow of ideas from the dominant to the subordinate culture groups with its implications of unequal relationships. Another trend is that part of the striving for national existence and for recognition by other political states has included the sports arena. Excellence in international competition is paramount to excellence in the athletic domain, thus sport has become a vehicle of social conflict as well as a model for understanding social conflict.

CULTURE AND HUMAN CONFLICT

Anthropologists and sociologists have long considered human conflict inherent in social relationships. Conflict arises from a basic need of resolution, thus conflict is the transition from ambiguity to hierarchy. Coser (1956:8) defines conflict as "a struggle over values and claims to scarce status, power and resources in which the aims of the opponents are to neutralize, injure, or eliminate their rivals."

The ultimate outcome of conflict can be physical death. However, predatory creatures, including humans, have developed modified kinetic behavior called "play fighting," which limits attack and defense, allowing expression without expiration. This conflict behavior in animals has been named ritualized aggression by Lorenz (1966). Bateson (1972:189) distinguishes instinctive programmed behavior of lower animals as "mood signs," and contrasts this with man's -- and some higher animals' -- ability to discriminate by meta-communication between mood-signs and other similar signs. Among these other signs are behaviors whose messages signal that "this is play"; they are deliberately sent and received as framing devices which identify these behaviors as modified conflict. For example, a playful nip of one animal by another, Bateson (1972:182) explains, denotes or represents what would be a bite for which the nip stands. But at that moment in that situation the "real" bite is fictional for it does not exist -- at least in that frame. One does, however, remember the bite which the nip has displaced in the play situation and realizes that the nip can also be replaced by the real bite if signals are misread. The fragility of the framing message of play is well known. Analogous to the above relationship of the nip to the bite is an institution among the Andaman Islanders of the Indian Ocean. Bateson (1972:182) reports that conflicts are often resolved by ceremonial striking or playful combat. Peace is concluded after each has been given ceremonial freedom to strike the other. The ritual blows of peacemaking are always liable to be mistaken for the "real" blows of combat. In that event, the peacemaking ceremony becomes a battle (Radcliffe-Brown, 1922).

What are the characteristics of sport behavior that qualify it as conflict? If the formal structure of sport is examined, one observes that it has two opposing sides competing for a limited resource, that of winning. As a result a differential or hierarchical relationship is created between participants, a relationship based on some specific standard, (e.g., comparing skill competency). One sees in sport the transition from ambiguity to hierarchy, or as Coser (1956:8) states, a struggle over values and claims to scarce status, power and resources. Nisbet (1970:70) defines competition as a form of conflict in which the object is to attain a goal rather than inflict damage directly on the opponent. Supporting this view, sport as competition modifies conflict in several features.

One feature is the competition between participants that the Greeks called striving together for the prize. The participants as players are striving or contesting in friendly rivalry against other humans, against their own past performances, and against obstacles (e.g., human, natural, or manufactured). I may try to run faster than my opponents, run faster than my past recorded time, or run faster while jumping over hurdles placed along a prescribed course. Lüschen (1970:21-22) has stressed that in sports competition there is a consensus of "association" grounded in a complementary and equi-librial alliance to compete or we might say, a planned ritualization or conflict.

The second factor is agreed-upon rules that are arrived at by consensus, rather than imperatives, as found in lower animal life. Although the differential outcome is important in sport competition, the kinds of maneuvers within the contest (conflict) situation center about opposing and complementary behaviors in a flowing sequence. Elias and Dunning (1966:389) refer to this as configuration or game-pattern, stating,

> The dynamics of this grouping and regrouping of players in
> the course of a game are fixed in certain respects and
> elastic and variable in others. They are fixed, because

without agreement among the players on their adherence to a unified set of rules, the game would not be a game but a "free for all."

Of course, rules can be misread or violated, resulting in alienation and aggression, as seen earlier in the Andaman Islanders' peacemaking blows. The modern counterpart is violence in sports (see Chapter 8 discussion for a fuller treatment of this topic).

The third factor integral to sport participation is the mutual interest in cooperative give-and-take through orderly procedures. Shared and understood methods of interacting that help to facilitate the relationships are observed. A controlled yet variable tension exists between members of one's own and opposing teams, individual and group goals, offense and defense, affectionate identification and hostile rivalry, competition and cooperation.

The fourth factor is the uncertain outcome of winning. To experience this hierarchical status as victor, one must fulfill the established criteria for winning. Caillois (1979:14) describes this process as "rivalry in some single quality (speed, endurance, strength, memory, skill, ingenuity, etc.) exercised within defined limits in such a way that the winner appears to be better than the loser in a certain category of exploits." In some specific criterion, such as score, time, or position, one side has achieved supremacy over the other(s). The prior uncertainty or ambiguity is now removed, and a winner is declared. This act of winning is unequivocal and a crystal clear characteristic of sport. Everyone knows who has won and who has lost. The meticulous record-keeping phenomenon in modern sports is testimony to the importance of this feature (Guttman, 1978). Even in an event in which the sides are determined equal for the moment, an overtime, sudden death, or rematch generally resolves the ambiguity of equality. This clarity is unlike the serious conflict situations in everyday life, in which winning is not so precise. In fact, the participant may not know exactly whether, or what, he or she has won or lost, because of multiple variables and the blurred criteria. For example, the top grade on a school test may mean to the student an academic "win," but a remark on the paper, "This is not your best work," by the teacher may imply a status "loss." A raise in salary in one's work situation might be inferred as a financial "win," but a simultaneous move to an office with less square-footage could be interpreted as a status "loss." The preciseness of sports winning may well be more absolute or "real" than in life itself. In like manner, sport is not a replica of social conflict, but a modification. Therefore, the mirror image theory of sport and conflict is misleading. The relationship between sport and other forms of conflict, such as war, needs further explication.

Sport has been dubbed in some circles as war without weapons and battle without bullets. Conversely, Caillois, in referring to the spirit of competition, suggests that other cultural phenomena conform to the code of game playing (e.g., the duel, the Medieval tournament, and certain aspects of the so-called courtly war). The ancient Chinese feudal war lords conducted their battles as if playing a board game. Sitting high and back from the battle, each lord ordered the field maneuvers of his soldiers in terms of "moves." At a set time the battle ceased and the troops' positions were marked for starting at that point the next day. The rival war lords would then gather together for refreshments, discuss the day's successes and failures, and compare their troops' performances. In truth, the battle was a form of entertainment for the nobility. Another example shows that by changing fighting implements and thereby removing a warrior's personal involvement, fighting becomes no longer honorable. When the gun was introduced to the South Pacific people it became available for the war parties. However, the Samoan warriors lost interest in fighting because the former personal skill and valor of personally striking an enemy with a well-thrown spear was absent. The men complained that strength and courage was not necessary if a gun were used and that even weak women and children could strike down the enemy. Therefore, the prestige of doing battle disappeared and the warrior was no longer set apart as special (Dunlap, 1951).

Chapple and Coon (1942:616, 628-35) conclude that primitive war is more closely related to game behavior than the warfare waged by modern nations. They argue that warfare between tribal peoples is often mutually planned and announced in the same manner that sporting events are arranged. This notion was refuted by Otterbein (1970:32-33) in his study of war. He suggested, contrary to the findings of Chapple and Coon, that most primitive peoples initiate war by surprise attack rather than by mutual agreement, mainly because it is a more successful tactic.

An intriguing notion of war as modern society's paroxysmic festival has been suggested by Caillois (1959:162-80). He feels that war corresponds to the festival, because the ordinary norms of preservation--thrift and decorum--are reversed and it is a time of excess, violence, and exorbitant waste of goods, people, and objects. Caillois (1959:175) suggests that war, which is now "pure crime and violation," in early times

> had most paradoxically accepted loyalty, respect for the enemy, and had outlawed the use of certain weapons, ruses, and tactics, had established a complicated ceremonial and rigorous etiquette in which one applied himself to emulation in good manners as well as bravery and audacity.

These agreed-upon rules and procedures of war seemed to parallel those of sports. Caillois (1959:174) further decried the total war of the modern world, stating,

> There is no longer a well-defined battlefield, which used to

constitute a reserved area, comparable to the lists, the arena, and the playing field. This enclosure dedicated to violence, at least left all around it a world ruled by more clement laws.

Caillois's statements that war and sport were similar are supported by entrepreneurs who argue that violence is inherent in such sports as football and ice hockey and to remove that violence would destroy the games. One needs only to read the sports section of the local newspaper to find terms of battle used to describe sports events: "ISU captures..., Indians scalp..., Lions seize..., Panthers kill..., Illini dead..., Braves bury..., Home Team escapes...." It seems that an argument is being made that whether the aggressive drive is innate or acquired, it accumulates within the individual, and society much like a steam valve must be released. War is considered one outlet; sports can also discharge the accumulative tensions, thus serving as an alternative for war. But does it?

Sipes (1973), in a classic study, investigates the relationship between war, sport, and aggression, and tests two rival models of behavior: the drive-discharge model given above, and the culture pattern model which purports that aggressive behavior is learned culturally in varying degress. He concludes that warlike or combative behavior is culturally learned rather than being inherited. Combative sports, according to Sipes, are those such as boxing, hunting, ice hockey, football, and wrestling. Noncombative sports include activities such as baseball, bowling, golf, and skiing. He defines combative sports as those including actual or obvious body contact or expanded warlike activity between opponents, either directly or through real or simulated weapons (Sipes 1973:68). Sipes (1973:80) suggests that : (1) sports, as a general category of behavior, and war manifest no functional relationship across time; (2) combative sports and war appear to reinforce each other but do not serve as alternatives in a society; and (3) war and combative sports appear to be components of a broader culture pattern. Thus, Sipes questions the proposition that sport serves as a substitute for war, and placed the responsibility of aggressive expression and its control upon individual societies.

We are still left with the gnawing issue that "sport is the most dramatic form of nonhostile combat in which humans participate" (1984 Olympic Scientific Congress, 1984:25). Sport often accommodates aggression and sponsors violence. Further study is needed to determine whether culturally directed sport induces or deters violent behavior and whether violent behavior sponsored by sport can be predicted and controlled. These issues are discussed in Chapter 8.

If one accepts Sipes' (1973) conclusions that combative sports and war are components of a larger cultural pattern, then one must also conclude that learning and practice of one activity reinforces the other and that both augment pervasive societal aggression. In other words, combative war and sport are both social devices for learning and expressing aggression. Therefore, combative sports can serve as preparation for war. Examples of this abound in primitive or traditional societies. One is found in the child-training practices of the Dani people of highland New Guinea. The Dani children's play almost exclusively imitates adult activities, such as the boys' emulation of the tribal warfare. In the game of war the boys divide into opposing sides on a field of tall grass. Each child attempts to hit his enemy with small pointed grass arrows thrown forcefully from the hand with motions similar to his father's spear-throwing. As the children advance, taunt, challenge, retreat, and even injure each other, an observer is startled by the replication of the adults' battlefield tactics. The Mesoamerican ballgame may have been used as preparation for war by the young Aztec noblemen. It has been assumed that these nobles played matches against rival groups between military campaigns to keep in top physical condition. The military exercise training program of the boys and girls of the ancient Greek city state of Sparta is an oft-quoted example of military enculturation. One cannot ignore the military toys, board, and electronic war games in the American child's play repertoire.

The consideration of sport as an alternative to war does not necessitate an understanding of sport as biological steam valve. Rather, it is thought of as a temporary cultural replacement or supplement to war. "Counting Coup" by the American Plains Indian warriors was the ultimate in dangerous sports. In the heat of battle, the "game" was to touch an enemy's body, paraphernalia, or weapons, but not to kill him. Some souvenir was shown as proof. A brave's honor and respect was based on the number and difficulty of "coup" successfully executed. In like fashion, the boys imitated their fathers by carrying out raiding parties into enemy camps to steal objects; thus practicing the skills of stealth, courage, physical prowess and the system of prestige which were to be used in adulthood. Training North American Indian boys in long-distance running was considered to be preparation for hunting and war. One wonders then why the girls, who did not hunt or fight, also participated in such training? There is a danger of attributing cause and effect relations to similar behavior patterns without analyzing other contributing factors and/or varying purposes of such behavior. Another problem in assuming that sport both prepares for war and serves as a substitute for it, is the fact that war demands total involvement. In a sense, any skill practice could be construed as preparation for war.

It has been verified cross-culturally that armed have been better able than unarmed tribal groups to defend and expand their territory and exert influence on their neighboring political communities (Naroll, 1966:19). Otterbein (1970:3;93) reports that out of fifty societies he studied, only four had no military organizations (i.e., Copper Eskimo, Dorobo, Tikopia, and Toda) and these apparently had been driven from more desirable lands into their present isolation. Thus, the importance of war as a negotiating tool in intersocietal relations cannot be disregarded. However, the seeming reinforcement of similar format and behavior patterns in war and sport provides opportunities to teach and develop less-violent behaviors as normative, especially since these behaviors are culturally evolved. If models of confrontation used in war, such as shock weapons (hand-to-hand combat) and projectile weapons (thrown from a distance) as extensions of human force plus the use of tactical formations of lines or ambushes (Otterbein, 1970:37-38) can be translated into the nonmortal combat of sport, a step has been made toward modifying war. If war could be reconstituted with the attributes and behavior of "sport," then aggression could be meaningfully decelerated and redirected as codified conflict. The relationship between the factions of the old Indian Creek Confederacy of the American Southeast provides an excellent example of codifying conflict through sport. Haas (1940) reports that the Creek villages were divided into district semidivisions named Red (war) and White (peace) towns respectively. Within one semidivision a village referred to another as "my friend." In the other, villages were called "my enemy," and hostile relationships generally existed. Thus, the setting for serious conflict was in place. However, the Creek avoided this. Haas (1940:479) notes, "A legitimate outlet for this feeling was provided by the ever popular two-goal game," the "stickball" or "racket game" referred to earlier. Through an elaborate contractual agreement between opposing villages a match was played. The disposition of the match was such that "if either town should defeat the other a given number of times, the losing town would be required to change over to the semidivision of the winning town" (Haas, 1940:481). This manipulation of intervillage relationships through the outcome of a stickball match ameliorated intergroup antagonism, and hostilities were substituted for by friendship. Sport was a viable substitute for war.

Sport might well be a vehicle for conflict management, sport being a less violent alternative to war. It may not be so much that sport and war are alike, but that our definition, meaning, and understanding of that behavior we have assigned to each dictates their perceived similarity. Sport's principal function relative to the problem of human conflict may be in its ability to modify the expression of conflict.

CULTURE AND MULTI ETHNIC SPORTS PROGRAMS

Another important application of anthropological theory to real sport situations is in the area of sport program development, in particular, those involving multiethnic, multicultural, or multiracial populations. While the section that follows does not enumerate specific procedures, it does identify cultural premises and caveats in the creation, development, and implementation of such programs.

There are many reasons for such programs' existence. Also, there are many issues: the meaning of ethnicity, ethnic contact variables such as assimilation versus cultural diversity or compatibility versus conflict. These programs are important in one sense as contexts in which positive and negative factors in association are played out. Barth (1969:9-10) has contended,

> Ethnic distinctions do not depend on an absence of mobility, contact and information, but do entail social processes of exclusion and incorporation whereby discrete categories are maintained despite changing participation and membership in the course of individual life histories. One finds that stable, persisting, and often vitally important social relations are maintained across such boundaries, and are frequently based precisely on the dichotomized ethnic statuses.

In other words, ethnic distinctions do not depend on social isolation but, quite to the contrary, are often the very foundations on which embracing social systems are built.

Important in these social interactions are the continuance of relations and the respect for separateness. The dialectic model of sports and games provides a plausible perspective. Sport represents a dialectic in the opposition of competing individuals or groups. This dual organization of sport is structurally and symbolically useful in understanding interethnic contact situations. The unordinariness of the event from the daily life style represents something separated. The nonthreatening nature of the encounter may signal that important or serious issues are not being addressed. The ruled order of the game provides a secure format countering uncertainty and potential disorder. In addition, the participants' roles and strategies are performed exclusively within the event. Within this bounded frame, the interaction can be maximized, and the permanency of status as symbolized by winning can be minimized. While one side is winning the contest and the other is losing, there is hope for reversal. This arrangement can keep ethnic groups in responsive communication.

The opinion that sport is considered part of the peripheral genre of a society's leisure, and so not at a society's core belief system, makes it useful at borders and boundaries between groups. At this margin, through sport events, nonthreatening relationships can be experienced and evaluated (Cheska, in press). As a buffer zone between the familiar and the new, sport can help make the process of adjustment or accommodation less traumatic. Nevertheless, the potential danger at the margins does not go unobserved. During an event, if symbolism assumes the collective power of the larger original group and its beliefs, then perceptions are magnified and extended beyond the local situation, and the event may be interpreted as vital, threatening, and dangerous. This raises the possibility of direct conflict rather than its indirect management within the gaming context. It is precisely at this border that there is the development of multiethnic sports programs ranging from integrating mixed-racial populations in a physical education class to orchestrating the cross-cultural athletic showcase of the world, the Olympic Games.

Sport programs must be founded on the assumption that the cultural variation affects and is reflected through behavior. Specifically, culture affects behavior in four critical ways: perception, expectations, motivation, and communication (Blanchard, 1976). Sports situations are not exceptions to these processes.

Culturally sensitive sports programs are desperately needed, but are difficult to achieve. Too frequently the proposed ethnic benefits are poorly perceived and expectations are not compatible with the receiving group's experience. For these reasons introducing values from one ethnic group to another is frequently unsuccessful. Let's start with a few examples of past efforts at cross-ethnic physical activity programs. Sometimes, because the members from a dominant culture group are appointed as change agents in a receiving culture, their programs are introduced to acculturate. As described earlier in this chapter, the teaching of "Red Rover" to Mexican children by an American teacher and of "Tip-Cat" to the Dani children by Indonesian teachers are examples of culturally laden games intended to introduce or accommodate other changes. In these cases, the basic value of competition was being promoted. But the first group rejected the introduced cultural feature and the second greatly modified the game.

As an example of motivation and communication, Allan Tindall's (1975a) study of cultural functions of physical education concentrated on the diverse ethnic messages that the Ute Indian and the Anglo-Mormon high school students transmitted in a physical education class in basketball. The Anglo-Mormon boys perceived that winning basketball games was done through concentration, teamwork, and self-sacrifice; that one received status through team wins; and that one obtained the skill level necessary for team participation by playing basketball together. Thus the Anglo-Mormons practiced their basketball skills by playing as a team during class time under the direction of the physical education teacher. The Ute Indian boys are affected by the cultural premise that one man cannot, and should not, control another. They perceived that one went about winning basketball games by using his individual skill to score points. One obtained status by being a skillful player whether he won or lost. To obtain skill one practiced and played alone, so that in games skills were demonstrated, not obtained. As noted, the two groups were operating from two different cultural motivations. Because the high school physical education class stressed skill learning through group practice and team competition, the situation complemented motivations of the Anglo-Mormon youth and they eagerly participated in the class. The Utes brought a different cultural premise to bear on the situation and did not wish to "practice" basketball in the class. The Ute boys were skilled basketball players and participated avidly in their own Ute recreational leagues. Clearly, messages sent by these youth to themselves and others concerning their social identity were based on different cultural motivations. Those participating in the physical education basketball class were in effect stating, "I am an Anglo-Mormon," while those not so participating were stating, "I am a Ute." If the instructor in this class had been aware of the differing ethnic motivations from which each group fashioned its basketball behavior, he could have developed a program which encompassed both cultural statements!

The Navajo Youth Physical Education, Recreation, and Health Program is an example of a culturally sensitive program which was well conceived and adequately implemented. In 1972 a vision of a New Mexico Anglo teacher was realized when she was permitted to initiate a youth summer recreation program on the Navajo Indian reservation. Beginning with five sites to which a small trained staff of Anglos and Navajos travelled over the summer, sports instruction in baseball, basketball, soccer, and track was offered. Swimming was taught in portable swimming pools. Art and craft objects were created from natural and scrap materials, emphasizing local Navajo themes. Because the average participant knew so few traditional techniques and games, these were stressed. By 1979 the program had expanded to thirty-six sites, several of which had become permanent all-year facilities staffed by Navajo junior college graduates trained in recreational leadership. With the cooperation of the Navajo Tribal Council, the Bureau of Indian Affairs (BIA) took over the program's administration and continued its expansion to reservation schools. In a real sense, the program reconstructed the tribal heritage in the lives of Navajo children and youth. The project's success was based in strong measure on the leaders' understanding of Navajo identity and values which were reinforced and renewed within the program's activities. The curriculum, so to speak, took into account the cultural context to which the activities related (Cheska, 1978a).

It is not enough to realize that sport behavior by members of a specific culture is an outcome of that culture. We need also to recognize that members of a specific culture use sport behavior to retain that culture. One example of sport encouraging ethnic retention, and thus inhibiting assimilation, was the ten soccer clubs founded from the 1920s to 1960s in the city of Milwaukee, Wisconsin, by Croatian, German, Hungarian, Italian, and Polish groups. As reported by Pooley (1981) these clubs fielded thirty-five sponsored soccer teams; stressed distinct ethnicity in club membership, policy, social events, and game play; and encouraged club members to speak their native language. Playing soccer was in itself an ethnic statement because it was the most popular outdoor sport in each of their countries of origin, but certainly not in America. These men used sport to accentuate their separate national entities, but at the same time they felt personally in tune with values, attitudes, and behaviors of American society.

Mathias (1981) illustrates the importance of the environmental context on the transformation in the form of games played by immigrants in America. Specifically she compares the fate of the popular Italian game of *bocce* played by people from central Italy who settled in the Iron Range of Minnesota and those from southern Italy who settled in South Philadelphia, Pennsylvania. *Bocce,* popular in both areas of Italy, is played by two teams, from four to eight men each. Players line up and choose a finish line in the distance. Then men take turns throwing and rolling stones over the fields and down the roads until they pass the finish line. The winner is either the first man to cross the finish line or the man who crosses the finish line with the fewest number of throws. The urban Italian factory workers of Philadelphia, because of congested and crowded living conditions, soon moved their *bocce* competition from the city streets to specially constructed courts and the sport has gradually lost its popularity. The semirural Italian iron-ore miners of Minnesota preserved the traditional open form of *bocce,* and it is still enthusiastically played today. Mathias' example suggests that the different environmental situations of otherwise similar incoming ethnic populations often lead to different local adaptations and game styles.

The celebration of ethnic diversity is reinforced by sports events held between nations. The most visible example is the Olympic Games, the late 1800s' brainchild of Frenchman Pierre de Coubertin. In the late 1900s it has become the athletic showcase of the world and is participated in by 155 countries. In fact, the 1976 Montreal Olympics were viewed, read about, or discussed by one-third of the world's population. The 1980 Moscow Olympics were planned to reach one half of the world's population, but that goal was not reached because of the boycott by some major countries. However, the 1984 Los Angeles Olympics may reach an even larger audience. The Olympics have touched the lives of more people than any other single event in history. The wish of de Coubertin, who acclaimed the Olympics as the festival of the world's youth, was that the striving for excellence in athletics would be a forum for cultural exchange and appreciation of diversity (MacAloon, 1981). This is what it has become.

The physical expertise, energy, money, leadership, and resources involved in this quadrennial spectacle may seem misdirected in terms of net results because technically there is only the verificaton of physical prowess. However, the symbolic transference of this kind of superiority to other sociopolitical facets of culture is extensive. The Olympics is only the tip of the intercountry sports exchange iceberg. There are world region games, such as the African, Asian, Central American, European, Near East, and and Pan American games. There are invitational games sponsored by host countries which invite other countries with common association to send participants. Such events include the British Commonwealth Games to which all nations and/or territories in political alliance with Britain are invited; the Maccabean Games sponsored by Israel to which all contestants of the Hebrew faith from over the world are invited; and the U.S.S.R. Spartakiad in which all ethnic groups within the U.S.S.R. are invited to enter. There are international championships conducted by the International Federations of many sports, such as badminton, skiing, soccer, and volleyball. The World Cup Soccer finals is the largest sport event in the world, involving almost two billion people. There are exchange sports programs sponsored by individual countries inviting another country's athletes to exhibit, compete, and tour with local teams. China conducted such a program for many years prior to its diplomatic recognition in the 1970s and continues to expand these programs. The vast sport exchange system within the world ranging from great international spectacles to people-to-people and club exchanges can enhance the respect of cultural diversity and the continuance of friendly multiethnic relationships. (For further discussion of this, see information on international relationships in Chapter 8.)

In sum, the following suggestions can be made relative to sports programs that involve multi ethnic or multi cultural populations.

(1) Multiethnic sports programs provide a protected preserve for cultural exchange.
(2) The two-sided structure of the sport event can be a model of and vehicle for multiethnic contact.
(3) Introducing new values through a sports program leads to acceptance only to the degree that the values are compatible with those values important to the borrowing ethnic group.
(4) The basic assumption of a sports program is that cultural variation affects and is reflected through participants' behavior in four important ways: perception, expectations, motivation, and communication.
(5) An ethnic group's sports content is modified to adjust to the differing local environmental and social situations.
(6) The respect for others' way of life, the recognition of humanness, and the joy of diversity can serve as criteria for the results of multiethnic exchange through the sports program.

Anthropologists are interested in the issue of cross-cultural understanding. By studying and working with other cultural groups, anthropologists compare the modes of living, believing, and adapting of other native groups with their own. There are two basic attitudes which filter the information available about other societies. One is ethnocentrism, the other is cultural relativism. Ethnocentrism is a feeling that one's own group is superior to all others. Thus, because "my" group is the center of everything, others are judged in reference to it and are often held in scorn. Even anthropologists need to be aware that they may inadvertently consider their own culture's way of living better than those they study. It seems that what is ours is judged more virtuous than any other. Cultural relativism is the interpretation by which the individual's own background, social norms, and beliefs influence one's perception and evaluation. This sounds like ethnocentrism, but it is based on the view that there is no single scale of values applicable to all societies. The phrase "each to his own way" may help explain the concept. Thus, judgments of comparative morality, virtue, or goodness between ethnic groups are not applicable, for each adapts in its own appropriate fashion to its own unique set of circumstances. Words like "tolerance," "appreciation," and "respect" describe the perception of each culture for the other.

Ethnocentrism is evident in sport. As an example, people in the United States delight in the sport of boxing, which is designed literally to beat an opponent into submission by the use of the fists, and appear unmoved by the cruelty of the conflict. Yet, most Americans abhor the Mexican/Spanish bullfight in which the bull is goaded, stabbed with sharp pics, and finally artfully speared to death in an extremely uneven fight. Each so-called sport is directed toward the total incapacitation or destruction of the opponent, but the ethnocentric-minded persons in the United States feel their own style is superior to others!

On the other hand, cultural relativism can also be observed in sport. For example, most Americans recognize the mutual legitimacy of the two versions of medieval football: one evolved into European-style soccer (which Europeans call football) and the other into American football. It can be concluded that each is an appropriate adaptation to a unique set of circumstances. Americans advance the ball with the hand by carrying, throwing, or running with it as well as from a stationary kick. Europeans advance the ball by various body parts, such as the feet, shoulders, and head without the hands touching the ball. Each group's technique makes for excitement and enjoyment, and neither should be called superior. It is worth noting that each sport has been introduced to the other group and is gaining in pooularity--soccer or European football in the United States and American football in Europe.

The basic components of the sport institution (e.g., two sides, ordered procedures, rules, criteria for winning, and uncertain outcomes) are evident in all sport situations. They seem to exist above cultural barriers. This being the case, these elements provide a common content for extra- and cross-cultural communication. In this sense, sport can be viewed as a universal language.

Cross-cultural understanding can be promoted through sport. In these multiethnic settings are the ingredients of understanding. By increasing contact between various culture groups, such as in sports settings, more information is available about each other to help decrease the need to lump others into undifferentiated stereotypes. As Barth (1969) has said, stable, persisting, and often virtually important social relations can be maintained across ethnic boundaries. Mutual contact, communication, and respect of each group's diversity are positive processes available through the vehicle of sport. At the same time, a recognition of the ethnic or cultural factor in sport program development is essential to program effectiveness.

SUMMARY

In this chapter sport has been defined as a context in which cultural change can be mediated. Sport can be employed to reinforce and strengthen a group's threatened values by adjusting or modifying cultural features introduced from the outside so that the new element better fits the borrowing group's perception of itself. Sport can subtly introduce novel ways of doing things, thus providing a reservoir of potential behaviors which, so to speak, are on "cultural hold."

General themes of culture change covered here include enculturation, cultural maintenance, acculturation, innovation, ethnicity, conflict, and conflict management. Of these, enculturation and cultural maintenance are dedicated to internal consistency within and continuity of a society. Changes in a society can be caused by processes such as discovery and invention; those innovations are usually shared by members within a society and also by diffusion to other societies. Two or more differing groups share each other's cultural features through contact; however, each group's ethnic integrity is protected in these transactions and the exchange is mediated by varying degrees of acceptance. A borrowing society's acceptance of a foreign cultural element is dependent on the feature's compatibility with the group's cultural traits and its perceived need. "Like attracts like" may be an appropriate adage here. Seldom is the borrowing society's belief system displaced by another society's feature, but the element itself is adjusted to better fit into the receiving group's belief system. The beauty of this complex process is that the ethnic group can have it both ways--it filters out foreign features which destroy societal continuity but also allows novelty to be introduced and absorbed in controlled measure. This delicate negotiative process can result in opposition between individuals and/or between ethnic/racial groups. In change, the potential for human conflict exists. Sport as a universal language of movement can provide a vehicle for conflict management, as it keeps channels of communication open and thus mediates and minimizes alienation of the ethnic groups. Sport can also provide a behavior pool that is less aggressive and violent than war. Ethnic understanding and respect can possibly be generated in the process. This same understanding is important in the development of sport programs involving different ethnic or cultural groups.

Exercises

Discussion questions:

1. Culture change is a prevalent force in the lives of contemporary Americans. Isolate and describe the types of changes that have occurred in our society over the past twenty years. What parallel changes have occurred in American sport?

2. In the process of becoming a sport enthusiast, either participant or spectator, one is actually "enculturated" into sport. What are the forces of enculturation that underlie this development?

3. One type of social change is the change that accompanies the movement from one social class to another within a society. What types of sport are associated with the major socioeconomic classes in American society? What changes in sport behavior tend to accompany social mobility, upward and downward, in the American system?

4. Syncretism is a process affecting the nature of borrowed sports in all societies. To what extent has the syncretism phenomenon affected that nature of particular sports as these are played in America (e.g., soccer, rugby, tennis, golf, football)?

5. Sport and war are related social phenomena. One of the most obvious similarities is in the language used in both institutions. Illustrate the use of "war" language in particular American sports. Which sports seem to employ the most such language? Which the least? Speculate as to the reasons for the differences.

6. Ethnicity is a factor in American sport. What ethnic stereotypes are associated with particular sports and positions in those sports? Also, what types of sport situations are likely to lead to the interaction of different racial, cultural, or ethnic groups? What can be done to manage these situations so that the results are positive rather than negative?

7. It is suggested that sport competition can lead to understanding between the combatants. Do you think this is true? Cite some examples from your own experience. How should this work in cross-cultural situations? In other words, how "should" sport competition work to facilitate the understanding of cultural differences? Does that always happen?

Special Projects:

1. Collect data on the history of a particular sport. What

major changes have occurred in the sport? Isolate the forces underlying these changes.

2.   Select one of the several theoretical models described in Chapter 3 (e.g., structural-functionalism, evolutionism, cultural materialism) and analyze the way in which that model might be used to study sport change.

3.   Collect information on the history of the Olympic Games focusing on the most memorable events. What Olympics and isolated incidents are the public most likely to remember? What does this suggest about the international, cross-cultural understanding ostensibly promoted by that major sporting event?

4.   Go to the library and find a detailed description of a game that is not played in America but is popular in another part of the world. What does the game tell you about the culture of the society in which it is played? How could the game be used to teach others about that culture?

82 year-old, Senior Olympic swimming star, Dr. Thomas Cureton is often referred to as the "Father of Physical Fitness"

8 Contemporary Issues and the Anthropology of Sport

Because of the popularity of sport in contemporary society, it is not unusual that sport issues have become standard fare in social science classrooms and frequent topics of discussion among professionals. The social scientist can no longer ignore sport, regardless of how he or she feels about frisbee football or nude sky-diving. In fact, many are admitting that they rather enjoy getting serious about sport-related issues.

Anthropologists in particular are interested in the social problems that characterize the sport institution, especially as these can be amplified from a cross-cultural persepctive. For example, knowing something about the mechanics of male and female inequality in Eskimo society and how this inequality is reflected in the Eskimo sport institution sheds light on the problems that surround female sport participation in our own society.

Of the major social issues with social problem dimensions, those most significant anthropologically include the role of women in sport, sport and the aging process, sport and violence, and sport and international relations.

THE ROLE OF WOMEN IN SPORT

"The subject of women in athletic competition is no longer even a controversial issue" (Shaffer, 1972:431)! So said Thomas E. Shaffer, M.D., at the 1972 national research conference in the United States on women and sport. However, there must be many people in the world who have not heard the news. Perhaps they have not recognized that change has been unfolding before them. Women's participation in sport has become increasingly acceptable.

Couched in the anthropological evolutionary model from band

233

societies to supraband societies, the redefined role of women in society is reflected in their involvement in sports--or lack of it. Women in the early band level societies, who with their male companions share in the general activity of living, gradually assume more private, specialized domicile and child-care responsibilities with the emergence of agriculture. The male assumes the more public, specialized, economic and religious responsibilities. According to anthropologist Friedl (1978:68-75), male power is closely related to the role that men play as producers and exchangers of the most valued items in a society. Friedl notes that men build dependent relationships and obligations in these transactions, which become the basis for power. Sport also establishes and reinforces bonds of power between competitors in gaining a scarce and valuable item, that of success. Therefore, as Tiger (1970) has suggested, male bonding through sport occurs as these opportunities for social reinforcement of males by males take place outside the family. Increasingly, as women fulfill the private domicile role, they are deprived of sport competition in the male power-oriented public context. The female in the supraband societies' sports context has usually been depicted in a supportive role, (e.g., a spectator, preparer of food, quasientertainer [pompon and cheerleader], enthisiastico). Only in recent decades has this passive image of femininity been modified as the female actively enters the sports arena as well as the stands.

If this evolutionary process is occurring (or reoccurring-- remember the earlier references of the primitive peoples' ample free time for leisure activities), then several issues about women's involvement in sport need to be addressed:
(1)   The image of femininity and its historical impact on female sport participation;
(2)   The nature and basis of differential access to and participation in sports between the sexes;
(3)   Female sport participation in other cultures;
(4)   Alternatives for the future of female sport participation.

It is assumed that each society's historical perspectives on the place and function of its women evolved and revolved about the cultural core of home, hearth, and child care. The female contribution was a private one, while that of the male was public. The female for the most part played or sported in seclusion from the males. The fate of the "peeping Tom" is illustrated in a Micmac Indian folk tale which tells of a brave who, knowing that the maidens were playing water games in the nearby lake, hid himself in the bushes beside the water. As the girls tossed the ball back and forth, it accidently fell into the bushes. As the females rushed toward it, the young man was discovered. The women so pelted him with stones and verbal tirades, that he never dared to observe them at play again (Rand, 1894). Apart from the overtones of sexual curiosity, the tale carries the message of female isolation in play activities.

Anthropologists until recently have considered sports a matter of secondary concern. Thus, it is not unusual that female sport roles have received so little attention. There are some additional reasons for the dearth of ethnographic information on women's sports participation: (1) the sports activities were generally separated by gender; therefore, female play was essentially by and among women; (2) the early anthropologist was usually male and thus excluded from the female activities; (3) the assumption by anthropologists of the minimal role sports held in the lives of observed people; (4) sports patterns and purposes in the "exotic" societies were unfamiliar to anthropologists and eluded their analysis; and (5) sports events in sacred ceremony were the purview of the men, and the females' role was to facilitate the general event (e.g., abstainer from sexual activity before the event, dancer, food preparer, spectator).

However, instead of wringing our hands over the lack of anthropological information on the role of women in sport, we should note what has been done in other social sciences such as history, sociology, psychology, and physical education, as a backdrop for further anthropology of sport analysis.

The Female Image and Female Sport

The specialized image of femininity in supraband society has limited the females' participation in sports. A brief review of the feminine image in the sports from the early classical civilizations to the modern era points out an erratic but progressive change toward active sport and game involvement by females.

The Pharaonic Egyptian society has left records of the "Dancing Gymnast" whose feats were commemorated on the painted wall mural in temples, tombs and palaces (Wilkinson, 1878, Petrie, 1927; Gardiner, 1930). The acrobats' short veil-like, see-through white costumes, framed by long, braided hair, enhanced their graceful somersaults, backbends, leaps and turns, as did the staccato clicks of the accompanying castanets. These women were considered entertainers in the palaces of the nobility. The wives and female children of the wealthy were not excluded from family physical recreation, for the wives frequently participated with their husbands in hunting expeditions along the Nile River, and boys and girls alike were taught to swim in the home's swimming pool or in the Nile (Abdou, 1961, 1970; Mutimer, 1970).

The Greek city states pose an intriguing dual ideal of "fertility and femininity." The girls and women of Sparta had an obligation to prepare for childbirth and bear strong offspring. The Spartans considered physical fitness a sacred obligation to the defense of the state. Thus, toward this end the girls as well as the boys daily practiced calisthenics, sports, and other strenuous physical activity (Gardiner, 1910:47; 1930:12). Edgar Degas, famous French painter, captured the teasing relationship of these practice sessions in a lighthearted painting, "Spartan Girls Provoking Spartan Youth" (1860) which hangs in the London National Gallery. The girls and women of

Athens were praised for their beauty and competence in the home (Gardiner, 1930:41-42; Ionannides, 1976:110). A few references to their physical recreation allude to the tossing of a light ball, probably in playful exercise after the bath (Harris, 1972:81). At the Heraean Games, an exclusively women's festival, girls and women competed in footraces and victors received crowns of olive, similar to the men's contests at the Olympic Games (Gardiner, 1930:42).

At the beginning of the Christian era women were becoming emancipated throughout the whole of the Roman empire (Harris, 1972:179), but this trend was short-lived. Historians are prone to note the passivity of the Romans in physical activity, except in a military context, and their affinity for observing rather than participating in sports as entertainment. Little is recorded for this era concerning women's sporting activity. However, we do know about the gladiatorial games of Rome, which were not games in the true sense but rather spectacles of death. The political leaders' strategy during the disintegration period of the Roman Empire, roughly from the third to the fifth centuries A.D., was to provide the restless, unemployed refugees from the far corners of the dying empire who crowded into Rome with food and entertainment. Women, men and children packed into the huge "sports" stadia to observe these pitiful, grotesque "sporting" masquerades of death. The fate of the gladiator was literally in the hands of the spectators; "thumbs up" signaled life; "thumbs down" condemned the person to death.

It is not surprising that during the long, desolate Dark Ages in Europe, the image of the female as "patronizing spectator" gathered credibility. By the Middle Ages it had become the norm. The grand jousting tournaments brought ladies of castle and countryside to the festive displays of horsemanship by armoured knights (Howell and Howell, 1980). The lady served as patron and provided an elegant reason for a knight's gallantry. Huizinga (1949:10) notes, "The lover wore the colours of his lady; companions the emblem of their confraternity; parties and servants the badges or blazon of their lords." Knightly exercises and courteous fashions with their worship of bodily strength, honors and dignities with their vanity and their pomp were raised to the level of virtue (Huizinga, 1949:40). According to Hardy (1974), the tourney as practice for warfare became more real than war itself. Toward the end of this period more knights were killed in the tourneys than on the battlefield. In time the feudal lords found the financial burden of keeping a standing and a reserve army in preparation for battle impractical, and the practice was abandoned. Also, the use of gunpowder made the lance and bow obsolete. In some ways the medieval period must have been exciting with its jousts, carnivals, fairs and town rivalries. Though women remained largely spectators, they were not excluded from sport participation. At the English fairs, for example, it was not uncommon for the "milkmaids" to participate in footraces for prize money (Strutt, 1876).

The concept of British amateur sports unfolded with the rise of the middle class and the emergence of a gentry who had the time, money, and facilities to participate in physical contests for the sheer enjoyment of them. Fair play was a gentlemanly custom developed as a mark of the moneyed, dilettante leisure class. Women were occasional observers, but the term "spectator" as we know it today probably is a bit too strong. From the British amateurism and leisure class mentality, the female image of "dabbler" grew. Women were considered the "fairer" sex--that is, in the upper class circles--and perpetuated the myth of frills, frivolity, and fertility. A dabbler was a female companion who at social gatherings played in mixed company such games as "tree tag," "blind man's bluff," and occasionally participated in an archery outing, a backyard croquet match, or maybe was pulled behind by a male skater across a frozen pond (Cheska and Gerber, 1981). When one considers the plight of the lower socioeconomic classes, the illusion of the dabbler in sports seems absurd, because the poorer citizens could hardly hold body and soul together, even with the whole family laboring in mines, factories, and farms. The quiet desperation of the destitute went unheeded. Interestingly, it was the upper-middle and upper-class women who enjoyed activities that could be considered sporting. This same social atmosphere underlay women's sports participation into the 1900s.

The democratization of sports did not begin in the United States until the twentieth century. The "social performer" image held sway until the mid-1900s. Starting with the East Coast schools and universities, "play for play's sake" was the popular slogan for female sports teams. The prevalent types of school-girl sports participation were "intramural programs" in which teams within the same shool played each other. At other times, there were "play days" in which girls from several nearby schools were mixed and matched, regardless of affiliation, to form teams of equal skill for a day of fun. The "sports day" in which each school entered its own campus sports team winners, and at which winners of events were recorded, represents an important transition. Prior to this type of competition, official winners were seldom announced, even though the players "knew the score."

Extramural sports competition between schools gathered momentum in the 1950s and 1960s, because public schools and higher education institutions were beginning to ascribe to the philosophy of opportunity for the female "sports competitor." Heretofore, such highly skilled female athletes had to seek practice, training, and competition in community and extra-school agencies, such as the Y.W.C.A., city recreation and industrial leagues, and private sports clubs.

In summary, the history of women's sport participation in Egypt, Europe, and later North America reflects a range of attitudes, some of which tend to reappear. The varying perceptions of the female-- the dancing gymnast of early Egypt, the fertility and femininity

Grecian images, the patronizing spectator of the Middle Ages, the dabbler of the Renaissance, the social performer of the Industrial Age, and the sports competitor of the late 1900s--actually fit today's various stances of femininity. For example, the Egyptian gymnast model as entertainer may be linked to her modern, free-exercise acrobatic cousins, cheerleaders and pompon squads. The sports competitor of the second half of the twentieth century, similar to track performers in early Greece, is gaining respect and emulation from younger sisters. Still, the general support role of the female continues as a main thread in the historical tapestry of femininity.

Nature and Bases of Differential Access to Sport

In the attempt to understand the differential access to sport participation by sex, the following oft-discussed positions are considered: (1) women are perceived as different from men both biologically and socially, thus leading to culturally defined gender roles; (2) differentiated rather than equal sex status in any societal context is modeled after human hierarchy; (3) sports by their very structure are hierarchical and have functioned chiefly in the homosocial (male) domain as models of power in industrialized or "modern" societies; and (4) women's sport participation is a social anomaly (Cheska, 1981b).

1. Women are perceived as different from men. Approximately one-half of the world's population is female, with internally oriented sex organs that provide the receptacle for the male's sex organ. From this fertile union, a new human being results. This new life's nurturance has been the female's responsibility, while the male historically has been the protector and keeper of territorial boundaries relating to the family. From this differentiation of labor and from its behaviors developed socially valued gender roles (Martin and Voorhies, 1975). Scholars have attempted to bridge the complementary equivalency of sex roles to that of gender roles, contending that the "protected" female gradually became recognized as the property of the male and as his status object. From this sexual divison of labor has emerged assumptions of hierarchy, power or prestige.

> In the relationship between the sexes, males have had a disproportionate amount of resources under their control. They could bargain their power, status, money, land, political influence, legal power, and educational and occupational resources (all usually greater than women's) against women's more limited range of resources, consisting of sexuality, youth, beauty, and promise of paternity. Men also could bargain their aggression, strength, competitiveness, and leadership capabilities against women's domestic and clerical services. In addition, men could offer women potential maternity, reciprocally the ultimate

validation (in a sexist world) of a woman's femininity
(Lipman-Blumen, 1976:17-18).

This reciprocal condition does not foster equality, but an uneven
distribution of access to and participation in power-related cultural
features.

2. *Differential sex status modelled after human hierarchy.* The
idea that sex status is modelled after the hierarchical human
condition is rationalized by the notion that this hierarchy is linked to
environmental exploitation. Power in social relations marks the
relative control each person has over elements of the environment.
Hence, power is a sociopsychological phenomenon (Adams,
1975:9-10). Yet, it must be remembered that when the symbolic
layers of power are stripped to the basic meaning, they translate into
the use of force for compliance. Social power has logically developed
from binary differentiation, classification, and ranking or
arrangement which is common to all human beings (Adams,
1975:106). This means that members of a society enjoy differential
right of access to basic resources (Fried, 1967:52). Fried implies that
it is impossible to classify any society as nonranked. The ranking of
objects (or humans) involves making a judgment based on differences
observed and then bestowing value. Given the differences between
the sexes biologicially and the classification, categories, or attributes
assigned to each sex as gender roles, the result is ranking.
Differences exist and they exist hierarchically.

3. *Sports are power models in homosocial domain.* The third
explanation, that sports by their very structure are hierarchical and
thus serve as models of power in the homosocial domain, is the logical sequel of the first two premises. A game is a competitive event
with the purpose of differentiating winner and loser in some unique
feature. Asymmetry is ordained by definition. Levi-Strauss (1966:32)
declared that "games thus appear to have a <u>disjunctive</u> effect: they
end in the establishment of a difference between individual players or
teams where originally there was no identification of inequality.
And at the end of the game they are distinguished into winners and
losers." Gruneau (1975:129) astutely observed, "Hierarchy, as a
concept, is a cornerstone of the sporting ethos." Thus, "the traits
of strength, aggression, competitiveness and leadership capabilities
can be played, practiced, and displayed in an athletic arena as an
exercise of symbolic power where strategy, chance and skill as merit
make a difference" (Cheska, 1981b:5). This playground of power
along with the human need for aggregation are powerful motivating
ingredients for homosocial exchange. The homosocial view of
gender role suggests that men are attracted to, stimulated by, and
interested in other men (Lipman-Blumen, 1976). The sport situation
allows men to practice their gender roles with each other (Maccoby
and Jacklin, 1974). Tiger (1970) claims that males "court" other
males and validate their maleness through interaction, often of an

aggressive, even violent nature. It also has been suggested that men identify with and seek help from other men because individuals identify with other individuals whom they perceive to be controllers of resources in any given situation (Lipman-Blumen, 1976). So, games and sports, as models of symbolic control, reinforce status in the homosocial arena where males interact with other males. The exclusivity of the male ceremonial house of the Iatmul peoples of New Guinea serves well to illustrate this point. The males of the village spend their waking hours in the company of other males, talking, debating, joking, working, sporting in common collegiality, retreating to their wives and homes only at night, if even then. The wives prepare and deliver food and other necessities to their husbands at the ceremonial house, but are not permitted entry. It is only in special reversal celebrations, such as *Naven*, when women are tolerated in the men's house and this is part of a transvestite ceremony (Bateson, 1958).

The counterpart to the above example is the all-male club system in Europe and the United States, which frequently centers about sport participation. In the United States it has been only since the advent of the 1966 Civil Rights Act and the subsequent Education Amendment Act known as Title IX (1972), that exclusion of females from sporting clubs has been challenged. Historically women have been excluded as inappropriate and ineffective game contenders, whose presence has been allowed in supportive roles (similar to the domicile roles) and as display commodities (property) within these social power transactions.

In past eras, games were both cultic (sacred) expressions and recreative (secular) enjoyments (Crawley, 1913; Culin, 1907; Cushing, 1883; Damm, 1970; Gini 1939; Henderson, 1947; Massingham, 1929; Simri, 1969; Guttmann, 1978). Games in which males competed were self-testing bouts, contests, or mass participations. The ritual game served to legitimize hierarchical power by ascribed godly power (the granting of favor by the supernatural). The recreational game legitimized hierarchical power by merit (the earning of power by achievement). Therefore, both models of power were available for males, but not recognized for females. Until recently, sport as a power symbol has been perceived as the homosocial domain, as control symbolized in attributes of competitiveness, strength, and prowess.

As suggested earlier, women's past sport participation has been largely expressive activity and agile body manipulation (e.g., dance or acrobatics, light-object manipulation or ball-tossing; Abdou, 1961; Klafs and Lyon, 1973; Metheny, 1965). These stress quality in performance such as a near-perfect balance-beam gymnastic routine, rather than the quantity of outcome in achieving power, such as winning a football match. However, over the past 100 years in the United States girls have been playing more games and sports classified as boys' activities. Boys, on the other hand, have been narrowing their games repertoire to sports (Kleiber, 1980; Lever, 1976; Sutton-Smith, 1979; Sutton-Smith and Rosenberg, 1961). This seems to indicate that the females in the United States are adopting the male kinetic model, seeking and achieving power in both procedures and rewards. If the same activities are particpated in by females as well as by males, then the same socially determined traits should be manifest in each gender. The question that arises is whether the scarce commodity of hierarchical power can logistically accommodate the increased gender participation. Simply stated, just how much room is there at the top? One technique used in the United States is to widen the number of situations in which individuals can claim the position of "number one." For example, a preschooler can be the number one ball-roller in his or her group; a fourth grader can be number one basketball dribbler in his or her school; a student-athlete can be number one guard on the high school basketball team. The point is that the pool of number one positions in diverse activities and in levels of these activities has expanded dramatically.

4. *Women's sport participation is a social anomaly.* Various sets of arguments have been employed to "prove" that sports competition by females is socially unacceptable. Talbot's (1981) adaptation of Douglas' (1966) framework is used here to show how women's sports participation has been interpreted by its opponents as a social anomaly. The first strategy identified by Douglas is to place the questionable behavior or anomaly into a category and deny its other attributes. Talbot observed that opponents of women's sports participation argue that because one category of women, housewives, are not interested in sport, then no women are interested. Other groups of females are completely overlooked. The second strategy is to remove the anomaly by physical control. Talbot reminds us that women have been traditionally excluded from club houses, golf courses, playing fields, and other sport facilities because these were considered male preserves. Only recently have women been allowed to play, albeit begrudgingly, at nonpeak times. The third argument is that the anomaly should be avoided as abhorrent. Thus, claims Talbot, myths have been promulgated that contact sports are not ladylike and that international sportswomen must be lesbians. Both of these statements attack the image of the sportswoman as unnatural and perverted. Talbot (1981) reports a recent statement by Ted Crocker, Secretary of the Football Association of England, 1978: "it's not natural for girls to play football." This attitude is not dead. The fourth observation sees that anomaly as highly dangerous and to be avoided. This myth suggests that strenuous sports activity harms women's reproductive functions. The truth is that the body cavity which contains the female sex organs is by far more protected than the male's sex organs. The fifth defense of the anomaly is the use of ambiguous and deleterious symbols in poetry, mythology and ritual. In sports literature, poetry, and picture, there are recurrent themes of the warlike athletic Amazons depicted as deformed women or as

semi-men, and the stereotype of the female athlete in field events as a steroided, bewhiskered, hpyermuscled, coarse-featured behemoth. While all of these five arguments claiming that women's sports participation as a social anomaly are spurious, a few additional observations may help dispel these myths for good.

The first notion, that because housewives are not interested in sport, no women are, is not defensible. The data suggest otherwise. For example, the rate of high school girls' participation in interscholastic sports increased dramatically in the 1970s. According to the United States Commission on Civil Rights (1980), girls' participation in organized sports programs in the United States increased from 194,000 in 1970-71 to over 2,000,000 in 1978-79, which is nearly a 700 percent increase, while the high school female enrollment decreased five percent. In colleges, intramural and intercollegiate women's sports programs increased during the 1970s 100 percent, while women's enrollment in colleges increased only 40 percent (U.S. Commission on Civil Rights, 1980). AIAW intercollegiate sports competitors grew from 1972 to a total of 100,000 in 1980, which compares favorably to 170,000 male competitors in 1980 NCAA intercollegiate sports (Leonard, 1980:202). It is of interest to note that the first tennis tournament for women took place in 1881, and the national women's singles championship, under the auspices of the United States Lawn Tennis Association, was established in 1887 (Cheska and Gerber, 1981:80). The first women's intercollegiate basketball game took place in 1896 between the University of California, Berkeley, and Stanford University (Cheska and Gerber, 1981; Emery, 1979). According to Cheska and Gerber (1981), women's first real venture into competitive sport in the United States began with croquet in the early 1860s, and there has been a steady growth except during the 1930s and 1940s during this century. Therefore, it is ludicrous to suggest women are not interested in competitive sports.

The attempt to limit sports participation by women through physical control has historical roots in the barring of women as performers or spectators at the ancient Olympics. Even in 1801, a female teacher in Salem, Massachusetts, was virtually ostracized when it was thought that she had instructed her female pupils in the techniques of skating. In Germany in 1851, a woman was nearly stoned to death for daring to ice-skate (Cheska and Gerber, 1981:78). Competitive sports and facilities at which they were played were considered the bastion of the male. "Going to the club" was a male prerogative, and women were excluded. It was not until the late 1970s that women were officially accepted into many fashionable tennis, golf, and ski sports clubs as full-fledged members, rather than as guests to occasional social dinner and dance events. With the passage of Title IX in 1972 female students could no longer be denied access to school sports facilities. This provided practice and playing space for girls' as well as boys' school sports teams. The past practice of confining women's sports to inferior or even worse, no facilities, is gradually changing, but the myth of exclusiveness fades slowly.

The third idea that women who participate in sports are somehow unnatural and perverted, is hard to erase because the attitude is in the eyes of the beholder. Appropriate gender behavior is socially determined and affective, not inherent. The controversy over the use of steroids (androgen) to build muscular strength in athletes has indirectly proven that females have naturally about one-half the muscle mass of males and that no diet, training, or exercise can measurably alter that. The prolonged use of steroids can increase muscle strength and produce secondary sex characteristics, but the price of this practice is so high in self-perception that it is seldom followed knowingly by females. The unusual nature of the practice makes it spectacular news, thus highlighting its uniqueness. The subtle prerequisite to skilled sports performance is the absence of bulky, heavy, inhibiting attire. The increase of sports participation by women in the early years of this century made imperative the development of the "bloomer" outfit for exercise. At that time exposure of the ankles and legs of female athletes was immodest. The analogy that followed was that nudity, which was considered exposure of any of the body parts, was immoral. Therefore, athletes were immoral. This questionable exposure of the female body still haunted the sportswoman in conservative regions of the United States and Canada during the 1930s and 1940s. However, the freedom of the 1920s had set a prototype which was to return after the depression and war years in the United States. Since the female body had been under "wraps" for so many centuries, it is understandable that the rapid exposure of the female form in this century was a radical change and was resisted as a moral issue. The positive image of the healthy, trim, firm-bodied sportswoman was promoted by sports clothing manufacturers in the mid-1900s, and eventually convinced American women that sports clothing is a must, whether or not worn by true sports participants. Other advertisers for products from brassieres to beer have joined in selling the sporting image and their wares as well. During the 1970s women sports champions became sportswear fashion plates photographed on the tennis courts, golf courses, and swimming pools.

Because strength and endurance sports events are still considered appropriate for males, while graceful sports are assumed appropriate for women, when women enter strength events such as field events of javelin, discus, shot put, or high jump, resistance is felt. Likewise, when men enter graceful sports, such as figure skating, the accusation of femininity is registered by some. Even in gymnastics, the female sequences stress fluidity, flexibility, and appearance of effortlessness; the male sequences stress power moves and endurance, and fluidity is used usually only in transition moves. The positive perception of feminine images in sports performances is gradually becoming the norm, but there is still a long way to go.

The fourth anomaly is that strenuous sports participation harms women's reproductive functions. Cheska and Gerber (1981) have noted that the normal female matures earlier than the male and produces a greater amount of estrogen and less androgen. The male produces significantly more androgen than estrogen. This is basic to the development of appropriate secondary sex characteristics (Wyrick, 1974). Compared with the male's bone and muscle structure, the female anatomical structure is characterized by less bone and muscle mass, a lower center of gravity, and more fatty tissue. Upon the advent of puberty, the female begins to experience sequentially the specific female life processes of ovulation, menstruation, pregnancy, and menopause. Menstrual cramps are common among adolescent girls. However, whether the cause is anatomical-psychological change or related to psychological factors, physical activity almost always has a beneficial effect. Menstruation need not interrupt performance of most games or sports. Generally, female athletes are able to achieve their average sports performance throughout the entire menstrual cycle, including menses (Shaffer, 1972; G. V. Mann, 1981). In the 1956 Melbourne Olympics, six gold medals were won by women who were menstruating (Heusner, 1966). Early research by Erdelyi (1960), Gendel (1971) and others indicates no reason to restrict physical activity of women because of the reproductive organs and no need for concern about later effects of sport competition on pregnancy, labor, and later health (Heusner, 1966). Wyrick (1974) has shown that women athletes who are in excellent physical condition have an easier delivery than other women. Injury to female reproductive organs in sports participation is highly unlikely. Because of the internal protective nature of the uterine cavity, it is considerably more protected than the male genitalia (Dunkle, 1974). The breasts of the female are just as amenable to protective equipment as are male gonads. It has been shown that severe bruises are not causal agents of breast cancer. The myth of reproductive injury through sports participation is as scientifically defensible as the flat-earth concept.

The fifth strategy in the argument against women's sport participation is the use of negative symbols in poetry, mythology, and ritual. This kind of rhetoric is slowly being replaced by positive imaging of the sportswoman in television, periodicals, and newspapers. A tentative respect for women sports competitors is increasing in the United States. However, the stereotype of the Amazonian athlete is still a concern. Snyder (Snyder and Spreitzer, 1978) asked 400 adults what types of sport participation would enhance a women's femininity. Over 50 percent cited swimming, tennis, and gymnastics, while fewer than 20 percent named softball, basketball, and track. When 328 college athletes were asked if they felt a stigma was attached to women who "participate in the sport you specialize in," 54 percent of the basketball players and 47 percent of the track-and-field participants said "yes," while only 38 percent of the swimmers and divers and 27 percent of the gymnasts answered in the affirmative. Sixty-five percent of a control group of 275 college women indicated that there was a general stigma attached to women's participation in sports. However, Kingsley, Brown, and Siebert (1977) revealed a positive social acceptance of female athletes by 240 nonathlete college women who reported no evidence of social stigma toward female softball players, as well as none toward dance performers. It may be that the negative stereotypes linger on, but not all our social interactions are determined by them (Rohrbaugh, 1979). Eleanor Metheny (1965) characterizes as acceptable sports for women those which rely on skill rather than on strength or force, employ a spatial barrier between opponents, use light implements to manipulate light objects, and display the body in graceful, flowing movements that are attractive to the male. Sports not acceptable for women, according to Metheny, are those which use physical force to overpower or subdue an opponent, show strength, and involve direct bodily contact during competition.

Although the myths surrounding women's sports participation as a social anomaly have been exposed for what they are, traditional attitudes die hard. The issue is still a contemporary one.

Girls are still more likely to be given dolls with which to play, while boys are encouraged to play with footballs, basketballs, and soccer balls (Sutton-Smith, 1979). According to Michener (1976), parents still prefer their daughters to be cheerleaders rather than competitive team members.

Female Sport Participation in Other Cultures

The male Western sports model of instrumentality has been exported to unlikely countries the world over, such as Mongolia and Tonga. However, women's sports in these areas have not substantially progressed. Not only is there no equal opportunity for female participation, there is no opportunity at all. In many developing nations, such as those of Africa, only the talented, highly trained male athletes compete in sports. The broad base of general athletic participation is missing. Under such conditions male athletes are singularly identified and intensely trained to compete internationally. It is not uncommon for coaches from countries, such as the U.S.S.R, the United States, or China, to be imported to help "develop" a national team. This has occurred only infrequently in women's competition to date. In a way, this practice could be likened to trying to spread the frosting on a cake without the cake. The international competitive participation and success is used for purposes of political and diplomatic export. (See the section in this chapter on sport and international relations.) But this plan can backfire. Since the 1970s a handful of highly trained female athletes have defected from their homelands to more favorable and affluent nations. However, this has occurred generally between more developed countries. Such women include Martina Navratilova, touted as the world champion female tennis player and originally from Poland, and China's national team tennis player, Hu Na, who in 1982 defected to the United States.

Anthropological research has demonstrated that some societies, such as the Choctaw Indians of Southeastern United States and American Southwestern Indian tribes, have healthy attitudes toward female sport, attitudes that seem more progressive than those typical of contemporary Euro-America. In these contexts the females' interest and participation in sport is encouraged and rewarded. The model Choctaw female is one who is actively involved in sports. The preferred young female image of Southwestern Indian tribes is one of active involvement in sports such as basketball, softball and volleyball. The support system of these young women is strong and gratifying.

The Future of Women in Sport

What do the data suggest about the future of female sport participation? Does she stay home and play checkers with the kids, take to the streets in protest, or develop novel alternatives? Of these alternatives the following appear most reasonable and likely.

The first of these alternatives involves moving toward the "equal valuation of male and female gender roles" as these are manifested in sport competition. Differences would be recognized but not used as a basis for differential access to power. The female would continue to perform expressively, displaying sympathy, affection, compassion, and tenderness, along with traits of sensitivity, warmth, and shyness. Likewise, the publicly oriented male would perform instrumentally, showing independence, assertiveness, ambition, aggression, and risktaking, along with traits of leadership, dominance, and competition; these traits combine to form a social image of masculinity (Duquin, 1978:90). A double standard of value or excellence would exist, even within the same sport. This is already the case in gymnastics. Gymnastics for men, for example, is based on strong tumbling activities involving varying degrees of danger and difficulty, with only transitional corner manuevers which could be described as "effortless." Gymnastics for women (free exercise) is based on agile, rhythmic dance manuevers with synchronized flow, elegance, and grace. Despite the differences, equal status would be accorded both male and female athlete under this type of a system.

A second alternative is "androgyny or valuing integrated human traits rather than separate gender traits." Because socially defined gender roles have served in the past to define specialization in most societies, such as in economic, political, religious, domestic, and leisure activities, the concept of nondifferentiated "humanness" seems difficult to envision. However, recent investigations of cross-sex-typed individuals by Maccoby (1966) and Bem (1975) have shown that persons who perceive themselves as both instrumental (maleness trait) and expressive (femaleness trait) show psychological well-being, behavior flexibility, and performance effectiveness. The combination of instrumental and expressive valuation of self is the essence of monoandrogynism, in which each individual develops both traditionally masculine and traditionally feminine activities.

The incorporation of both gender roles in an ideal model of sport participation is given credibility by Duquin's (1978:101) notion that sport is basically human movement and as such has an infinite variety of qualities that need to be recognized. For example, the traditional Eastern orientation to sport is more of a process-product approach that emphasizes body awareness, sensitivity, meditation, and joy. Also, Adam Smith (1975) has suggested that the path of sensitivity to the expressive element in sport culminates in quality performance. The Esalen Sport Institute of California is a prototype of an androgynous perspective toward sport. The institute conducts sports programs stressing feeling at home with one's body, introspective quality, the aesthetic nature of human movement, complementarity in moving and responding, and communicating nonverbally with others.

A third future alternative is the "adoption of male gender traits by females (or vice versa)" in the same sport activities. Because modern sport is outcome-oriented, it may be that sport participation must be weighted toward masculine traits. Duquin (1978:99) contends, "Sport, conducted as an instrumental activity, would give primary attention to the more talented and serious sport pursuers as opposed to the less instrumental, more expressive participant". Research conducted in the United States points to females participating in competitive sports and displaying male traits such as aggressiveness, assertiveness, competitiveness, mastery of the physical environment (Balazs, 1975; Gerber et al., 1974; Harris, 1973; King and Chi, 1979; Kingsley, Brown and Siebart, 1977; Rohrbaugh, 1979). The philosophical approach of parity in sport opportunities and competition inherent in the Title IX of the Educational Amendments Act of 1972 reinforces the instrumental approach to sports participation. With the greater equivalency in school sports programs, the assumption is that the girls' opportunities will be brought closer in line with those of the boys. In other words, the male model serves as the standard. One cannot help making reference to the increasing display of male characteristics by female competitors in sports as well as in business, political and public leadership endeavors. Recent research has shown that when females receive training regimens similar to those of males, women are more physiologically similar to males in lean body mass and cardiovascular performance than previous researchers assumed (Burke, 1977; Drinkwater, 1973). The females also perform similarly to the males. Increasingly, research points to the potential equality of female performance even in male-dominated physical activities, such as track events.

Of these three alternatives the latter appears to be the mostlikely direction of the immediate future. As the world moves into the postindustrial era, women continue to play a more vital role in economies and concomitantly invade the games and sport domains once the exclusive property of males. In this process, it appears that females are adopting the male kinetic model.

Additional Questions

There are several additional issues which anthropologists should explore in this attempt to understand and interpret the role of women's sports in society. These include the following:

1. Why have the differences in the reproductive organs of the male and female rather than other body similarities been used to define gender behavior?
2. Why have "male sports" been considered appropriate public contests while "women's sports" generally have not?
3. What evidence do we have of reversal or exceptions to the above model of women's sports participation? What cultural ramifications surround this reversal?
4. Why have females in developed societies adopted the male competitive model of success in sports?
5. Are there other cultural traits of game participation available in addition to the competitive model for both sexes?

SPORT AND AGING

Until recently, minimal attention has been paid by scientists to the issue of sport and aging. As a result, there is little documented evidence regarding the benefits or possible dangers of sport participation by the elderly. Sport is a subcategory of physical activity that has many dimensions: psychological, economic, social, and symbolic. In order to be understood, the broader issue of the elderly and their general role in society needs to be put in perspective. In other words, how society regards the older segment of its citizenry and how these persons regard themselves and their roles are vital to sport as issues with implications for the elderly.

Images of Old Age

Before examining sport as valuable to the elderly and to the elderly's place in society, it is necessary to review the panhuman phenomenon of old age itself. The first obvious fact is that old age is the vestibule of death. Weiss (1981) suggested that aging is a process genetically programmed into the human animal; that the physiological maximum of somewhere between 90 to 100 years represents the top limits on human life, except in unusual cases. According to the

United States Congress Senate Committee on Foreign Relations Report (1980), the world population in the mid-1980s was estimated to be 4.4 billion. In 1980 the world population under age 15 was 35 percent while those over age 64 was only six percent. The startling discrepancy is seen in the comparison of developed and developing countries. In the former, 1980 statistics suggest that 24 percent of the population was under age 15, with 11 percent over 64. In the developing groups, these percentages were 39 and four, respectively. It appears that the aging issue is an issue of the developed countries of the world. Worldwide, life expectancy is 61 years. However, in the less-developed areas it is only 57 but 72 among the more developed groups. In this century, the average life expectancy in the United States has increased more than 25 years, from 47 in 1900 to over 73 in 1981 (Fries and Crapo, 1981:74).

In the later part of the life span, physiological deceleration is inevitable. Both the length of the life span and physical demise are universals. Everybody dies. Biologically there is an arrest of the growth process, a reversal of size, a decline in body efficiency, and a deterioration of the body structure. These changes are called primary aging and are initially determined by heredity. However, this process can be modified by environmental factors as can secondary aging resulting from accidental damage and illness, which accelerates primary aging. It is the modification of the primary and secondary aging factors in human life to which this section addresses itself. Specifically, it centers on two questions: (1) Is sports participation a reasonable way to deter aging? (2) Can the elderly contribute to society through their involvement in sports?

Disengagement vs. Activity

In order to address these concerns, an examination of two views of old age must be understood. One view regards the decline accompanying old age as inevitable, so the older person should withdraw from past activity, even though this results in mutual disengagement between him or herself and the rest of society (Cumming, and Henry, 1961). The other view suggests that the older person should fight against or postpone old age by continuing an active life. The elderly should maintain social ties and engage in as many activities as possible. These two theoretical approaches to old age, disengagement or activity, reflect in differing ways the general structure of a society, its intergenerational relationships and its cultural value system.

In the activity model, the elderly can continue to contribute to a society in productive, repository, educative, and symbolic ways. Where subsistence techniques have remained traditional, as in hunting-gathering and herding societies, the elderly often are able to contribute throughout their extended life spans. For example, women provide child care, and men supervise ritual ceremony. Simmons (1945), in his study of the social status of the aged in relation to the material culture and formal social structure in primitive societies, found that aged women tended to retain their property rights longer than men, in hunting, fishing, and gathering societies. However, the aged men were better able to preserve the control of property in farming and herding societies. In communities which lack written processes, the human mind and speech are the major mechanisms of information storage and transmittal. Thus, the elderly can serve not only as instructors in the technology but as repositories of the society's wisdom. Their role as story-teller brings to the young the important rationale and personalization of abstract societal values. Often paralleling these functions in tribal societies, the revered elderly serve as moral evaluators, hearing and passing sanctions on transgressors of societal norms.

On the other hand, the productive technology may become obsolete within one or two generations in modern society. This may lead to the devaluation of traditional technical knowledge and gives support to the withdrawal model of old-age adjustment. This process has occurred in several African tribal groups as modernity has encroached on their rural communal life. The book by the anthropologist and former President of Nigeria, Jomo Kenyatta (1965), addresses this issue. When information, as in our modern day, can be recorded and retrieved accurately, efficiently, and almost universally by mechanical means (e.g., writing, printing, computer), the memory of the elderly is superfluous. When the transmittal of the societal mores is embedded in formal specialized educative and jural systems. then judgments by the elderly are ignored. For example, the United States, as a rapidly changing society, epitomizes this approach to the elderly. The aged inferentially are considered obsolete and in turn are conditioned to accept withdrawal as the appropriate model of successful aging. This negative valuation of the elderly may reflect a hold-over attitude from our earlier history in which the environmental necessity for physical strength, endurance, experimentaton, and abandon was needed to "tame" the land. Youthful values were extolled because innovative and daring rather than traditional solutions were needed to solve perplexing growth problems. Presently, Americans seem to have transferred the "throw-away" attitude of our material culture to our view of the elderly. When he or she is thought to be no longer fully productive, the older worker is retired. A further extension of this attitude is seen in the begrudging treatment of old people who require custodial care and supervision for physical or mental reasons. In Western societies such care is a social responsibility of conscience. In primitive societies where environmental resources are marginal and survival requires great effort, the elderly are often abandoned. For example, among traditional Arctic Eskimo, those elderly members no longer able to contribute equal to their consumption of precious food resources were ceremoniously killed or voluntarily committed suicide.

Nevertheless, in the United States and northern Europe the

retired citizenry can be classified as the leisure class, for they have been provided the necessities of life exclusive of work. Their condition is one of freedom from work; the older person has become the user of leisure time (Neugarten, 1974). If the older can retain"relative good health, education, purchasing power, free time, and political involvement, they are not likely to become the neglected, the isolated or the expendables of the society" (Neugarten, 1974). Because the withdrawal/disengagement perspective is inconsistent with the basic quality of sports, attention here is directed toward the more appropriate activity model.

Sports Contribution to Older Americans

Does sport, in fact, as a version of physical activity, in any way assist in deterring the debilitation of aging in the life cycle? Anthropologists have not attended specifically to sports as an agent in postponing physical deterioration, but they have had a broad interest in the role of the older person in society, and their observations show a correlation between continuous vigorous physical exercise and longevity. Researchers have found in studying active, long-lived individuals in the Caucasus of southern U.S.S.R., the Hunza people of West Pakistan, and the Vilacamba of the mountains of Eduador, one basic commonality: a high level of physical fitness conditioned by a great deal of physical exertion. In these diverse peoples' daily activities a high degree of cardiovascular (heart and circulatory) fitness is sustained along with other physiological systemic benefits (Leaf and Launois, 1975). This finding is significant because sports participation is one way to achieve a high level of physical exertion in complex modern societies where the demand of the physical attributes on the human body in productive work, daily maintenance, and even leisure activities does not reach the body's organic optimum. In the process of aging, the anticipation of physical debilitation and reduced social involvement increasingly militate against one's systemic well-being, but a regimen of vigorous sport participation may feasibly deter physiological decline and increase social expectancies.

Although one might hope that older Americans would spend a lot of time in sports participation, this does not seem to be the case. In a national survey, Harris (National Council on the Aging, 1975:59) found that of people over the age of sixty-five, about one-fourth spent a lot of time walking or participating in recreational activities, while only three percent regularly participated in more physically demanding sports such as swimming, tennis, or golf. Zborowski (1962) studied the relationship between aging (as opposed to age) and sports activity. He found a consistency of physical activity patterns in older men and women; both groups engaged in activities similar to those of their younger years. However, in both populations, male and female, group activity, such as team sports, decreased noticeably after forty. Conversely, Zborowski noted that solitary sports participation such as walking declines less. He concluded that the withdrawal influence of age-related negative expectations and corresponding restrictions on behavior became self-fulfilling prophecies. Harootyan (1982) compared the kind and frequency of physical activity by men and women under sixty to those over sixty years of age. Of 160 activities mentioned by the younger group, 129 were noted by the older group. He found that older people who remained at least partially active tended to substitute less strenuous, solitary activities for the more strenuous and group-oriented physical and sports activities of the earlier years. Less strenuous activities most frequently cited were walking, conditioning exercises, and gardening. Except for the somewhat strenuous activities of swimming, jogging, tennis, and golf, older people did not generally pursue sports in the later years of life, especially group-oriented sports such as baseball, basketball, football, handball and hockey. For the few people who did, a consistent pattern of lifetime physical activity was the key factor. Harootyan (1982:143) concluded:

> The physiological decrements that occur with age due to decreases in physical activity over the life cycle have been documented. But it is known, too, that these physiological decrements need not occur to the degree that they do. If one's goal is to improve the general health and well-being of people in old age, it is clear that higher levels of consistent physical activity should be fostered during young adult and middle ages.... It seems then, that the potential exists for increased participation by older men and women in sports activity, perhaps, best exemplified by swimming, golf, softball, volleyball, tennis, handball, track/field, bicycling, and hiking (i.e., noncontact sports that nevertheless require medium to high levels of physical activity). Even contact sports such as touch football, soccer, and field hockey are feasible sports for older people, given appropriate rules of play and medical standards for participation. Regardless of which kind of sports activity is involved, it is known that over 60 percent of the older population in general are not hampered in activity by chronic illnesses, creating a potential pool of over 15 million people age sixty-five and over from which to draw.

Several researchers have looked at the reasons given by physically active Americans, including the elderly, for their participation in sport and recreation. These include a sense of well-being, health, sociability, habit, self-worth, and fad (Anderson, 1959; Fasting, 1979; Harootyan, 1982; Miller, 1982). In general, these motivations are viewed as positive factors in the delay of physical deterioration and the enhancement of life quality.

Some elderly persons find satisfaction in participating in

organized competitive sports programs. Yves Jeannotat (1980:480) quotes Dr. Andrivet, former head of the French National Sports Institute:

> I can see no deep-rooted reason why veterans (skilled participants) should refrain from precisely that which renders sport so attractive, namely the element of competition. All hinges, however, on their level of physical fitness and the training programme they put themselves through by way of preparation for competition.... We know how to measure our efforts, but only competitive sport gives us the opportunity of assessing our physical worth.

Various local, state, and national competitive events for older groups are becoming more common in the United States. For example, the state of Virginia held its first Golden Olympics in 1979, "combining sports and games with entertainment, dancing, fellowship, and fun" (Kendrick and Wyatt, 1981:41). The specific competitions included track and field events, softball hit and throw, riflery, billiards, horseshoes, tennis, duck pin bowling, ten pin bowling, golf, croquet, swimming, miniature golf, and bridge. Throughout the United States and Canada various senior citizen organizations promote sports for the elderly; for example, the National Senior Sports Associations, who reserve membership for men and women fifty years of age or older. The most highly organized official senior sports competitions are the Senior Olympics in track and in swimming. These were founded in Santa Monica, California in 1969, and held in 1970, the first competition for people age forty and over. Age brackets are in five-year groupings up to the oldest participant. Several states, including California, Illinois, Indiana, Ohio, and Virginia, sponsor their own competitions. Master's Sport competition is held in each sport; those best known are golf, swimming, tennis, and track and field (Cureton, 1982). Swimming tournaments, relays, and telegraph meets involve thousands of competitors striving to better their own record and possibly break a world's record for their own age group. National and regional tennis tourneys are held on grass, clay, and hard court surfaces by the Super Senior Tennis organization in cooperation with the United States Tennis Association (Selder, Roll, Carter, 1980).

Ever since the Older Americans Act of 1965 and the subsequent amendment in 1975, which broadened the definition of social services for older persons, there has been an increasing public awareness in the United States of the needs of older citizens. This may be symptomatic of the country's gradual acknowledgement that retirement without purpose, program, or vitality is counterproductive to the public welfare (Murphy, 1977). Underlying the choice of physical activity by the aging is a far greater social issue, the worth of the elderly to society. This issue is far from resolution in the United States.

Older Americans' Contribution Through Sports

The second question concerning sport and aging, "Can the elderly contribute to society through their involvement in sports?" takes the issue beyond sport as simply physical involvement. Too frequently we think of only the physical benefits of sports to the individual participant. However, there is a wide range of additional benefits that accompany sport involvement. The social context in which physical activity occurs can enhance the participant's experience. This sharing with others contributes to enjoyment as well as the potential continuance of the physical activity. Often, as individuals age, their support network of relatives, friends and acquaintances diminishes to leave the person increasingly separated from others. As a survivor, life's alternatives for social activity shrink perilously. This condition is reflected in the decrease of group sports among the elderly. This need not be the norm. A counter-movement to combat this loneliness is the senior citizen centers which have sprung up over the United States. Myerhoff (1978) notes the importance of such a center in the lives of Jewish survivors in Los Angeles.

A role for elders not frequently considered in sports, but extremely important in a culture's historical perspective, is the elderly as myth-tellers. Older persons either have a first-hand experience of "the great game" or have at their memory's fingertips accounts that they were given by their seniors. Their story-telling provides historic continuity, preservation of heroes, symbolic depth, and record of communal expression, from which youth can evaluate their society and themselves. Another role of the elderly in sport is in the administration of the sport event. Consider the Trobriand situation. The men who see themselves as too old to actually play in the intervillage cricket match are of much value as umpires, scorekeepers, and general critics of performance. In addition, their pre-game conversation keeps the game's history and meaning in perspective. This oral transmission of the past is a means of intergenerational understanding and cultural continuity. Without individuals filling these roles and providing this information, the game would suffer from lack of historical depth.

The role of the elderly as teacher is also important. Advice can take the form of skill instruction, as coaching, improving players' performance, and teaching strategies effective in past situations that could be useful in present conditions. This historical pool of knowledge is valuable to the present generation of performers and to the rich cultural heritage of the group. The Cherokee shaman trains and supervises the village's team that competes against other villages in the racket game, and clearly fills these functions (Mooney, 1890). The elderly bring past information, experiences, and symbolic meanings of association with the sport to the value system of the group. Lancy's (1977) description of the older men teaching *Malang*, a mathematical counting board game, to the young Kpelle boys of Liberia, Africa, points to the important social behavior taught by the game participation. When the youth were drawn away from this instruction by the intrusion of foreign highway construction crewmen and truck drivers, who taught them the games of *Ludo* and checkers, the social fabric and the traditional deference to the older men taught through *Malang* was endangered.

The elderly in communal sports events perform roles of administration, instruction, interpretation, and elaboration. They become the principal "myth tellers" in their respective communities. They are important to the sport process.

VIOLENCE IN SPORTS

The violence surrounding modern sporting events has reached alarming proportions. Examples are myriad: fist and stick fights between ice hockey players in North America, hooliganism at soccer matches in England, spectator abuse of game officials in South America, and verbal diatribes of baseball and basketball coaches toward officials in the United States. Strangely, these are considered normal in many circles.

What really constitutes violence? In general it is characterized by rough and injurious physical force, action, or treatment. It can also be rough or immoderate vehemence, as of feeling or language (Urdang, 1968). Inherent in violence is aggression, which may be viewed as the intentional response a person makes to inflict pain or harm on another person (Alderman, 1974:225). Alderman distinguishes two types of aggression, reactive and instrumental. Reactive or hostile aggression is the delivery of physical or psychological punishment as an end rather than a means (Silva, 1979:202). Berkowitz (1965) calls it "angry aggression" because the aggressor is often perturbed with the target of the act, "with both perception of the other person as a threat or noxious stimuli and the emotion of anger being necessary concomitants" (Alderman, 1974:229). Instrumental aggression involves an intent to inflict pain or injury as a means to an end, tangible reward as money, victory, or praise (Silva, 1979:202).

Violence in sport is reactive and/or instrumental aggression committed by a person attending, engaging in, or otherwise involved in an athletic event upon any other player, spectator, coach, game official, public and/or private official or enterpreneur, or property. A subcategory of sports violence not often considered is the physical abuse of animals by perpetuating aggression between them, usually leading to the death of one or more of the contenders. Examples include cockfights and pit-bull terrier dog fights. Modern bullfights also lead to death of the bull by the hands of humans, in the name of sport.

Sport violence is not unique to modern times. Its presence over the ages is obvious (Atyeo, 1978; Lasch, 1979). Historians have noted the violent extremes of athletes in the Roman and Byzantium Empires. Allan Guttmann (1981), in summarizing violence at the Roman games, cites the fighting among spectators in Pompeii, which caused that city to lose the right to stage games for an entire decade. Guttmann also noted the arrest of a favorite charioteer in 390 A.D., which touched off riots that ended only when Theodosius I had the army slaughter 30,000 of the rioters. In Justinian's time (483-565 A.D.) chariot racing was not so much a sport as a form of political contest. The two leading teams, the Greens and the Blues, were supported by different political factions whose violent rivalry led to the bloody riots and to the fiery destruction of Constantinople in 432 A.D. (Bryer, 1967; Encyclopedia Americana, 1964; Cameron, 1976). The shadowy evidence of ritual killing in the Mayan rubber ball game, *Pok-ta-Pok*, and its later variant, the Aztec *Tlatchi* ball game (300-1500 A.D.), attests to the ultimate price of participation. Medieval football, its origins embedded in seasonal festivals, was a rough-and-tumble free-for-all between two villages or rival groups. The violence and mayhem surrounding this ball game in Europe are well-documented (Elias and Dunning, 1971; Renson, 1981). Accidental killing was not uncommon (Olmert, 1981). Renson (1981) recorded a complaint about the game of *souille* (variant of football) submitted in 1780 to the Council of Brabant, Belgium. The indictment read:

> On the day of the battle, more than a thousand people gathered on the battlefield, both players and observers. When the local magistrate threw up the ball, more than 400 people hurled themselves on it and did violence to each other until the ball reached its goal. After this scene was played out, some returned full of blood, others were overheated, and the rest were half asphyxiated, so that most of them were obliged to stay in bed, if not that day then the next. And it was even more distressing for the poor farmer, who found his land completely trampled, his ditches destroyed, and his hedgerows ripped out. In a word, his land looked as though the enemy had camped there (Renson, 1981:5).

Clifford Geertz (1972:27) in his account of the modern Balinese cockfight claims:

> Every people, the proverb has it, loves its own form of violence. The cockfight is the Balinese reflection on theirs: on its look, its uses, its force, its fascination. Drawing on almost every level of Balinese experience, it brings together themes -- animal savagery, male narcissism, opponent gambling, status rivalry, mass excitement, blood sacrifice -- whose main connection is their involvement with rage and the fear of rage, and, binding them into a set of rules which at once contains them and allows them play, builds a

symbolic structure in which, over and over again, the reality of their inner affiliation can be intelligibly felt...Balinese go to cockfights to find out what a man, usually composed, aloof, almost obsessively self-absorbed, a kind of moral autocosm, feels like when attacked, tormented, challenged, insulted, and driven in result to the extremes of fury, he has totally triumphed or been brought totally low.

As Geertz points out, violence grows out of the cultural context of a society. It is a customary and repetitive procedure for dealing with aggression (rage) and creates a metaphor or social commentary (meaning) on individual and collective existence. It also provides an exciting reversal of ordinary life.

Factors Underlying Sport Violence

Instinctive A variety of theories have been proposed to explain the human penchant for violence. One of the most frequently cited explanations is the so-called "instinctive" or "drive-reduction" theory. Basic to this perspective is the notion that humans, like other animals, have an instinctive bent toward aggression (Lorenz, 1966). This aggression is basic to species survival; it is there and must be expressed or released. The physical contest furnishes a socially approved "throw away, nonserious" drain-off vehicle for the expression of that explosive quality of human nature. Sport in this sense is a controlled detonation.

Among the Trobriand Islanders, cricket has often been viewed as a substitute for intratribal warfare. The British actually introduced the game with that expressed purpose in mind. They outlawed war and gave the natives the game of cricket in its place. And, to no one's surprise, the Trobriands adopted the game in that spirit, even though the war symbols continue to temper the game process. The cricket ball pitch-style is the same as that associated with throwing the war spear. The body decorations of the players include war colors and designs. Also, the field entry and exit formations and the team chants have many warfare connotations.

Another example of seemingly displaced aggression is the Balinese cockfight. The Balinese people are nonaggressive. Their daily lives are marked by social decorum and calm. Yet, the ferocity of the cockfight is replayed regularly for the great majority of Balinese males, who find it compellingly and thoroughly satisfying. While cockfighting is outlawed, its popularity has not diminished; the game has merely been taken underground. In the United States, cockfighting is still common though illegal in most states. It is estimated that as many as 500,000 Americans have some direct contact with cockfights each year (Herzog and Cheek, 1979). Is this an important alternative to other forms of American violence?

The increase in modern sports violence, viewed from the perspective of the instinctive aggression theory, may be a result of society's repression of the aggressive behaviors available to people in earlier periods of human history. For example, early man had social warfare and other forms of physical retribution (e.g., explosive rituals of reversal), and physical exertion (e.g., hunting, chopping trees, handling a plow, carrying heavy burdens). The ordinary quality of modern life does not offer the variety of excitement that man needs to release the innate pressures toward aggression. Therefore, he seeks alternatives (Elias and Dunning, 1970). Lofland (1982:372) sees this search for alternatives as basic to crowd joy. The excited sport crowd responds to a staged contest as though it were a dramatic form of conflict (La Piere, 1938:477). The spectators become vicarious participants in the violence on the field. But, when they take the conflict literally, rather than symbolically, the crowd behavior becomes fan violence (Lofland, 1982:375).

Social learning The social learning theory is probably the most widely accepted aggression theory. It is based on the proposition that aggression is learned social behavior (Bandura, 1973). In other words, violence teaches violence. Bandura (1973) has demonstrated, for example, that children exposed to aggression learn and use that aggression in later behavior. Liebert and Baron (1972) have documented the powerful influence of the media on aggressive behavior in children. Television, movies, radio, and printed matter do affect child violence. In the Liebert and Baron study, those children not exposed to adult-modeling aggressive behavior tended to be less aggressive than those so exposed. Also, the children who witnessed aggressive behavior became more aggressive than they were prior to exposure. They seemed to learn from witnessing the specific aggressive styles that they later employed in their increased level of violent behavior.

It is thus suggested that sport violence is learned. Smith (1972:102) claims that the approval of violence in sport is not only an influence on the endurance of sport violence, but is also a factor in the reinforcement and legitimation of violence in general.

Crowding Another explanation for sport violence is the crowding phenomenon. There appears to be a correlation between crowding and violent acts. Research with animals has demonstrated this connection in a variety of populations (Storr, 1969). Perhaps the human system is biologically unable to remain in a confined space. Sitting in the midst of 100,000 football fans on a warm September afternoon may trigger that innate aversion to crowding, provoking a violent reaction, a reaction expressing the need to escape.

Related to the "crowding" explanation is the idea that pheremones can provoke violence. Pheremones, scents emitted by animals, including humans, which function primarily as sexual stimuli, can also initiate violence in the right setting. It is suggested that among males, pheremones increase testosterone levels. In erotic or romantic settings, this leads to some form of sexual release. In crowded situations, it can precipitate violence. For example, in some

European soccer stadia, crowding is such that men find it easier to roll up their programs and urinate on the concrete floor immediately in front of them rather than climb over their fellow spectators and use the public restrooms. Urine contains high levels of pheremones, so that a potentially dangerous scent often fills the air surrounding the already agitated spectators. The results can be explosive. The fans are driven to violence by their inability to escape the message that the overpowering pheremones are sending to their hormones.

Frustration-Aggression   Another proposition sometimes employed to explain human violence is the so-called "frustration aggression" theory (Dollard, Miller, Mowrer and Sears, 1939; Martens, 1975). This suggests that violence results when one is unable to reach a desired goal because of blocked access to the goal. The child wants a cracker, but his mother has secured them in a cookie tin with a tight-fitting lid. After tugging, shaking, and pulling unsuccessfully, the child gives up and, in anger, throws the tin on the floor, and caves in the lid with his size-six Buster Browns. Likewise, adults, especially in modern society, face a variety of stress resulting from the frustration of their efforts to achieve success. After rational pathways have not produced the desired results, some persons may revert to irrational aggressive action.

Mann (1979:354) has suggested that frustration aggression can explain some forms of spectator violence in sport. For example, when access to the stadium is blocked, or services not available, or when the fan feels an official has made an unjust call, the reaction can be a violent one. Someone gets punched, a beer bottle is tossed toward home plate, or a urinal is ripped off the restroom wall. Likewise, on the field, repeated failures can lead to aggression. Consider the fleet-footed halfback who on a normal Sunday afternoon would gain 150 yards but on this particular day has gained only 15 yards on a total of twenty-one carries. It's the fourth quarter, the team is losing, and he's hot. After being slammed to the ground for another loss, he leaps to his feet and pokes his fist into the space between the face guard and the helmet of a surprised opponent. Frustration aggression can work on spectator and participant alike.

Miscellaneous   One explanation for crowd violence at sporting events is the presence of alcohol. Fans drink, get surly, and start beating up on each other. Edwards and Rackages (1977) recount several incidents of spectator violence against athletes that involved liquor bottles or beer cans. The influence of booze on crowd decorum was demonstrated in Cleveland in 1974. The publicity department of the Indians' baseball team sponsored an "all you can drink ten-cent beer night." The results were chaos in the stands and the eventual wholesale destruction of property in both stadium and infield areas (Case and Boucher, 1981).

Kleinman (1960), in studying crowd behavior at basketball games, found that mobile and emotional coaches along with lax school administration policies facilitated the increase of crowd outbursts.

Similarly, Leach (1960), in examining fan behavior, concluded that the player's poor sportsmanship and the conduct of the coach were the prime factors underlying crowd behavior problems at sporting events. In a long-range study of crowd behavior at ice hockey games Meehan (1979) indicated that overt aggressive actions by players and/or coaches can have a marked effect on the nonverbal behavior of the crowd. Research indicates that observing aggressive models or even certain types of athletic events--such as wrestling, football, and ice hockey, as opposed to gymnastics and swimming--tends to heighten the potential in the observer for aggressive responses (Goldstein and Arms, 1971; Arms, Russell, and Sandelands, 1979; Lennon and Hatfield, 1980). Smith (1975) recorded that in thirty-four major crowd outbursts reported in the *Toronto Globe and Mail* newspaper from 1963 to 1973 that some sort of assaultive behavior preceded three-fourths of the action.

Cultural setting Some social scientists have concluded that culture defines acceptable levels of violence and aggression, and that such incidents are largely the manifestation of what is consistent with culture norms. This is suggested by Sipes (1973) in his cross-cultural analysis of the relationship between sport and war.

Culture acts to affect perception of violence, and this may be the key to sport violence levels in any society. For example, Blanchard (1981) has compared the reactions of two samples, Choctaw- and Anglo-Americans, to a series of hypothetical football situations: pictures showing various forms of verbal or physical confrontations that might occur in a typical football contest (see pages 84-86). The responses were instructive.

> In comparison with members of Anglo-American sample, the Choctaws were less likely to envision fighting between members of the same team, quicker to express disapproval of scenes of obvious violence, and slower to express concern over rule infractions. Where brutality was evident, the Choctaws expressed strong disapproval; the Anglos generally voiced approval. Where the reality of excessive violence was not clear, the Choctaws interpreted the event as having only competitive overtones; the Anglos tended to deal with these same events as violence. In general, while witnessing the same event, the Choctaw spectator would be likely to perceive less deliberate conflict than his Anglo counterpart (Blanchard, 1981:90).

This differential perception of violence probably lies somewhere in the cracks between the various theories that have been proposed. Certainly, no one explanation is satisfactory in itself. Perhaps, as Coakley (1981:52) has suggested, "actual displays of aggressive behavior...depend upon a combination of this context (sporting event), general social conditions and specific precipitating events between individual spectators."

Reducing Violence in Sport
    William Hechter (1977:44) in his definitive article on criminal law
and violence in sport observed, "No rules or practice of any game
whatever can make that lawful which is unlawful by the law of the
land; and the law of the land says you shall not do that which is likely
to cause the death of another." According to Hechter the use of
assault and battery in the course of the playing of a game cannot be
tolerated, even if the persons agree to do what the law says shall not
be done. In spite of the above admonition, the immunity of persons
indulging in assaultive practices, by claiming that aggression is "part
of the game," has long been claimed. For example, body contact in
football, boxing, and wrestling is assumed imperative to the structure
of the game. Messner (1981:54-5) states, "one of the striking features
of the sport of football is its violent nature. It is true that the
expression of violence in football is regulated by formal rules, but,
nevertheless, success in the game requires that the participants
behave in a violent manner much of the time." In ice hockey, soccer,
and basketball, excessive physical contact has become accepted as
strategy.
    Countering this belief, Michael Smith (1981:5) explains,

> When body contact assumes an importance far out of
> proportion to that required to play the game--when
> viciousness and ferocity are publicly extolled as virtues,
> when inflicting pain and punishing opponents are
> systematized as strategy--a stage of brutality can be said to
> have been reached. These practices may strain the formal
> rules of sport but do not necessarily violate them.

Horrow (1981a:9) claims that despite the enormous pressures working
to keep sports violence cases out of litigation, an increasing number
of cases are reaching the law courts. He reports the argument
advanced by a Minnesota prosecutor in the sports violence case, State
vs. David Forbes, 1975:

> The mere act of putting on a uniform and entering the sport
> arena should not serve as a license to engage in behavior
> which would constitute a crime if committed elsewhere. If a
> participant in a sporting event were allowed to feel immune
> from criminal sanction merely by virtue of his being a
> participant, the spirit of maiming and serious bodily
> injury...may well become the order of the day. (Horrow,
> 1981a:9)

This possibility has been dramatically fantasized in the science fiction
film of the 1970s, *Roller Ball*, a game that combined the roller
skating derby and basketball, in which the players were political
pawns with license to kill. But we do not have to have recourse to
fantasy, for devastating attacks upon players by other players are

becoming almost commonplace. In some instances excessive physical contact has been condoned by management as instrumental strategy. Such organizational deviance, according to Santomier, Howard, Plitz, and Romance (1980:29-30), is characterized by four conditions: (1) the deviant act must be contrary to the norms outside of the organization; (2) the deviant act must find support in the norms of a given level or division of the organization; (3) the deviant behavior must be known to the dominant coalition of the organization, either passively or actively (passive knowledge includes failing to prevent the acts from occurring); and (4) new members must be socialized to participate in the deviant action. While Santomier *et al.* (1980) do not specifically mention excessive aggressive acts, conditions they present set the context for instrumental violence. It is extremely difficult to prove that player violence is part of an official organization's strategy, whether it be that of professional sports or of the local amateur league, but some examples leave little doubt about intent. In one case, written on the locker room blackboard during the half-time by the coach of the women's basketball team were the following words, "I want that player hurt!"

Michael Smith (1981) listed sport violence by players in descending order of legitimacy. First is body contact performed according to the official rules of a given sport (e.g., body blocking in football). Second are instances of borderline violence that are assaults (e.g., late hitting in football, high tackling in soccer, baseball brushback pitch, or basketball elbowing and bumping for position). A bit more serious is the quasi-criminal violence that violates not only the formal rules of a given sport, but also the informal norms of player conduct. The awarding to Houston Rocket basketball player Rudy Tomjanovich in 1979 of 3.3 million dollars for injuries which he received during a game from a bone-breaking blow of Kermit Washington is such an example (Horrow, 1981a). The most flagrant form of violence is criminal violence which is so serious to be outside the boundaries of the game and handled from the outset by the law. Death is often the result.

Instinctive explosive injury inflicted on another player leading to court trials are cited by Horrow (1981a). One was the September 21, 1969, incident when Boston Bruin hockey player Ted Green was struck by a long-splitting stickslash to his head by Wayne Make of the St. Louis Blues. Concussion and massive hemorrhaging resulted in two brain operations and only partial restoration. Another involved a lawsuit, Hackbart versus Cincinnati Bengals. It resulted from a September 16, 1973, football "incident" in which Bengal Charles Clark struck Bronco safety Dale Hackbart on the back of his head, causing three broken vertebrae; muscular atrophy of the arm, shoulder and back; and the loss of strength and reflexes in his arm.

In legal cases, the courts find most difficult the distinction between aggressive play and excessive violence; the separation of legitimate hard play from excessive illegal contact is not clear. Such violence by professional athletes may constitute a small percentage of all societal violence. However, the vast media exposure and the overpowering role-model influence these athletes wield magnifies their impact drastically.

Making coaches, managers, and owners responsible for their players' behavior, as well as requiring players to accept legal responsibility, may deter official condoning of brutality as game strategy. Because professional teams are motivated by profit, imposing sizable fines (financial, missed practices, banning from events) might affect the offending team's and player's pocket books. Tactics by players stressing skill and finesse rather than inordinate body contact, quicker and more exacting penalties called by game officials, negative reinforcement by the media of observed violence, coupled with minimal reference to such acts all might contribute to reduced sport violence.

Understandably, player violence will not decrease measurably until both professional and amateur management and players feel violence is unprofitable. Horrow (1981b:65) was encouraged to discover that 45 percent of hockey players would prefer less fist fighting in games, while 82 percent like the idea of less illegal stick work. Canadian hockey players who played under less-violent international rules found those games more rewarding experiences than league games. Increasingly, persons experienced in public relations feel that violence may not be critical to the box office. Also, a feeling is growing that in television brutality is not the salable quality it used to be. Sports fans today differentiate between contact and brutality, and are looking for more skill, finesse, and reflex action, not violence and brutality.

A potent tool of sports violence control in the professional ranks may be some legal definition and sanction, such as a Sports Violence Act. Even the threat of such legal action might deter aggression. At the turn of the twentieth century when collegiate football was perceived as becoming intolerably brutal, President Teddy Roosevelt threatened to ban the sport. Almost instantaneously, rule changes reformed the game and reduced the violence.

Preventing overt aggressive behavior from starting is the best deterrent to its spreading. Thirer (1981) contends that only when society can find effective methods for curtailing and discouraging violence in the broader society will sport violence decrease proportionately, but it would appear that we cannot wait for something or someone to reverse the trend. At least some actions regarding sports spectators can be taken immediately. Physical and time factors at sports facilities are known to adversely effect and agitate spectators' behavior. For example, Russell and Drewry (1976) found that crowd size was positively related to participant aggression. Architectural features which reduce spectator stress include wider, safer ingress and egress routes, well-monitored patterns of traffic flow to and within athletic facilities, demarcation of individual seating spaces, separation of sectional seating, wider aisles, reduced crowding, more impenetrable physical barriers between spectators and arena, and limited access (Parker, 1977). Plexiglass screening or high rotating walls, low bush and flower gardens, and even moats have been used. In Argentina some soccer fields are surrounded by moats filled with water and broken glass (Jackson, 1982). This does not seem like too drastic a measure when one realizes that in 1950 an official, following his controversial decision in a Buenos Aires soccer match, was beaten to death by players and fans (Eitzen, 1981). Offering afternoon contests when families can attend, rather than night events, can reduce obstrusive behavior. Youthful males who attend more night performances are more likely to display disruptive behavior than a family-oriented person.

Additional Questions

Additional questions that might be addressed by anthropologists relative to sport violence include: (1) Are there common cultural prerequisites leading to collective aggressive behavior? (2) In what ways do varying societies differ in their aggressive behavior? (3) Is aggressive behavior linked to frustration of perceived needs by members of varying societies? (4) Is aggressive behavior linked to practice of such behavior in multiple settings, serving as reinforcement rather than substitute situations? (5) Is violence more prevalent in certain age stages of the life cycle?

SPORT AND INTERNATIONAL RELATIONS

Introduction

Sport is gaining credibility as a tool for both cultural exchange and international political negotiations. The major financial commitments of nations to "showcase" their top athletes has paid off in the past and is expected to continue to add to the coffers of status. A country's reputation in the family of nations can be enhanced almost magically by the symbolic transformation of physical prowess to political prestige.

The term international relations can be confusing because it is intertwined with so many differing facets of one society interacting with another. National refers to a nation-state, which can be described as a body of people associated with a peculiar territory and which has sufficient unity to possess a government of its own. These people traditionally have a common or shared language, race, and ethos. Exceptions to this pattern abound, such as Czechoslovakia with its two distinct ethnic patterns, Czechs and Slovaks. It is also a practice for political units of government that may not be recognized as nations to engage in international sport competition. Puerto Rico is a case in point, for it is recognized by the International Olympic

Committee (IOC) as an independent entry in the Olympic games, despite its being a commonwealth associated with the United States (MacAloon, 1983). The IOC in 1950 tried to convince East Germany and West Germany, who were functioning as independent political units, to enter one representative German team in the 1952 Helsinki Olympic Games. Only at the last minute was this agreement aborted by East Germany. Several years later the IOC, in an unprecedented political coup, convinced the two Germanies to march as one unit at the 1956 Winter Olympics at Cortina d'Ampezza, Austria (Lowe, Kanin, Strenk, 1978:vi-vii.).

In international sports the central political unit of government is frequently involved in the sport promotion. A nation either tacitly (e.g., the United States up until 1978) or openly (e.g., U.S.S.R from 1925) commits its sport resources to the furthering of its national interests. Governmental concerns revolve around selecting and/or training athletes, financing and supervising the transaction, and producing successful athletes.

The term transnational refers commonly to sports exchange beyond national boundaries by nongovernment sponsoring units of a nation, such as the national sports federations, Amateur Athletic Union (AAU), Young Men's and Young Women's Christian Association, colleges, universities, high schools, and even multinational industrial corporations. These kinds of sport competition are often less publicized and promoted than government sponsored events.

International Relations in this context may be described as various forms of significant association or interaction between or among persons, peoples, or countries. This connection or link between groups takes place through some action, event, or declaration of intent. Communication occurs in the process of relating. One important use of sport in international relations is diplomacy between nations. For example, the Republic of China employed a 1971 international table tennis tournament between the United States and China as a diplomatic "ice breaker" on the road to official recognition of China by the United States. This "ping pong diplomacy" was one step along the patient road of the Chinese government toward diplomatic recognition by other nations (Kanin, 1978).

Sport as a Vehicle for International Understanding

Recognizing that some degree of sharing between nations commonly means understanding, we must consider the difference between understanding and relations. Both imply communication between groups. However, "understanding" moves closer to compatibility and even friendliness than does the more neutral term "relations," which does not necessarily imply reciprocal affability.

The principle of striving is basic to the fabric of sport. The nobility of the contest between two worthy opponents sparks the imagination of all. Huizinga (1950:64) extolled the transcendent quality of excellence which the Greeks called *arete*, as meaning fitness by exercise through contests. *Arete* expresses the idea of always doing and being the best, excelling over others with nobility and honor. Huizinga felt that civilization, which has been founded on *arete* coupled with fair play, was in jeopardy. As he watched peace being eradicated in Europe during the 1930s, he also lamented the fate of sport as if the two were connected. He argued,

> sport has become profane, "unholy" in every way and has no organized connection whatever with the structure of society, least of all prescribed by the government.... Sport and athletics showed us play stiffened into seriousness but still being felt as play...business becomes play...play becomes business (Huizinga, 1950:197-200).

His admonition went unheeded. Almost as a grotesque taunt to Huizinga's words, the spectacularly bigoted Berlin Olympics of 1936 (frequently called "The Nazi Olympics"; Mandell, 1971), whose sponsoring government Huizinga detested, showed other nations the controlling power a government can wield in sports.

However, the quality of honorable striving together in sports is still revered by many. In fact, the ideals of Pierre de Coubertin, the founder of the modern Olympics, are echoed in the 1978 Olympic Charter:

> The development of those finest physical and moral qualities comes from contests on the friendly fields of amateur sport. They bring together the youth of the world in a great quadrennial sports festival, thereby creating international respect and good will and helping to construct a better and more peaceful world (International Olympic Committee, 1978).

In 1896 just following the Athens Olympics, de Coubertin was convinced that the Olympics generated true knowledge of other peoples, and even after thirty-three years of trying to sell this ideal, he wrote with strong conviction,

> To ask the peoples of the world to love one another is merely a form of childishness. To ask them to respect one another is not in the least utopian, but in order to respect one another it is first necessary to know one another.... Universal history is the only genuine foundation of a geniune peace.... To celebrate the Olympic Games is to appeal to history (quoted in MacAloon, 1981:268).

Heinila (1966:31), a Finnish sociologist, stated,

> According to sport, and especially Olympic ideology, one of

the fundamental functions of international sport is to promote international understanding and good will among world youth. Sport has been referred to as one of the most influential movements of peace. No doubt, the history of international sport and that of the Olympic Games give numerous evidences of the functions of sport for building friendship ties between the different countries.

In that spirit of sharing and understanding between athletes from varying nations, the 1932 Los Angeles Olympics initiated the Olympic Village. It provided for friendly interaction between Americans and the visiting athletes of the world. It proved such a success that later Olympics incorporated the common living quarters for all athletes. This mixing tended to personalize other culture and ethnic mores. The vital process of international understanding which Pierre de Coubertin envisioned continues. However, such personalized exchange in recent Olympics has been greatly eroded by isolation of national sports teams from the local community. Ironically, the Los Angeles Olympic Games Committee reportedly proposed complete elimination of such exchange because of security risks to the athletes.

Historically, the involvement of Americans in sport competition with foreigners has been based on individual entrepreneurship, friendship, and interclub comaraderie and has been more transnational than international. As early as 1844, a young man from New Haven, Connecticut, George Seward, went to England and beat every man who ran against him in all distances up to a quarter-mile. He offered headstarts to all competitors and beat all existing short-distance records for running, skating, and jumping on skates. He finally returned to America the acknowledged sprinting champion of the world (Curtis, 1900:350). In 1857 the America's Cup boat race was instituted between the United States and England for friendly competition by yachts of different countries. In 1863, Louis Bennett, a Seneca Indian known as Deerfoot, went to England, running in many races at distances near ten miles. Bennett defeated all of England's best men and established the world's record for running twelve miles in one hour. During that period it was not unusual for Americans of various East Coast athletic clubs to challenge their English, Scottish, and Irish counterparts. The visits were reciprocated. In 1884 a team of athletes from Yale University crossed the Atlantic to compete in track events against Oxford and Cambridge Universities. In April of 1896 several American athletes paid their own way to compete in the first modern Olympics at Athens, Greece. The group, containing no amateur champion and only one record-holder, surprisingly won almost every event they entered. This small band of amateurs was the first of a long series of United States Olympic competitors.

Nationalism was part of Americans' early interest in international sports competition, and the ripple effect was inevitable. Other nations quickly adopted the tendency to couple sport and national interest.   Andrzej Wohl (1970:123), a Polish sociologist, has observed that

> Top-class athletes have become traveling salesmen of
> international cooperation. Competitive sports recognizes no
> local, national, or racial barriers or differences of world
> outlook and it could not exist at all if one wanted to set up
> such limitations for sport. And that is why it is an excellent
> instrument for the fraternization of the peoples of the
> world, for the fraternization of young people from all the
> continents.

Wohl (1970) has also noted that competitive sport has succeeded in breaking through national barriers and in setting up international federations, associations, and forums, such as the Olympic Games, at times when various political, scientific, or artistic organizations had yet to expand across cultural boundaries at that level. He suggests that this was due to the international language of sport, the universal form of human motor activity, the special language of competition, and the constant need to break new records in sport (something that can be measured with utmost accuracy even in cross-cultural settings). In no other area of human international cooperation has there been such regularity and systematic order as in competitive sport (Wohl, 1970:123).

The twentieth century has seen the phenomenal growth of the superstructure of international and transnational sport organizations, providing a cornucopia of sport competition. In 1980, organizations that were involved in sports administration in different countries of the world from Afghanistan to Zambia totaled 135 national Olympic committees, 73 national sports councils and associations, 42 international information documentation centers, and some 96 international sport federations and related governing associations. These federations ranged from the International Archery Federation (FITA) to the International Yacht Racing Union (IYRU). Examples of international governing organizations are the International Olympic Committee (IOC), which governs the Olympic Games; the International Workers Sports Association (IWSA), which has 14 national federations totalling 1,150,000 members in 12 countries; the General Association of International Sports Federations (GAIF), which provides a forum for 55 international sports federations; International University Sports Federation (FISU), which conducts the World University Games with participant-students from 56 countries; and the International Sports Organizations for the Disabled (ISOD), which sponsors the Para-Olympics (Special Olympics) every Olympic year with participants from 17 countries (Timmer, Gordon, Tadeusz, and Recle, 1980). Over 50 countries are expected to participate in the 1984 Wheel-Chair Olympics, to be hosted by England.

The concern for international understanding through sport generated a worldwide Congress on Sport and International Understanding, held in Finland in July, 1982. Questions posed for delegate discussion included: (1) What is the significance of international relations in sports in the world today? (2) In what way has international exchange through sports promoted or hindered understanding between nations? (3) What are the opportunities and prerequisites of sports to strengthen common understanding? (4) What challenges will cooperation through sports face in the coming decades? (Congress on Sport and International Understanding, 1982:130).

The plethora of international sports organizations attests to the ability of sport to bring together peoples from all lands in a climate of cooperation. The ninety-six international sport federations represent transnational structures that were formed by persons interested in an umbrella of common rules, procedures, and recordkeeping within a specific sport. These multinational sport-governing groups have created an environment for fair athletic exchange.

Beauty of movement need not be grasped only in a fleetingly observed aesthetic instant; it can be savored on the television slow motion, replay, and videotape so common in the late 1900s, as well as through other traditional descriptive media, such as radio, motion pictures, photographs, newspapers, periodicals, and biographical and autobiographical books. It has been estimated that the 1976 Montreal Olympics were watched or listened to by 1.5 billion people, or about one out of every three persons then alive on the earth (MacAloon, 1981:ix). This represents the largest audience of any event ever held in the world throughout history. The global proportions of this international understanding generated through sports should not be underestimated!

The role of sport as a vehicle for international and cross-cultural understanding is difficult to document with any degree of specification. Yet as Jones (1959:170) has noted, it is hoped that

> Sport may, indeed, become a tremendously positive factor for improving international understanding. All those engaged in sports may become agents of goodwill between the peoples of the world. Theirs is a great opportunity. It is the sacred responsibility of all sportsmen that this opportunity shall not be missed.

Sport and International Politics

Sport has certain characteristics which perhaps impel it more readily than other human activities toward an association with politics. Sport, especially competitive sport, tends to identify the individual with some group and the individual welcomes this identity. Even the lone runner cannot escape his association with club or town, county or country (McIntosh, 1963:190).

Loyalty, prestige, and pride of accomplishment in sport is easily translated into an exchange commodity between nations; it is easily politicized. The fact of the sport-politics relationship need not be debated. However, one might argue over the impact that politics has had on international sport. Is politics abusing sport or has it extended the positive qualities of sport to other levels of competition?

Edwards (1973:125) contends that the sport team represents the earliest form of societal organization and that it is a natural method of socializing youth into patriotism.

It was Natan (1969) who contended that in a world where success in sport and play is considered as a measure of national vitality and national prestige, one must be reconciled to the fact that sport has become the tool of politics. Ultimately it is a significant social phenomenon (Natan, 1969:210). However, the negative connotation of using sport in politics is evidenced by Natan's (1969:205-09) slogans: "Nationalism is sports' deadliest enemy.... International competitive sport has become an arena for ideologies.... The idea of carrying out military training under the cloak of 'sport' is the basic principle...in all the nations of the Eastern bloc...; sport can be used as a powerful political factor even in a democracy."

The use of sports for political purposes should not be summarily dismissed as an exploitation or misuse of sport. As Strenk (1977) has described, there are several ways in which sport may be used as an international political or diplomatic tool, and each may be legitimate in the proper context.

1. *Instrument of Diplomacy* International athletic contests have become a form of public diplomacy. There has been no Olympiad in recent years in which some major diplomatic negotiations were not being transacted. The German Democratic Republic (GDR) had dedicated as much as two percent of its gross national product to developing an outstanding sport reputation. Sport facilities, medical centers, coaching institutes, housing accommodations, talent search, medical testing, drug research, job subsidies for sportsmen and premiums and bonuses for record-breaking athletes were part of the effort. According to Strenk (1977) "diplomats in track suits" were busy campaigning from 1956 to the 1970s for international recognition for East Germany. Gradually the barriers went down; first with international sports federation recognition. Then, the IOC granted GDR the right to compete as a separate team in the Olympic Games. Finally, the North Atlantic Treaty Organization (NATO) ended its boycott of GDR athletes. Sport proved a valuable weapon in the GDR's fight for diplomatic recognition.

The People's Republic of China has effectively utilized its sport personnel through its "friendship first, competition second" policy to establish a positive national image over the world (Tien and Matthews, 1977). China sent its sports teams around the world, astutely matching the talent of its various athletes to the local athletes' abilities. There was a far more important goal at stake. Goodwill leading to diplomatic recognition was more vital than winning a sport event (Kanin, 1978; Kolatch, 1972). Finally her struggle for diplomatic recognition and membership in the International Olympic Committee was realized when Taiwan, the People's Republic of China rival for participation in the Summer Olympic Games of 1976, was forced by the Olympic Committee to either compete under a name which excluded the word China or bow out of the Olympics. Taiwan withdrew (Espy, 1979). With their international sports competition well established in the 1970s, the Chinese sports enthusiasts of the 1980s acclaimed international victories with shouts of "China is the best" and "China is number one" (Breeze and Findlay, 1982:32). In April, 1983, because the United States granted political asylum to the Chinese female tennis star Hu Na, China cancelled all sport and cultural exchanges with the United States. Nevertheless, the Chinese national diving team was allowed to compete that spring in the world diving championships held in Houston, Texas. At this event, "The Chinese team almost immediately won the affection of local fans with its good will, sportsmanship, and curious habits (bowing to the pool after each dive)" (Neff, 1983:60). A dual political strategy was being used by the Chinese government. One strategy was the official diplomatic protest, through the use of sports, of another government's action that also related to sports. The other strategy was maintaining their internatonal sports prestige by participation in a world sports championship.

2. *Vehicle for Ideology* Sport can serve as a vehicle for ideology and propaganda. The U.S.S.R. is a stellar example of a nation utilizing the sports competence of its youth as an ideological statement. Riordan (1977) acknowledged that the Soviet Union had demonstrated that the highest realization of human potential can be most effectively achieved through the planned application of societal resources toward that desired end. The Soviet leaders assign sport personnel such tasks as demonstrating the superiority of and winning support for the communist system; encouraging friendly, commerical and good-neighborly relations with the U.S.S.R.; and, within the socialist bloc, achieving unity on Soviet terms (Riordan, 1977:340). The sports emissaries were thought to do more than diplomats to recommend their political philosophy and way of life to the outside world. The pattern of foreign sports competition of the U.S.S.R. and other communist countries closely followed the course of their foreign policy and has clearly demonstrated the effectiveness of this union (Riordan, 1977;1981).

3. *Acquisition of Prestige* Sport plays a role in the quest for

prestige. Competition between athletes has been promoted not only by large industrialized countries, but by developing nations as well. The track victories of the Kenyan athletes Heino, Temu, and Biwott in the Mexico City Olympic Games in 1968 focused attention on their country. The four elegantly bedecked Manchurian athletes marching in the Montreal Olympic Games opening ceremony left a mark on the minds of the observers. Manchurian inclusion in the Olympics was an unsurpassed opportunity for recognition not available in any other way. The potential beyond publicity for the event itself, which is assured by the insatiable interest of world television, radio, newspaper and magazines, is in the tourist, vacation and commercial potential of a specific country. Japanese culture was magnificently portrayed in coverage of the 1964 Olympics. The price tag was $1.5 billion, but the benefits to Japan, specifically its reinstatement into the family of nations, tourism, and increased trade, have far overshadowed the cost.

4. *Instrument of Foreign Policy* Sport as tool in foreign policy serves to further international understanding and peace. Melvin Lasky (quoted in Strenk, 1977:7) frames this maxim:

> Nothing less than great sporting rivalries, which enlisted the overwhelming emotions and impassioned enthusiasms, could serve to reinforce the new needed structure of the twentieth-century world peace.... Patriots were still needed, not to fight battles at dawn, but for matches under arclights at night -- the historic mutation. High-powered sports could be the replacement for power politics.

The idea that sport can help promote understanding has been the stance of the United States Department of State. The United States Senate was told in 1973 that "the doors to better international understanding have been opened" by the following endeavors: the Partners of the Americas Sports Program, the Peace Corps Sports Corps, and the Department of State's International Athletics Division and People-to-People program. The spokesman tried to clarify the official position of the United States government, "Since sports in the United States is a nongovernmental activity, the State Department's role reflects this basic concept in international sports. Our interest is in furthering international mutual understanding and communication through sports" (Reich, 1973:20274). A scant five years later and only one year after the President's Commission on Olympic Sports (1977), the United States government moved from a lukewarm involvement to an aggressive promotion of sport. The Amateur Sports Act of 1978 was introduced to confirm the United States Olympic Committee as the coordinating body for amateur athletic activities in this country, to protect the rights of amateur athletes, and to provide a mechanism by which the right to govern the particular sport is awarded to the most representative and capable amateur sports organization.

An authorization of $30 million was recommended to carry out the mandate, of which $12 million was earmarked for the support training centers, for a sports medicine program, and for the dissemination of sport information. The Amateur Sports Act makes the government motive clear:

> the Congress finds that amateur athletic activity is an important part of American society, providing benefits to both the general public and individual amateur athletes. Furthermore, Congress finds that it is important that the full benefits of amateur sports, both for domestic and international point of view, are realized through the minimization of organization conflicts (U.S. House of Representatives, 1978:10).

5. *Medium for Political Protest* Sometimes sports events provide an international forum for an internal national problem. The black power protest of Americans Tommie Smith and John Carlos in the 1968 Mexico City Olympics is a case in point. The seeking of asylum by athletes and sometimes spectators in another country has often posed an embarrassment to some Eastern bloc nations. Another form of protest is the boycotting of sports events by an international team or governing body, such as that of the West German track and field delegation to the 1969 European Championships in Athens. The United States tennis federation boycotted the 1976 Davis Cup matches in protest against the intrusion of South Africa's apartheid politics into the Davis Cup competition. Countries also have boycotted international sports events (e.g., the United States boycott of the 1980 Moscow Olympics).

6. *Catalyst for Conflict* Sport can enter the international scene as a catalyst of conflict as Goodhart and Chataway (1968) have so aptly stated in the title of their book *War Without Weapons.* The Nazi general and IOC (International Olympic Committee) member von Reichenau once defined sports as "war with friendly arms." Since the Olympics provides a world stage, it has also provided the backdrop for "actors in conflict." Probably the most dramatic and tragic action was in the 1972 Munich Olympics when Black September Arab terrorists seized nine Israeli athletes as hostages to hold in exchange for the release of 200 Palestinian prisoners held in Israeli jails. The death of the hostages and five of the terrorists did not resolve the issue or stop the Games.

A different twist to conflict was experienced in the "soccer war" of 1969 between Honduras and El Salvador, a continuance of their long-standing political and economic disagreements. Following riots, spectator attacks upon the visiting team, and deaths, during the three-game series to determine which country would advance to the World Cup in soccer, El Salvador protested the series outcome. The mounting hostility broke into a full-scale war when "violations" occurred at the border between those two central American countries (Wright, 1977:32).

7. *Significance of Sports in International Politics* In examining the many ways in which sport can be used in political activities, one realizes that the issue is no longer whether sport is apolitical, but the degree in which it is related to political interests, goals and policies. Guldenpfennig and Schulke (1980) have advocated the political research on sport as a general social development. Sands (1976:10) summarized the issue of competitive sport as an arena for international politics:

> It appears that politics and sport will never be separated in the international sphere--competition, nationalism, and wining are too important.... The greatest question is whether society in general will consider the problems of politics in sport great enough to overcome them.

Sport and International Business

Another concern relative to sport and internationalism is the role of multinational corporations. The sale of sports programming and equipment is big business. Little needs to be said about the sky-rocketing interest in viewing sports on television and the money this generates in advertising. The ultimate in sport investment costs is the Olympic Games. For example, NBC (National Broadcasting Company) offered to pay the U.S.S.R. $80 million for telecast rights to the 1980 Moscow Olympics.

The multinational sport corporation that provides facilities, equipment, personnel, and training and development programs to other countries is an already thriving but expanding enterprise. This kind of sport expertise for sale is exemplified in the United States Sports Academy, an Atlanta, Georgia corporation, which contracts with small nations to develop sports programs for their citizens. Bahrain and Saudi Arabia have such agreements with them.

In another vein, multinational corporations specializing in sports equipment have increased their sales through Olympic endorsement. A common fund-raising technique by the United States Olympic Committee is the permission to use the copyrighted Olympic seven-ringed logo along with the Olympic "endorsement" of certain products for a specific Olympiad. The German shoe company, Adidas, using the 1972 Olympics as a launching platform, was able to capture a lion's share of the world tennis-shoe market in part through popularizing its products by gifts to international athletes.

SUMMARY

This chapter on sport and contemporary issues has examined the decreasing resistance to participation by women in sport; the use of physical activity and sport in deterring the onset of old age; the conflicting theories of sport as augmenting or providing a substitute for violence; and the use of sports as a tool for international exchange.

Because the evolutionary perspective upon which this volume is based inherently endorses change, the authors propose that the issues of the contemporary world will change, as accommodations to the changing natural and human environment. Adjustment or adaptation is not always directed to the status quo but to potentiation. It may be that the movement of man into outer space will require additional game models, models that take him beyond competitive sports. When small collections of humans are placed in these hostile or semirestrictive environments, different sport forms stressing mutual benefit and equitable distribution of resources may be more appropriate. It may be then that the equivalency of cooperative forms of physical activities of band societies could again become useful in social interaction. Therefore, the traditional band model should not be forgotten. We cannot afford to disregard the valuable social strategies of our past.

In the future, the generic term "sports" may become androgynous in that women and men will make sport choices based on personal preference rather than gender. The aged may be healthier and remain active longer by engaging in more physically demanding activities. Violence may be allowed, but only in specially controlled sport settings. Aggression and violence in sport will be reduced for the average person through educational programs. Sport in international relations may be less pyramidal than today, when only the best compete. Broader, informal bases of personal participation between individuals and small groups of differing political territories may surpass large-scale international sports events. In this sense, contemporary issues in sport are issues for the future. The anthropology of sport provides a workable framework for understanding these issues, as they affect past, present and future.

Exercises

Discussion questions:

1. It might be suggested that the inequalities that characterized the female participation in sport historically paralleled those characteristic of society in general. Using a symbolic anthropology model, analyze the role of the female athlete in American society as a reflection of the American female role in general.

2. As you contemplate the prospect of old age, which alternative would you choose regarding your own life? Would you disengage yourself from the rest of society or would you fight against or postpone old age by continuing to be involved in physical activities and sports? What are your

reasons for choosing one path and not the other? What extenuating circumstances would cause a reanalysis of your plan?

3.   How would a structural-functionalist explain the physical aggression characteristic of American sport? What about a cultural materialist explanation?

4.   You are assigned to a nongravitational space station with thirty-one other young male and female adults from Canada, Japan, and Egypt to monitor satellite equipment and relay interplanetary communications. A special recreation zone fifty feet square by eighteen feet high can be created by activating retractor modular paneling. What kind of vigorous physical activity and sport can you modify for your leisure pursuits? Invent your own game. What sports could you devise if you were independently mobile in your space suit outside the station and could move in all directions by small jet propulsion mechanisms?

Special Projects:

1.   Go to a high school girls' basketball game. Describe the evidence for female athletic inequality that you observe. Would you describe this as discrimination? As sexism? If you had the power to make any changes necessary, what steps would you take to correct the observed inequalities?

2.   Set up a socio-drama role-play situation. The situation is the International Olympic Committee's Executive Council meeting in Geneva, Switzerland in January, 1997. Seven members are in attendance in addition to the President of the International Olympic Committee. Dedicated to a smaller Olympic Games, you wish to limit athletes from each nation to 200. To do this you propose to exclude all team sports except soccer (European football) in the upcoming twenty-seventh Olympic Games to be held in the year 2000 in Lago, Nigeria, Africa. What resistance would you expect and from what Executive Council members? What arguments would you set forth to convince the world sectors represented at the meeting of your plan? What might their counterarguments be? Consider what impact the exclusion of any team sports other than soccer might have on the world international sports competition.

Epilogue

Sport is an institution with universal significance. Whether it is baseball in Japan, soccer in Brazil, ice hockey in Czechoslovakia, cricket in England, or football in America, sport is a significant component of the human experience. The anthropology of sport treats this experience from a cultural perspective, appreciating its worldwide significance and its role in the evolution of culture. However, the anthropological approach to sport does not stop there. It addresses contemporary issues and suggests ways in which anthropological understandings might be useful in real problem solving, decision making, and program development. It also provides the student, the educated layman, the professional, and the informed citizen with a range of valuable skills, understandings, and knowledge. The following are the most important of these.

1. *Understanding sport and its significance as an institution.* It is important to know what sport is and to understand its role in society. Sport goes beyond the strenuous though relaxing fun of an October afternoon touch football game in a neighbor's backyard. It creates industry, it generates dollars, it changes community relationships, it affects personality development and career choices, and it turns the mild-mannered grocery clerk of Monday morning into the lunatic fan of Sunday afternoon. It is important that one understand and monitor these sport related forces in his or her personal, family, and community lives.

2. *A critical perspective on the sport institution.* It is important that one be realistic about the role of sport in the contemporary world. Unfortunately, athletic programs sometimes "get out of hand," and participants lose sight of their original objectives. In the professional ranks playing for pay replaces playing for enjoyment and contests become more business than sport. In interscholastic circles the game becomes more important than

277

education, more work than play, and more physical abuse than physical education. In some ways, such developments are predictable. Institutions surrounded with unquestioning enthusiasm and emotional fervor can quickly let their excesses mask their initial intentions. The history of religious cults provides many excellent illustrations of this tendency. The informed citizen needs to be alert to the dangers of unchecked enthusiasm in any institution, but in this case, athletics. The problem is an especially sensitive one in education circles. In recent years, high schools and colleges have had a tendency to let their excitement over building winning teams undermine basic educational goals. More money is spent for new locker room facilities than for library books, basketball players who can average 20 points per game cannot read the daily newspaper, and scholarships are given to athletes whose academic records predict certain failure in college. The good news is that the public, the courts, regulatory agencies (e.g., NCAA), and the student athletes themselves are taking steps to correct these abuses. The educated professional, especially one with a personal interest in sport, should be familiar with the issues and prepared to take a position in the discussion surrounding the movement toward reform in interscholastic athletics.

3.   *Appreciating and maintaining the play element in sport.*
The importance of play in human life is becoming increasingly evident, especially in scholarly circles. It is now generally accepted that play is vital to human survival and a critical factor in the evolutionary process. One of the authors of this book has suggested in another context:

> . . . play is an important mechanism of adaptation . . . in fact, play is adaptation. In the process of primate evolution, adaptation and survival increasingly become cognitive (as opposed to mechanical or instinctive). Human beings, in comparison to other anthropoids, are forced to think more about and reflect on, the mechanics of adaptation. It is both a gift and a dread responsibility of self-consciousness. Whether it be the anxiety that comes with contemplating the inevitability of death or the pleasures of anticipating a tasty meal or an exciting sexual encounter, this unavoidable reflecting on existence represents an important dimension of human adaptation. In other words, the human struggle for survival is not a mindless struggle. It is in many ways a symbolic act. And, it is a source of tension, a tension generated by the conflict between the perceived demands of survival and the will to act. At an instinctive level, such tension is at best limited. But, at symbolic levels, the tension is both unavoidable and intense.

This is the evolutionary importance of play. Play is a mechanism which human beings employ to remove themselves from the angst of reflecting on the realities of existence. Play is a symbolic distancing that relieves or at least limits that tension. Yet, it is not a form of escapism; not pure fantasy. Play still addresses those vital issues of survival, but indirectly. Play may reverse or abstract, but deals with the fundamental problems of adaptation nonetheless (Blanchard, 1984).

Ideally, sport has an important play element. It should be fun. As such, play has an endless array of mental and physical health possibilities. The educated sport enthusiast should keep that in mind. Some of the saddest stories in the annals of sport history are those of athletes driving themselves to a type of sport burn-out: the basketball player who pushed so hard in his playing years that the joy was eradicated; the ex-tennis pro who refuses to pick up a racket because of all the pain the memories bring. Effective sport participation maintains its playfulness. The anthropological study of play provides the rationale.

4.   *Understanding theoretical approaches to the analysis of sport.* The understanding of the theoretical process is one of the contributions that a good education makes toward one's preparation for life. The educated person has the ability to objectify and analyze those implicit theoretical propositions that affect every dimension of his or her daily life. In this particular case, this means the application of social scientific theory to the sport institution and its complex array of problems and issues.

The educated professional realizes that there are many ways of looking at sport, and that often these many ways contradict each other. However, that does not negate the significance of particular theoretical models. For example, the structural-functional and conflict model approaches to the analysis of athletic competition's impact on one's local community may lead to mutually exclusive conclusions. For example, use of the structural-functional model might prompt the observation that such competition is good because it promotes community cohesion. Yet, at the same time, the conflict model might suggest just the opposite--athletic competition is bad because it legitimizes social class competition. Neither is totally right or wrong. However both direct the interested observer to a more detailed understanding of athletic activities.

5.   *Understanding the evolution and history of sport.* Events, athletics or otherwise, do not occur in a temporal vacuum. Rather, they are products of previous events. A knowledge of the mechanics of sport evolution and the history of particular events gives the sport professional or educated enthusiast an advantage in understanding contemporary sport history.

6.   *Understanding sport and change.* The role played by sport in change, at both social and individual levels, is an area of understanding also critical for the educated person. In particular, he or she should be aware of the influence that sport has on the

enculturation and socialization of young persons in our society. The internalization of values by children, teen-agers, and young adults, is often a direct result of some athletics-related influence. The contributions of sport anthropology can be useful in minimizing the negative and maximizing the positive benefits of such influences.

7.   *Knowledge of sport in "other" cultures.* The sophisticated sport professional or enthusiast is one who knows more about sport than the fundamentals of one or two patently American games. Perhaps there is something virtuous about someone who "lives, sleeps and eats" his or her particular sport. However, overspecialization has its limitations. Knowledge of games and sports played by other social groups and in other countries, coupled with an intellectual curiosity and unbiased willingness to experiment, gives one a wealth of possibilities for creating novel physical fitness regimen and recreational programs.

8.   *Being aware of the meaning of sport at a personal level.* The ability to deal with the sport dimension of one's own life is fostered by the social scientific investigation of sport and is important to the education of all persons interested in the sport phenomenon. The joys, the agonies, the anticipation and excitement of athletics, whether as participant or spectator, send ripples so deeply into the human psyche that neither the casual observer nor the thinking "sports nut" can allow them to go uninvestigated. He contemplates, analyzes, and rationalizes those often incomprehensible feelings. He must. It is part of the game. Anthropology provides an interesting perspective for this introspection.

These are the most immediate issues addressed by the anthropology of sport. Whether you are a classical archeologist, dollhouse cabinet maker, nuclear physicist, broccoli salesman, FBI agent, robot recreation specialist, or pet mortician, in the sport-obsessed world in which we live, these issues are unavoidable and the anthropological approach valuable, though the extent of that value may vary. If you hate to sweat, your only physical exercise is lifting a beer can, and the one spectator sport you find tolerable is the recreational sex on late-night HBO, it is important. But, if you read the Sunday morning paper from the sports page, throw your shoe at the television screen when your team fumbles away a sure win, and play tennis in the rain, it is essential.

Sport is an experience, a serious enterprise, and an all-encompassing institution that has become an important topic of social scientific investigation. The anthropology of sport is one facet of that investigation.

References

Abdou, Kamal Saleh 1973 Sports and Games in Ancient Egypt. In, History of Sport and Physical Education. Ed, Earle F. Zeigler. Champaign, Ill.: Stipes Publishing Co., 57-65.

_____ 1961 Sports and Games in Ancient Egypt. Unpublished Ph.D. Dissertation, Indiana University, Bloomington.

Adams, Richard N. 1975 Energy and Structure: A Theory of Social Power. Austin: University of Texas Press.

Alderman, R. B. 1974 Psychological Behavior in Sport. Philadelphia: W. B. Saunders.

Allison, Maria T. and Gunther Lüschen 1979 A Comparative Analysis of Navajo Indian and Anglo Basketball Sports Systems. International Review of Sport Sociology 14:75-86.

An-che, Li 1937 Zuni: Some Observations. American Antropologist 39:62-76.

Anderson, John E. 1959 The Use of Time and Energy. In, Handbook of Aging and the Individual. Ed, James E. Birren. Chicago: University of Chicago Press.

Anderson, Nels 1964 Dimensions of Work: The Sociology of a Work Culture. New York: David McKay.

Anderson, Wanni Wibulswasdi 1974/75 Song Duel of the Kobuk River Eskimo. Folk 16/17:73-81.

Arens, William 1975 The Great American Football Ritual. Natural History 84:72-81.

Arms, Robert, Gordon W. Russell and Mark L. Sandelands 1979 Effects of the Hostility of Spectators of Viewing Aggressive Sport. Social Psychology Quarterly 42(3):275-79.

Atyeo, D. 1978 Blood and Guts. New York: Paddington Press. Avedon, Elliott M. and Brian Sutton-Smith 1971 The Study of Games. New York: John Wiley.

Azoy, G. Whitney 1982 Buzkashi: Game and Power in Afghanistan. Philadelphia: University of Pennsylvania.

Bailey, Flora L. 1942 Navajo Motor Habits. American Anthropologist 44(2):210-34.

Balazs, E. 1975 In Quest of Excellence. Waldwick: Hoctor Products for Education.

Balikci, Asen 1978 Buzkashi. Natural History 87 (February):54-63.

Bandura, A. 1973 Aggression: Social Learning and Personality Development. Engelwood Cliffs, N.J.: Prentice-Hall.

Barnett, Lynn 1976 Current Thinking About Children's Play. Quest 26:5-16.

Barry, H., M. K. Bacon, and I. L. Child 1957 A Cross-Cultural Survey of Some

Sex Differences in Socialization. Journal of Abnormal and Social Psychology 55:327-32.

Barth, Fredrik 1969 Ethnic Groups and Boundaries. Boston: Little, Brown and Co.

Bateson, Gregory 1958 Naven. Stanford, Calif.: Stanford University Press.
_____1972 A Theory of Play and Fantasy. In, Steps to an Ecology of Mind. Ed, Bateson. New York: Random House, 177-93.

Bekoff, Marc 1972 The Development of Social Interaction, Play, and Metacommunication in Mammals: An Ethological Perspective. Quarterly Review of Biology 47:412-34.

Bem, Sandra 1975 Sex Role Adaptability: One Consequence of Psychological Androgyny. Journal of Personality and Social Psychology 31(4):634-43.

Benedict, Ruth 1934 Patterns of Culture. Boston: Houghton Mifflin.

Berkowitz, Leonard 1965 The Concept of Aggression Drive: Some Additional Considerations. In, Advances in Experimental Social Psychology. Vol. 2. Ed, Leopold Berkowitz. New York: Academic Press.

Berlyne, D. E. 1960 Conflict, Arousal and Curiosity, New York: McGraw-Hill.
_____1971 What Next? Concluding Summary. In, Intrinsic Motivation: A New Direction in Education. Eds, H. I. Day; D. E. Berlyne, and D. E. Hunt. Toronto: Holt, Rinehart and Winston.

Best, Elsdon 1924 The Maori, Vol. II. Memoirs of the Polynesian Society. Wellington: Tombs.
_____1952 The Maori as He Was. Wellington: R. E. Owen, Government Printer.

Bilby, Julian 1923 Among Unknown Eskimo. London: Seeley, Service and Co.

Blanchard, Kendall 1974 Basketball and the Culture-Change Process: The Rimrock Navajo Case. Council on Anthropology and Education Quarterly 5(4):8-13.
_____1975 Choctaw Conflict Language and Team Sports: A Problem in Language Borrowing. Unpublished paper presented at the annual meetings of the Southeastern Conference on Linguistics, Nashville (March).
_____1976 The Critical Cultural Component in Recreation and Intramural Programs. Unpublished paper presented at the annual meetings of the National Intramural-Recreational Sports Association, San Diego (April).
_____1979a Stickball and the American Southeast. In, Forms of Play of Native North Americans. Eds, Edward Norbeck and Claire Farrer. St. Paul, Minn.: West Publishing Co., 189-208.
_____1979b The Tribe and the Evolution of Modern Sport Behavior. Unpublished paper presented at the annual meetings of The Association for the Anthropological Study of Play. Henniker, N.H. (April).
_____1980 The Social Meaning of Peasant Sport in Medieval Europe: The Use of Anthropological Models in the Analysis of Historical Data. Unpublished paper presented at an international conference on sport sponsored by the Center for Medieval and Renaissance Studies, University of California, Los Angeles (June).
_____1981 The Mississippi Choctaws at Play: The Serious Side of Leisure. Urbana: University of Illinois Press.
_____1984 Play and Adaptation: Sport and Games in Native America. Oklahoma University Papers In Anthropology (in press).

Blom, Franz 1932 The Maya Ballgame Pok-ta-pok. Middle American Research Series, Pub. 4, No. 13. Tulane University Press.

Boas, Franz 1888 The Central Eskimo. Sixth Annual Report of the Bureau of American Ethnology (1964 edition). Lincoln: University of Nebraska Press.

Bogoras, Waldemar 1904-1909 The Chukchee. Memoir of the American Museum of Natural History. New York. Vol. 7.

Breeze, Richard and Ian Findlay 1982 Football Demos Are Just Not Cricket.

Far East Economic Review 115:31-33.

Brewster, Paul G. 1956 The Importance of the Collecting and Study of Games. Eastern Anthropologist 10(1):5-12.

Bridges, Esteban Lucas 1947 Uttermost Part of the Earth. New York: Dutton.

Brozek, Josef and A. Henschel (eds.) 1961 Techniques for Measuring Body Composition. Washington, D.C.: National Academy of Sciences--National Research Council.

Bryant, Alfred T. 1970 The Zulu People, As They Were Before the White Man Came. New York: Negro University Press.

Bryer, Anthony 1967 Byzantine Games. History Today 17(7):453-59.

Buck, Peter 1949 The Coming of the Maori. Wellington: Whitcombe and Tombs.

Buhler, Charlotte 1928 Kindheit und Jugend. Leipzig Hirzel.

Burke, E. J. 1977 Physiological Effects of Similar Training Programs in Males and Females. Research Quarterly 48(3):510-17.

Buros, Oscar Krisen (ed.) 1974 Tests in Print II. Highland Park, N.J.: Gryphon Press.

Caillois, Roger 1959 Man and the Sacred. Glencoe, Ill.: The Free Press of Glencoe.

_____1969 The Structure and Classification of Games. In, Sport, Culture and Society. Eds, John Loy and Gerald Kenyon. New York: Macmillan Publishing Co., 44-55.

_____1979 Man, Play and Games. New York: Schocken Books. (Originally, Les Jeux et les hommes, 1958) Paris: Librairie Gallimard).

Cameron, Alan 1976 Circus Factions: Blues and Greens at Rome and Byzantium. Oxford: Clarendon Press.

Cardinall, A. W. 1927 Ashanti and Beyond. London: Seeley, Service and Co.

Carpenter, C. R. 1964 Naturalistic Behavior of Nonhuman Primates. University Park: Pennsylvania State University Press.

Case, Robert W. and Robert L. Boucher 1981 Spectator Violence in Sport: A Selected Review. Journal of Sport and Social Issues 5(2):1-14.

Chapple, Eliot D. and Carleton S. Coon 1942 Principles of Anthropology. New York: Henry Holt.

Charlevoix, Father Pierre Francois 1721 Historical Journal. In, Historical Collections of Louisiana. Ed, B. F. French. New York: D. Appleton (1851 edition). Vol. 3, 119-96.

Cheska, Alyce Taylor 1975 Stewart Culin: An Early Ethnologist of Games. The Association for the Anthropological Study of Play, Newsletter 2(3):4-13.

_____1978a Navajo Youth Health, Physical Education, and Recreation Program Evaluation. Unpublished report, Navajo Tribal Council & BIA, Gallop, N.M.

_____1978b The Study of Play from Five Anthropological Perspectives. In, Play: Anthropological Perspectives. Ed, Michael A. Salter. West Point, N.Y.: Leisure Press, 17-35.

_____1979 Native American Games as Strategies of Societal Maintenance. In, Play Forms of Native North Americans. Eds, Edward Norbeck and Claire Farrer. St. Paul, Minn.: West Publishing Company, 227-47.

_____1981a Native American Youth Sports' Choices and Game Attraction Factors: Part I: Recreational Choices of Native American Youth. Unpublished paper, University of Illinois, Urbana, Ill.

_____1981b Women's Sports -- the Unlikely Myth of Equality. In, The Female Athlete: A Sociopsychological and Kinanthropometric Approach. Eds, J. Borms, M. Hebberlinck, and A. Venerando. Basel, Switzerland: S. Karger, 1-11.

_____1981c Games of the Native North Americans. In, Handbook of Social Science of Sport. Eds, R. F. Gunther Lüschen and George H. Sage. Champaign, Ill.: Stipes Publishing Co., 49-77.

_____In Press. Sport as Ethnic Boundary Maintenance: A Case of the

American Indian. International Review of Sport Sociology.

_____ and Ellen W. Gerber 1981 Women in Sport. In, Encyclopedia of Physical Education, Fitness, and Sports. Vol. 1: Philosophy, Programs, and History. Eds., James S. Bosco and Mary Ann Turner. Salt Lake City, Utah: Brighton Publishing Co., 78-94.

Churchill, Llewella Pierce 1899 Sports of the Samoans. Outing 33: 562-68.

Coakley, Jay 1981 Sport in Society: Issues and Controversies. St. Louis: C. V. Mosby Co.

Coe, Michael D. 1962 Mexico. New York: Frederick A. Praeger.

_____ 1966 The Maya. New York: Frederick A. Praeger.

Cook, Sherburne 1946 Human Sacrifice and Warfare as Factors in the Demography of Precolonial Mexico. Human Biology 18:81-102.

Congress on Sport and International Understanding 1982 Announcements: Quest 9(1): 130-31.

Coser, Lewis 1956 The Function of Social Conflict. New York: Free Press.

Cozens, Frederick W. and Florence Stumpf 1951 Implications of Cultural Anthropology for Physical Education. American Academy of Physical Education. Professional Contributions, No. 1. Washington, D.C.

Crawley, A. E. 1913 The Book of the Ball. London: Methuen & Co., Ltd.

Csikszentmihalyi, Mihaly 1975 Beyond Boredom and Anxiety. San Francisco: Jossey-Bass.

Culin, Stewart 1889 Chinese Games With Dice. Philadelphia:Oriental Club.

_____ 1895 Korean Games with Notes on the Corresponding Games of China and Japan. Philadelphia: University of Pennsylvania Press.

_____ 1903 American Indian Games. American Anthropologist 5(1):58-64.

_____ 1907 Games of the North American Indians. Twenty-fourth Annual Report of the Bureau of American Ethnology. Washington, D.C.: Government Printing Office.

Cumming, E. and W. Henry 1961 Growing Old: The Process of Disengagement. N.Y.: Basic Books.

Cureton, Thomas K. 1982 Personal Interview. Champaign, Ill., June 1.

Curtis, William B. 1900 Bygone International Athletic Contests: What Americans Have Accomplished. Outing 36(4):350-57. (July).

Cushing, Frank Hamilton 1883 My Adventures in Zuni, Vol. III. The Century Illustrated Monthly Magazine 16(1):28-48.

Cushman, Horatio B. 1899 History of the Choctaw, Chickasaw and Natchez Indians. Stillwater, Okla.: Redlands Press (1962 edition).

Damm, Hans 1970 The So-Called Sport Activities of Primitive People: A Contribution Toward a Genesis of Sport. In, The Cross-Cultural Analysis of Sport and Games. Ed, Gunther Lüschen. Champaign, Ill.: Stipes Publishing Co.

Danquah, Joseph Boayke 1928 Gold Coast: Akan Laws and Customs. London: G. Routledge.

Davidson, D. S. 1936 The Pacific and Circum-Pacific Appearances of the Dart Games. Journal of the Polynesian Society 45(3 and 4): 99-114; 119-26.

Dead Birds 1977 In, Films for Anthropological Teaching. Ed, Karl G. Heider. Washington, D.C.: American Anthropological Association, 51.

de Brebeuf, Jean 1636 Relation of 1636. In, The Jesuit Relations and Allied Documents. Ed, Reuben Gold Thwaites. Vol. 10. Cleveland: Durrows Bros. (1897 edition).

DeGrazia, Sebastian 1962 Of Time, Work and Leisure. New York: The Twentieth Century Fund.

Denzin, Norman K. 1975 Play, Games and Interaction: The Contexts of Childhood Socialization. The Sociological Quarterly 16 (Autumn): 458-78.

de Paina, Father Juan 1676 Origin and Beginning of the Ball Game Which the Apalachee and Yustaga Indians Have Been Playing From Pagan Times

Up to the Year 1676. In, Archivo General de Indias Seville Escribania de Camara Legajo 157, XXX. Julian Granberry, transcript and translation, for incomplete study by John M. Goggin. Photostats in Stetson Collection, Gainesville: University of Florida Library.

Diem, Carl 1971 Weltgeschichte des Sports. Frankfurt: Cotta. Vol. I (3rd edition).

Dolhinow, Phyllis 1971 At Play in the Fields. Natural History, Special Supplement (December):66-71.

Dollard, J., N. Miller, H. O. Mowrer, and R. R. Sears 1939 Frustration and Aggression. New Haven: Yale University Press.

Douglas, Mary 1966 Purity and Danger. London: Routledge & Paul.
_____ 1970 Natural Symbols. New York: Vintage Press (1973 edition).

Drinkwater, Barbara L. 1973 Physiological Responses of Women to Exercise. In, Exercise and Sport Sciences Reviews. Ed, Jack Wilmore. New York: Academic Press.

Dunkle, M. C. 1974 What Constitutes Equality for Women in Sport? Newsletter for the Project on the Status and Education of Women. Association of American Colleges, Washington, D.C.

Dunlap, Helen L. 1951 Games, Sports, Dancing, and Other Vigorous Activities and Their Function in Samoan Culture. The Research Quarterly 22(3):298-311.

Dupree, Louis 1966 Aq Kupruk: A Town in North Afghanistan. Part I: The People and Their Cultural Patterns. American Universities Field Staff Reports. South Asia Series. Vol. 10.

Duquin, Mary E. 1978 The Androgynous Advantage. In, Women and Sport: From Myth to Reality. Ed, Carole A. Oglesby. Philadelphia: Lea & Febiger, 89-106.

Duran, Fray Diego de 1971 Book of the Gods and Rites and the Ancient Calendar. Trans., Fernando Horcasitas and Doris Heyden. Norman, Okla.: University of Oklahoma Press.

Edwards, Harry 1973 Sociology of Sport. Homewood, Ill.: The Dorsey Press.
_____ and Van Rackages 1977 The Dynamics of Violence in American Sport: Some Promising Structural and Social Considerations. Journal of Sport and Social Issues 1(2):3-31.

Eifermann, Rivka R. 1973 Rules in Games. In, Artificial and Human Thinking. Eds, Alice Elithorn and David Jones. San Francisco: Jossey-Bass, 147-61.

Eitzen, D. Stanley 1981 Sport and Deviance. In, Handbook of Social Science of Sport. Eds., Gunther R. F. Luschen and George H. Sage. Champaign, Ill.: Stipes Publishing Co., 400-14.

Ekholm, Gordon F. 1961 Puerto Rican Stone "Collars" as Ball-game Belts. In Essays in Pre-Columbian Art and Archaeology. Eds., Samuel K. Lothrop, et al. Cambridge, Mass: Harvard University Press, 356-71.

Elias, Norbert and Eric Dunning 1966 Dynamics of Sport Groups with Special Reference to Football. British Journal of Sociology 17:388-402.
_____ 1970 The Quest for Excitement in Unexciting Societies. In, The Cross-Cultural Analysis of Sport and Games. Ed, Gunther Luschen. Champaign, Ill.: Stipes Publishing Co., 31-42.

Emery, Lynne 1979 The First Intercollegiate Contest for Women: Basketball, April 4, 1896. Unpublished paper presented at the annual meetings of the North American Society for Sport History, Austin, Texas (May).

Encyclopedia Americana 1964 Justinian. Vol. 16:267. New York: American Corporation.

Erdelyi, Glyula F. 1960. Gynecological Survey of Female Athletes. Paper presented at National Conference on Medical Aspects of Sport, American Medical Association, Washington, D.C. (November).

Erikson, Erik H. 1963 Childhood and Society. New York: W. W. Norton &

Company. Second Edition.

Espy, Richard 1979 The Politics of the Olympic Games. Los Angeles: University of California Press.

Evans, Arthur 1921 The Palace of Minos at Knossos. London: Macmillan and Company.

Fagen, Robert M. 1981 Animal Play Behavior. New York: Oxford University Press.

Fasting, Kari 1979 Sport and Television: Research on the Inter-relationship. Notater og Rapporter Fra Norges Idrettschogskole. Oslo, Norway: Norges Idrettschogskole (Norwegian School of Physical Education).

Firth, Raymond 1929 Primitive Economics of the New Zealand Maori. New York: E. P. Dutton

_____ 1930/31 A Dart Match in Tikopia. Oceania 1:64-97.

Fogelson, Raymond 1962 The Cherokee Ball Game: A Study in Southeastern Ethnology. Unpublished Ph.D. Dissertation. University of Pennsylvania, Philadelphia.

Fox, J. R. 1961 Pueblo Baseball: A New Use for Old Witchcraft. Journal of American Folklore 74:9-16.

Fox, Steven J. 1977 A Paleoanthropological Approach to Recreation and Sporting Behaviors. In, Studies in the Anthropology of Play. Ed., Phillips Stevens. West Point, N.Y.: Leisure Press, 65-70.

Frederickson, F. S. 1960 Sports in the Cultures of Man. In, Science and Medicine in Exercise and Sports. Ed., W. R. Johnson. New York: Harper and Row, 633-38.

Freeman, Derek 1983 Margaret Mead and Samoa: The Making and Unmaking of an Anthropological Myth. Cambridge, Mass.: Harvard University Press.

Freud, Sigmund 1922 Beyond the Pleasure Principle. Trans., C. J. M. Hubbeck. Vienna, Austria: The International Psychoanalytical Press.

Fried, Morton H. 1967 The Evolution of Political Society. New York: Random House.

_____ 1975 The Notion of Tribe. Menlo Park, Calif.: Cummings.

Friedl, Ernestine 1978 Society and Sex Roles. Human Nature 1(4)68-75.

Fries, James F. and Lawrence M. Crapo 1981 Vitality and Aging. San Francisco: W. H. Freeman and Co.

Gardiner, E. Norman 1910 Greek Athletic Sports and Festivals. London: Macmillan & Company, Ltd. (Reprinted by Wm. C. Brown: Dubuque, Iowa, 1970).

_____ 1930 Athletics of Ancient World. Oxford, England: Clarendon Press.

Geertz, Clifford 1972 Deep Play: Notes on the Balinese Cockfight. In, The Interpretation of Cultures. Ed., Geertz. New York: Basic Books, 412-53.

Gendel, Evalyn S. 1971 Fitness and Fatigue in the Female. Journal for Health, Physical Education and Recreation 41(8):53-4, 56-8.

Gerber, Ellen, Jan Felshin, Pearl Berlin and Wyneen Wyrick 1974 The American Woman in Sport. Reading, Mass.: Addison-Wesley.

Gilbert, Bill 1967 What Sports for Girls? Today's Health 45(10):20-23.

Giles, Herbert A. 1906 Football and Polo in China. The Nineteenth Century and After 59:508-13.

Gini, Corrado 1939 Rural Ritual Games in Libya (Berber Baseball and Shinny). Rural Sociology 4:282-98.

Gipe, George 1978 The Great American Sports Book. Garden City, N.Y.: Doubleday.

Glassford, Robert Gerald 1976 Application of a Theory of Games to the Transitional Eskimo Culture. New York: Arno Press.

Gmelch, George 1972 Magic in Professional Baseball. In, Games, Sports and Power. Ed., Gregory P. Stone. New unswick, N.J.: Dutton, 128-37.

Goldstein, Jeffrey H. and R. L. Arms 1971 Effects of Observing Athletic Contests on Hostility. Sociometry 34(1):83-90.

Goodhart, Philip and Christopher Chataway 1968 War Without Weapons. London: W. H. Allen.
Goodman, Mary Ellen 1967 The Individual and Culture. Homewood, Ill.: The Dorsey Press.
_____ 1976 The Culture of Childhood. New York: Teacher's College Press.
Grattan, F. J. H. 1948 An Introduction to Samoan Custom. Apia, Western Samoa: Samoa Printing and Publishing Co.
Gruneau, Richard S. 1975 Sport, Social Differentiation and Social Inequality. In, Sport and Social Order. Eds., Donald Ball and John Loy. Reading, Mass.: Addison-Wesley, 117-84.
Guldenpfennig, Sven and Hans-Jurgen Schulke 1980 The Need for Politilogical Research on Sport and Its Relation to the Sociology of Sport. International Review of Sport Sociology 15(1):127-37.
Gusinde, Martin 1961 The Tamana: The Life and Thought of the Water Nomads of Cape Horn. Trans., Frieda Schutze. New Haven, Conn.: Human Relations Area Files (HRAF).
_____ 1975 Folk Literature of the Selknam Indians. Los Angeles: University of California Press.
Guttmann, Allen 1978 From Ritual to Record: The Nature of Modern Sports. New York: Columbia University Press.
_____ 1981 Sports Spectacular from Antiquity to the Renaissance. Journal of Sport History 8(2):5-27.
Haas, Mary R. 1940 Creek Intertown Relations. American Anthropologist 42:479-89.
Haddon, A. C. 1898 Study of Man. London.
Halbert, Henry S. 1897 Indian Schools. In, Bienniel Report of the State Superintendent of Public Education to the State Legislature, for the Scholastic Years 1895-96 and 1896-97. Jackson, Miss.
Hardy, Stephen H. 1974 The Medieval Tournament: A Functional Sport of the Upper Class. Journal of Sport History 1(2):91-105.
Harner, Michael 1977 The Ecological Basis for Aztec Sacrifice. American Ethnologist 4:117-35.
Harney, W. E. 1952 Sport and Play Amidst the Aborigines of the Northern Territory. Mankind 4(9):377-79.
Harootyan, Robert A. 1982 The Participation of Older People in Sports. In, Social Approaches to Sports. Ed., Robert M. Pankin. London: Associated University Presses Ltd., 122-47.
Harris, Dorothy V. 1973 Involvement in Sport: A Somatopsychic Rationale for Physical Activity. Philadelphia: Lea & Febiger.
Harris, H. A. 1972 Sport in Greece and Rome. Ithaca, N.Y.: Cornell University Press.
Harris, Janet C. and Roberta J. Park (eds.) 1983 Play, Games and Sports in Cultural Contexts. Champaign, Ill.: Human Kinetics Publishers.
Harris, Marvin 1974 Cows, Pigs, War and Witches: The Riddles of Culture. New York: Vintage Books.
_____ 1979 Cultural Materialism: The Sturggle for a Science of Culture. New York: Random House.
Haury, Emil W. 1968 The Hohokam: First Masters of the American Desert. National Geographic 131(5):670-95.
Hechter, William 1977 The Criminal Law and Violence in Sports. The Criminal Law Quarterly 19:425-53.
Heider, Karl G. 1970 The Dugum Dani: A Papuan Culture in the Highlands of West New Guinea. Chicago: Aldine.
_____ 1977 From Javanese to Dani: The Translation of a Game. In, Studies in the Anthropology of Play. Ed., Phillips Stevens, Jr., West Point, N.Y.: Leisure Press, 72-80.
_____ 1979 Grand Valley Dani: Peaceful Warriors. New York: Holt, Rinehart and Winston.

Heinila, Kalevi 1966 Notes in Inter-group Conflicts in International Sport. International Review of Sport Sociology 1:31-38.

Henderson, Robert W. 1947 Ball, Bat and Bishop: The Origin of Ball Games. New York: Rockport Press. (Reprint: Gale Research Company, Book Tower, Detroit, 1974).

Herzog, Harold and Pauline B. Cheek 1979 The Anatomy of Cockfighting. Southern Exposure 7(2):36-40.

Heusner, William W. 1966 Basic Physiological Conecpts as They Relate to Girls Sports. In, Proceedings: Second National Institute on Girls Sports. Washington, D.C.: American Association for Health, Physical Education and Recreation.

Higgs, Robert J. 1982 Sports: A Reference Guide. Westport, Conn.: Greenwood Press.

Hildebrand, J. R. 1919 The Geography of Games. National Geographic 36(2):90-143.

Hoebel, E. Adamson 1954 The Law of Primitive Man. New York: Atheneum (1972 edition).

Hoffman, Walter J. 1896 The Menomini Indians. Bureau of American Ethnology, Annual Report 14.

Hole, Frank and Robert Heizer 1977 Introduction to Prehistoric Archaeology. New York: Holt, Rinehart and Winston.

Holmes, W. H. 1907 Introduction. Twenty-Fourth Annual Report of the Bureau of American Ethnology. Washington: Government Printing Office. ix-xl.

Horrow, Rick 1981a The Legal Perspective: Interaction Between the Private Lawmaking and the Civil and Criminal Law. Arena Review 5(1):9-18.
_____ 1981b Sports Violence: The Prospects for Reform. Arena Review 5(1):63-64.

Howell, Maxwell L. and Lorne W. Sawula 1973 Sports and Games Among the Etruscans. In, A History of Sport and Physical Education. Ed., Earle F. Zeigler. Champaign, Ill.: Stipes Publishing Co., 79-91.

Howell, Maxwell L. and Reet A. Howell 1980 Women in Sports and Games in the Medieval and Renaissance Periods as Depicted in the Art. Unpublished paper presented at the Congress of Women in Sport, Rome, Italy.

Howitt, A. W. 1904 The Native Tribes of South East Australia. London: MacMillan.

Hughes, Linda 1983 Beyond the Rules of Game. Why are Rooie Rules Nice? In, The World of Play. Ed., Frank E. Manning. West Point, N.Y.: Leisure Press, 188-99.

Huizinga, Johan 1949 The Waning of the Middle Ages. Garden City, N.Y.: Doubleday.
_____ 1950 Homo Ludens: A Study of the Play Element in Culture. Boston: Beacon Press.

Humphrey, Robert L. 1981 Play as Life: Suggestions for a Cognitive Study of the Mesoamerican Ball Game. In, Play as Context. Ed., Alyce T. Cheska. West Point, N.Y.: Leisure Press, 134-49.

Hutt, Corrine 1966 Exploraton and Play in Children. Symposium of the Zoological Society of London 18:61-81.

Ibraham, Hilmi 1975 Sport and Society. Long Beach, Calif.: Hwong Publishing Company.

International Olympic Committee 1978 Olympic Charter. Lausanne: Comte International Olympique.

Ioannides, Ion P. 1976 Physical Culture of the Greek Antiquity. In, The History, the Evolution and Diffusion of Sports and Games in Different Cultures. Eds., R. Renson, P. P. deNayer and M. Ostyn. Leuven, Belgium: B.L.O.S.O., 105-15.

Jackson, Steven J. 1982 Spectator Violence. Unpublished paper, Department of Physical Education, University of Illinois, Urbana.

Jeannotat, Yves 1980 Sport and the Older Man. Olympic Review 155:585-86.

Johnson, Irving and Electra 1955 South Seas' Incredible Land Divers. National Geographic 107(1):77-92.

Johnson, William (ed.) 1980 Sport and Physical Education Around the World. Champaign, Ill.: Stipes Publishing Co.

Jokl, Ernst (ed.) 1964 Medical Sociology and Cultural Anthropology of Sport. Springfield, Ill.: Charles C. Thomas.

Jones, R. W. 1959 Sport and International Understanding. Report of the UNESCO Congress "Sport--Work--Culture." Helsinki, Finland, 159-70.

Kagan, Jerome 1973 A Conversation with Jerome Kagan. Saturday Review 1(3):41-42.

Kando, Thomas M. 1975 Leisure and Popular Culture in Transition. St. Louis: C. V. Mosby.

Kanin, David B. 1978 Ideology and Diplomacy: The Dimensions of Chinese Political Sport. In, Sport and International Relations. Eds., Benjamin Lowe, David B. Kanina and Andrew Strenk. Champaign, Ill.: Stipes Publishing Co., 263-78.

Kaplan, David and Robert A. Manners 1972 Culture Theory. Englewood Cliffs, N.J.: Prentice-Hall.

Kauffman, H. E. 1941 Die Spiele der Thadou Kuki in Assam (The Play of the Thadou Kuki in Assam). Zeitschrift für Ethnologie 73:40-71.

Kennedy, John G. n.d. Contemporary Tarahumara Foot Racing and its Significance. In, The Tarahumara. Ed., Ralph Beals. Los Angeles: University of California, 86-104.

Kendrick, Karen A. and Chuck Wyatt 1981 Going Strong in the Golden Olympics. Parks and Recreation 16(12):41-44.

Kenyatta, Jomo 1965 Facing Mount Kenya. New York: Vintage Books.

Kenyon, Gerald 1969 A Conceptual Model for Characterizing Physical Activity. In, Sport, Culture and Society. Eds., Loy and Kenyon. New York: Macmillan, 71-81.

King, John P. and Peter S. K. Chi 1979 Social Structure, Sex Roles, and Personality: Comparison of Male/Female Athletes/Nonathletes. In, Sports, Games, and Play. Ed., Jeffrey H. Goldstein. Hillsdale, N.J.: Lawrence Erlbaum Associates.

Kingsley, Joan L., Foster L. Brown, and Margaret E. Siebert 1977 Social Acceptance of Female Athletes by College Women. Research Quarterly 48(3):727-33.

Klafs, Carl E. and M. Joan Lyon. 1973 The Female Athlete: Conditioning, Competition and Culture. St. Louis: C. V. Mosby Company.

Kleiber, Douglas A. 1980 The Leisure Experience of Males and Females: A Context for Androgynous Behavior. Unpublished paper, University of Illinois, Urbana.

Kleinman, Seymour 1960 A Study to Determine Factors That Influence the Behavior of Sport Crowds. Unpublished Ph.D. Dissertation. Dept. of Physical Education. Ohio State University, Columbus.

Kluckhohn, Clyde and William Kelly 1945 The Concept of Culture. In, The Science of Man in the World Crisis. Ed., Ralph Linton, 78-106.

Kluckhohn, Clyde and Dorothea C. Leighton 1974 The Navajo. Cambridge, Mass.: Harvard University Press.

Kolatch, Jonathan 1972 Sport, Politics and Ideology in China. Middle Village, N.Y.: Jonathan David.

Kroeber, Alfred L. 1948 Anthropology. New York: Harcourt, Brace and Co.

Kukushkin, G. I. 1964 Growth, Physique and Performance. In, International Research in Sport and Physical Education. Eds., E. Jokl and E. Simon. Springfield, Ill.: Charles C. Thomas, 254-61.

Lancy, David F.   1977   The Play Behavior of Kpelle Children During Rapid Cultural Change. In, The Study of Play: Problems and Prospects. Eds., David F. Lancy and B. Allan Tindall. West Point, N.Y.: Leisure Press, 84-91.

La Piere, R.   1938   Collective Behavior. New York: McGraw-Hill.

Lasch, Christopher   1979   The Culture of Narcissism. New York: W. W. Norton.

Laudonniere, Rene   1562   History of the First Attempt of the French to Colonize the Newly Discovered Country of Florida. Trans., Richard Hakluyt. In, Historical Collections of Louisiana and Florida. Ed., B. F. French. New York: J. Sabin and Sons (1869 edition), 165-362.

Lawick-Goodall, Jane   1971   In the Shadow of Man. New York: Houghton-Mifflin.

Leach, Edmund   1954   Political Systems of Highland Burma. Boston: Beacon Press.

Leach, Jerry W.   1976   Structure and Message in Trobriand Cricket. Unpublished paper written to accompany the movie Trobriand Cricket. Berkeley, Calif.: University of California Extension Media Center. This film is available for rental or purchase from the University of California, Extension Media Center, Berkeley, Calif. 94720, as well as from other university film services.

Leach, G.   1960   Solving the Spectator Problem. School Activities 31 (Dec.):99-101.

Leaf, Alexander and John Launois   1975   Youth in Old Age. N.Y.: McGraw-Hill.

Lee, Richard B.   1968   What Hunters Do For a Living, or, How To Make Out on Scarce Resources. In, Man the Hunter. Eds., Richard Lee and Irven Devore. Chicago: Aldine, 30-48.

Lennon, Joseph X. and Frederick C. Hatfield   1980   The Effects of Crowding and Observation of Athletic Events on Spectator Tendency Toward Aggressive Behavior. Journal of Sport Behavior 3(2):61-68.

Leonard, Wilbert M.   1980   A Sociological Perspective of Sport. Minneapolis: Burgess.

Lesser, Alexander   1933   The Pawnee Ghost Dance Hand Game: A Study of Cultural Change. Columbia University Contributions to Anthropology, 16. New York: Columbia University Press.

Lever, Janet   1976   Sex Differences in the Games Children Play. Social Problems 23(4):478-87.

_____   1983   Soccer Madness. Chicago: University of Chicago Press.

Levi-Strauss, Claude   1966   The Savage Mind. Chicago: University of Chicago Press.

Lewis, Thomas M. N. and Madeline Kneberg Lewis   1961   Eva: An Archaic Site. Knoxville: University of Tennessee Press.

Liebert, R. M. and R. A. Baron   1972   Some Immediate Effects of Televised Violence on Children's Behavior. Developmental Psychology 6(1):469-75.

Lipman-Blumen, Jean   1976   Toward a Homosocial Theory of Sex Roles: An Explanation of the Sex Segregation of Social Institutions. Signs: Journal of Women in Culture and Society 1:15-31.

Little, Kenneth   1965   Western African Urbanization: A Study of Voluntary Associations in Social Change. Cambridge: University Press.

Loether, Herman J. and Donald G. McTavish   1974   Descriptive Statistics for Sociologists. Boston: Allyn and Bacon.

Lofland, John   1982   Crowd Joys. Urban Life 10(4):355-81.

Lorenz, Konrad   1966   On Aggression. Trans., Marjorie Kerr Wilson. N.Y.: Bantam Books.

Lowe, Benjamin, David B. Kanin, and Andrew Strenk   1978   Sport and International Relations. Champaign, Ill.: Stipes Publishing Co.

Loy, John W.   1969   The Nature of Sport. In, Sport, Culture and Society. Eds., John W. Loy and Gerald Kenyon. New York: Macmillan, 56-71.

_____, Barry D. McPherson and Gerald Kenyon 1978 Sport and Social Systems. Reading, Mass.: Addison-Wesley.

Lumsden, Charles L. and Edward O. Wilson 1981 Genes, Mind, and Culture. Cambridge: Harvard University Press.

Lüschen, Gunther 1970 The Interdependence of Sport and Culture. In, The Cross-Cultural Analysis of Sport and Games. Ed., Gunther Lüschen. Champaign, Ill.: Stipes Publishing Co., 85-99.

MacAloon, John J. 1981 This Great Symbol. Chicago: University of Chicago Press.

Maccoby Eleanor E. 1966 Sex Differences in Intellectual Functioning. In, The Development of Sex Differences. Ed., Eleanor E. Maccoby. Stanford, Calif.: Stanford University Press, 25-55.

_____, and Carol N. Jacklin 1974 The Psychology of Sex Differences. Stanford, Calif.: Stanford University Press.

Maccoby, Michael, Nancy Modiana and Patricia Lander 1964 Games and Social Character in a Mexican Village. Psychiatry 27:150-62.

Malina, Robert 1972 Anthropology, Growth and Physical Education. In, Physical Education: An Interdisciplinary Approach. Eds., Robert N. Singer, et al. New York: Macmillan, 239-309.

Malinowski, Bronislaw 1939 The Group and the Individual in Functional Analysis. American Journal of Sociology 4:938-64.

_____ 1948 Magic, Science and Religion. Garden City, N.Y.: Doubleday (1960 Anchor Books edition).

_____ 1967 A Diary in the Strict Sense of the Term. New York: Harcourt, Brace and World.

Mandell, Richard 1971 Nazi Olympics. New York: Macmillan.

Mann, G. V. 1981 Menstrual Effects of Athletic Training. In, Women and Sport: An Historical, Biololgical, Physiological and Sportsmedical Approach. Eds., J. Borms, M. Hebbelinck and A. Venerando. Basel, Switzerland: Karger (Volume 15, Medicine in Sport Series), 195-99.

Mann, Leon 1979 Sport Crowds Viewed from the Perspective of Collective Behavior. In, Sports, Games, and Play: Social and Psychological Viewpoints. Ed., Jeffrey H, Goldstein. Hillsdale, N.J.: Lawrence Erlbaum Associates, 337-68.

Manning, Frank 1981 Celebrating Cricket: The Symbolic Construction of Caribbean Politics: American Ethnologist 8(3):616-32.

Martens, Rainer 1975 Social Psychology and Physical Activity. New York: Harper and Row.

Martin, M. Kay and Barbara Voorhies. 1975 Female of the Species. New York: Columbia University Press.

Massingham, Harold J. 1929 Origins of Ball Games. In, The Heritage of Man. London: J. Cape Publishers, 208-27.

Mathias, Elizabeth 1981 Italian-American Culture and Games: The Minnesota Iron Range and South Philadelphia. In, Play as Context. Ed., Alyce Cheska. West Point, N.Y.: Leisure Press, 73-92.

McIntosh, Peter C. 1963 Sport in Society. London: C. A. Watts & Co. Ltd.

Mead, George H. 1934 Mind, Self, and Society. Chicago: University of Chicago Press.

Mead, Margaret 1928 Coming of Age in Samoa: A Psychological Study of Primitive Youth for Western Civilization. New York: William Morrow.

_____ 1937 The Samoans. In, Cooperation and Competition Among Primitive Peoples. Ed., Margaret Mead. New York: McGraw-Hill, 282-312.

Meehan, J. 1979 Aggression in Human Performance: Dealing with Violence. Paper presented at the National Association for Physical Education in Higher Education Annual Conference. Milwaukee.

Menke, Frank G. 1947 The New Encyclopedia of Sports. New York: A. S. Barnes (1960 edition).

Mergen, Bernard 1977 From Play to Recreation: The Acceptance of Leisure in the United States, 1880-1930. In, Studies in The Anthropology of Play. Ed., Phillips Stevens, Jr. West Point, N.Y.: Leisure Press, 187-200.

_____ 1978 Work and Play in an Occupational Subculture:American Shipyard Workers, 1971-1977. In, Play: Anthropological Perspectives. Ed., Michael Salter. West Point, N.Y.: Leisure Press, 187-200.

Messner, Steven F. 1981 Football and Homicide: Searching for the Subculture of Violence. In, Sociology of Sport: Perspectives. Eds., Susan L. Greendorfer and Andrew Yiannakis. West Point, N.Y.: Leisure Press, 53-60.

Metheny, Eleanor 1965 Connotations of Movement in Sport andDance. Dubuque, Iowa: Wm. C. Brown.

Michener, James A. 1976 Sports in America. N.Y.: Fawcett Crest.

Millar, Susanna 1968 The Psychology of Play. Harmondsworth, Middlesex, England: Penguin Books Ltd.

Miller, Judith 1982 Sport Spectatorship and Participation Among Adults. Unpublished M. A. Thesis. University of Illinois, Urbana.

_____ 1983 Description of Games and Sports in Tonga. Paper presented at the annual meetings of The Association for the Anthropological Study of Play, Baton Rouge, Louisiana (February).

Miller, Stephen 1973 Ends, Means, and Galumphing: Some Leitmotifs of Play. American Anthropologist 75(1):87-98.

Moncrieff, John 1966 Physical Games and Amusements of the Australian Aboriginal. The Australian Journal of Physical Education 36:5-11.

Mooney, James 1890 The Cherokee Ball Play. American Anthropologist 3(2):105-32.

Morgan, W. P., J. A. Roberts, F. R. Brand and A. D. Feinerman 1970 Psychological Effects of Chronic Physical Activity. Medicine and Science in Sports 4:213-17.

Murdock, George P. et al. 1961 Outline of Cultural Materials. New Haven, Conn.: Human Relations Area Files (HRAF).

Murphy, James F. 1977 Leisure, Aging, and Retirement: Changing Patterns and Perspectives. Journal of Health, Physical Education and Recreation 48(8):30-31.

Mutimer, Brian T. P. 1970 Play Forms of the Ancient Egyptians. Proceedings, 1st Canadian Symposium on the History of Sport and Physical Education. Ottawa, Canada: Department of National Health and Welfare, 569-78.

Myerhoff, Barbara 1978 Number Our Days. New York: E. P. Dutton.

Nabokov, Peter 1981 Indian Running. Santa Barbara, Calif.: Capra Press.

Naroll, Raoul 1966 Does Military Deterrence Deter? Trans-action 3(2):14-20.

Natan, Alex 1969 Sport and Politics. In, Sport, Culture, and Society. Eds., John W. Loy and Gerald S. Kenyon. New York: Macmillan, 203-10.

National Center for Health Statistics 1980 Vital Statistics for the United States, 1977. Volume 2, Section 5. Hyattsville, Maryland: National Center for Health Statistics (DHEW Publication PHS 80-1104).

National Council on the Aging 1975 The Myth and Reality of Aging in America. Washington, D.C.

Neff, Craig 1983 A Double Victory with a New Twist. Sports Illustrated 58(19):60-61.

Nickerson, Elinor 1982 Racquet Sports. Jefferson, North Carolina: McFarland & Company.

Nisbet, Robert A. 1970 The Social Bond. New York: Alfred A. Knopf.

Neugarten, Bernice L. 1974 Age Groups in American Society and the Rise of the Young-Old. American Academy of Political and Social Science Annal 415:187-98.

Norbeck, Edward 1971 Man at Play. Natural History Magazine, Special Supplement (December):48-53.

_____(ed.) 1974 The Anthropological Study of Human Play. Rice University Studies 60(3).

Norman, James 1976 The Tarahumaras: Mexico's Long Distance Runners. National Geographic 149(5):702-18.

Oakley, Fredericka B. 1976 Methodological Considerations for Studies of Play in Primates. In, The Anthropological Study of Play: Problems and Perspectives. Eds., David Lancy and Allan Tindall. Cornwall, N.Y.: Leisure Press, 173-78.

Ogawa, Keiko 1978 Culture Change and the Symbolic Interactionist Approach. Unpublished Master's Essay, Department of Anthropology, University of Illinois, Urbana.

Oliver, W. H. 1960 The Story of New Zealand. London: Faber and Faber.

Olmert, Michael 1981 Points of Origin. Smithsonian 12(6):40-46.

Olsen, Fred 1974 On the Trail of the Arawaks. Norman, Okla.: University of Oklahoma Press.

Olympic Scientific Congress Program (1984) Eugene, Oregon.

Opler, M. E. 1944 The Jicarilla Apache Ceremonial Relay Race. American Anthropologist 46(1):75-97.

Opler, M. K. 1945 A Sumo Tournament at Tule Lake Center. American Anthropologist 47(1):134-39.

Ortiz, Alfonso 1969 The Tewa World. Chicago: University of Chicago Press.

Otterbein, Keith F. 1970 The Evolution of War. New Haven, Conn.: HRAF Press.

Palmer, Denise and Maxwell L. Howell 1973a Archaeological Evidence of Sports and Games in Ancient Crete. In, A History of Sport and Physical Education. Ed, Earle F. Zeigler. Champaign, Ill.: Stipes, Publishing Co., 67-78.

_____1973b Sport and Games in Early Civilization. In, A History of Sport and Physical Education. Ed., Earle F. Zeigler. Champaign, Ill.: Stipes Publishing Co., 21-34.

Parker, R. 1977 Football Violence Study Shows Critical Influence of Grounds and History. The Times of London (April 9): C-2.

Petrie, Flinders 1927 Objects of Daily Use. London: British School of Archaeology in Egypt. University College.

Perry, W. J. 1923 The Children of the Sun. London: Methuen and Company.

Pfuetze, Paul E. 1954 Self, Society, Existence. New York: Harper and Row.

Piaget, Jean 1962 Play, Dreams and Imitation in Childhood. New York: W. W. Norton.

Pooley, John 1981 Ethnic Soccer Clubs in Milwaukee: A Study of Assimilation. In, Sport in the Sociocultural Process. Eds., Maria Hart and Susan Birrell. Dubuque, Iowa: Wm. C. Brown, 430-47.

Popenoe, David 1974 Sociology. New York: Appleton-Century- Crofts.

Radcliffe-Brown, A. R. 1922 The Andaman Islanders. Cambridge, England: Cambridge University Press.

_____1952 Structure and Function in Primitive Society. London: Oxford University Press.

Rajagopalan, K. 1973 Early Indian Physical Education. In, A History of Sport and Physical Education. Ed., Earle F. Zeigler. Champaign, Ill.: Stipes Publishing Co., 45-55.

Rand, Silas T. 1894 Legends of the Micmacs. New York: Longmans, Green and Company.

Rattray, Robert Sutherland 1916 Ashanti Proverbs: The Primitive Ethics of a Savage People. Oxford: Clarendon Press.

Raum, O. F. 1953 The Rolling Target (Hoop-and-Pole) Game in Africa. African Studies. 12:104-21.

Reagan, Albert B. 1932 Navajo Sports. Primitive Man 5:68-71.

Redfield, R., R. Linton and M. J. Herskovits 1936 Memorandum for the Study of Acculturation. American Anthropologist 38:149-52.

Reich, Alan 1973 Sports--Gateway to International Understanding. Congressional Record. 93rd Congress, 1st Session (June 19, 1973), Vol. 119, No. 85, 20273-20275.

Reigelhaupt, Joyce A. 1973 Review: (Three volumes on Sport). American Anthropologist 75:378-81.

Renson, Ronald 1981 Folk Football: Sport and/or-as Ritual? The Association for the Anthropological Study of Play Newsletter 8(1):2-8.

Riordan, James 1977 Sport in Soviet Society. London: Cambridge University Press.

_____1981 Sport Under Communism. 2nd edition. London: C. Hurst and Company.

Roberts, John M., Malcolm J. Arth, and Robert R. Bush 1959 Games in Culture. American Anthropologist 61:597-605.

Roberts, John and Brian Sutton-Smith 1962 Child Training and Game Involvement. Ethnology 1(2):166-85.

Robinson, Christine E. 1978 The Uses of Order and Disorder in Play:An Analysis of Vietnamese Refugee Children's Play. In, Play: Anthropological Perspectives. Ed., Michael Salter. West Point, N.Y.: Leisure Press, 137-45.

Rohrbaugh, Joanna Bunker 1979 Femininity on the Line. PsychologyToday 13(3):30; 32; 35; 41-42.

Rooney, John F., Jr. 1974 A Geography of American Sport. Reading, Mass.: Addison-Wesley.

Roth, Walter E. 1902 Games, Sports and Amusements. North Queensland Ethnography. Bulletin No. 4. Brisbane: George Arthur Vaughan, Government Printer.

Royce, Anya Peterson 1982 Ethnic Identity: Strategies of Diversity. Bloomington, Indiana: Indiana University Press.

Royce, Joseph and T. Murray 1971 Work and Play in Kapingamarangi, Past and Present. Micronesia 7(1/2):1-17.

Russell, G. and B. Drewry 1976 Crowd Size and Competitive Aspects of Aggression in Ice Hockey: An Archival Study. Human Relations 29(8):723-35.

Sack, Allen 1977 Sport: Play or Work? In, Studies in the Anthropology of Play. Ed., Phillips Stevens, Jr. West Point, N.Y.: Leisure Press, 186-95.

Sage, George H. 1974 Sport and American Society. Reading, Mass.: Addison-Wesley.

Sahlins, Marshall 1972 Stone Age Economics. Chicago: Aldine.

Salter, Michael A. 1974 Play: A Medium of Cultural Stability. In, Proceedings from the Third Canadian Symposium on History and Physical Education. Ed., Louis Young, Halifax, Nova Scotia, 1-22.

Samarin, William J. 1967 Field Linguistics. New York: Holt, Rinehart and Winston.

Sands, Robert 1976 International Sport is Politics. Australian Journal Health, Physical Education and Recreation. 72:7-10.

Santomier, James P., William G. Howard, Wendy L. Piltz, and Thomas J. Romance 1980 White Sock Crime: Organizational Deviance in Intercollegiate Athletics. Journal of Sport and Social Issues 4(2):26-32.

Sasajima, Kohsuke 1973 Early Chinese Physical Education and Sport. In, A History of Sport and Physical Education. Ed., Earle F. Ziegler. Champaign, Ill.: Stipes Publishing Co., 35-44.

Schroeder, Albert H. 1955 Ball Courts and Ball Games in Middle America and Arizona. Archaeology 8(3):156-61.

Scotch, N.A. 1961 Magic, Sorcery, and Football among Urban Zulu: A Case of Reinterpretation under Acculturation. Conflict Resolution 5(1):70-74.

Selder, Dennis J., G. Fredrick Roll and J. E. Lindsay Carter 1980 Profiles of Super Senior Tennis Players. The Physician and Sportsmedicine 8(9):101-05.

Service, Elman 1962 Primitive Social Organization. New York: Random House.

_____1963 Profiles in Ethnology. New York: Harper and Row.

_____1968 War and Our Contemporary Ancestors. In, War: The Anthropology of Armed Aggression. Eds., M. H. Fried, M. Harris, and R. Murphy. Garden City, N.Y.: Natural History Press, 160-67.

Shaffer, Thomas E. 1972 Physiological Considerations of the Female Participant. In, Women and Sport: a National Research Conference. Ed., Dorothy V. Harris. University Park: Pennsylvania State University, 321-31.

Sharer, Robert J. and Wendy Ashmore 1979 Fundamentals of Archaeology. Menlo Park, Calif.: Benjamin/Cummings.

Sherif, Muzafer 1958 Superordinate Goals in the Reduction of Intergroup Conflict. American Journal of Sociology 63:349-56.

Silva, John M. 1979 Assertive and Aggressive Behavior in Sport: A Definitional Clarification. In, Psychology of Motor Behavior and Sport. Eds, Claude H. Nadeau, Wayne Halliwell, Karl Newell and Glyn Roberts. Champaign, Ill.: Human Kinetics Press.

Simmons, L. W. 1945 The Role of the Aged in Primitive Society. New Haven, Conn.: Yale University Press.

Simri, Uriel 1969 The Religious and Magical Functions of Ballgames in Various Cultures. Proceedings of the First International Seminar on the History of Physical Education and Sport. Netanya, Israel: Wingate Institute of Physical Education, 2.1-2.12.

_____1973 The Ball Game of Antiquity. In, A History of Sport and Physical Education. Ed., Earle F. Zeigler. Champaign, Ill.: Stipes Publishing Co., 93-99.

Sipes, Richard 1973 War, Sports, and Aggression: An Empirical Test of Two Rival Theories. American Anthropologist 75(1):64-86.

Smith, Adam 1975 Powers of Mind. New York: Random House.

Smith, Jerald C. 1972 The Native American Ball Games. In, Sport in the Sociocultural Process. Ed., M. Marie Hart. Dubuque, Iowa: William C. Brown, 340-58.

Smith, Michael D. 1972 Aggression and the Female Athlete. In, Women and Sport: A National Research Conference. Ed., Dorothy V. Harris. University Park: The Pennsylvania State University.

_____1975 Sport Collective Violence. In, Sport and Social Order: Contributions to the Sociology of Sport. Eds., Donald W. and John W. Loy. Reading, Mass: Addison-Wesley Publishing Company, 277-330.

_____1981 Sport Violence: A Definition. Arena Review 5(1):2-8.

Snyder, Eldon E. and Elmer Spreitzer 1974 Sociology and Sport: An Overview. The Sociology Quarterly 5(4):467-87.

_____1978 Social Aspects of Sports. Englewood Cliffs, N.J.: Prentice-Hall.

Soustelle, Jacques 1961 Daily Life of the Aztecs on the Eve of the Spanish Conquest. Trans., Patrick O'Brien. Stanford, Calif.: Stanford University Press.

Special Committee on Aging 1980 A Report of the Special Committee on Aging, United States Senate -- Part 1: Development in Aging, 1980. Washington, D.C.: Government Printing Office. (97th Congress, 1st Session; Report No. 97-62).

Spencer, Baldwin and F. J. Gillen 1927 The Arunta: A Study of a Stone Age
        People. The Netherlands: Oosterhout. Vol. I, (1966 edition).
Stern, Theodore 1949 The Rubber Ball Games of the Americas. American
        Ethnological Society Monograph 17. Seattle, Washington: University
        of Washington Press.
Stevens, Phillips, Jr. 1973 The Bachama and their Neighbors: Non-kin Joking
        Relationships in Adamawa, Northeastern Nigeria. Unpublished Ph.D.
        Dissertation. Northwestern University, Evanston, Ill.
_____1975 Social and Cosmological Dimensions of Bachama Wrestling.
        Unpublished paper presented at the annual meetings of the American
        Anthropological Association, San Francisco (December).
_____1980 Play and Work: A False Dichotomy? In, Play and Culture. Ed.,
        Helen B. Schwartzman. West Point, N.Y.: Leisure Press, 316-23.
Stewart, Elbert W. 1981 Sociology. New York: McGraw-Hill.
Storr, Anthony 1969 Human Aggression. N.Y.: Atheneum.
Strenk, Andrew 1977 Sport as an International Political and Diplomatic Tool.
        Arena Newsletter 1(5):3-10.
Strickland, Donald A. and Lester F. Schlesigner 1969 Lurking as a Research
        Method. Human Organization 23:248-50.
Strommenger, Eva 1964 5000 Years of the Art of Mesopotamia. New York:
        Harry N. Abrams.
Strutt, Joseph 1876 The Sports and Pastimes of the People of England from the
        Earliest Period to the Present Time. London: Chatto and Windus
        (originally published in 1801).
Stumpf, Florence and Frederick W. Cozens 1947 Some Aspects of the
        Role of Games, Sports, and Recreational Activities in the Culture of
        Modern Primitive Peoples: The New Zealand Maori. Research
        Quarterly 18:198-218.
Suomi, Stephen J. and Harry F. Harlow 1971 Monkeys at Play. Natural History
        Special Supplement (December):72-75.
Sutton-Smith, Brian 1972 Games of Order and Disorder. In, The Dialectics of
        Play. Ed., Brian Sutton-Smith. Schorndorf, West Germany: Verlag
        Hoffman.
_____1973 Games, the Socialization Conflict. Canadian Journal of History
        of Sport and Physical Education 4(1):1-7.
_____1975 Play as Adaptive Potentiation. Sportswissenschaft 5(2):103-18.
_____1979 The Play of Girls. In, Becoming Female: Perspective on
        Development. Eds., Claire B. Kapp and Martha Kirkpatrick. N.Y.:
        Plenum Press, 229-57.
_____and John M. Roberts 1981 Play, Games, and Sports. In, Vol. 4,--
        Developmental Psychology. Handbook of Cross-Cultural Psychology.
        Eds., Harry C. Triandis and A. Heron. New York: Allyn and Bacon,
        425-71.
_____and C. G. Rosenberg 1961 Sixty Years of Historical Change inthe
        Game Preference of American Children. Journal of American Folklore
        74:17-46.
Talbot , Margaret J. 1981 Women and Sport: A Leisure Studies Perspective.
        In, The Female Athlete: A Sociopsychological and Kinanthropometric
        Approach. Eds., J. Borms, M. Habbelinck, and A. Venerando. Basel,
        Switzerland: S. Karger, 30-40.
The Hunters 1977 In, Films for Anthropological Teaching. Ed., Karl G. Heider.
        Washington, D.C.: American Anthropological Association, 78.
Thirer, Joel 1981 The Psychological Perspective: Analaysis of Violence in
        Sport. Arena Review 5(1):3-43.
Tien, H. Yuan and Josephine A. Matthews 1977 Transforming Society Through
        Sports: The Games That the Chinese People Play. Unpublished paper,
        Social Science Research Council, University of Chicago.

Tiger, Lionel 1970 Men in Groups. New York: Random House.

Timmer, Rob; Alan Bell Gordon, Szubra Tadeusz and Josef Recle (eds.) 1980 International Directory of Agencies Responsible for the Administration of Physical Education and Sports Programs 2:1/2 The Hague: International Association for Sports Information.

Tindall, B. Allan 1975a The Cultural Transmissive Function of Physical Education. Council on Anthropology and Education Quarterly 6(2):10-12.

_____ 1975b Ethnography and the Hidden Curriculum in Sport. Behavioral and Social Science Teacher 2(2).

_____ 1976 Questions about Physical Education, Skill, and Lifetime Leisure Sports Participation. Position paper presented to UNESCO on behalf of the Association for the Anthropological Study of Play. First International Conference of Ministers and Senior Officials Responsible for Physical Education and Sport for Youth (April).

Tylor, Edward B. 1871 Primitive Culture: Researches into the Development of Mythology, Philosophy, Religion, Language, Art, and Custom. London: J. Murray.

_____ 1879 The History of Games. The Fortnightly Review, London: Chapman and Hall, 25, n.s. (Jan. 1 - June 1): 735-47. Also, *In*, The Study of Games. Avedon and Sutton-Smith, 1971, 62-76.

_____ 1896 On American Lot-Games as Evidence of Asiatic Intercourse Before the Time of Columbus. International Archives for Ethnographie, Supplement to Vol. 9:55-67. Also *In*, The Study of Games. Avedon and Sutton-Smith, 1971, 77-93.

Urdang, Laurance 1968 The Random House Dictionary of the English Language. New York: Random House.

United States Commission on Civil Rights 1980 More Hurdles to Clear: Women and Girls in Competitive Athletics. Clearinghouse Publication No. 63. Washington, D.C.: U. S. Government Printing Office.

U. S. Congress Senate Committee on Foreign Relations. 1980 Hearings on U.S. Population Policy. April 29; June 5.

U. S. House of Representatives 1978 Committee on the Judiciary -- Subcommittee on Administrative Law and Governmental Relations. Hearings: Amateur Sports Act of 1978. Washington, D.C. Government Printing Office.

U. S. President's Commission on Olympic Sports 1977 Final Report, V. 1-2. Washington, D.C.: Government Printing Office.

Weiss, Gerald 1973 A Scientific Concept of Culture. American Anthropologist 75(5):1376-1413.

Weiss, Kenneth M. 1981 Evolutionary Perspective on Human Aging. *In*, Other Ways of Growing Old. Eds., Pamela T. Amoss and Stevan Harrell. Stanford, Calif.: Stanford University Press, 25-58.

Weule, Von Karl 1925 Ethnologie des Sportes. *In*, Geschichte des Sportes aller Volker und Zeiten. Ed., G.A.E. Bogeng. Leipzig.

White, Leslie 1949 Science of Culture. New York: Grove Press.

_____ 1965 Anthropology 1964: Retrospect and Prospect. American Anthropologist 67:629-37.

Whiting, Robert 1982 Japan's Passionate Affair with Baseball. Asia 5(1):10-15.

Wilkinson, Sir J. Garner 1878 The Manners and Customs of the Ancient Egyptians, Vol. II. New York: Scribner and Welford.

Wilson, Edward O. 1980 Sociobiology (abridged edition). Cambridge, Mass: Harvard University Press.

_____ and Charles L. Lumsden 1983 Promethean Fire. Cambridge, Mass: Harvard University Press.

Wohl, Andrzej 1970 Competitive Sport and Its Social Functions. International Review of Sport Sociology 5(1):117-30.

Wright, Quincy 1942 A Study of War, Vol. I. Chicago: University of Chicago Press.
Wright, S. 1977 Are the Olympics Games? The Relationship of Politics and Sport. Millennium 6:30-44.
Wyrick, Waneen 1974 Biophysical Perspectives. In, The American Women in Sport. Eds., Ellen W. Gerber, Jan Felshin, Pearl Berlin, and Waneen Wyrick. Reading, Mass: Addison Wesley, 403-515.
Zborowski, M. 1962 Aging and Recreation. Journal of Gerontology 17:302-09.
Zibro, Joyce 1970 A Child Goes Forth. Bulletin of the Field Museum 41(11):6-7.

Index

Chariot racing, 256
Chataway, Christopher, 273
Cherokees, 16–17, 114, 254
Cheska, Alyce, 24, 25, 110, 242, 244
Chichen Itza, 100, 102, 105
Chicken pull game, 154
Chiefdom, 167–168
Child, I. L., 206
China, 96, 97, 98, 227, 265, 270–271
Chinese, 219, 265, 271
Choctaw Fair, 171
Choctaws, Mississippi, 12, 45, 52, 56,
    59, 72–73, 84–86, 192, 193, 246, 260
Chou Dynasty, 97
Chugan, 16
Chukchi, 155–160
Chunkey, 93
Churchill, Llewella Price, 179
Civil Rights Act, 240
Cleveland Indians, 259
Coakley, Jay, 260
Cochiti Pueblo, 22–23, 71
Cockfighting, 255, 256–257
Coe, Michael, 100, 105, 107
Cognitive development, 206, 207;
    domains, 75
Combative sports, 220
Comparative linguistics, 11
Competition, 57, 117–118, 179
Conflict, 57, 216;
    enculturation, 206, 207;
    management, 199
Congress on Sport and International
    Understanding, 269
Consensus of association, 217
Constructive games, 207
Cook, James, 174
Coon, Carleton, 219
Copan, 100
Coser, 216, 217
Counting coup, 221
Cozens, Frederick W., 25, 45
Creeks, 222
Crete, 97, 98
Cricket, 74, 139, 177, 181, 215, 254, 257
Criminal law and sport, 261
Crocker, Ted, 241
Croquet, 242
Cross-cultural understanding through
    sport, 228–229
Cikszentmihalyi, Mihalyi, 44, 51, 212
Culin, Stewart, 17–19, 21, 26, 110,
    112, 113

Cultural maintenance, 229;
    materialism, 71, 203;
    relativism, 12, 227, 228;
    transmission, 206
Culturally sensitive sports programs,
    224
Culture, 12, 34–36, 59;
    dynamic model of, 203;
    process, 10;
    static model of, 202
Cushman, Horatio B., 170

Damm, Hans, 56, 203
Dancing Gymnast, 235
Dani, 41, 160–163, 221, 224
Danquah, Joseph Boayke, 188
Dart throwing *(teka; tika),* 176–177,
    180, 182, 192, 196
Darwin, Charles, 9
Dead Birds, 4, 161, 165
de Cubertin, Pierre, 226, 266
Deep play, 24
Degas, Edgar, 235
DeGrazia Sebastian, 38, 39
Denzin, Norman K., 46
Descriptive linguistics, 11
Diem Karl, 56
Direct historical approach, 110
Discovery, 200
Douglas, Mary, 55, 74, 241
Draw-A-Man, 82
Drewry, B., 263
Dunlap, Helen L., 182
Dunning, Eric, 217
Dupree, Louis, 130
Duquin, Mary E., 247
Duran, Fray Diego de, 103, 106

East Germany (GDR), 270
Ecological meaning, 194–195
Edwards, Harry, 32, 47, 49, 259, 270
Egypt, 96, 97, 98, 196, 235, 237–238
Eifermann, Rivka R., 210
Ekholm, Gordon F., 102
Elderly as myth-tellers, 254, 255;
    as teachers, 254
Elias, Norbert, 217
El Salvador, 273
Emic, 77, 85
Enculturation, 199, 200, 205–206, 213,
    229
English fairs, 236
Epikoinos, 15